German Expressionist theatre: the actor and the stage considers the powerfully stylized and anti-realistic styles of symbolic acting on the German Expressionist stage from 1916 to 1921. It relates this striking departure from the dominant European acting tradition of realism to the specific cultural crises that enveloped the German nation during the course of its involvement in World War I. Unlike any of the very few publications in English on stage Expressionism, this book describes three distinct Expressionist acting styles, all of which in their own ways attempted to show how symbolic stage performance could be a powerful rhetorical resource for a culture struggling to come to terms with the crises of historical change. The examination of previously untranslated portions of Expressionist scripts and actor memoirs allows for an unprecedented focus on description and analysis of the acting itself.

GERMAN EXPRESSIONIST THEATRE

GERMAN EXPRESSIONIST THEATRE

The actor and the stage

DAVID F. KUHNS

Professor of English Literature and Theatre, Geneva College

CAMBRIDGE
UNIVERSITY PRESS

PUBLISHED BY THE PRESS SYNDICATE OF THE UNIVERSITY OF CAMBRIDGE
The Pitt Building, Trumpington Street, Cambridge CB2 IRP, United Kingdom

CAMBRIDGE UNIVERSITY PRESS
The Edinburgh Building, Cambridge CB2 2RU, United Kingdom
40 West 20th Street, New York, NY 10011–4211, USA
10 Stamford Road, Oakleigh, Melbourne 3166, Australia

First published 1997

Printed in the United Kingdom at the University Press, Cambridge

Typeset in Baskerville 11/12½ pt

A catalogue record for this book is available from the British Library

ISBN 0 521 58340 3 hardback

for Pam and Chloe

Contents

Acknowledgements

I should very much like to acknowledge the assistance of the following German theatre and literary archives in the research for this project: Theatermuseum des Instituts für Theater-, Film- und Fernsehwissenschaft der Universität zu Köln; Akademie der Künste, Berlin; Stiftung Deutsche Kinemathek, Berlin; Märkisches Museum, Berlin; Staatsbibliothek zu Berlin–Preussischer Kulturbesitz; Deutsches Theatermuseum, Munich; Handschriften-Sammlung der Stadtbibliothek München; Deutsches Literatur-Archiv, Marbach am Neckar. I am greatly indebted to Professors Dennis Kennedy, Simon Williams, and Christopher Innes for their careful readings of and suggestions for this manuscript in its various stages of revision. I also wish to thank Victoria Cooper and her splendid editorial staff at Cambridge University Press for their help in the final preparation of the manuscript. Finally, I am very grateful to my dear wife, Pam, and my daughter, Chloe, for their loving encouragement throughout the several intermittent seasons of this project's development.

ce

Introduction

The late Wilhelmine and Weimar eras are notable for the fascination they continue to hold for historians of art, literature and, particularly, the theatre. One reason for this is the distinct relationship between forces of socio-political change and revolutions in aesthetic philosophy and artistic form moving through these periods. From the turn of the century until the outbreak of world war a spirit of artistic revolution waxes in German culture. The general result thereafter is that the arts – again, notably the theatre – are prepared as never before in German history to articulate the experience of historical change. German society – particularly from the end of the war through the brief "revolutionary" period, 1918–19 – is in such a state of turmoil that one can accurately speak both of a culture in transformation and of a crucial role for the arts in the process.

Among various artistic strategies active in this historical situation Expressionism was the most prominent. Yet the exact nature and specific features of this new and undeniable "movement" in the arts eluded definition. The artists who acknowledged and embraced it debated its aesthetics and struggled over its goals to such a degree that in the end it seemed, as one scholar has written, that there was "not one Expressionism but a number of loosely connected and subtly – or not so subtly – differentiated Expressionisms."[1] Yet notwithstanding the marked divergence of its stylistic modes, ranging from primitivist emotionalism to abstract geometrism, the Expressionist movement was decisively about cultural transformation. In social consciousness and ethical commitment, as well as artistic form and aesthetic philosophy, Expressionism sought to revolutionize German society and renew its faith in humanity.

No where was this more evident than in the theatre. However, most subsequent scholarly attention has focused on the plays and relatively little on their performance. The present study assumes, by contrast, that the historical significance – that is, the formative connections between a mode of dramatic art and its cultural moment – can best be concretized in production research. It is in the production of a script, after all – in the concrete matrix of resources and initiatives shaping the work of directors, actors, designers, and critics – that the play's historical materiality begins to come clear. In the case of Expressionism, in particular, I shall argue that the cooperative efforts of the productions' artists converged definitively on the body and voice of the actor. What distinguishes Expressionist performance in the history of the early Modernist avant-garde is the degree and manner in which the process of cultural transformation was inscribed in the body of the actor itself and thereby performed on stage. What distinguishes the theatre of Expressionism, in other words, is the extent to which it "textualized" actors. Radically suppressing their traditional mimetic function, Expressionist productions foregrounded actors' bodies and voices as complex thematic stage signs. In this way, audiences were virtually impelled to "read" the performance as an Expressionist text about, rather than a mimetic imitation of, the contemporary state of German culture.

Central to the argument of this text was the issue of expressive power itself. For this reason it is important to stress from the outset that this book is about a kind of "performing" whose standards and challenges were markedly different than those associated with traditional mimetic or rhetorical notions of stage acting. The distinction is necessary for an understanding of what it was that theatrical Expressionism attempted to accomplish in its conception and use of the stage actor. The Expressionist strategy in the theatre for coming to terms with the crises of contemporary German history was to anthropomorphize them abstractly in the body and voice of the actor. The basic assumption was that to give history expressive form in such a way was to acquire some measure of influence over the course of historical events. Clearly such an ambitious undertaking went well beyond traditional ideas of acting as either realistic impersonation or declamation. Rather, what the Expressionist actor sought to demonstrate, to textualize, was the historical power of "expression" itself. To this idea of acting I shall apply the term "performance." Thereby, I mean to denote a kind of stage art that foregrounds the performer's expressive powers as capable of "performing," bringing about directly, some effect in real life. The Futurists and the Dadaists, of course, experimented with something like this idea of performance;

but the real effects of the stage events they performed were limited to sensationalist sensory stimulation or expressions of cultural protest. What distinguishes Expressionist performance from practices such as these was that the efficacy it sought was nothing less than the regeneration of German society as a whole.

Whether they have privileged aesthetic form or psychological credibility, technique or inspiration, theories of acting from ancient times to the modern era have generally assumed some sort of social, moral, and/or spiritual public influence as a consequence of the actor's art. In this context, the view of acting as a species of rhetorical art – the dominant view until the end of the nineteenth century – conceives of this influence as a direct affective impact on an audience. The principal alternative conception – arising in the mid eighteenth century and culminating in the tradition of Stanislavskian psychological realism – is that the actor's art affects an audience indirectly, as a by-product of its central effort to create a mimetic illusion of individual emotional experience. The sort of efficacy sought in Expressionist performance, ambitious though it was, must be understood in terms of the first tradition just mentioned, that of the rhetorical stage. I distinguish Expressionist "performance" from mimetic psychological acting chiefly in order to show the degree of Expressionism's faith in the power of rhetoric to reach beyond the theatrical frame and directly influence the ethical, social and political behavior of audiences.

However, when one realizes the centrality of the stage director in Expressionist production, it also becomes clear that the actor was not expected to shoulder the rhetorical burden of performance efficacy alone. A common feature of the various modes of theatrical Expressionism was the use of scenic design and lighting conceptions to shape the expressive work of the actor, whose performance in turn infused the stage environment with great energy. Hence, the present study is not simply about acting. Rather, it considers the ways in which the Expressionist actor functioned as the central dynamic force in a rhetorical totality that included all the visual and aural elements of the production. Expressionism's distinctive way of integrating acting, costuming, make-up, set design, lighting, and music rendered all of these elements "active" on stage. It was the Expressionist production's overall style, not just its human actors, that was expected to "perform" the desired rhetorical effect upon an audience.

It is in this context that the following study examines the nature of German Expressionist performance in its several distinct modes. The period in question is 1916–21, during which Expressionism achieved the greatest clarity as a theatrical movement. Though the study takes an historical attitude, however, it is neither solely a factual reconstruction nor a social history of Expressionist performance. Rather, elements of both methods are employed in a hybrid approach which seeks to account for the fact that a variety of contemporaneous but clearly distinct performance modes were all termed "Expressionist" by their practitioners. Thus, while detailing the distinctions between these modes, I am also about the project of synthesizing them. What emerges is a conception of German theatrical Expressionism as a cohesive (if not always coherent) movement whose purpose was to influence performatively the historical process of transformation from late-Wilhelmine culture to a more ethically advanced, humanitarian society.

The eclecticism of my approach was necessitated by the particular paucity of available research resources. The primary source material for the study is of four basic types: reviews of Expressionist productions by contemporary newspaper critics or theatre historians; memoirs or statements by actors, directors, theorists, and reviewers; theoretical manifestoes written by Expressionist playwrights and aestheticians; and finally the language and stage directions of selected Expressionist scripts. None of these sources alone provides a complete account of the details of Expressionist performance. All of them, however, provide some valuable information which helps in describing the movement. These materials are generally available only in German and all translations are mine except where indicated in the text which introduces the quotation or in the accompanying reference citation.

Theoretical treatises – such as those of Felix Emmel, Kasimir Edschmid, Vassily Kandinsky and Lothar Schreyer – are important in that they articulate the aesthetic and social goals of theatrical Expressionism. However, like the language and stage directions of the plays, they are only a record of the expectations for, not necessarily the achievements of, the Expressionist stage. Neither type of primary resource provides the sense of practical experience in Expressionist performance which is afforded in the statements of the actors and directors. Unfortunately, such personal accounts by these artists themselves are scarce. Of those that I have been able to locate, only Fritz Kortner's lengthy autobiography affords any significant detail about what an actor experienced as he attempted to meet the demands of Expressionist staging. Kortner's Berlin career was launched on the Expressionist stage and he quickly became Expressionism's most renowned performer. But while that small portion of his memoir dealing with Expressionism is a valuable record of his own relationship to the movement, it is, after all, only one actor's statement. His observations about other actors, such as Albert Bassermann, and directors, such as Leopold Jessner, are clearly subjective. On the other hand, he generally attempts to convey both the strengths and the weaknesses of the artists with whom he was associated.

By far the most extended statement about Expressionist production by a director is that of Lothar Schreyer.[2] However, since Schreyer is known to have sacrificed strict historical accuracy, at times, for the sake of theoretical argument in his memoirs, his account is primarily valuable only as a theory of Expressionist performance, not as a reliable record of practical achievements. The problem here, it should be noted, is not one of systematic fabrication but rather of the inevitable distortions of recollection: the primary memoir, *Expressionistisches Theater* (1948), was written three decades after the period in which he worked at the Sturm-Bühne and the Kampfbühne. None of the other important Expressionist directors has left anything more than an isolated remark here or there, in an interview, a letter, or a program note, as to his *practical* methods or objectives. Nonetheless, I have taken such comments as are available to be significant evidence of directorial strategies – as, for example, where Jessner states that he sought to turn his actors into "transcendental sculptures."

The newspaper reviews, one might imagine, move us a little closer to an objective description of Expressionist performance techniques. However, the rhetoric of the theatre critics, as much as that of the playwrights or theorists, reveals their own sense of cultural mission. Moreover, the reviews of the earlier Expressionist productions lack specificity. Typically, the acting is not described but rather evaluated in a general phrase or two at the end of the review after the critic has discussed the script at length. Even where descriptions of acting are most detailed, however – in the reviews of late Expressionist productions in Berlin from approximately 1918 to 1921 – the critic typically spends more time discussing the play than the production. In some cases, his objectivity is compromised by an evident positive or negative bias with regard to Expressionist aesthetics generally or to the particular style of "Expressionist" performance in the production being reviewed. Where the critic levels a harsh judgment it is often in the context of his distinction between genuine and counterfeit theatrical Expressionism.

Thus, in addition to what may be gleaned about Expressionist acting itself, the newspaper reviews are also valuable for the variety of conceptions of theatrical Expressionism which they reveal. Herein, however, lies the danger mentioned above: namely, the inevitable rhetorical skewing of the critic's report. Hence, I have throughout the study sought to address the audience dimension of Expressionist performance specifically in terms of how audience response as well as the actors' work on stage is constructed by the critics in their reviews. When any theatre reviewer critiques a production he or she inevitably constructs, implicitly if not explicitly, an audience response as well. Even the most individual critical reactions carry *ex officio* institutional authority in print; and every review, therefore, implicitly argues a certain definition of the community and what it requires of the theatre. Though such allowances obviously must be made in reading any account of a performance, past or present, they are especially significant in the case of Expressionist-era production reviews. This is because German theatre criticism at this time was practiced with a seriousness and sense of social responsibility both traditional, dating at least from the age of Schiller and Weimar classicism, and uniquely modern, reflecting the urgent contemporary sense of cultural crisis felt and articulated by many of the critics.

While the printed journalistic record is of great use, there exists little helpful photographic documentation of the varieties of Expressionist acting. The few publicity photos of famous Expressionist actors – such as Kortner, Werner Krauss, Ernst Deutsch, or Agnes Straub – and the handful of action stills which are extant pertain mostly to late Expressionist performance in Berlin. Also, like most production stills, their informative value is limited because they are obviously posed rather than taken spontaneously in the course of the action. I have been unable to find any visual record of acting in the earliest, provincial Expressionist productions; although some few pencil sketches of settings and their lighting effects, or of actor positions on stage, are available. At his Hamburg Kampfbühne theatre Schreyer would not even permit reviews of productions, let alone photographs of them. I have been able to locate a few stills of partial masks and puppet models used in his stagings. This is supplemented by graphic evidence in the form of sketches and complete color renderings of the full-sized body masks typically worn by his actors. Here a dominant costuming agenda appears to have transformed actors into walking abstract Expressionist paintings. However, these kinds of visual documentation – production stills, sketches drawn during performances, and mask renderings – finally shed no definitive light on what the actors actually did in performance. Therefore inclusion of such photos and illustrations as are available seemed to offer little advantage. Instead, I have chosen simply to describe the visual details of the various Expressionist performance modes on the basis of the more detailed kinds of evidence noted above, chiefly newspaper reviews and memoirs.

Another part of the visual record are the few extant Expressionist films. I have chosen to discuss the cinema version of Kaiser's *Von morgens bis mitternachts* and Robert Wiene's *The Cabinet of Dr. Caligari*. Yet these films fail to capture the experience of live Expressionist performance which the newspaper reviews and artists' statements describe from either side of the footlights. An extended discussion of Expressionist cinema would reveal more about the art of the Expressionist director and film editor than it would about the work of the Expressionist stage actor. Also, I have omitted consideration of the so-called "Kammerspielfilm" of the 1920s which, in the style of the "New Objectivity" subsequent to Expressionism, typically depicts proletarian economic hardship and resultant moral depravity. Though such films make ample use of Expressionist atmosphere in the mise-en-scène, the acting is psychological and realistically understated – everything, in short, against which all modes of Expressionist performance were in rebellion.

Notwithstanding the cinema-like fluidity of space and time in some of them, the plays of the Expressionist era were written either for stage production or, in the case of Kandinsky, as theoretical exercises. The scripts which are given extended discussion in this study are those which seem most significant for the development of Expressionist performance. I have included, that is, those plays whose style of composition and/or production treatment most clearly defined distinct modes of performing. Thus, along with the famous productions of Expressionist plays or classic scripts – such as *Der Sohn* [*The Son*], *Der Bettler* [*The Beggar*], *Die Wandlung* [*Transfigura-*

tion], *Masse Mensch* [*Man and the Masses*], Schiller's *Wilhelm Tell*, and Shakespeare's *Richard III* – less well known premières, such as those of Paul Kornfeld's *Die Verführung* [*The Seduction*] or the Sturm-Bühne production of Stramm's *Sancta Susanna*, are examined. On the other hand, well-received productions of dramas such as von Unruh's *Ein Geschlecht* [*One Race*] or Kaiser's *Gas* trilogy, to name only a few, are not considered. Though such plays marked important *thematic* consolidations or advances in the development of Expressionist dramatic art, they appear to have made no significant new performance demands beyond the established mode of intense character acting epitomized in Reinhardt's Deutsches Theater ensemble and the productions of Das junge Deutschland.

The question of theme in Expressionist drama, however, may have been significant for Expressionist acting because of social issues the plays failed to address. The typical functions of women in Expressionist scripts, for example, are conceived in blatantly sexist terms. In plays as distinct as Sorge's *Der Bettler* and Stramm's *Sancta Susanna*, women are figures of either inspiration or corruption, true to a Judeo-Christian literary tradition dating from the epochs of Biblical composition. Often they function simply as derivative spiritual factors in the central male figure's progress toward his vocation and destiny. In the few cases where they have an identity of their own – as, for example, in *Sancta Susanna* or Paul Kornfeld's *Die Verführung* – it is morally diabolical.[3] Stramm's conception of the vicious principal female character in *Kräfte* [*Forces*] is nothing short of outright misogyny. Critics who reviewed Agnes Straub's portrayal of this figure characterized her performance in bestial terms and compared it to the animal-like, "demonic" acting of Gertrud Eysoldt in Wilde's *Salomé* (Kleines Theater, Berlin, 1902) and Tilla Durieux in Hebbel's *Judith* (Deutsches Theater, Berlin, 1910). In my analysis of the development of distinct modes of Expressionist performance, I shall have occasion to comment on the influence of sexism, both in the plays and in proto-Expressionist performance genres such as the cabaret. The sexist pattern is most evident in the darkly sensual spirituality which became characteristic of female performances in Expressionist theatre.

Where possible, I have consulted all four types of primary source material – reviews, memoirs, manifestoes, and scripts – in order to achieve as detailed and balanced an account of Expressionist performance as possible. Where specific historical evidence seems most reliable – chiefly in the reviews – I have used it as the foundation for inferential reconstruction of details which are missing. As a principal aid in this procedure, I have drawn upon the language and stage directions of the plays and the arguments of the theorists to help fill in the gaps. In some cases the preponderance, or the sole source, of available information is strictly subjective – Schreyer's memoirs, for example, are virtually the only extended account of Kampfbühne Expressionist performance. Nevertheless, I have utilized such resources in the belief that subjective information – properly qualified as such, of course – is better than none at all. It at least reveals something of the aesthetic intention and thematic concerns which were likely to be influential in the development of performance methods, even though full factual details of those practices themselves might prove finally unrecoverable. My synthesis of primary sources is based on the conviction that the statements of theorists, the language and stage directions of the scripts, the practical work of the actors and directors, and the reactions of the critics all informed one another. The material from memoirs, of course, comes after the fact, and it undoubtedly suffers to some degree from the distortions of hindsight. Yet it does give some indication of how the actor, director, theorist, or critic may have contributed to the general climate of artistic experimentation which characterized the Expressionist era.

More than any programmatic quality, what gave theatrical Expressionism a degree of coherence as a movement was the loosely defined, sometimes contentious, theatrical community it created. Nonetheless, care must be taken, in the context of theatre history, when speaking of "the Expressionists." This is a point about which many studies of Expressionism are careless. Strictly speaking, the movement's programmatic dimension was most evident, as Roy Allen has amply demonstrated, in the various Expressionist literary circles organized in the pre- and post-war eras.[4] Associated in a basic program of aesthetic and ethical principles, these writers' fellowships met regularly in such informal venues as cafés or publishing offices to share the results of their often quite distinct practical working methods. Such literary Expressionists were nurtured by a relatively stable collective identity and community of support. But aside from Schreyer's coterie theatre group, the *Kampfbühne* (itself a derivative of Herwarth Walden's interdisciplinary Expressionist *Sturm* circle), and the short-lived *Das junge Deutschland* association at Reinhardt's

Deutsches Theater, Expressionism "moved" within the theatre in a much less concerted way.

Whereas Expressionist literary circles had been active since 1910, it was not until mid-way through the war – thanks to the pioneering efforts of some of the provincial theatres – that Expressionist drama began to appear on stage. While some dramatists worked in connection with the literary circles, the majority of contributors in these programmatic associations were lyric poets whose principal subject was the cultural bankruptcy of contemporary German society. Initially, these poets wrote in a symbolic and metaphysical, rather than a political or social, vein. It may be that their formalist bias had its origin in the era of the Prussian victory over France in 1871. Since that time, German society had enjoyed a widespread sense of socio-political and economic security. Hence, in the years just before World War I, politics had come to be ignored by the older generation and disdained as anti-intellectual by the younger. By 1915, however, the full horror of the human catastrophe being wrought by the war had shaken the German people into a new, unavoidably historical consciousness. Whereas pre-war Expressionists had apprehended the decay of Wilhelmine culture in spiritual and philosophical terms, now the need for a socio-political literary praxis was urgently apparent. Thus, stage Expressionism appeared in a context of cultural emergency with the implicit mandate of articulating a new, *historical* understanding of contemporary German society. Yet, because of the political and social turmoil of this era, its development was more discontinuous and diversified than pre-war literary Expressionism. Therefore, to speak of "Expressionist theatre" is to speak of a wide variety of work by artists loosely associated in their historical situation rather than to signify a well-defined coterie united by aesthetic agreement and geographic proximity. The pre-war literary circles had been urban artistic collectives functioning exclusively in a given German city. During the war years, by contrast, the styles of Expressionist theatre productions emerged in a much more de-centralized way, having no such clear-cut geographical identity.

While the Expressionist lyric had offered aesthetic escape from traditional Wilhelmine philistine culture, the Expressionist theatre struggled to enable Germans both to deal with the present devastation and to believe in a future recovery. For many involved in the Expressionist movement, the fulfilment of this faith depended on the success of the so-called November Revolution of 1918. By about 1920, however, the turmoil following the armistice had produced not a radically new and enlightened society but an unstable young republic already hampered at every turn by political conflict and compromise. At this point, most Expressionists cynically conceded not only the "failure of the revolution" but the death of their movement as well. Yet Expressionism continued to influence theatrical production for some three or four years more, in the course of which many critics proclaimed the degeneration of Expressionist theatre into mere sensationalism and commercial opportunism. This period of "black Expressionism," so-called, marks the profoundly cynical, last gasp, phase of the movement. The question lingers, then: who were "the Expressionists" in the theatre? Are we speaking of committed social visionaries, nihilistic pariahs, or simply stylistic opportunists who drew on the Expressionist vogue with greater or less commercial success?[5]

Throughout this study my use of the phrase "the Expressionists" is meant to signify only that relatively small group of theorists and journalists, playwrights, directors, and designers who sought *in writing or other public statement* to define theatrical Expressionism as a movement. To be sure, the production work of a few other influential directors – Reinhardt and Fehling, for example – was regarded by many as definitive of Expressionism in practical terms. However, I include neither these latter directors nor virtually any of the principal actors, producers, or theatre critics under the rubric of "the Expressionists." Rather, one objective of this study is to clarify the relationships between this discrete, relatively small group and the larger theatre community which it so powerfully, if briefly, engaged.

With this qualification in mind, it may be noted that the importance of communal bonding was a paramount theme for the Expressionists. And for a time, their message spoke eloquently to the larger theatrical community, articulating a broadly felt longing for cultural wholeness shared by many Germans. More than any other modern European avant-garde movement, German Expressionism was the product of a crisis of national identity. The most common experience of the Expressionist generation was the feeling of social and spiritual fragmentation, a feeling intensified nearly to the breaking point by the end of the war. Initially, the theatrical response to this crisis was to forge images of human spiritual wholeness. Later, the political, social and economic instability of the young Weimar Republic engendered a cynicism that began to erode Expressionist confidence in the spiritual renewal of German culture. At this point the earlier optimism turned into its opposite – a demonstration of life's inevitable and hopeless spiritual corruption. What remained constant in the theatre through the duration of the movement, however, was the fundamental belief that "expression" was not merely a matter of emotional self-indulgence but rather of the artistic synthesis of life's tragic contradictions. Typically, this synthesis was embodied in the plays in a central figure who had the ability to experience life passionately and to express that experience with great inspiration. The Expressionist orator-hero took decisive control over life through his gift for giving it dynamic expressive form.

The nature of such expressive power was considered to be both private and public; its source was intensely personal yet also to be found in a universal empathy – or, at the end, disgust – with mankind. This contradictory philosophy of expression presented a great challenge to the actors and directors who sought to actualize it on the stage. Their general practical strategy was to develop a kind of performance which synthesized certain of the abstract expressive properties of music, dance, mime, sculpture and painting. In this way, the representation of subjective personal feeling was supposed to become fused with the presentation of "absolute," and therefore universal, artistic form. The "acting" which resulted was not based on the psychological motives and bourgeois individualism implicit in realist performance. Rather, it presupposed the "instrumental" view of the actor dating from Goethe and the era of Weimar classicism. In Expressionist theatre, the actor forfeited the mimetic function as it had been developed in the tradition of Hamburg realism in order to become a synthetic agency of poetic expression, so to speak; a kind of "medium" *through which* the "essential" truths of humanity – as Expressionist playwrights and directors understood them – were poetically expressed. This synthetic strategy characterized the movement across the spectrum of its divergencies of genre and style.

Some of the most prominent artists associated with Expressionism chose to work in several media instead of limiting themselves to only one. For example: Kandinsky wrote plays and poetry in addition to his principal work as a painter; Kokoschka, the painter, was also a playwright, producer and director; Barlach, the sculptor, wrote several well-received plays; Herwarth Walden, the journalist and art exhibitor, composed music for Expressionist productions; Arnold Schönberg, the revolutionary inventor of twelve-tone music, produced several paintings with Der blaue Reiter. Particularly in the seminal case of Kokoschka, the result was work bearing a hybrid character in which properties of the various arts commingled to synthesize new modes in playwriting and theatre production.

As for the actors of Expressionist drama, however, the majority were professionals contracted to commercial theatres in the provinces or in Berlin. With the notable exception of Schreyer's coterie ensemble of amateur performers at the Kampfbühne, Expressionist actors were not Expressionists; they espoused no particular commitment to either the aesthetic programs or the social visions of the movement. None of them worked in the interdisciplinary manner of artists like those just mentioned. Aside from the influential proto-Expressionist actor/playwright Frank Wedekind, I know of no other major professional German actor of this era who wrote plays, painted, composed music, or otherwise produced significant Expressionist art. In fact, the evidence rather suggests that for most of the actors Expressionism was simply another ephemeral style to master. Yet here was a kind of theatre performance that required, like no other, every fiber of emotional energy and physical commitment. The efficacy of Expressionist theatre – in which the scripts, directors, and audiences exacted the highest expectations of performance virtuosity – most depended on the actors; and, more often than not, they seem to have responded well to the challenge. Accordingly, how they succeeded without any apparent ideological fervor becomes a central question for this study. To an unprecedented degree, these actors exemplified Diderot's famous paradox; and their situation, as we shall see, gave new meaning to the old debate about inspiration versus technique.

In comparison with script and scenographic analysis, the subject of performance in Expressionist theatre scholarship has generally received scant attention. German-language studies of Expressionist theatre have tended only to touch on it, typically in the course of analyzing literary and thematic features of the plays. In an early commentary such as Felix Emmel's *Das ekstatische Theater* (1924), even the section specifically entitled "ekstatische Schauspielkunst" is a theoretical polemic, not a descriptive analysis. Emmel is more interested in advocating the replacement of psychological acting with performance based on "ecstasy of the blood" [die Ekstase des Blutes] than he is in explaining specifically what such a stage art might involve. Bernhard Diebold's influential *Anarchie im Drama* (1921) develops a typology of Expressionist drama based on how various plays position the hero ethically and socially. But neither this contemporary thematic approach nor later studies examining, variously, sociological imagery, theoretical application, and even stage directions, attempt to document or theorize the specific functional situation of the actor on the Expressionist stage.[6]

English works on stage Expressionism generally conceive of it scenically, emphasizing the design elements as the most "Expressionist" aspects of the productions. They acknowledge a deliberate artificiality in Expressionist performance but typically attribute its specific characteristics to the influence of stylistic features in script, setting and lighting. Yet, while elaborating the range of variation in design style or language and characterization, these works frequently assume a more or less uniform stylization in the acting. Mel Gordon acknowledges a variety of Expressionist performance modes in his article, "German Expressionist Acting" (1975); however, he merely glosses their stylistic differences and makes no attempt to analyze them as expressive strategies with specific ideological purposes.[7] In his *The Revolution in German Theatre: 1900–1930* (1981), Michael Patterson identifies two basic tendencies – primitivism and abstractionism; but in the process he ignores significant stylistic variations in both primitivist and abstractionist performance. He provides no consideration, for example, of the evocative neo-symbolist abstractionism of Lothar Schreyer's Kampfbühne ensemble. Yet Schreyer was the chief performance theorist and stage director in the *Sturm* circle, arguably Berlin's most influential Expressionist association. In the only other English publication specifically on acting style, Dennis Calandra attempts to convey "the nature of Expressionist performance" by analyzing a film adaptation of one Expressionist play, Kaiser's *Von morgens bis mitternachts*.[8] While his description of the acting is valuable, it by no means encompasses the richness and diversity of live Expressionist stage performance; much less does it account for its "nature."

The present study is an attempt to render such an account. Since the available evidence supports Gordon's argument that there were three basic types of Expressionist performance, I have retained his tri-partite framework rather than Patterson's dualist model. Bearing in mind the dangers inherent in any overly rigid scheme of classification, I accept Gordon's rubrics "Schrei" and "Geist" as basically apt labels for two of the three general kinds of acting. Indeed, the emotional intensity of early provincial stage Expressionism often culminated in a climactic scream outburst; and the abstract, evocative choral performances of Schreyer's Sturm-Bühne/Kampfbühne ensemble did resemble the Symbolist theatre's concentration on the "Geist," in the sense of "spiritual," mode of consciousness in acting. However, I take up these two terms as starting points for a very different kind of analysis. Whereas Gordon's concern was purely stylistic, mine is also rhetorical. That is, I propose to examine the varieties of Expressionist performance style as modes of "discourse," not simply as sensational formal experiments. For some of its practitioners and aficionados, stage Expressionism was certainly the latter. However, I am drawn to the former way of thinking about Expressionist performance because its stylizations were a serious attempt to find an empowering historical rhetoric for a society in crisis.

That, obviously, is what discourses are for. They rhetorically structure perceptions of social situations for the tactical and strategic advantage of some group – they are a means to power. The difference between style and discourse is that the former is a relatively individual matter of conscious and intentional rhetorical choice whereas the latter arises, more collectively and less directly, out of an ideological base. Style produces deliberate and distinct constructions; discourses reveal pervasive ideological orientations. Whatever particular style an individual writer may use, discourse, to some degree, uses, "writes," every writer. Thus, it is possible for several unique styles to express the same basic discourse. This principle is the theoretical keystone of the present study. Expressionist performance styles, though quite distinct from one another, partook of the same essential discourse of poetic social empowerment. Yet this is not to argue that Expressionist style is somehow less important or worthy of analysis than Expressionist discourse. My argument, rather, is that theatrical Expressionism is distinctive in the way that it cultivated a symbiotic relationship between the two. Every mode of Expressionist acting conveyed and was driven by a discourse of historical crisis and "expressive" empowerment. Thus, when I speak of a "Schrei" or "Geist" Expressionist performance mode, my goal is a kind of combined discourse/style criticism that examines both the ideological base and the material tropes of Expressionist theatrical rhetoric in terms of each other.

Conceived thus, the book is intended to address both those readers just getting acquainted with theatrical Expressionism and those who may wish to consider a new approach to a familiar subject. A cursory exposure to this era of German stage history evokes images of intense accents in scenic design, lighting, stage movement and speech. But aside from its sensational interest, exactly what and how did such an emphatic performance grammar signify? The answers are not self-evident. It is not enough simply to say that the emphatic stylizations of Expressionism expressed alienation from bourgeois culture or the horrors of the war experience; beyond this, Expressionist performance was an attempt to *do* something about these problems. The what and the how of this, therefore, has to do not only with the circumstances of Expressionist performance in the theatre itself, but also with the cultural background out of which Expressionism, as a strategy for dealing with history, emerges.

Accordingly, Chapter One of this study is a brief description of the philosophical traditions and socio-economic forces which shaped the values that produced Expressionist theatre in Germany. I have chosen to provide only a synopsis of the material such a chapter might contain because to describe and analyze in full detail the history of German culture at this time is obviously a book-length study in itself, one which has been done well several times in English as well as German.[9] Having laid this necessary foundation, the ensuing chapters explore Expressionist discourse at the technical, stylistic level of rhetoric. Chapter Two discusses the major theatrical antecedents of Expressionist performance as a way of defining artistic strategies upon which the actors and directors of stage Expressionism could have drawn in attempting to meet the demands of the scripts. Such background is essential to – indeed is a part of – the particular historical argument this book advances about the nature of Expressionist performance. For those readers having little familiarity with the Expressionist era it is necessary preparation for the later chapters. On the other hand, readers with expertise in the field may wish to skim the first two chapters and engage my argument in detail beginning at Chapter Three. From this point to the end of the study, historical analyses of specific Expressionist performance modes reference and apply, as needed, the background material set forth in Chapters One and Two.

My intention in the first two chapters of the book is to describe the cultural environment which facilitated the emergence of Expressionist performance, not to argue for some clear evolutionary line of development. Indeed, such a reductive model would miss the distinctive geneses of the different kinds of performance which, though related synchronically as discourse, were stylistically quite undiachronic. For this reason, the final three chapters are an attempt to consider the varieties of Expressionist performance each in their own terms. The third chapter examines the Schrei mode, while analysis of Geist acting is the business of Chapter Four. In his article, Gordon identifies a third performance mode as the "Ich" ("ego" or "confessional") style in which a solitary individual performed in the Schrei manner against a background choral ensemble of stereotyped, two-dimensional characters. However, I shall argue in Chapter Five that both the "Ich" rubric and its definition are misconceived and must be replaced by a more appropriate model which I term "emblematic performance."

My ultimate objective is both to distinguish the stylistic features of the three modes and to identify assumptions about the historical nature of stage "expression" which they held in common. In this way, as I said earlier, I hope to make some sense of the term "Expressionism" as it was applied to quite disparate modes of performance and, consequentially, to arrive at a fundamental understanding of the Expressionist actor as the central operative in a theatrical program of cultural revolution. Across the various modes, the basic "expressive" goal appears to have been quite uniform: namely, to create the experience of "ecstasy" – as a mode of historical consciousness – in both actors and audience. In every type of Expressionist performance, the poetic word was regarded as the kernel from which the playwright's ecstatic vision, as a force of cultural transformation, was to be unleashed. Often, however, it was the director rather than the actor who was regarded – by himself, as well as the actors and critics – as the liberator of "expression." Therefore, in examining the varieties of Expressionist performance on their own terms, I also give necessary attention to the actor–director relationship. Typically, the most successful Expressionist directors were auteurs who boldly shaped the acting to serve their ideas of the scripts, even if those interpretations differed markedly – as they sometimes did – from the stated intentions of the playwrights.

However, the interpretations of the directors – together with the nature of the scripts, the formulations of the theorists, and the judgments of the critics – must finally be understood as reflective of the most decisive influence on the development of theatrical Expressionism: that is, the relatively sudden emergence of a new, historical consciousness in the German people. Before 1914, as the eminent theatre critic Herbert Ihering later recalled,

it was a time of peace. Our hearts stand still when we hear this word. Peace. People were at peace in their beliefs, in their consciousness, and in their imagination. At peace also in their blindness. Because they had faith, they did not see.[10]

Virtually until the day of mobilization, German political life had slumbered in the complacent assumption of a natural and gradual socio-economic progress which transcended any threat of political disturbance, not to mention the undreamt-of possibility of war on German soil. Thus, by 1915 what had befallen many Germans was an unexpected and troubling awareness of impending historical crisis. At this point, support of the war effort became the great water-shed dividing German society. Those who prosecuted the war did so ultimately as a last stand against the passing of the old Wilhelmine order. Those who resisted the war were fighting, more generally, for the birth of a new Germany. For the latter, among whom the Expressionists were most articulate, the salvation of Germany was synonymous with opposition to the war. For the former – the conservative, militarist camp – only final defeat and royal abdication could compel an acceptance of historical change. Whether it was welcomed or abhorred, this new and fundamental understanding of contemporary German life could no longer be avoided.

So it was that the theatre, along with every other aspect of culture, became increasingly politicized and polemical from the closing years of the war through the brief revolutionary period following the armistice. This was especially the case with late Expressionist performance in Berlin. In the final analysis, however, what becomes clear is that the Expressionist theatre – even in the work of its most political writer, Ernst Toller – was never able effectively to address the political complexities of the early Republic. In place of dialectical reflection, it offered a kind of aesthetic faith that life could be made whole through an art of intense expression. To this end, the actor – as raw material for the director, and sometimes raw meat for the audience – became the medium in which theatrical Expressionism performatively inscribed its discourse of cultural renewal.

CHAPTER I

Abstraction and empathy: the philosophical background in the socio-economic foreground

OVERVIEW

The two most distinctive characteristics of the Expressionist movement in literature and drama were its theme of cultural regeneration and the self-conscious artificiality of its creative methods. The idea of renewal took on a variety of practical postures ranging from defiant, emotional rejection of Wilhelmine culture to mystical, spiritual transcendence of it.[1] Accordingly, "Expressionism" manifested itself in markedly divergent forms, and this situation was no where more evident than in the theatre productions themselves. Stylistically, what most clearly linked the varieties of theatre performance which were called "Expressionist" was a firm rejection of the mimetic representation of social life in favor of an abstract, or at least overtly theatrical, rendering of it. Why Expressionism in the theatre developed a strategy of deliberate artificiality to effect its vision of social regeneration is the question this opening chapter will address. The short answer is that modern European anti-realist artists – the Germans not least – assumed that a revolution in aesthetic form amounted to a full scale cultural revolution.[2] Why the Expressionists, in particular, made that assumption is the underlying question that requires a more detailed analysis of the particular sensibility which blossomed in young German artists and intellectuals in the first two decades of the twentieth century. The germs of that sensibility are to be found generally in the philosophical tradition shaped by Kant, Schopenhauer, Nietzsche, and Bergson, and particularly in the socio-economic dynamics of middle-class Wilhelmine culture.

In their rejection of mimesis, the Expressionists certainly did not abandon the Naturalist artistic program of social utility; rather, they simply located social "reality" not in empirical experience but in what they regarded as the more fundamental and comprehensive realm of the "spiritual." The social utility of art was evident in its unique power to access this realm and connect it to contemporary social life. Because of the particular social instability of late Wilhelmine Germany, moreover, the relationship between innovative theatrical performance and historical change is unusually evident. My purpose, therefore, is to explore the ways and means by which Expressionist theatre "performed" the demise of Wilhelmine society and its transformation into what would later be known as Weimar culture. Initially this requires a description both of the aesthetic of "autonomous art" that emerged from the philosophical traditions of German idealism and of the spirit of cultural rebellion provoked by Wilhelmine authoritarian social structures. The former resulted in an insistence on the non-representational self-sufficiency of art. The latter produced in many young Germans a strong need to declare, in specifically *emotional* terms, their individual liberation from Wilhelmine patriarchal values. Together they engendered a conviction of the absolute validity of subjective expression as the mode of cultural resistance necessary for the renewal of German culture.

In *Abstraktion und Einfühlung* (1908) – the theoretical treatise on modern art which, together with Vassily Kandinsky's *Über das Geistige in der Kunst* (1912), most influenced the development of Expressionist aesthetics – Wilhelm Worringer argued that the work of art is an "autonomous organism." As such, it "stands beside nature on equal terms and, in its deepest and innermost essence, [is] devoid of any connection with it, in so far as by nature is understood the visible surface of things." It arises not out of the mimetic urge, whose "gratification has, [in principle], nothing to do with art," but rather out of "absolute artistic volition" [*das Kunstwollen*]. Worringer defined this principle as

that latent inner demand which exists *per se*, entirely independent of the object and of the mode of creation, and behaves as *will to form*. It is the primary factor in all artistic creation and, in its innermost essence, every work of art is simply an objectification of the *a priori* existent absolute artistic volition. [italic emph. mine][3]

With this concept, Worringer provided Expressionist painters, particularly in Kandinsky's *Blaue Reiter* group, with both an aesthetic and a social theory of subjectivity. In every individual artist, subjectivity *wills* its own unique expressive forms; yet it does so from within a faculty, "absolute artist volition," which is common to all humanity and therefore of a specifically social character in any given epoch. Subjectivity is conceived as both individual and collective, and the contradiction between self and other is thus mediated.

This principle, for Worringer, was a function of human spiritual development. Both primitive man, seeking security in the presence of the noumenal forces he apprehends in nature, and sophisticated modern man, who renounces and wishes to transcend the material world, take up the artistic strategy of abstraction. At the outset, it is important to realize that "abstraction" – as Worringer and the Expressionist artists he influenced understood the term – did not refer simply to an aesthetic of non-representational formalism such as that developed by Kandinsky in painting around 1910. Rather, it signified a general rejection of mimesis which was expressed in a variety of styles ranging from cool geometrism to highly emotional primitivism. This rejection occurred, argued Worringer, because the particular "will to form" in both primitive times and the age of Modernity stands opposed to empirical reality and its materialist differentiations. In these epochs, the forms into which subjectivity wills itself bond humankind in a symbolically abstract, non-materialist, and hence "spiritual" art. For the Expressionists, rejection of mimesis defined their generation in terms of a collective subjectivity whose particular "artistic volition" emerged as a will to resist the authoritarian materialism of Wilhelmine culture. Going well beyond the promptings of individual subjectivity, this art of "Expression" was matter of social liberation.

The origin of the term "Expressionism" itself is somewhat obscure. Rudolf Blümner, an actor, performance teacher, and aesthetic theorist who was associated with the drama section of the influential *Sturm* Expressionist circle in Berlin, wrote in 1921 that the concepts of "impression" and "expression" were distinguished, in religious terms, as early as the thirteenth century by St. Thomas Aquinas.[4] According to John Willett, however,

the earliest printed appearances of the word "expressionist" were a reference to 'the expressionist school of modern painters' in *Tait's Edinburgh Magazine* in July 1850; an allusion to 'the expressionists, those who undertake to express special emotions or passions' in a lecture on modern painting given by Charles Rowley in Manchester on 23 February 1880; and the title given to a group of writers, 'The Expressionists', in the novel *The Bohemian* (1878) by the *New York Times* critic Charles De Kay, who was the American consul-general in Berlin between 1894 and 1897.[5]

In 1901, the French painter Julien-Auguste Hervé had employed the word "Expressionism" in order to describe an exhibition of his paintings at the Salon des Indépendents in Paris. Subsequently, the term was used by Hervé and other French artists and critics to characterize the work of such painters as Cézanne, Van Gogh, Matisse, Gauguin, and Pechstein. In Germany, the term "Expressionism" came into general use when Worringer, referring to these same artists, wrote about the "young Parisian Synthetists and Expressionists," in the August 1911 issue of *Der Sturm*. By 1914 the word was commonly employed in German avant-garde periodicals for designating the work of a certain group of poets and painters whom, since 1910, they had been calling variously "die Jungen," "die Jüngeren," "die Jüngsten," "die neuen Dichter," "die fortgeschrittenen Dichter," etc. Hugo Ball was among the first to talk of an "Expressionistic theatre," as early as 1914. However, it was not until 1916 that this idea was formally proclaimed by Walter Hasenclever in a series of *Die Schaubühne* essays on "the theatre of tomorrow . . . the call for a spiritual stage."[6] This was also the year which saw the first self-proclaimed "Expressionist" drama, Hasenclever's *Der Sohn*, on the German stage.[7]

The Expressionist impulse originated in painting and German Expressionist painters had organized themselves into associations such as Die Brücke (Dresden, 1905) and Der Blaue Reiter (Munich, 1912). But German Expressionism as a movement was most clearly defined in literature and through the medium of literary circles and such related journals as *Der Sturm, Die Aktion, Die weißen Blätter*, and *Die Schaubühne*.[8] The lyric was the dominant genre of literary Expressionism from approximately 1910 until the latter stages of the war when drama emerged as the chief Expressionist vehicle. Like its literary antecedents, Expressionist drama was symbolic and rhetorical, not analytic and representational. Therefore, the basic material of Expressionist theatrical performance was poetic image, not psychological insight. "Acting," for the Expressionists, was not a matter of imitating goal-oriented actions but rather of presenting a series of more or less abstract images on stage. For this reason it bore close relation to the arts of music, dance and sculpture, which certainly have mimetic potential but, since the beginning of the modern era, frequently have been used abstractly to embody non-mimetic poetic ideas and images.

The place of poetry as a mode of cognition in traditional German culture is well reflected in Peter Gay's remark that "Germany can be said to be the only country that could have taken seriously Shelley's famous sweeping dictum that 'poets are the unacknowledged legislators of the world'."[9] Before post-war cynicism began to erode their hope of cultural regeneration, the literary Expressionists' most fundamental assumption about poetic art was based on the well-established traditional belief in its power of "Bildung," its ability literally to shape society with its inspirational effect. Initially articulated by Schiller in his *Letters on the Aesthetic Education of Man* (1795), this traditional faith was particularly embraced by Expressionist playwrights and performance theorists for whom the modern avant-garde theatre resembled that of ancient Greece. The Expressionist stage, like the ancient theatre, was not intended as a place of mere entertainment; rather, it claimed for itself the status of a sanctuary wherein the deepest spiritual truths of the culture were embodied and apprehended.

Expressionist theorists looked to ancient drama as the highest dramatic form and, in their own peculiar way, they sought to use it as their model. Ivan Goll, for example, conceived of Greek drama as "an immense heightening of reality, the deepest, most mysterious, Pythian surrender to boundless passion, to consuming pain, represented in a supernatural manner." For Lothar Schreyer, Aeschylus was an "Expressionist" while Euripides was a "Naturalist." In the plays of Aeschylus, as Schreyer read them, the focus of the drama is not the man of action but the man "who suffers the pain of revelation." According to Goll, modern drama, by comparison, had not been able to give expression to the full life of the community. The "law of the mask" had to be re-established, he argued, because the mask is "fixed, unchangeable and penetrating. It represents Fate, and each individual wears his mask, which is what antiquity calls guilt."[10] Expressionist theatre – particularly in its early, provincial phase between the years 1916 and 1919 – sought to recapture this full life of the community. In place of the scapegoat king of ancient drama the early Expressionist playwrights created the "New Man," whose capacity to experience "the pain of revelation" would lead to social renewal through his inspirational expression of that experience. In effect, the New Man became the Ur-mask of contemporary German culture; like the mask of the ancients, this figure seemed to possess a numinous power of penetrating to and revealing essential truth about the human condition.

Walter Sokel has argued that the "New Man" was an embodiment of the young German intellectual's conflict between the longing to be bonded to his fellow men, on the one hand, and an inescapable sense of aloofness from communal life, on the other.[11] Yet such a generalization doesn't really specify how the early Expressionist intellectuals and poets related to their own contemporaries, aside from their rejection of their fathers' generation. It begs the question of how and to what degree the New Man actually represented his "fellow men." Notwithstanding the rhetoric of "universality," with whom did the Expressionist really long to be bonded? To whom did he actually address his impassioned plea for brotherhood – some comprehensive idea of generational community or only an elite cadre of his fellow intellectuals and aesthetes? From whom did he at the same time withhold his fellowship? It was in the theatre, as no where else in the arts, that these questions were sociologically concretized and explored. Indeed, a detailed study of Expressionist performance reveals how the German actor's body and voice, in their very physical and socio-economic materiality, wrestled with the trope of the New Man. The striking and quite unintentional by-product of this struggle was an on-going critique of Expressionist sociology, which conceived of the poetic image and the power of rhetoric as significant forces of historical determination. More than the readily pliable mediums of words, musical sounds, paint or clay, the refractory physical and social materiality of the actor rigorously tested this conception. It was not the Expressionist dramatist but the Expressionist actor who truly represented, embodied, the historical situation which Expressionism attempted to shape.

Clearly the New Man concept expressed a theory of social formation analogous to the substitutionary scapegoat pattern of ancient drama and its essentially nationalist idea of "mankind." The appeal of this dramatic paradigm of historical change is understandable when one considers that the German federation, like the fifth-century Athenian polis, was still relatively isolated politically and culturally from its neighboring states. It is therefore not surprising that – as in the drama of classical Athens, so for the Wilhelmine Expressionists – the power of rhetoric, of impassioned speech, should seem to have about it the force of historical determinism understood as universal destiny. Within such a conception of society the idea of the New Man as the representative of all men, like that of the polis king as he is represented in Periclean drama, seemed credible. And as in the ancient theatre, so in the theatre of Expressionism, the enactment of this messianic myth had profound implications for the art of acting. An appreciation of them begins with a look at the heritage with reference to which Expressionist writers defined themselves and constructed their own version of the past, the present, and the future. This heritage was spawned in German philosophical idealism and specifically shaped by the Wilhelmine academic institutionalization of the German classical tradition.

Both the alienation of young German intellectuals and their longing for social wholeness were aspects of the general realization that Wilhelmine Germany lagged behind the rapid and radical remaking of culture elsewhere in Western Europe. German Naturalism had dramatized the social consequences of rapid economic and technological progress. Expressionism attempted to show how these historical developments necessarily reconstituted the individual subject as an existential pariah whose only viable social option was to inhabit an alternative mythical realm of the "spirit." Naturalism had defined humankind as a specimen, a datum; Expressionism declared material existence essentially metaphorical, the very flesh and bones of the human body itself the symbolic vehicle of a fundamental, spiritual level of reality. Many Expressionist writers concretized this reality through the trope of "suffering," which they conceived as the common bond of all people. This, in fact, was their principal rhetorical strategy for coming to terms with the process of historical change in Germany. It became the task of German actors in the Expressionist theatre to perform the process of cultural change symbolized in this trope. In a variety of modes, the stylistic choices of Expressionist performance textualized the body of the actor by inscribing in it "young Germany's" story of estrangement and longing, a script that German intellectuals had been rehearsing ever since Kant's *Critique of Pure Reason* (1789) created the philosophic basis of modernism itself.

I. THE PHILOSOPHICAL TRADITION

According to Kant, "nature" is not an objective context in which man occupies a preordained place, but rather it is a subjective construct that man projects upon phenomena. It follows therefore that both mimesis and revelation are impossible as bases of art. That is, "objective" nature does not exist as an object to be imitated, and revelation is impossible because the human mind is incapable of apprehending ultimate truth (or the "Ding-an-sich" – the "thing in itself"). Rather, argued Kant, art is essentially solipsistic. Since the artist creates his own universe, man becomes like God in the creative act. His art is therefore "autonomous"; it exists apart from the dictates of empiricism and moral law, as an end unto itself. Empirical experience is formulated in the conceptual language of "logical ideas"; but the form of art, Kant maintained, is the "aesthetic idea," which is embodied in metaphor. The aesthetic idea he defined as "that representation of the imagination which induces much thought, yet without the possibility of any definite thought whatever, i.e., concept, being adequate to it."[12]

The significance of the aesthetic idea in human experience is that it replaces reason with intuition as the mode of cognition. Art is autonomous because the intuitive significance of aesthetic ideas is self-contained and self-authenticating rather than referential; aesthetic "meaning" exists as a matter of mythic faith rather than empirical proof. Here originates the modern assumption of a quasi-religious redemptive power in art, an attitude which emerges in the work of Wagner, flourishes in French symbolism, and finally becomes the Ur-theme of the anti-realist tendency in modernism as a whole. Here is also the philosophical basis for a view of "expression" as something more than merely the vehicle of content; instead, expression becomes content itself.

In Romantic philosophy this identity of form and content was conceived as the "organic" property of art. The concept of "Organismus" or organism was developed primarily by Kant, but it was Schiller – to be sure, under the influence of Kant – who formulated its revolutionary practical implications for art. In his *Letters on the Aesthetic Education of Man* (1795), Schiller maintained that the meaning of a work of art is not to be found in its individual aspects but only in how their working relationships comprise a dynamic whole; that is, art is meaningful not in terms of content but only in terms of form:

In a true work of art, the content should effect nothing, the form everything; for form alone has an effect upon the whole man, while subject-matter by contrast affects only individual faculties. The content, then – however sublime and comprehensive it may be – is always restricted in its influence upon the spirit; and only from form can true aesthetic freedom be anticipated. Therefore, the mystery of the master artist exists in this: that the form does away with the content.[13]

Schiller here anticipates what the Expressionist painter and play-wright Vassily Kandinsky would say about "non-objective art" in *Über das Geistige in der Kunst*. In this treatise, one of Expressionism's most influential theoretical documents, Kandinsky argued that

it is never literally true that a form is meaningless and "says nothing." Every form in the world says something . . . There are artists who even today experience abstract form as something quite precise and use it to the exclusion of any other means. This seeming stripping bare becomes an inner enrichment.[14]

Interestingly, however, German Romanticism also arrived at the principle of "autonomous art" from a cynical perspective. In this view, mimesis was regarded as a pathetic fiction effective only in deluding any fool who really did believe that poets are the unac-knowledged legislators of the world. Though art might indeed reflect the superficial data of sense experience, so the argument ran, it was unable to reveal or represent any essential reality. Kleist, for example, read Kant very pessimistically. For him, the insight that man can have no ultimate insight was devastating. Though he appears to have battled this sense of despair with such chauvinistic pieces as *The Prince of Homburg* (1811) (written in the year of his suicide), *Käthchen von Heilbronn* (1809) and *Hermannsschlacht* (1810), the plays of his near contemporaries Büchner and Grabbe are thor-oughly imbued with a cynical rejection of any redemptive hope for humankind. The basic theme of these dramatists is the impossibility – or, in Büchner's case, perhaps, the hostility – of a higher, transcendent reality in a predatory world driven by human appetite and self-interest. For them art could only imitate a fragmented world of alienation; it had no power to generate, much less reveal, any compensatory synthesis of life's contradictions.

Chief among such pessimists in philosophical writing was Arthur Schopenhauer, who argued that neither the metaphorical nor the rational faculties could ever be truly creative or liberating because they were inescapably mired in the rational limitations of language. They merely masked the ultimate absurdity of human existence itself in the face of the unknowable "Ding-an-sich" which Kant had postulated. This "thing in itself," which Schopenhauer termed the "Will," Kant had conceived as benignly irrelevant, in its final unknowability, to human affairs. Schopenhauer, by contrast, char-acterized the Will as the ultimate Cosmic force, which disguises itself in phenomenal experience and impels the universe onward with the force of its own ruthless self-assertion. Granting Kant's point about the limitations of human understanding, the Will thus appeared cruelly indifferent to all human intentions just as it compromised them at every turn. Human life, then, could only be viewed as meaningless and absurd. Therefore, to congratulate oneself on the accomplishments of one's culture or, indeed, of civilization as a whole, argued Schopenhauer, was the equally cruel delusion underlying all human unhappiness. The way out of this trap was to recognize and accept the uniformity of the Will behind the rationally differentiated, and therefore illusory, categories which determine human motives. Only with the acceptance of the fundamental identity of all things could man transcendentally perceive the world as "Idea" and become free.

As "Will," life could amount only to nihilistic chaos; but as "Idea" it became the complete freedom of will-less contemplation, through the pure form of absolute art. For Kant, the artist's subjectivity – his own God-like individuality – was the best possible human *approximation* of ultimate reality. Truth was rationally projected form. Schopenhauer's artist, by contrast, could *know* the Truth, but only by divesting his art of all rational elements of representation. For Schopenhauer, only music had the power to work the transfiguration of Will into Idea because "Music is by no means like the other arts, the copy of the Ideas," (i.e., essences) but it is "the copy of the Will itself."[15] Music, he argued, speaks directly to our intuitive feelings. Unhampered by the medium of ideas and language, it reveals the Will immediately, as it exists before assuming the disguises of natural individuation. For this reason, argued Schopenhauer, all art should aspire to the condition of music, which represents nothing and thus, in representational terms, is formless. Artistic formlessness, in this sense, is itself the form, the "Idea," of the Will.

The importance of this conception as a legacy to Expressionism is evident in that every type of Expressionist performance drew upon the non-representational model of music. However, Schopenhauer's significance for the Expressionist theatre is also clear in what he has to say about the Will's expression of itself in the human body and in human character:

The act of will and the movement of the body are not two different things objectively known, which the bond of causality unites; they do not stand in the relation of cause and effect; *they are one and the same* . . . The action of the body is nothing but the act of the will objectified. This is true of every movement of the body . . . *the whole body is nothing but objectified will* . . . The parts of the body must therefore completely correspond to the principal *desires* through which the will manifests itself; *they must be the visible expression of these desires. Teeth, throat and bowels are objectified hunger; the organs of generation are objectified sexual desire* . . . As the human body generally corresponds to the human will generally, so the individual bodily structure corresponds to the individually modified will, the character of the individual. [italics mine][16]

That Schopenhauer's words here adumbrate a theory of Expressionist acting is suggested by comparison of them with remarks by Expressionist performance theorists. Paul Kornfeld, for example, argued that

. . . the actor who merely performs is truer in his expression than many an individual who is subject to an actual destiny. Discretion with regard to many things in real life hinders a person from expressing himself completely: the memory of many things binds him up and the rays of a thousand events cross through him. So at any moment he can only be a changing complex of behavior.[17] However, the actor is free of all that. He is not a complex, but always a *unity* and is in no way falsified. Therefore he can only be clear and straightforward. And since he is *only* this unique embodiment of unity, he can be it completely and magnificently. By shaping that embodiment, the actor will find the emotion which expresses its essence.[18]

The key idea in both of these passages is that of "embodiment." As "the whole body is nothing but objectified will" for Schopenhauer, so acting is essential "embodiment" for Kornfeld. This is what the Expressionist theorist Kasimir Edschmid was getting at in his remark that the actor playing a sick man plays "not merely the cripple who suffers; he becomes sickness itself."[19] The principle was also articulated by the stage director Leopold Jessner at the height of the Expressionist movement. His 1919 Staatstheater production of *Wilhelm Tell*, he said, sought to enact "not the story but the idea behind the story."[20]

What Walter Sokel says of Ernst Barlach's sculpture "The Avenger" aptly describes the basic technical objective of the kind of acting Jessner had in mind: "The expressive gesture of movement possesses the figure to such a degree that the figure becomes the carrier of the expression, a means for making an emotional state visible."[21] Through a sculptural use of his body, the Expressionist actor became possessed by the form of expressive gesture. In this way, he sought abstractly to capture images which illuminated the essence of human life. With such an approach to acting he attempted to become "dissolved in humanity," to use the Expressionist playwright Georg Kaiser's phrase.[22] The sculptural element in Expressionist acting is a topic to which I shall return in Chapter Five in relation to Jessner's productions of *Wilhelm Tell* and *Richard III*. Here I simply observe that Expressionist acting incorporated a sculptural principle of plasticity as part of its general synthetic performance strategy for expressing essential truth.

When the Expressionists talk of "essentializing" they are seeking to capture, in a communal way, something very like a direct experience of Schopenhauer's "Idea." Here we encounter the problem of the audience, or more broadly, the sociological question. The Expressionists, unlike Schopenhauer, could not allow themselves to side-step this issue and be content with talk of the natural aristocracy of genius and its inevitable social isolation. The experience of World War I led most Expressionist artists and theorists to the conclusion that personal insight was valuable only insofar as it created community; that vision was given primarily for social redemption, not merely individual enlightenment. Though Schopenhauer greatly influenced the philosophical tradition which gave the Expressionists their understanding of the nature of art, his basic elitism wasn't much help in defining its social value. For this the Expressionists initially looked to Nietzsche.[23]

At first thought, Nietzsche would appear as unlikely a source of inspiration as Schopenhauer for a vision of collective social regeneration; at least the Nietzsche of Zarathustrian elitism. Unlike Zarathustra, the Expressionist New Man must find a way to overcome the isolation of his creative genius. His vision is but a nightmare if it cuts him off from his fellow men; indeed, it is precisely for humankind that he suffers the vision at all. But though Zarathustra disdains the commonness of mankind, Dionysus ecstatically plummets to its primal depths; and it was in this latter Nietzschean persona that Expressionist dramatists found a compelling theoretical model. In practice, however, Expressionist sociology amounted to a fusing of these two extremes: intellect and instinct. The conception of the latter faculty as developed by Nietzsche, and later Henri Bergson, was not of a blind biological compulsion but rather of an innate and direct cognition of ultimate reality unmediated by intellect and its rational constructs. Human initiative was truly productive – i.e., creatively progressive – only as it accepted the risk of yielding itself fully to the force of "instinct." The "New Man" was to possess the superior wisdom and vision of Zarathustra and also the daring leadership and joyful self-sacrifice of Dionysus. Art, the necessary medium for this fusion, would produce a new and transcendent mode of existence characterized by what Nietzsche had called a mood of "tragic optimism."[24] What we learn from the Greeks, he had argued, is the power of art to conquer the pessimism that life inevitably inspires in us. By making their suffering the subject of their drama the Greeks discovered that it is "only as an esthetic phenomenon . . . that existence and the world appear justified."[25] The knowledge born of "tragic optimism" is a knowledge of suffering which all men share; and, most importantly, because it is an *instinctual* awareness they are bonded by it.

The cognitive power of "instinct" was both a prominent theme in Expressionist drama and a basic theoretical principle of "ecstatic" performance. As we shall see in Chapter Two, it is particularly associated with Vitalism, whose influence on Expressionist dramaturgy and acting originates generally in Bergson's philosophy of "creative evolution" and specifically in the playwriting and the performing of Frank Wedekind. It was Bergson who, along with Nietzsche, so forcefully maintained that the innate operation of human intuition was our only means of directly apprehending ultimate reality. Only by means of this faculty, argued Bergson, can we know the essence of our lives, which is the intuitive consciousness of, and instinctive communion with, the *élan vital.* It is this comprehensive and mysterious vital force which drives all life creatively to fulfilment and beyond that to new potentiality. Likewise for Wedekind, and the Expressionists who modeled their work on his example, the cultivation of instinctual consciousness was not merely libertarian self-indulgence but a principle of both individual human development and social progress. If this principle appeared nihilistic, it was because it involved a good deal of personal risk in its unavoidable confrontation with the social inhibitions and cultural taboos which atrophy human growth. For, as Bergson had argued, ". . . in the evolution of life, just as in the evolution of human societies and of individual destinies, the greatest successes have been for those who accepted the heaviest risks."[26]

Vitalism was nihilistic, that is, only to those who could not recognize its essential spirit of self-sacrifice. Indeed, Nietzsche had emphasized this self-sacrificial spirit in man's developmental progress

to "superman" [*Übermensch*]. The very predicate of Dionysian instinctual knowledge, it was as essential to the enlightened consciousness of the superman as Zarathustrian intellectual vision. As
Nietzsche had said in *Thus Spake Zarathustra*:

I teach you superman. Man is a something that shall be surpassed. What
have ye done to surpass him? . . . What is great in man is that he is a bridge
and not a goal: what can be loved in man is that he is a *transition* and a
destruction. I love those who do not know how to live except in perishing, for
they are going beyond. I love the great despisers because they are the great
adorers, they are arrows of longing for the other shore. I love those who do
not seek beyond the stars for a reason to perish and be sacrificed, but who
sacrifice themselves to earth in order that earth may some day become
superman's . . . [27]

What is most striking about this passage is the relationship, which
Nietzsche stresses (the italics are his), between the idea of destruction
and the idea of transition. In the resulting concept of evolutionary
self-sacrifice, the Nietzschean legacy that unites Expressionist aesthetics and Expressionist sociology into a coherent vision is apparent.
From this perspective, the juxtapositions of nihilism and salvation, of
ecstasy and contemplation, of primitivism and abstraction, are
comprehensible. The key juxtaposition is that of instinct and intellect, which appear to be antitheses only because they are at opposite
ends of the same cognitive continuum. The point here is not that the
two are different faculties; rather they are different degrees of the
same faculty because, as Nietzsche argued, "instinct is the most
intelligent of all kinds of intelligence which have hitherto been
discovered."[28]

Hence, theatrical "ecstasy" was not merely sensationalist or
provocative (it was certainly these); but, more importantly, for the
Expressionists it was humankind's most advanced mode of intelligence. In their view, it was this evolving knowledge that would be
mankind's salvation. To be sure, such knowledge was a rare
experience because, in practice, the balance of intellect and instinct
was fragile: if intellect predominated, then the visionary power of
instinct was compromised, while the reverse yielded only incoherent
raving. For Nietzsche, of course, the very possibility of tragic drama
depended upon a synthesis of Dionysian freedom and Apollonian
restraint. However, for his young Expressionist disciples this dialectic immediately found a specific and very personal sociological
application.

II. THE PROVOCATION OF EXPRESSIONIST SENSIBILITY

The position of the young German intellectual at the beginning of the Expressionist literary movement in 1910 was one of great emotional complexity. He was the product of an authoritarian, tradition-bound educational system. With its oppressive emphasis on philological training and the stigma it attached to academic failure, Wilhelmine school life was a major factor in the wave of suicides which had taken the lives of 1,152 German adolescents in the last two decades of the nineteenth century.[29] In this context, Wedekind's *Frühlings Erwachen* [*Spring's Awakening*] (1891) is an important proto-Expressionist play thematically as well as stylistically. It demonstrates, in Sokel's words, the relation between "the two cults which dominate German youth in the early twentieth century, the cult of suicide and the cult of passionate irrationalism."[30]

The educational system was the complement of Wilhelmine nuclear family life, and Wedekind's play dramatizes its principal characteristic – the puritanical suppression of adolescent sexuality. The importance of sexuality in Expressionist literature is an index of the degree of institutionalized frustration and humiliation this generation experienced in the home and at school. Since the family and the educational system were the bulwarks of Wilhelmine prudery, they became the prime targets of Expressionism's assault on Wilhelmine moral values. In literature, the prostitute became a figure of liberation from domestic oppression. On stage, proto-Expressionist performers like Wedekind helped to inspire the vitalist spirit of defiance which the sons of late Wilhelmine Germany hurled at their fathers' rigid system of social and sexual taboos. Fritz Kortner, whose portrayals of tyrants made him one of Expressionism's most celebrated actors, created several of those roles on the basis of encounters with abusive professors in his early adolescence.[31]

However, though sexual liberation is a prominent motif in Expressionist ideology, it should be understood, along with the rejection of academic pedanticism, as an aspect of a general rebellion against the traditional concept of cultural authority itself. Thus, defiance of the father's dominance over family life and of the teacher's power in the classroom were but early versions of the larger rejection of the culture of the Fatherland, particularly when the catastrophe of the war had destroyed any remaining vestige of Wilhelmine leadership credibility. On the other hand, the Expressionist vision of social order was not anarchic; the idea of strong cultural leadership itself, far from being discredited, was central to the sociology of Expressionism.[32] Indeed, this was the central meaning in the trope of the "New Man." He was conceived as something of a philosopher king, a destined leader whose gift of superior social enlightenment qualified him to guide the masses by means of his power of inspired expression. In Expressionist drama this leader appeared in two distinct figures: the vitalist/nihilist rebel (e.g., Bitterlich, the central character in Kornfeld's *Die Verführung* [1913)] who smashes spiritually enslaving cultural taboos; and the visionary poet (e.g., Friedrich, the hero of Toller's *Die Wandlung* [1918]) who inspires faith in the future redemption of society through universal brotherhood.[33]

In both cases the objective was to counteract a pervasive assumption about the German middle class: namely, that its historical viability depended on abdicating any effort at collective self-determination. What Wilhelmine authoritarianism had revealed was the intransigence of the aristocratic spirit and the obsolescence of its feudal social temperament in the industrial era in Germany.[34] The most significant consequence of this, according to one social historian of Wilhelmine culture, was that "the German bourgeoisie never formed into a class. It remained a set of aspiring individuals in the class-destroying situation of competing for social status."[35] Since a middle-class revolution never forced the aristocracy to abdicate its social prerogatives, German society remained bound to the caste values embodied in aristocratic privilege. The aristocratic tradition of rigid social organization, and the habit of subordination and obedience it demanded, continued to assert themselves through the main channels of socialization – the educational system and the family.

The feverish pace of economic growth which began with the establishment of the Second Reich in 1870 also helped to entrench the authoritarian social structure. In countries such as England, the more leisurely pace of industrialization had fostered the development of liberal democratic consciousness based on private enterprise capitalism. But Germany's rapid industrial development, being overseen by tight state control, served to consolidate the traditional authoritarian political order. Thus, late Wilhelmine culture, while highly sophisticated technologically and industrially quite competitive, lacked the progressive spirit typical of mature capitalism elsewhere in Europe. Yet there were powerful economic countertendencies as well, which were undermining Wilhelmine authoritarianism. Egbert Krispyn, another social historian of the era, has argued that the ultimate effect of industrialization and urbanization on the bourgeoisie, "from which the Expressionists almost to a man were recruited, . . . was the final dissolution of the patriarchal pattern of existence." Urbanization had swelled the bourgeois as well as the proletarian populations of the cities. In such a setting the traditional large-clan patriarchal way of life gave way to smaller nuclear families ruled by fathers who pretended to the old patriarchal authority. But the discrepancy between this pretense and the typical father's actual, more modest, socio-economic position was painfully obvious. The more a father over-compensated by asserting his authority, the more his son confronted him defiantly with the truth.[36]

However, there is a danger in viewing the father–son antagonism in this era as such a specific and uniformly pervasive pattern in domestic social life. Indeed, the rebellion appears rather to have been fraught with contradictions. Many young German intellectuals found themselves in the ambivalent position of having no personal conflict with their own fathers while being swept along in the general wave of father-hate. The situation is well rendered by Franz Werfel, for example, in his story *Nicht der Mörder, der Ermordete ist schuldig* (*Not the Murderer, but the Victim is Guilty* [1920]). The son in the story asks his father the following rhetorical question: "Are we both subject to an incomprehensible law that we must seek each other out at a distance but hate each other in proximity?"[37] Or consider this remark by Kafka in his *Brief an den Vater* (*Letter to Father*): "I believe that you are entirely guiltless of our alienation, but likewise, I am also not to blame."[38] The fact is that youthful defiance was directed not only at fathers but also, and more generally, at father figures – school teachers and professors, priests, magistrates and judges.[39]

The father–son conflict was truly generational; more than simply a societal pattern of domestic turmoil, it expressed a widely shared anti-authoritarianism. As a theme in Expressionist literature – and particularly in Expressionist drama – this rebellion concretized and symbolically enacted the younger generation's understanding of the processes of historical change. A play like Hasenclever's *Der Sohn*, where the title character strides triumphantly over his father's corpse into a future full of glorious potential, attempted to articulate a concept of historical transformation. Other plays of generational conflict in the years following Hasenclever's 1916 drama similarly sought to perform the triumph of youth in the struggle over Wilhelmine authoritarianism.

The enactment of cultural revolution in the theatre, of course, is never a substitute for the real thing; but always the hope is that theatre can raise consciousness and reshape values, thereby motivating social change. As Brecht repeatedly insisted, social relationships must be analyzed practically in the theatre if any real-life praxis is to emerge. Expressionist theatrical innovation and the idealistic vision that fueled it never yielded any such useful strategic insight, much less any effectual praxis for the reformation of values. Failing to produce any real change in society, the performance of historical change on the Expressionist stage ultimately proved solipsistic. Though it aspired to address humanity at large, Expressionist theatre succeeded only in speaking to and transforming itself; it converted no one outside of its own coterie. Further, while Germany's sons rebelled against the Wilhelmine ideology and culture of father and Fatherland, their program of social renewal also reflected the optimism of that culture and ideology. The Expressionists' confidence that they could redeem culture through art was no less an article of faith than their fathers' belief that Wilhelmine culture was inevitably progressing in and of itself. The two notions of "progress," to be sure, were light-years apart: economic and political expansion versus ethical and intellectual growth. Yet, for a short time, these two models of social development co-existed in a strangely symbiotic relationship. This was evident when, at the outbreak of war, their radically differing social attitudes briefly merged in nationalist spiritual fervor.

The Expressionists' initial hope that the war would galvanize German ethical life reflects their own sense of personal struggle with the contradiction between individual and social identity. Before World War I most Expressionists were apolitical, preferring lyrical individualism over social activism. However, their initial enthusiasm for the war indicates that the political dimension of Expressionism begins not with the anti-war movement of 1915, but with the idea of national identity which the war initially promised in 1914. This first year of the war saw the publication of a million and a half nationalist war poems, with not a few Expressionists among the authors represented.[40] Many Expressionists ardently answered the call to arms, and several – including such pioneer dramatists as Stramm and Sorge – perished. The Expressionist conception of the "nation" as an ethical community was intimately linked to its notion of social "progress." Both assumed a society of ethically responsible individuals, not a phalanx of obedient automatons. As Ernst Toller later argued, such ethical individualism was the product of an almost religious devotion to a politics of ethical feeling:

The basic prerequisite of the political writer (who is somehow always a religious writer) is this: to feel responsible for himself and everyone of his brethren in the human community. To repeat: he must be a human being who feels responsible.[41]

Because of the nationalism which sent the young Expressionists into combat, the war's inability to support such an ethical objective was not apparent at the outset. What the unprecedented horror of those first months of fighting quickly taught German youth was the irrelevance of national identity in such circumstances. For the Expressionists, the vision of a united Germany was replaced by one of a united humanity. As a result, the tides of internationalism and social activism rose up to begin the final assault on Wilhelmine culture.

Not surprisingly, it was at precisely this point, in the latter years of the war, that resistance to social criticism and political change reached its apex in the Wilhelmine ruling classes, as well as in the bourgeoisie. This was most clearly reflected in the pervasive public censorship of the press and other forums, including the theatre. Censorship, of course, was nothing new to the German avant-garde theatre community. Since the inception of the Second Reich in 1870, the growing political strength of Catholicism, for example, had pressured liberal monarchist administrations in Bavaria to prevent "obscenity" and "blasphemy" on the stage.[42] Particularly in the Bavarian capital of Munich, where German theatrical modernism had first developed, the avant-garde's battle with the censor raged in the press and in the courts. By 1917, however, the practice of censorship had become coordinated nationally under the direct supervision of the military leadership. Things had been difficult enough under the scrutiny of the "theatre security police" (*Theatersicherheitspolizei*, a division of the *Sittenpolizei* or "moral police") because the moral judgments of these artistically unqualified officials were enormously influential in censorship decisions. When Expressionist plays first came upon the stage in 1916, "any piece which could be held to undermine the war effort or the morale of the public was certain to be banned from public performance."[43] Consequently, as with so many avant-garde stagings of playwrights like Ibsen and Strindberg in the 1880s and 90s, the earliest Expressionist productions were forced to resort to expedients such as the private performance.

The initial effect of such performances on the Expressionists themselves was to reinforce an elitism which came into conflict with the broader social mission which their drama espoused. For a certain group of Expressionists, however, this protective closing of ranks was not simply intellectual defensiveness. These artists regarded official public rejection of their work through censorship as but another form of the cultural stigma that had marked their whole lives;[44] for no one better understood what it was to be misunderstood than the Expressionist who was also a Jew. Though Jews accounted for less than one percent of the German population, their influence on German culture in the first decades of the twentieth century was enormous. At this time, according to Istvan Deak,

The owners of three of Germany's greatest newspaper publishing houses; the editors of the *Vossische Zeitung* and the *Berliner Tageblatt*; most book publishers; the owners and editors of the *Neue Rundschau* and other distinguished literary magazines; the owners of Germany's greatest art galleries were all Jews. Jews played a major part in the theatre and in the film industry as producers, directors, and actors. Many of Germany's best composers, musicians, artists, sculptors, and architects were Jews. Their participation in literary criticism and in literature was enormous: practically all the great critics and many novelists, poets, dramatists, essayists of Weimar Germany were Jews.[45]

A significant number of the Expressionists were Jewish. More than thirty percent of the contributors to one of the earliest and most important Expressionist anthologies, *Menschheitsdämmerung* (*Twilight of Mankind* [1920]), were Jews. The percentage jumps to over forty in Karl Otten's retrospective Expressionist prose anthology, *Ahnung und Aufbruch* (1957). Two of the three most influential Expressionist actors, Fritz Kortner and Ernst Deutsch, as well as Expressionism's most renowned director, Leopold Jessner, were Jewish.

In view of this, it is not surprising that anti-Semitism is a significant factor in the pervasive sense of loneliness, isolation, and "outsidership" which Krispyn calls "the central experiences in the life of the Expressionists' generation." The Jew of late nineteenth- and early twentieth-century Germany daily experienced in real life what many

Expressionists only understood imaginatively, as artists who felt misunderstood. For those Expressionists who were Jews, the conflict between the longing to belong and the sense of inevitable isolation was especially poignant. Artists such as Franz Kafka, Franz Werfel, Carl Sternheim, Ivan Goll, Alfred Ehrenstein, and Ludwig Rubiner spent their lives in restless and aimless wandering.[46] Werfel once described his life as one rendered silent by "a new, horrible *aloneness*" ["eine neue entsetzliche Einsamkeit macht das Leben stumm"]; and Rubiner thought of the Expressionist's isolation as his "original sin." Among Expressionist dramatists, Toller writes most directly of his sense of "being different" as a result of the anti-Semitism of his neighbors toward his family. In his autobiography, *I Was a German* (1934), he recalls a feeling of not only being different but also, as a well-to-do Jewish boy in the company of poorer Christian playmates, of feeling guilty about it. Fritz Kortner, at the height of his early career on the Berlin Expressionist stage, was repeatedly accused of using his influence in an effort to have only Jewish actors and staff hired at the Staatstheater.[47]

In another sense, the isolation of many Expressionists – and not only the Jews among them – was the result of a freely exercised, yet somehow fated, "choice." This was the existential element in Expressionist identity. The relationship between Existentialism and Expressionism is evident in Paul Kornfeld's 1918 essay "Der beseelte und der psychologische Mensch." In this, one of Expressionism's major theoretical documents, Kornfeld draws a distinction between "psychological man," an object of external observation and analysis, and "inspired man," who is experientially defined "from within."[48] Much as the Expressionists longed to belong to the society of their fellow men, they could not avoid the sense of existential isolation which authenticated their sense of individuality. The uniquely spiritual cast of German Expressionist existentialism – as compared to the later French existentialism, for example – is evident in that the individual becomes isolated because of his ability and choice to become "inspired." In the Expressionists' view, however, this kind of isolation was not fatal to the possibility of community. Rather, existential aloneness – because it was shared by all men, like the experience of suffering mentioned above – became a communal truth, a principle of spiritual bonding. Isolation paradoxically linked one man to another.

Two existential images, isolation and wandering, particularly dominated Expressionist drama. In complementary relation, they became the twin predicates of the great Expressionist themes of rebellion and regeneration. Their convergence gave rise to the central motif of Expressionist drama: the journey of the soul, a journey which often ended either in a triumphant sense of messianic vocation (Toller's *Die Wandlung*) or in vitalistic self-annihilation (Kaiser's *Von morgens bis mitternachts*, Kornfeld's *Die Verführung*). In both directions, the progress of that journey was typically a function of the central figure's expressive growth in the course of the play. Such visions were spawned principally in the imaginations of the playwrights, theorists, and, to a lesser extent, the directors of theatrical Expressionism; to the actor fell the traditional burden of donning someone else's persona and conveying its emotional urgencies and ideological agenda.

For the Expressionist actor this motif – the dynamic growth of expressive capability in the service of human progress – typically had little autobiographical impetus, aside from being the central and most formidable technical challenge of his or her performance. Still, the actor was expected to commit fully to this general theme as an idea of acting. In practice, demonstrating the historical power of expression became a matter of transforming one's body and voice into an imperative theatrical event, a decisive encounter for the audience. In this way, Expressionist acting was both a powerful experience and a persuasive argument about the potential relationship between performance and cultural development. The task assumed by the Expressionist theatre was not simply rendering the individual spiritual journey. Beyond this, or by way of it, these artists sought to develop a theatrical discourse which could do no less than mediate the fundamental contradictions between intellect and emotion, society and self. This mission characterized the entire Expressionist movement, not just its theatrical aspect. "We were not Bohemian in the usual sense," recalls Ernst Blass, "we had a sharply defined feeling of responsibility, [we] were radical and middle-of-the-road."[49]

This statement perhaps best describes the position of that other definitive member of the Expressionist theatre community, the reviewer. Since the inception of the Modern era, the theatre critic has exercised great influence in establishing the terms and standards by which a culture defines the significance of its theatrical activity. As John Willett has pointed out in his fine study of Weimar theatre, this

was particularly true of the German press in the late Wilhelmine and
Republican eras. Many of these critics were accomplished dramaturges, directors, and actors; therefore they spoke with authority and
sophistication on matters of theatrical production. But even more
importantly, as Willett notes, they believed in the vital importance of
what they wrote as it bore upon the formative influence of theatre art
on German cultural history. Thus, the critics – along with the
playwrights, theorists, directors and actors – understood their work
as "artistic" in the traditional, Schillerian sense of *"Bildung"*: i.e.,
having an historically consequential impact on the ethical as well as
aesthetic development of a culture. A significant element in understanding Expressionist theatre's representation of historical change,
therefore, is a careful analysis of the rhetoric in which the critics of
the era reconstructed in print what they saw on the Expressionist
stage. Because their reports of these productions are the principal
surviving evidence of their nature and qualities, the critical discourse
of the reviewers is as significant an aspect of "Expressionist performance" as the work of the actors and the rest of the artists involved.

Generally, Expressionism can be seen as one of many phases in the
modernist revolution. But the Expressionist movement, as Sokel says,
was also "a vital chapter in the catastrophic history of modern
Germany."[50] Accordingly, the theatre which crowned that movement primarily addressed not merely the difficulties of modern life in
general but the peculiar problems of being a modern German. For
the young artist and intellectual, life in Wilhelmine society clarified
those problems; and the Expressionists found in the traditions of
Kant, Schopenhauer, Nietzsche, and Bergson an aesthetic and social
philosophy which offered guidance. Because the poets and playwrights sought to make the poetic word into a significant cultural
force, the actors of the Expressionist movement sought to mold their
bodies and voices into forceful poetic form. Primarily, they approached this challenge with the practical resources of their own
adaptive instincts and technical training. Through the influences of
playwrights, dramaturges, and to some extent, directors, the spirit of
cultural rebellion and an appreciation for the idea of an autonomous,
self-validating art of "expression" no doubt inspired them. But their
chief source of stimulation for technical strategies in Expressionist
acting came from the manifold directions in performance experimentation which had already begun to revolutionize the theatrical avant-
garde of their era.

CHAPTER 2

The poetics of Expressionist performance: contemporary models and sources

Expressionism, like any of the artistic movements of the early twentieth century, did not develop or progress in the orderly fashion of a moving army, as a term such as "avant-garde" implies. Rather, in John Willett's words, it was "more like a current in the sea. Shapeless, it is at the same time continually changing shape; it has no outlines, just marginal areas where nobody can say which way it is going or if it is moving at all."[1] So the Expressionist era must have seemed to those artists caught up in it. Nonetheless, Expressionism ultimately assumed the coherence of a movement; and it did so in painting and literature earlier and more clearly than in the theatre. This was largely due to the formation of artists' groups such as "Die Brücke" and "Der Blaue Reiter" and literary circles like "Sturm" and "Aktion" which found an identity in the exhibitions and periodicals they sponsored.

For Expressionist theatre the only such group of any importance – within the context of commercial theatre – was the Berlin association, Das junge Deutschland; and it too was essentially a literary and theoretical vehicle. Aside from the Sturm-Bühne coterie, the actors of Expressionist drama themselves were not significantly associated with such societies, but rather found stimulation and support in the practical setting of the theatres to which they were contracted. In general, therefore, they were not as ideologically grounded in Expressionist aesthetics as the literary and graphic artists and, of course, the theorists. Where Expressionist ideology touched the details of their daily work, directors were the main channel of influence. However, Expressionist journals such as Walden's *Der Sturm* and Franz Pfemfert's *Die Aktion* extensively debated among themselves the nature and goals of the new art. Hence, as I noted at the beginning of this study, synthesizing the various "Expressionisms" which corresponded to these disagreements is a challenging problem. This is true of the Expressionist theatre for the additional reason that its practical sources, as well as its theoretical under-pinnings, were manifold.

Indeed, there were several contemporary trends in performance experimentation which provided more or less direct and usable examples for both actors and directors. The Symbolist theatre had modulated the Independent Theatre movement by redefining the stage as an ethereal, poetic realm and the actor as a sort of aestheticized spiritual medium. In the work of such proto-Expressionists as Wedekind and the young Kokoschka a daring lack of inhibition inspired an openness in actors for the physical and vocal extremities which Expressionist performance would later require. The cabaret tradition broke down the barrier between performer and public and provided a protean experimental space which challenged *status-quo* Naturalist conceptions of the actor, the stage, the audience, and the auditorium. The theoretical writings of Gordon Craig were translated and widely read by 1905 in Germany, near the beginning of the Expressionist movement in the arts. Contemporary developments in Middle-European dance re-vealed a tension between an earth-bound, free-form primitivism and a precisely choreographed abstractionism. The impact of Futurism came in the form of exhibitions, articles, and lecture/performances hosted by avant-garde impresarios such as Herwarth Walden.

The strongest foreign impression on Expressionist playwrighting itself, of course, came from the proto-Expressionist dramaturgy of August Strindberg. During the period 1913–15, moreover, numerous German stagings of such dramas as *To Damascus*, *A Dream Play*, and particularly, *Ghost Sonata* clearly influenced the early Expressionist theatre's revolutionary conceptions of dramatic space, action, and characterization. This is a point to which I shall return later in a discussion of the first ground-breaking productions of pre-war Expressionist scripts in the provincial theatres. However, more than Strindberg's plays, it was the dramatic art of Frank Wedekind – and particularly the figure of the author on stage attempting to perform his own bizarre characters – that first and most clearly revealed the radical implications of the new anti-realist dramaturgy for the actor.

I. WEDEKIND

"At the beginning stands Wedekind," wrote Rudolf Kayser in 1918.
He is the first Expressionist; the intensity of his instinctual emotions breaks
through the conventional walls of his century. For the first time since Sturm
und Drang and Classicism, the identity between poet and poetry here
shows itself. Wedekind doesn't artistically mold or shape, rather his passion
gushes forth from a unique, visionary realm. Through the harsh personality
of his creativity he became the enemy of a colorless and mechanistic age.
He perceived the falsehood of his era and that made of him a moralist.[2]

Here Kayser is referring to Wedekind the playwright. But for similar
reasons, Hugo Ball saw Wedekind the actor as representing the end
of morality. The impact of Wedekind's acting was such, he argued,
that it transcended the issue of moral propriety. In performances that
were "as gruesome as hara-kiri," Ball recalled in 1914, Wedekind
"tore and hacked himself to pieces . . . cursed sadistically, spat forth
wit and scorn." The chief consequence of this was that he destroyed
the social barrier between internal and external impulses, between
private and public life. Specifically referring to portrayals of his own
characters, such as Buridan in *Die Zensur* [*Censorship*, 1907],[3] Ball says
that it tore one's soul to watch him; but more disturbingly, the
"Gothic berserkness" in Wedekind's "shocking self-exposure"
enticed, tempted the audience. Though he may not always have
moved the spectator emotionally, his effect on him was nonetheless
"hypnotic."[4]

This intimidating aura apparently carried over into Wedekind's
off-stage life. In 1911 Fritz Kortner – later to become one of the most
celebrated of Expressionist actors – recalls a chance encounter with
Wedekind in a Munich bathhouse. As he swam, he noticed

a man in water which only came up to his hips, who, as though he were
innocently naked, stood motionlessly and thought. He fascinated me even
before I realized that it was Frank Wedekind . . . Only today, now that I
see him again in my memory standing in the bath, do I recall that when I
was fifteen I fainted at a performance of *Frühlings Erwachen* and had to be
carried out. The cold thrill I had had at that time – as well as from an
Erdgeist performance a year later – again crawled up my naked back as I
stood intimidated and speechless in the cold water, face to face with the
poet.[5]

Bertolt Brecht, recalling the "brittle voice, slightly monotonous and
quite untrained," with which Wedekind sang his cabaret songs, states

flatly: "No singer ever gave me such a shock, such a thrill. It was the man's intense aliveness, the energy which allowed him to defy sniggering ridicule and proclaim his brazen hymn to humanity, that also gave him this personal magic . . . His greatest work was his own personality."[6]

Through his published works, in the daily press, at the literary café, in the censorship courtroom, on the dramatic stage – in all these venues of public life Wedekind performed Wedekind, a fascinating drama of self-enactment situated in the central enigma of his public persona. In particular, Wedekind's scandalous reputation as a playwright – largely a media creation resulting from several sensational censorship trials – gave new meaning to the idea of "presence," both on and off the Wilhelmine stage. More than any specific technique of performance, it was his darkly charismatic persona that so influenced Expressionist conceptions of acting and stage presence. As an habitué of the literary café world, his "real-life" appearances, as much as his stage performances, virtually personified a subversive freedom of expression that seemed capable of shaking establishment culture to its foundations.[7]

This was precisely the concept of the stage – as locus of a rhetorical presence powerful enough to become an historical force – which was taking shape in organized Expressionist circles which gathered in the literary cafés. In Berlin, Munich, and other progressive artistic communities throughout Germany, many of the avant-garde rallied to Wedekind's support in the battle with censorship. More than simply another comrade, he became an inspiring and representative figure for them. As courtroom defender of free speech, as iconoclastic playwright, and as actor working in his own unique "Wedekindstil," he encapsulated the historical situation of expressive struggle against Wilhelmine culture by which the young German avant-garde defined itself. In this way, his persona became something of a cultural "text" – both a biographical reflection of the avant-garde community and a walking historical polemic about the current state of German culture.[8]

To be sure, Wedekind's stage performances were idiosyncratically focused on his own work as a writer. In this sense, of course, the "crises" he performed were quite distinct from those underlying the work of later Expressionist actors performing plays they had not written about a struggle for expressive freedom that had become the problem not of a single embattled author but of a whole generation of young artists. His character portrayals on stage dramatized his own highly individual struggle for self-expression. Nearly all contemporary descriptions of Wedekind as an actor note how his performance charisma paradoxically emerged from what seemed an amateurishly wooden physical and vocal technique. Yet the spastic clumsiness of movement and metallic harshness of voice which these accounts record defined a radically new performance grammar born out of Wedekind's desire to communicate clearly.[9] His good friend and first biographer, Artur Kutscher, maintains that in fact Wedekind decided to become an actor only because he felt that his plays were being misrepresented to the public by actors who didn't understand the characters he had created. And indeed, though he acted other playwrights' characters adequately, he truly excelled by all accounts only in roles he had written. Throughout his stage career, the great preponderance of his creative energy was devoted to demonstrating the proper method of acting his own plays. In short, remarks Kutscher, "the poet Wedekind found his most essential advocate in the actor Wedekind."[10]

As a result of Reinhardt's successful production of *Erdgeist* in the 1902 première season of his "Kleines Theater," Wedekind's reputation as a playwright was greatly enhanced. At the same time, he was also coming into increased demand as an actor, and his title role appearance in *Marquis von Keith* at Munich's "Academic-Dramatic Society" in 1902 stimulated vigorous positive and negative critical reaction.[11] Undaunted, he continued to act in his own plays to continued mixed critical response. In 1905 he began touring his own productions of them around Germany, usually with himself in the leading roles. That year also he acted again the role of Keith (Barnowsky / Kleines Theater / Berlin), and he and his future wife Tilly starred as Jack and Lulu in the Vienna première of *Büchse der Pandora* (1904) (Kraus / Trianon-Theater). In 1906 he created the role of the Masked Man in the famous Reinhardt première of *Frühlings Erwachen* (1891), and in 1907 he played the role of the Consul Kasimir in Reinhardt's Kammerspiele production of *Keith*. In 1909 he appeared in a seven-play cycle of his works at the Munich Schauspielhaus, and from then until his untimely death in 1918 at the age of 54, he was most frequently seen as a touring guest performer in productions of his own plays. Throughout his career, Wedekind's reputation for sheer stage presence as an actor flourished among his professional theatre colleagues. The great Josef Kainz declined to attempt the lead role of *Der Kammersänger* after Wedekind had acted it; and Leopold Jessner declared that "the day when Wedekind began to make an impression as an actor across the country [was] the beginning of a new era."[12]

Within the personal shadow he cast upon this era, Wedekind's dramatic writing and stage work exercised specific practical influence on Wilhelmine theatre artists. As Julius Bab, a contemporary critic and historian of the era, observed,

Wedekind . . . who was hardly an actor, but indeed an overpoweringly fanatic speaker, became something like the precursor of an Expressionist performance art. Here ended the greatest of all the theatrical means of illusion, the physical transformation of an actor into another figure. What remained on the stage was a savage [*wütend*] speaker who accentuated his penetrating speech only through certain fitfully stiff gestures. An actor like Fritz Kortner was, at least in his beginnings and in his fundamental tendencies, hardly other than a technically perfected Wedekind.[13]

The peculiar vocal characteristics of Wedekindstil resulted from the fact that Wedekind's stage career actually involved three distinct types of performing: acting for the dramatic stage, public readings of his works, and cabaret entertainment. The first, as noted above, grew out of his dissatisfaction with the playing of his characters by other actors. The last grew out of financial necessity and the notoriety of his bohemian reputation. But Wedekind's public readings of his plays were also important vehicles of self-performance on the stage. The contemporary writer Artur Holitscher remembered these readings for their

extraordinary art of accentuation [*Betonung*], which later as an actor of his own pieces, [he] developed to a mastery. It was a special pleasure to listen to Wedekind. When he read he was in love, one might almost say, with each of his words. With voluptuous joy he fashioned a creation out of vowel and consonant. He willed [*fügte*] sentences into the manifest fullness of a harmonious form. In these readings, his dialogue achieved, and his characters received, a contour and depth as they never did on the stage . . . Through an imperceptible retardation of tempo, a tiny pause before or after a word, what he said took on a meaning which could sooner be apprehended intuitively than intellectually . . . While he read he appeared to be completely certain of the effect of each of his words and of every detail of his poetic art.[14]

Something implicit in this last remark of Holitscher's, namely Wedekind's authority with his audience, together with an incredible performance stamina, made no less an impression on Brecht. On the occasion of an Autumn 1917 public reading by Wedekind of his recently composed *Herakles* (1917), Brecht was

astonished at his brazen energy. He read for two-and-a-half hours without a pause, without his voice sagging at any time – and what a strong pitiless voice it was! Without taking a minute's breath between the acts [of the play reading], he stood motionlessly bent over the table delivering, half from memory, these verses cast in bronze, while continually looking deeply into the eyes of each audience member one by one.

For the influential contemporary critic Siegfried Jacobsohn, in fact, Wedekind was chiefly fascinating as "a speaker . . . a word fanatic." Specifically, Jacobsohn noted how "he spoke, with a sharp edge, joltingly and almost uniformly loud, above all taking pains to deliver the content of his utterance clearly to the ear."[15]

The quality of voice alluded to by Brecht in the context of public readings was also evident in Wedekind's cabaret singing, in reference to which Brecht characterized Wedekind's voice as "metallic, harsh, dry . . . somewhat monotonous and quite untrained." Indeed, according to Rudolf Kayser, when he sang to his own lute accompaniment,

it was not at all singing, but only musical speech in an unassuming melody. The sharp accentuating voice [was] oddly urgent, compelling, enticing. Wedekind's countenance remain[ed] motionless. The eyes fixed upon one place in the room; no smile about the thin, compressed mouth. The ballad had an ice-cold sound; almost sad. Neither did the audience laugh, but rather, without knowing why, we felt unnerved.[16]

Such descriptions of Wedekind as public reader and cabaret singer make it clear that he created both a unique persona and a specific performance style for these modes. In his cabaret act, he performed luridly satirical ballads of his own composition, accompanying himself on guitar and lute. His brutal lyrics and bizarre melodies evoked the world of the street in images of lust, prostitution, and murder. His singing voice took on a brittle, cutting edge which utilized the "Zungen-R" (roll of the tongue) effect to achieve its harsh power. Heinrich Mann recalled his magnetic presence as follows:

The ribboned lute in clumsy hands, this elusive apparition, come from God knows where . . . advanced upon the refined world of that aestheticizing age . . . Small steps, "Here I come, you can't escape me." Stocky, head with the sharply cut profile of a Caesar, brow lowered mischievously, hair jaggedly close-cropped. Inexplicably, offensively, the eyes twitched with irritation and sudden melancholy. Vexed strumming, and then the performance. Nasal, caustic, ringing – but in meaningful pauses, the singer coiled and writhed amidst his own secret thoughts. He tolerated himself only with difficulty, and the public not at all. At a moment's notice, he would provoke them with shameless mimicry.[17]

Interestingly, what is missing from these accounts of Wedekind's public readings and cabaret work is any reference to the kind of frenzied physical intensity which Ball notes in his description of Wedekind's dramatic acting, cited above. Wedekind the reader/ singer appeared poised or coolly perturbed and withdrawn. But Wedekind the actor projected such an intense yearning, such an urgency about communication that his performances on the dramatic stage – quite beyond his initial purpose of simply indemnifying his intentions as a playwright with respect to characterization – appear to have foregrounded the art of acting itself as newly problematic.

At the heart of Wedekind's acting style was his struggle with his own body in its search for a physical grammar of expression that would complement, instead of compromise, his singular style of vocal delivery. For example, his performances as Dr. Schön in *Erdgeist* over the course of nearly twenty years (1898–1917) generally seem to have been characterized both by a vigorously immediate verbal delivery and a physical awkwardness, which latter quality, for one critic, conveyed "a powerful effect similar to that of a woodcut."[18] Of his début performance in this role in the 1898 première of *Erdgeist*, the director, Karl Heine, later remarked that "Wedekind's speech at times reminds one of the way a politician speaks before a large crowd." Indeed, as the contemporary actor Eduard von Winterstein recalls in his memoir, Wedekind on stage "did not want to act or experience anything; he wanted to preach what he, as a poet, had spoken – fanatically to preach it." Karl Zeiss, a contemporary director who particularly appreciated Wedekind's performing style, described him as "a mixture of actor, poet and propagandist in one person. These three elements [were] held together by virtue of an unprecedented ardor, by the vehement fanaticism of his *self-awareness*" [emph. mine].[19]

Zeiss's emphasis on Wedekind's particular kind of "self-awareness" – in which the performer is seized, physically and vocally, by the expressive moment – identifies the central proto-Expressionist quality in Wedekind's stage acting. I have already noted how, in his public readings, he made riveting eye-contact with each individual audience member while yet remaining totally enraptured by the sound of his own voice caressing the words of the dramatic text he had written. On the dramatic stage his "fanatic preaching" of his own play text transported him to a similar degree. In the words of Tilla Durieux, a well-known early twentieth-century German actress who often appeared with Wedekind on the stage, the poet–actor's "glowing eyes bored with such fanaticism into the audience that famous actors paled next to him."[20] At the same time, though Wedekind initially had sought to refine his physical technique through classical movement and dance training, he appears nonetheless to have retained a stiff, spasmodic, awkwardness of gesture in his acting. Consistently throughout his stage career, he was damned – by critics and friends alike – for the clumsiness in which he often seemed to "entangle himself" ("er verfängt sich," as one commentator put it). Yet that very struggle with his body on stage reflected the fitful contours of his diction and seemed the essential form of that powerful, unnerving charisma for which he was universally praised. Moreover, Wedekind's physical stage presence and bearing seems most to have impressed those performers who had been trained in and had perfected the subtleties and polish of the opposite style, naturalism. Durieux, for example, remarked that

as an actor Wedekind is difficult to describe, for although his characters staggered awkwardly about the stage, although he made a dilettantish impression . . . he thus analyzed the idea of the character so clearly . . . Wedekind the dilettante, the actor without suppleness, the one who was derided, was the strongest [performer] among us. To be sure, we had greater means at our disposal to express what he intimated; but these intimations were so strong that none of us could achieve them . . .[21]

The notion of the *physical* analysis of the *idea* of a character is further clarified in Karl Heine's description of Wedekind, both the playwright and the actor, as an "episodist."[22] Or, in the words of a modern scholar of Wedekindstil, Hans-Jochen Irmer, "instead of experientially creating organic character developments, Wedekind presented rapidly changing points of view, spasmodic attitudes." Essentially, this amounted to a kind of liminal acting: instead of smooth naturalistic continuity Wedekind emphasized transition in a rhythm of rapid-fire erasure and revision. The result was a kind of quick succession of snapshots of the character in a progression of attitudes, a modern visual analogy of which might be that of the strobe light effect on dance movement. Such a performance style conveyed an absence of stable identity, a liminal sense of existence located in-between social roles which perfectly captured the anomie of his characters, his audiences, and his own life. Arising out of the unique qualities of his dramaturgy, this customized performance grammar turned out to be one of discontinuity.[23] What Wedekind's plays required, that is, was a mode of acting whose eloquence went beyond language, expressing the true complexity of human consciousness when it is not rationalized in traditional bourgeois moral discourse. Accordingly, he strove for a type of performance suited to presenting human experience not as a naturalistic synthesis but rather as something like a palimpsestic text, wherein life's contradictions continually inscribe and reinscribe themselves, without resolution, upon one another.

In Wedekind's Lulu sex tragedies, for example, the title character is presented as a beautiful monster who instinctively – almost naively – preys upon her lovers. However, the principle of dramatic agency Wedekind employs here is strangely contradictory. Lulu essentially functions as a sexual *tabula rasa*, exerting her deadly erotic power over men by passively allowing herself to be constructed and reconstructed by them according to their own customized sexual fantasies. Each of her three husbands, who all perish as a result of attempting to possess her by marriage, give her a different name – Nellie, Eve, Mignon – and require her to dress and behave sexually to order. Here, paradoxically, powerful dramatic agency is signified by passivity. In the dialogue this is effectively conveyed, for example, at the end of Act I of *Erdgeist*, immediately after Lulu's first husband has dropped dead in a fit of jealous rage. Schwarz, the interloper who will soon become her second husband and next victim, assails her with questions such as "Can you tell the truth? . . . What do you believe in? . . . Do you have a soul?" – to which her repeated answer is "I don't know."[24] Even in *Frühlings Erwachen*, where Wedekind had celebrated the blossoming of sexual awareness, there is a clear sense of the monstrously tragic possibilities lurking within the joy of human sexuality when it is brutalized by bourgeois moral rhetoric. In Wedekind's poetics, the fact of human vitality is most compelling when the inability of language to encompass it is demonstrated. Along with Lulu's "I don't know" scene, the fragmented, almost stream-of-consciousness monologues of the children in *Frühlings Erwachen* are among the clearest examples.

These early plays discover a complex and tragic relationship between the limits of speech and the power of sensuality. Yet in *Frühlings Erwachen* Ilse's description of Moritz's brains dangling from the bushes after he has shot himself in remorse over failing his high school examinations, and Moritz's ghost holding his severed head at his side in the final graveyard encounter with his friend Melchior, are images of a beautifully eloquent grotesquery; just as Lulu herself is a figure of beautiful monstrosity. More than anything else, this grotesque beauty characterized both Wedekind the playwright and Wedekind the performer. As a dramatist he used this aesthetic to explore the spiritual relationship between morality and sensuality. But even more so in his acting, especially as described by Ball, Wedekind discovered what could be called an element of the "monstrous." It was this uniquely grotesque rendering of the human condition on stage that seemed so apt a tool of cultural criticism in the context of contemporary German history. Rudolf Kayser, it will be recalled, maintained that Wedekind was the "first Expressionist" because he told the truth, and that made him a "moralist." In this regard, his great importance for stage Expressionism was his discovery of how to tell historical truth performatively, allowing it to be written imagistically in his own body and voice. By submitting himself physically to the ravages of his own tragic vision of Wilhelmine culture on stage, Wedekind discovered a powerful bodily rhetoric of historical representation.

Though theatre historians segregate Wedekind, as a prototype, from the movement proper, the Expressionists themselves clearly viewed him as a founding father – and not just in terms of playwriting. In the final years of his life his stage work was much discussed by Expressionist theorists. For example, the writer and aesthetician Kasimir Edschmid[25] – for whom Wedekind's performing was, quite simply, the "greatest acting I have ever experienced" – saw an important "baroque" quality in his work. Until Wedekind, he argued, Germany had had actors but no *bona fide* national theatrical tradition; "but in the presentations of this dilettantish actor the fanatic ardor of the greatest German dramatists thrust itself forward with a truly national baroqueness." Paradoxically, however, what inspired one was the "helplessness" of Wedekind, through whose unprepossessing form a great poet, flooded with his "colossal yearning," created each character on stage both intentionally and by impulse, out of human nature as well as idea.[26]

Ball, too, caught this sense of raw humanity, noting that Wedekind could at once be diffident, irritated, embarrassed, tactless, brutal and sarcastic while performing. He was capable of an intensity, Ball claims, which could produce paroxysms in his neck, throat, legs – even his skull. Working himself into a mad frenzy, he could yet remain "as naive as a pony." In these reactions one senses something of the expectation of the carnival freak-show spectator. Indeed, it is precisely this kind of fascination Ball identified in a typical Wedekind audience who demanded of him his "obligatory Satanism" for its "child-scare" thrill:

We amuse ourselves with this pony. We smile when he goes limp-footed. He is full of mischief and trickery, arabesque and show. He has rediscovered acrobatics for the stage of the future . . . He flies and rides, soars through the air by his bent knees. His greatest advantage is that he traveled with the circus in his younger days.[27]

Here Ball is referring to an approximately two-year period, between early 1892 and the end of 1894, when Wedekind worked backstage in the circuses of Paris. He loved the circus because he discovered in it an aesthetics of motion which, beyond mere sensory stimulation, revealed both a moral argument and a social praxis. In a fascinating early essay entitled "Thoughts on the Circus" ["Zirkusgedanken," 1887] Wedekind observed that the governing principle of the circus ring is "elasticity, the plastic-allegorical representation of life's wisdom."[28] This elasticity, he suggests, has not only a spatial but also a temporal dimension which allows for past failures and future contingencies to be subsumed in the triumph of the moment. In the circus feat both performer and spectator are challenged to the limits of their physical and imaginative abilities, respectively. Yet while representing – through a kind of physical allegory – life's dares and challenges, the circus does away with its consequential finality. For always below the high-wire artist the net waits invisibly: either to catch her in the event of an unplanned slip, or to surprise the audience at the last terrifying second where an intentional, heart-stopping dismount into the void below climaxes the performance. When a famous jumping horse finally leaps the barrier successfully, after twice boldly approaching it only to shy at the last minute, the public's chagrin is instantly transformed into thunderous applause.[29] The elasticity of the circus performance extends to the audience whose responses take on its supple adaptability.

The horse's ignorance of any past failure as it takes a proud exit in the glow of present success, Wedekind argues, contains a more valuable lesson for us than "all the teachers, venerable elders, guardians, instructors, governesses or dancing masters taken together" could ever impart. The "wonderful virtuosity" of the circus act affords us the opportunity, in a carefully crafted moment of excitement, to capture the "golden, sunny joy of youth, the harmless enjoyment, laughing play, and sweet dreams" which in real life we restlessly pursue in vain.[30] Here Wedekind's aesthetic reveals its moral dimension; that is, the "true" and the "good" are evident in one's mastery – even if only imaginatively – over the physical dimension of life and the harmonious feeling such capability produces. On a practical level, what Wedekind is getting at here is the edifying effect, on performer and audience, of physical virtuosity in theatrical expression. But this idea of performance virtuosity, as I noted a moment ago, goes much deeper than sensory stimulation. Rather, physical expression becomes an exploration of the "good" and "true" relationship between body and spirit. For Wedekind, the circus was the purest embodiment, the circus act was the purest expression of a morality of the flesh.

That the figure of Wedekind on stage should remind Ball of the circus clown, or that for Edschmid Wedekind's "helplessness" on stage projected a powerful creative energy, are perceptions that point to the unique kind of performance virtuosity Wedekind inspired. For the Expressionist actor, Wedekind's work on the dramatic stage demonstrated the importance of uninhibited physical vulnerability and commitment, as well as athletic vocal elasticity. Given these qualities, effectual critiques of contemporary culture, comprised of vivid images and rhythms arising out of the dramatic text, could be inscribed performatively in the actor's body. In purely technical terms, Wedekind's public readings of his plays were powerful models of the kind of stage charisma and sheer stamina in performance that many Expressionist plays would later require. His cabaret performing contributed much to the tradition of iconoclastic fellowship between stage and audience which became the definitive hallmark of the early European theatrical avant-garde. Encompassing all of these performance modalities, however, Wedekind's persona – the real subject of his dramatic art and the essential character he performed – was seized upon by his contemporaries as a text of the times.

II. THE CABARET AND REINHARDT

For Wedekind personally, some measure of fulfilment came with dramatic acting because it was so effectually related to his life-long mission of self-vindication as a dramatist. His comparatively brief cabaret stint, on the other hand, quickly became a bad joke which financial necessity had forced upon him. As early as the end of his première March-July engagement in 1901 at the Elf Scharfrichter, he began to feel, in the words of one recent scholar, "like a monkey parading for an audience who ignored his true wares."[31] Thereafter he grew increasingly resentful of the financial need that bound him to the cabaret stage. "I will thank God," he wrote Carl Heine in August 1901, "when the whole Überbrettl movement is over and done with, and for my part I would do my best to expedite the process."[32] The paradox of Wedekind's disillusionment with the cabaret was that its style of performing appealed to the very side-show mentality which he despised in the audiences. The problem was that this recent French import, the variety cabaret, catered to a popular audience whose nearest reference point was the German variety show or "Tingeltangel." As early as 1895, however, Wedekind and the young poet Otto Julius Bierbaum together had envisioned the possibility of a new, artistic kind of Tingeltangel.[33]

It was precisely for the purpose of combating the philistine sensibility exploited by the popular Tingeltangel that Bierbaum, inspired by the tradition of the French *chanson* he had experienced in Montmartre, published his *Deutsche Chansons* in 1900. Through circulating this collection of singable poems, Bierbaum hoped to realize the potential he had seen in the French sung lyric for bringing art to the people. The variety show, Bierbaum argued, had enormous influence on the cultural life of the masses. Thus by raising its content to the level of serious art, one could reasonably hope to "ennoble" the popular sensibility.[34] Through the vehicle of the "applied lyric" – a poem of literary quality, attractive and accessible to the public by virtue of its singability – the variety stage, "as the stage of the future," could become "not a moral but an aesthetic institution."[35]

From its origins in the carnival, its oldest ancestor, the variety cabaret had emerged as a natural vehicle for this purpose. Like the carnival, the variety cabaret created an atmosphere of popular festivity and gay mocking laughter. The madness of both genres, in fact, could be viewed as an expression of that Dionysian vitalism which Nietzsche had identified. Such, at least, was the argument of early theorists/entrepreneurs of German cabaret like Bierbaum and Ernst von Wolzogen.[36] At the turn of the century, of course, Nietzsche's works were appropriated for all sorts of polemical purposes. But specifically, what advocates of cabaret found in his writings was a theory of humor that defined the energy released in iconoclastic laughter as a significant force of cultural development. Along with the idea of libidinal release, the spirit of a pervasive cultural criticism was central to this theory. By caricaturing the rhythms and manners of modern bourgeois life in a montage of outrageous images, the cabaret stage offered its perverse, Nietzschean version of "Bildung."

The principal mode of criticism on the cabaret stage was parody – through physical caricature as much as verbal mockery. The physical parodies of Philistinism in the variety cabaret paralleled the side-show distortions of the human body in the carnival (e.g., the contortionist, the sword-swallower). At the beginning of the German cabaret era, for example, the members of the coffee club Die Brille (the Eyeglasses) wore giant-sized spectacles during a mockingly ceremonious ritual in which initiates were consecrated as "clair-voyant knights."[37] The point of this caricature was that such large eyeglasses would enable the initiates to acquire aesthetic insight,[38] and thereby presumably to "see" the true state of German culture for the first time. Twenty years later, the contortionist/dancer Valeska Gert had come to epitomize this particular strategy of cultural criticism on the cabaret stage. Among the earliest of feminist critics to express her insights in dance, Gert caricatured such bourgeois mechanical reductions of the female body as those repre-sented by the chorus-girl kickline popular with variety stage audi-ences on both sides of the Atlantic.[39]

Even as a flagrant carnality on the cabaret stage encouraged an openness to physical experimentation in performing, the cabaret's sensual energy and humor stimulated the sexually repressed sensi-bility of Wilhelmine audiences. In this way, variety cabaret per-forming also explored a darker side of the carnival spirit. In the 1880s, the variety show entertainer Yvette Guilbert was among the first to pursue this direction. Guilbert, who had developed in the café-concert music hall performance tradition, was, in the words of one historian of cabaret, a woman of sharp angular gestures and bright, reddish hair, . . . her presence and delivery were a set of contradictions which enticed her audiences. She was at once the weary, aging, cynical coquette, and the pure English governess longing for a spiritual love. Her hoarse, mournful voice with its touch of hysteria could both bring to life [Aristide] Bruant's harlots and infuse meaning into a sentimental lyric. Guilbert was an actress in song, an authentic diseuse who "spoke, sang, prophesied" her numbers, and her mode was to be recreated in cabarets for the next half century.[40]

The specific genre of Guilbert's performances might be termed "portraitist performance." That is, Guilbert's art, like modern portrait painting, depended on capturing the particular character in a given moment of experience. Here one thinks of Wedekind's strobelight-like stage characterizations, previously discussed. However, this kind of hybrid performance, as the critic Clayton Hamilton observed, "is not acting, it is not singing, it is not recitation, yet it combines the finest beauties of all three . . ."[41] That is, beyond the strategy of depicting snapshots of the character as did Wedekind, Guilbert's work anticipated Expressionist acting in the way it synthesized the expressive properties of the arts into a performance which rendered character in an essential attitude.

Guilbert was representative of the Montmartre spirit of melancholic anomie imported into Germany at the turn of the century by the avant-garde in Munich and Berlin. In the hands of such performers as Wedekind and Gertrud Eysoldt, however, the Montmartre tradition became a more grotesque exploration of human existence in terms of death and sexuality. This kind of "dark performance" depended on the actor's instinctual ability to evoke a sexual/spiritual tension in the spectator. Localizing a sense of alienated existence in a kind of exciting but dangerous erotic aura, these kinds of performances – though they involved more than mere burlesque titillation – clearly exploited the female performer as a sexual object. Eysoldt particularly established a sexist paradigm in her portrayals of Wilde's Salomé and Wedekind's Lulu. Her stage persona was that of a sexual vampire, a woman who seemed to exist only to seduce men to their destruction. In both the cabaret, and the "Kammerspiele" theatre tradition which grew out of it, the image of woman reduced to purely sexual terms was proffered as a model of liberating Eros. A sketch of a nude woman in an erotic posture, in fact, became the virtual logo for the famous Munich cabaret, Die Elf Scharfrichter, on its program covers. Perhaps the best that can be said of this perverse sexual iconography is that the art of Wedekind, Eysoldt, and the tradition begun by Guilbert eventuated in an effective performance strategy of sexual caricature. This served to foreground the human body as cultural text to be interrogated for what it had to say about the moral situation of contemporary German society.

In both of its dimensions – parody and eroticism – the variety cabaret, like the carnival, was a place of escape. Within its giddy, smoke-filled confines, performers and public alike took a much-needed holiday from the repressive mores of their everyday lives. For the performers it also provided an alternative theatre space which enabled them to break the oppressive Naturalism of the establishment stages. This was due to the fact that, particularly in Germany, the cabaret was one of the only available venues at the turn of the century for introducing new anti-naturalist playwrights. In the Elf Scharfrichter, the prologue of Wedekind's *Erdgeist* was performed by the author in November 1901; and his pantomime *Die Kaiserin von Neufundland* was given its première staging in March 1902.[42] Max Reinhardt's Schall und Rauch cabaret became heavily involved in producing one-act plays by avant-garde authors; and so, of necessity, it also became a workshop for exploring the acting of their new anti-Naturalist pieces. Along with conveying the new dramatic material, the cabaret greatly reduced the dimensions of stage and auditorium, compelling a reconsideration of conventional assumptions about "aesthetic distance" between actor and audience. Concomitantly, it also redefined the theatre performance space as a rhetorical domain: instead of a mimetic window revealing Naturalism's stable, if sordid, sense of reality, it became the locus of polemical cultural representation. In place of an a-historical affirmation of traditional aesthetic and social values, the cabaret offered its stage as a palimpsest: a site whereon contending critical perspectives and rhetorical constructions of contemporary German culture were inscribed upon one another in the style and rhythm of montage.

Accordingly, in some artistic circles – such as Kurt Hiller's literary club "Der neue Club" – the cabaret setting took on a distinctly intellectual character. Indeed, it is chiefly due to this development that the German language today distinguishes between "Cabaret," referring to a strip-tease show, and "Kabarett," denoting a stage program of satirical cultural sketches and socio-political criticism.[43] Such relatively refined cabarets as the latter appear to have been the offspring of Bierbaum's *literary* Tingeltangel concept, adopted by student intellectual fellowships as an activist strategy for putting their critical insights into practice by performing them. Organizations such as these functioned more as laboratories for the public reading of new poetry, plays, and essays than as a place of sensualist escape. In this way, they also played no small part in the political education, as well as the literary development, of their members;[44] and it was in these venues that many of the young German intellectuals who would spearhead the Expressionist movement learned to practice cultural criticism forensically as well as in writing. Hiller's Der neue Club in particular, as well as the secessionist group "Das Gnu" which he led after his break with the original organization, provided some of the earliest and most influential performance opportunities for Expressionist writers. Because of the literary cabaret's markedly activist conception of literary production, the link between writing and the *performance* of written work was strongly established early on in the history of Expressionist literature.

Yet, while the literary cabaret stage cultivated the serious perfor- mance of cultural criticism, it typically also took care to preserve the spirit of satirical gaiety pioneered in the variety cabaret and honed to razor sharpness by performers like Wedekind. Der neue Club, for example, called its performance series "Das neopathetische Ka- barett"; and in his 1 June 1910 opening night speech, Hiller defined this "new pathos"

not as the measured gesture and gait of suffering sons of the prophets, but as universal gaiety, the laughter of Pan. Hence it follows that we see nothing unworthy and ignoble about mingling the most serious items of philosophy amid songs and (cerebral) jokes: on the contrary, precisely because for us philosophy has not an academic, but a vital significance, is not just something to be taught, a job, morality or expenditure of perspiration, but – experience – it seems to us to be more appropriate for a cabaret than for a lecture-room or a learned journal. But these last words do after all sound like an attempt at justification; they move with steps as clumsy as the spirit of gravity; they do not dance confidently, like that merry intellectualism we long for.[45]

Herein, Hiller articulated the growing view of such societies as his that intellectual insight and its aesthetic expression, in order to have any historical relevance or social effect, must be driven by the so-called "instinctual" promptings – often designated by the word "feeling" – associated with the popular sensibility. Along with the idea of synthesizing intellect and feeling, which was the basic gloss on "neues Pathos" offered by the leaders of Der neue Club, the further and much more ambitious implication of the term was the goal of reaching beyond intellectual circles to the broad mass of humanity with the message of cultural renewal through literary and artistic activism. To this end, the drama, more than the lyric or the essay, proved effectual; it was the literary cabaret, in fact, which first provided a stage for public readings of Expressionist drama. At a Spring 1914 performance of Das Gnu – virtually its last before being disbanded by the outbreak of war – Walter Hasenclever read sections of his recently completed play, *Der Sohn*. Two years later, the Dresden Albert-Theater première of this self-proclaimed "Expressionist" drama inaugurated the era of German stage Expressionism.

In the same year as the première of *Der Sohn*, 1916, the literary cabaret tradition merged with the more aggressive style of the variety cabaret in Hugo Ball's Cabaret Voltaire, which spawned the Dada movement. Like Futurism – from which it borrowed its spontaneous, confrontational methods – this new hybrid cabaret fostered a performance style based essentially on the principles of provocation and response. Though some elements of the Voltaire's programs – literary readings, musical performances, dramatic readings – resembled those of the pre-war literary cabarets, the marked difference was a circus-like atmosphere of mad-cap stimulation frequently proceeding from multiple, simultaneous performance events. These Dada "manifestations," as they were sometimes called, took their initial inspiration from the perceived insanity of global warfare. With a correspondingly more militant spirit than the pre-war literary cabaret, the Voltaire Dadaists carried the performance of activist cultural criticism beyond the boundaries of the footlights. As did Futurism, Dada radically repositioned the audience as participants in the performance event. This revolutionary rethinking of the stage/ audience transaction accorded well with ideas about desirable audience response and the necessary relationship between theatrical performance and socio-political life upon which Expressionist litera-ture, particularly the drama, after 1916 were based. Several of those Expressionist artists who managed to escape being caught up and killed or severely traumatized in the war became the anti-war refugees who frequented this international theatrical cross-road in Zürich. What the Voltaire demonstrated for them was one strategy for completing the activation of the stage begun before the war in the literary cabaret.

All told, and beyond the opportunities it presented to the German avant-garde artistic community for formal experimentation and iconoclastic fellowship, the cabaret movement did much to move the German stage toward a new historicity. Yet, despite the rich stage tradition of cultural satire spawned by them, the variety cabarets themselves – and such permutations as Reinhardt's theatre parody performance group, Schall und Rauch – never developed into politically committed activist theatres. Restrained both by government censorship and the fickle tastes of the public, variety cabarets may actually have defused social tensions. By venturing close to the limits of tolerance – particularly on the subjects of sex and politics – without consistently and defiantly crossing them, the variety cabaret both maintained its political viability and provided a release for a public more than willing to pay for its escapist needs.[46] Nonetheless, this innovative stage tradition helped to clarify how the place of performance might become a site of socio-political action, a venue wherein the artistic enactment of cultural criticism could have some real-life clout.

The satire and social commentary aspects of the tradition imported from France were preserved in the German cabaret. But what seems to have interested German theatre artists even more was the evocative potential of the cabaret setting for instilling a strong sense of atmosphere. Particularly in this regard, the influence of cabaret on "legitimate" dramatic performance itself brings us to the figure of Max Reinhardt. Among theatre producers and directors at the turn of the century none would become more quickly aware of the potential of cabaret intimacy for manipulating theatrical atmosphere than the young actor, Reinhardt. As he once wrote, "all depends on realizing the specific atmosphere of a play, and on making the play live . . ."[47] The cabaret stage afforded the flexibility required to do this; and it was from his early directing experiences in this venue that Reinhardt developed the famous tradition of atmospheric specificity that later Expressionist directors would adapt for their own rhetorical purposes.

Though he always spoke of serving only the play itself, Reinhardt too appreciated the rhetorical potential of atmospheric directing. In views expressed some twenty years after his break from Otto Brahm and Naturalism, Reinhardt argued that the cultural value of the theatre lay in its ability to address a wide spectrum of society. "The stage is the most powerful form of art," he said,

... because it appeals not to the individual only but to the public in general, and because it has the power of mastering and influencing that public. Every other art presupposes that he who receives has a certain amount of knowledge, a musical ear, a well-trained eye, and so forth. Every other art, therefore, appeals chiefly to the individual, while the theatre presupposes nothing and, in its best productions, addresses itself both to the most cultured individual and to the great masses . . .

Moreover, what draws one to the stage, according to Reinhardt, is an overwhelming desire for self-transformation, "a demonic impulse to disclose oneself."[48] This last phrase nicely captures the spirit behind performance innovations such as those introduced by Wedekind and fostered in the cabaret; it also suggests the strongly confessional element in avant-garde precursors of stage Expressionism. Yet it would be quite mistaken to conceive the idea of self-exposure in this context as simply a matter of emotional disrobing. Particularly as fostered by Wedekind's acting and shaped by Reinhardt's directing, this confessional aspect of early twentieth-century avant-garde performance involved not an array of psychological techniques for accessing the deep recesses of the actor's emotional life, but rather the development of a stylized vocabulary of physical and vocal gesture.

It was precisely the variety cabaret's emphasis on the gestural and the visual in its performances that guided Reinhardt's first work as a director in the Schall und Rauch cabaret. The innovation of this particular cabaret venture was that, initially at least, its parodies focused almost exclusively on theatre itself instead of broader social, political and cultural issues. Schall und Rauch, in fact, had been founded by a group of actors from Otto Brahm's Deutsches Theater ensemble as an alternative to the then dominant use of the theatre as a venue for Naturalism. Having evolved rapidly out of the actors' social group Die Brille, mentioned above, its initial impact was to apply the performance grammar of parody and caricature to an interrogation of both traditional and contemporary theatre paradigms. The opening night program on 23 January 1901 targeted everything from Wagner's *Walküre* to the arcane symbolist plays of Maeterlinck to Schiller's *Don Carlos*.[49] The great success of this and several such programs over the next few months, however, was largely due to the fact that the Schall und

Rauch's audience was not a broad section of the public but a relatively elite cadre of theatre artists, critics, and cognoscenti. When the group moved after its first season to a larger but less intimate venue in order to play for the general public, their audiences quickly tired of theatre in-joking.

A brief foray into political satire with the creation of the popular Serenissimus character[50] maintained Schall und Rauch's financial stability for the next several months, during which Reinhardt and his colleagues made the transition to experimental avant-garde drama which they evidently had envisioned from the start. The cabaret setting – with its discontinuous vignettes and parodic frivolity – had only been a starting point. By the Fall of 1902 Schall und Rauch had cast off all such features of cabaret and in January 1903 began calling itself, simply, Kleines Theater. At this point its program was comprised of full-length serious dramas; and thereafter the mission of Kleines Theater was to be thoroughly eclectic in its production of new works. This orientation too had grown out of Schall und Rauch's early parodies of dramatic genres and the resulting proliferation of supposedly distinct acting styles, of the pretensions of which Reinhardt in particular had always been impatient. Fully six years before the opening of Schall und Rauch he had complained in a letter to a friend: "Earlier there were good and bad actors. Today there are pathetic, naturalist, declamatory, modern, realist, idealist, pathological, extrovert and introvert actors, mood actors, emotional actors . . . Ibsen actors, Hauptmann actors, stylized actors, and so on."[51] What the Kleines Theater retained of its cabaret origins was Reinhardt's emphasis on theatricality and his great appreciation of gestural, visual, and musical elements in the variety cabaret tradition. Consequently, his well-known emphasis on the actor would stress the physical and gestural as much as the verbal elements in performance.

As early as 1905 Reinhardt took over control of the Deutsches Theater and inaugurated formal training for his actors. His emphasis, according to the contemporary director Carl Heine, was on persuading the actor "of his own free will to surrender to the ensemble . . ." In this way many of Expressionism's greatest actors – Fritz Kortner, Werner Krauss, Ernst Deutsch, Gertrud Eysoldt, Helene Thimig – were each trained "to work out his own salvation," as Reinhardt put it.[52] In practical terms, according to Martin Esslin, this meant that

. . . Reinhardt was able to show an actor not how he, Reinhardt, would act the part, but how that particular actor or actress should do it in order to give full expression to his or her essential individuality . . . The rehearsal process for Reinhardt thus developed its own peculiar dialectic. Watching a given actor, the character-actor Reinhardt learned to capture that actor's optimum personality and expressive individuality; having mastered this, he reproduced it to the actor who was thus confronted, as it were, with his ideal self in the ideal realization of the part. Thus Reinhardt never imposed his way of acting a part on the actor.[53]

Though it might be argued that Esslin's last statement does not follow from the rest of the passage cited, what is interesting in this description is the idea that the actor has an essential identity that emerges under strong directorial influence. Locating the source of this individuality not internally in the actor's personal emotional life but rather externally in the gestural realm of mimicry would become one of Expressionism's central performance strategies. No Expressionist director equalled the wide range and prestige of Reinhardt's production accomplishments, but many approached their work with the actor in just this way.

The cabaret had stressed the principle of ensemble performance, and Reinhardt's work with each of his actors reinforced their sense of group identity in the way it opened them to the expansion of their physical and vocal resources through stylization arising out of directorial suggestion. "Full of emotion," Eysoldt wrote, "he passes on to us light, form, color and sound, and [he] rejoices at the echo he finds in us."[54] Remarking that "even the greatest genius among actors falls short in his personality alone of all the suggestive power he needs," Ernst Deutsch, later to become one of Expressionism's definitive actors, described Reinhardt's influence as "nothing but the immense suggestive power which he communicates to the actor, thus enhancing to a phenomenal degree the latter's means of expression."[55] Or, as Heine rendered it, "with the patience and keen sense of an Indian, he sneaks around the actor, and lures him into the mask of the figure he is to represent."[56] Here then was a principal element of the background which the above named actors, and others similarly trained by Reinhardt, brought to the Expressionist stage: a strong sense of ensemble based on the actor's susceptibility to strong directorial influence and shaping of his expressive resources. Reinhardt's ability to develop these two qualities in actors – ensemble spirit and pliancy in stylization – was the aspect of his directing which marks his most influential early contribution to the development of Expressionist performance.

Typically, however, the molding of the actor's work on the Expressionist stage was less subtle in its process and more heavy-handed in its result. It varied markedly depending on a given director's idea of theatrical Expressionism: how it was supposed to look and sound on stage and what it was intended to do for, or to, the audience. So it was that the Expressionist theatre could build richly on the actor-centered ensemble tradition of Reinhardt and yet also work in the spirit of Edward Gordon Craig, for whom the accomplished actor could only serve as an "Übermarionette."

III. PROTO-ABSTRACTIONISM: CRAIG, THE DANCE AND FUTURISM

No director courted Craig more enthusiastically and persistently than Max Reinhardt. But Craig repeatedly declined Reinhardt's invitations to direct at the Deutsches Theater because he never felt that he would have the kind of total control over all elements of production that he required.[57] This does not really indicate a distinction between the two directors because both were master-controllers of their productions; both were auteurs. But Reinhardt, as we saw, exercised control through instinctive knowledge and encouragement of his actors; his objectives coalesced around the potential he saw in bringing certain actors to bear on a given script. Craig, by contrast, was first and last a designer, not an actor like Reinhardt. For him, the theatre became an art only when arrived at "by design." In this conception, there was no room for the "accidental" influence of man's unpredictable emotional behavior; human inconsistency was the "enemy" of design, hence of art. "Emotion," argued Craig,

is the cause which first of all creates, and secondly destroys. Art, as we have said, can admit of no accidents. That, then, which the actor gives us, is not a work of art; it is a series of accidental confessions.[58]

Because the mind – which might attempt to maintain a consistent design – can at any time be overpowered by emotion and thus become its slave, the human body is "*by nature* utterly useless as a material for an art" [emph. Craig's].[59]

The answer to this dilemma is not to abolish the actor. For actors to be of any service at all to the theatre, however, they must liberate themselves from the bondage of the flesh.

They must create for themselves a new form of acting, consisting for the main part of symbolical gesture. Today they *impersonate* and interpret; tomorrow they must *represent* and interpret; and the third day they must create. By this means style may return.

For Craig, style was to return from an ancient past, a time when the stone image of divinity "glowed with such earthly splendor and yet such unearthly simplicity . . . [that] it proved an inspiration which cleared the mind even as it intoxicated." Style would return, that is, when the actor was replaced with "the inanimate figure – the Übermarionette we may call him, until he has won for himself a better name." Marionettes are the descendants of those mysterious stone images in the ancient temples. Their present incarnation as puppets is a model for actors because though

the applause may thunder or dribble, their hearts beat no faster, no slower, their signals do not grow hurried or confused; and, though drenched in a torrent of bouquets and love, the face of the leading lady remains as solemn as ever . . . The Übermarionette will not compete with life – rather will it go beyond it. Its ideal will not be the flesh and blood but rather the body in trance – it will aim to clothe itself with a death-like beauty while exhaling a living spirit.[60]

In terms of Wedekind's example the actor is a kind of animus – an animating, if somewhat hostile, spirit; in Craig's conception, by contrast, the actor becomes an icon, a deathless symbol. If Wedekind is the father of the vitalist/primitivist tendency in Expressionist performance, Craig with equal clarity is one of the chief theoretical precursors of abstractionist/mystical Expressionism on the stage. For the practical roots of abstractionism, however, we must also look to the impact of Mid-European dance.

Craig's theoretical writings were avidly read in Germany in the first two decades of the twentieth century, a time when puppet theatre was very popular there. "Hence not surprisingly," as J. M. Ritchie observes, "from Wedekind on, German intellectuals seem obsessed with puppets, marionettes and mime."[61] This so-called obsession, however, appears to have been another part of the interest in developing a new grammar of physical expression simultaneously evident in Wedekind's acting and the performances of cabaret parodies. When, in 1904, Craig saw Isadora Duncan dance in Berlin, what most excited him was her inspired improvisational interpretations, on an empty stage, of the music of Gluck, Beethoven, and Chopin. The love affair between Duncan and Craig which quickly grew out of this first encounter was in part a product of the passionate belief both artists shared in movement as the essence of drama. As a result of their influence this view received considerable attention – particularly through the translation and publication in 1905 of Craig's *On the Art of the Theatre* in Germany.[62]

Around 1910, a number of Middle-European dance/movement theorists also began to influence German theatre with philosophies of rhythmic movement training. Chief among these were the Swiss composer Emile Jacques Dalcroze and the Hungarian dance theorist Rudolf von Laban. The fact that both Dalcroze and Laban founded movement schools at this time, in Dresden and Munich respectively, also did much to raise movement consciousness in theatre circles throughout Germany. In 1910 Dalcroze opened a school at Hellerau, near Dresden, which taught movement based on his concept of "eurhythmics," a system founded on a musical model which inculcated precise movement training and practice. The idea was that performers would learn to express emotions stimulated by various musical sound rhythms in precisely correspondent postures, movements and gestures. Specifically, students were taught to discover a unique arm and leg movement for each different rhythm or tempo in musical compositions whose physical interpretations they practiced daily. Yet the fundamental concept underlying this system was that the body itself, conceived as a cultural product, was the source of rhythmic creativity. In an essay entitled "The Nature and Value of Rhythmic Movement" (1922), Dalcroze argued that

From its birth music has registered the rhythms of the human body of which it is the complete and idealized sound image. It has been the basis of human emotion all down the ages. The successive transformations of musical rhythms, from century to century, correspond so closely to the transformations of character and temperament that, if a musical phrase of any typical composition is played, the entire mental state of the period at which it was composed is revived; and, by association of ideas, there is aroused within our own bodies the muscular echo or response of the bodily movements imposed at the period in question by social conventions and necessities.

Interestingly, this correspondence of musical and bodily images is conceived as an historical function: rhythmic awareness awakens the body to historical consciousness. By means of musical composition history inscribes itself in terms of style in the human body; and performance accordingly becomes historical. Beyond this, rhythmic correspondences, for Dalcroze, revealed in the movement of the body something like the structure of universal reality:

All the laws that govern the harmonizing of our bodily rhythms govern that of the specialized rhythms, and set up relations between the arts dealing with sight and those dealing with sound, between architecture and mechanics, between mechanics and music, between music and poetry, between poetry and art, between art and science, between science and life, between life and society.[63]

This theory that the human body, in rhythmic sound and movement performance, incarnates history textually strikingly resembles Expressionist conceptions of the actor's historicity. Expressionism, however, conceived of "history" less as a record of past cultural transformations and more in the sense of a currently unfolding process of cultural change, embodied as text in the actor on stage.

The influence of his approach to the music/movement relationship spread in Germany as Dalcroze opened other smaller studios and as his rhythmically stylized opera productions were seen throughout Central Europe. Its practical impact on theatre production was greatly enhanced through his association with Adolphe Appia, whose major collaboration with Dalcroze produced the famous 1913 staging of Gluck's *Orpheus and Eurydice* at Hellerau. A little-known theorist until his work on this production, Appia had written extensively on how to unify all elements of production to achieve an ideal, absolute beauty on stage. Inspired by the operas of Wagner and his theory of the Gesamtkunstwerk, he argued for a three-dimensional, dynamically plastic conception of the performance space whose masses and volumes would be integrated and molded by rhythmically progressive changes in lighting. In the Hellerau production of Gluck's opera, it was Appia's spare set, with its right-angled arrangement of connecting staircases and directional lighting, that most impressed audiences. With the coordinated rhythmic movements of Dalcroze's performers in this setting, repeatedly transformed by shifting light sources, *Orpheus and Eurydice* introduced an unprecedented degree of abstract reduction and suggestion in its conceptions of stage and dramatic action.

Appia's work in theory and production – along with the writings of Craig and the movement pedagogy of Dalcroze – were to contribute a great deal to the development of abstract Expressionism on the German stage. However, an opposite tendency in Middle-European dance, based on Isadora Duncan's intuitive and earthy choreography of individual expression, also influenced German theatre artists. In contrast to the typically deliberate rhythms and stateliness of the Dalcroze approach, Duncan's "skirt dance" style of performing allowed for abrupt transitions between moments of subdued lyricism and sudden flashes of emotional outburst. This kind of performance rhythm particularly came to characterize what I shall later call the "Schrei" ecstatic acting of early, provincial stage Expressionism. At times, individual Expressionist actors appear to have amalgamated the two models. But sometimes – particularly in late Expressionist productions in Berlin – those acting the principal "ecstatic" characters were set stylistically in relief with a choral ensemble performing in a Dalcroze-like monumental style. Where Expressionist production featured no such principal figures, as in Lothar Schreyer's Sturm-Bühne stagings, the ensemble seems to have taken the Dalcroze spirit to an almost hieratic level in its abstract orchestrations of sound, gesture, and movement. Indeed, the choral concept – in the Dalcrozian sense of a disciplined group performance of precisely coordinated, rhythmic sound/movement patterns – influenced Expressionist ensemble acting more than any other principle. For that reason the "movement choir" experiments of Rudolf von Laban are also relevant to the development of Expressionist performance.

Although Laban's early experiments in dance and movement theory were just developing in the Expressionist era, they were already well known in Germany and Switzerland. His work appeared as early as 1910 in Munich, where he founded his first dance company and school. For the next four years he produced workshops and performances there, but his influence was not generally felt until 1914 when he moved to Switzerland.[64] There he came into a close association with the Dadaists which enhanced his stature in avant-garde dance and theatre circles. Following the war, Laban's prestige was pervasive throughout Central Europe and particularly in Germany where he trained many students at his school in Stuttgart.[65] The extent of Laban's direct effect on Expressionist performance is conjectural. On the one hand, he deliberately distanced himself from those aspects of Expressionist art which he considered destructive of "a healthy sense" of aesthetic form.[66] On the other, this stance was taken nearly a decade after the passing of the Expressionist era, when his work had been much appreciated and discussed. However, some degree of influence can be inferred from his prominence in the dance world generally and his association with the Dadaists, particularly Hugo Ball; and it is probable that his ideas were considered by Expressionist performance artists who visited Ball's Cabaret Voltaire, which Laban frequented during the war. Laban's presence there was noted in Dada publications and some of his most prominent students participated in the last Dada performance in Zürich in 1919. Since many Expressionists were involved in the war, however, they might otherwise have come into contact with Laban's work through Hans Brandenburg's *Der moderne Tanz* (1917), which was one of the first dance treatises to discuss his theories.[67] In 1926, John Schikowski – who some nine years earlier had been the first director of the Sturm-Bühne – devoted several pages of his *History of Dance* to the "actual creator and founder of modern innovative dance [Kunsttanzes], Rudolf von Laban . . . who laid its theoretical and practical foundations and showed the way and purpose of its fulfilment."[68]

Though he was not directly involved in Expressionist performance, Laban's work related to both the ecstatic and the abstractionist directions in Expressionist performance. All human movement, he taught, should essentially be viewed in terms of such polarities as "central and peripheral orientation," "growing and shrinking," and "recurrence and free rhythmicality."[69] Peripheral arm movements, for example, might have a radiating or scattering quality; while central arm movements could take the form of a scooping or grasping gesture. Both kinds of movement were employed in Expressionist ecstatic acting and can be seen in the film *The Cabinet of Dr. Caligari.* Laban is best remembered, however, for that branch of his movement theory which he called "eukinetics." This discipline he defined as the study of the expressive qualities of dance considered specifically in terms of three aspects of movement – sequentiality of time, strength of force and extension in space. It was these three factors, he taught, which chiefly give movement its intended expression.[70] Laban developed movement-choirs to explore his theories; often, however, he worked with them either in an environment of silence or of exclusively percussive rhythms. Unlike Dalcroze, who believed that musical stimulation necessarily precedes movement exploration, Laban located the source of rhythmic insight in the purely plastic four-dimensionality of the body moving through space and time. "Movement," he once wrote, is first and fundamental in what comes forth from a human being as an expression of his intentions and experiences. One must always remember that all sound productions, such as speaking, singing and shouting, spring from physical actions, or in other words from movements. Whether I bang on a table and make it resound, or vibrate the air with shouts, it is always the same thing – movement made audible . . . The dancer of our cultural era . . . understands rhythms and sounds as a kind of audible gesture and dance as a visible language.

At a later point in the work just cited, however, Laban qualifies this view. Speaking of what he calls "Asian" acting and its emphasis on the visual through movement, in contrast to the western emphasis on sound via the spoken word, he remarks that

it would be most interesting to explore thoroughly the grammar and syntax of the Asian movement languages. But is it a question of movement language at all? Isn't it rather body positions and attitudes which mean the same as, for instance, a rune? Are they not characters or letters represented by the body, or even words and sentences written by it in space?

To be sure, dance signifies both syntagmatically as a kind of language and paradigmatically as a structure of images. But what Laban is getting at is the idea of the rhythmically moving body as a text – as a site of communication whereon meaning is inscribed and read, and therefore as a medium of social nexus. Like Dalcroze, Laban was an educator who viewed kinesic awareness as historical awareness. Through his movement choirs, he sought to make dance available to everyone so that "thousands of people can now experience the benefit of the rhythm and flow of dance . . . of the joy of moving." The historical nature of this kind of movement experience is evident in how it always refers to and redefines community. "Alongside the arts," Laban's movement students were required to

do a healthy job, preferably farming, gardening or something of that kind, for in both form and content the artistic work must grow out of the community in which I should like to bring them together.[71]

Towards the realization of this goal Laban led his students to explore rhythmic movement both as it arose out of their social existence and also as a purely abstract phenomenon. The exclusion of music in some of the movement choir exercises was a reflection of his fundamental vision of dance in this latter regard. As his most famous student, Mary Wigman, stated, Laban

liberated dance from its slave-like association with music, and reinstated its independence and beauty as an absolute language. He pursued movement in its smallest detail and proved that its liberated material can be brought into an organically unified compositional form.[72]

A former pupil of Dalcroze, Wigman went to study with Laban in 1913 at the suggestion of the painter and graphic artist Emil Nolde, a member of the Dresden Expressionist group known as Die Brücke who particularly appreciated Laban's explorations in dance without music.[73] Among individual dance performers, her work most closely resembled Expressionist patterns of stage movement – especially ecstatic patterns. Most often associated with the emergence of a new, more individually expressive genre known as the "Ausdruckstanz,"[74] she infused a great dynamism, emotional intensity, and freedom into her style. Her performance typically was characterized by spasmodic physical shifts from a state of aggressive thrusting tension to one of complete bodily withdrawal or collapse. This style had no derivative relation to Expressionist aesthetic philosophy, being developed out of Laban's purely formalist aesthetics. But its relevance to Expressionism was that it championed the principle that artistic expression could and should break free from its traditional status as mere vehicle and become its own subject.

This principle, of course, had become the hallmark of Modernist artistic experimentation throughout Europe by 1912, the year that saw the emergence of Berlin as an international crossroad for avant-garde eclecticism. At this juncture, influential European currents of several years' standing in the fine arts – such as Fauvism and Cubism – metamorphosed into new interdisciplinary movements with comparatively distinct national identifications – such as German Expressionism and, particularly, Italian Futurism.[75] Initially, the main point of intersection for these trends in Berlin was Herwarth Walden's publication *Der Sturm* and particularly the series of literary recitals and art exhibitions produced by the Sturm circle of avant-garde artists, critics, and theorists. *Der Sturm* had provided Oskar Kokoschka's dramatic work with its first influential exposure by publishing the text of *Mörder Hoffnung der Frauen* in 1910. Similarly, in March of 1912, Walden opened the Sturm Gallery with an exhibition of paintings mainly by Kokoschka; and a month later he introduced Futurist painting to Germany. The "Foundation and Manifesto of Futurism" (1909), written by the movement's leader F. T. Marinetti, had been published in Germany in 1911 and his poetry was translated in a 1912 German edition. His novels – for example, *Marfarka le Futuriste* (1909), whose hero is a sort of flying, bionic superman – were also translated around this time and read by the German avant-garde. Perhaps most influential, however, was the lecture Marinetti himself delivered on the occasion of the Sturm Gallery's first Futurist exhibition in 1912. The primary thrust of the Futurist position was that the arts required the inspiration of the industrial age. Marinetti rejected French symbolism's mysterious imagistic transcendence of mundane reality in favor of a more conceptual model based on the glorification of technology as the relevant expression of the human will.[76] Considering the machine to be the most contemporary evidence of the power of human creativity, the Futurist, as R. S. Furness has aptly written, "looked upon man as the modern Prometheus, the machine (train, aeroplane or motor-car) as guarantor of freedom and escape."[77]

From its founding, Italian Futurism[78] resembled German Expressionism insofar as it was an interdisciplinary, programmatic movement which rejected an atrophied cultural past and sought to revolutionize not only the arts but all of life.[79] However, the Futurists' fascination with exploring performance techniques and audience reaction *per se*, as well as their general attitude of self-conscious belligerence, tended to obscure rather than clarify their social goals. For its part, however, the German avant-garde by and large preferred to concentrate on the formal models of Futurist art and performance rather than the movement's celebration of technology or its political agenda. Even when the violent nationalism of some of the most prominent Futurists blazoned forth in late 1914, Herwarth Walden was not dissuaded from his continuing advocacy in *Der Sturm* of their aesthetic principles and strategies. Franz Pfemfert's *Die Aktion* – after initially rejecting the Futurist manifestoes[80] – featured Futurism in two special 1916 issues, more than a year after the erstwhile Futurist periodical *Lacerba* had turned militantly anti-German in early 1915.[81] These two issues of *Aktion* were particularly responsible for acquainting Hugo Ball and Johannes Becher with Futurist ideas. Within the German theatrical and literary avant-garde, Ball and Becher were among the most influential in the development of Expressionism.

The Italian Futurists particularly captivated their German audience in multimedia presentations which created an instantaneous, highly energized consciousness of immediacy. Though they proclaimed themselves heralds of the future, all of their performance efforts in fact were focused on stimulating a sensory experience of the present moment in a simultaneous evocation of its socio-political, phenomenological, and aesthetic contexts.[82] The Futurist understanding of immediacy resulted in the performance of "simultaneity" as the necessary and authentic state of contemporary historical consciousness: liberated from a dead past and alive to the present-day synchronic interpenetration of biological energy and technological power. "Futurism," wrote the Expressionist theorist Kasimir Edschmid, represented "the final destruction of impressionist reality ... through its representation of the world as a simultaneous juxtaposition of sense impressions."[83] Yet German Expressionism's stage representation of the world produced a very different sense of historical presence, one which was more diachronic and social. For the Futurist, history was the "future" phenomenologically summarized in concise images and rhythms of the techno-cultural present. For the Expressionist, immediate historical consciousness was apprehended as prophetic vision. It was evolutionary, not synchronous; a brave new world just beginning to dawn.

Since 1910, the Futurists had aggressively presented their program in Italy through a variety of media, including exhibitions, lectures, street theatre, mass meetings, congresses, posters, airplane leafletting, newspaper ads and inserts.[84] But their primary vehicle was a kind of eclectic performance called the "serate." These events typically sought to overwhelm audiences with multimedia stimulation: poems would be shouted, manifestoes declaimed, "noise-music" generated, garishly lit paintings displayed. The general intent of the serate was to provoke audience reaction through sensory assault and verbal insult; a strategy which not infrequently culminated in fisticuffs. Characteristically, such performances targeted the masterpiece tradition: the theatre, according to Marinetti, should be used to

systematically prostitute all of classic art on the stage, performing for example all the Greek, French, and Italian tragedies, condensed and comically mixed up, in a single evening. – Put life into the works of Beethoven, Wagner, Bach, Bellini, Chopin, introducing them with Neapolitan songs. – Put Duse, Sarah Bernhardt, Zacconi, Mayol, and Fregoli side by side on the stage. – Play a Beethoven symphony backwards, beginning with the last note. – Boil all of Shakespeare drama down to a single act. – Do the same with all the most venerated actors.[85]

A pervasive concept of "velocity" drove these performances and infused them with a positive sense of contemporary urban life and the hectic, disjunctive rhythms of communication and social interaction it had engendered. At the same time, the Futurists assaulted their audiences' traditional ideas of cultural history by demanding the destruction of museums and libraries. This negative idea of history as an obsolete past that had to be destroyed, they argued, was the only way of moving toward a more dynamic future. This, as I noted a moment ago, they represented as a sudden sensory consciousness of the present moment. Their own attempts at machine-age art ran the entire spectrum of genres. They created "picture poems" using a variety of print types deployed on the page in such a way as to stimulate a rapid activity of eye. They infused movement into the plastic arts with "kinetic sculptures"; and, along with the Cubists, employed the collage to explore pictorial composition as a modern procedure of assemblage and juxtaposition. In their "art of noise," complex orchestrations of sounds – musical, mechanical, street noises, etc. – were performed in concerts featuring instruments called *intonarumori* (literally, "noise-intoners").[86]

A guiding practical principle for Futurist performers was that of the mechanization of the human body. This in turn arose from the central performance concept of "declamation" whereby the performer violently articulated "words-in-freedom" with his legs and arms as well as his voice. Specifically, the voice was to be "dehumanize[d] . . . systematically doing away with every modulation or nuance"; and movement was to be executed "geometrically," in imitation of the sound and movement rhythms of machines. "Gesticulate in a draftsmanlike, topographical manner," Marinetti advised, "synthetically creating in mid-air, cubes, cones, spirals, ellipses etc."[87] In Giacomo Balla's *Macchina tipografica* (*Printing Press*) twelve performers enacted and intoned the pistons and wheels of a printing press in carefully rehearsed mechanical synchrony while uttering an assigned onomatopoetic sound.[88] Along with those of the machine, the rhythms of puppetry inspired Futurist stage movement in performances which featured life-size marionettes, sometimes performing in combination with live actors.[89] Marinetti's manifesto "Futurist Dance" (1917) acknowledges Dalcroze's "very interesting rhythm gymnastics" but argues for the need to surpass "muscular possibilities" in favor of machine-like movement patterns. In the composition *Dance of a Flyer*, for example, the performer, "lying on her stomach," was to "simulate with jerks and weavings of her body the successive efforts of a plane trying to take off."[90]

The Futurists also experimented with "actor-free" performances using only light and sound to create dramatically evocative experiences. Their principal scenic artist, Enrico Prampolini, was chiefly responsible for the characteristic Futurist emphasis on variety in scenic effects and the subordinate role of the actor's body in relation to them. In the essay "Futurist Scenography" (1915) he called for the replacement of painted scenery with "dynamic stage architecture that will move." Instead of externally projected lighting sources, scenic elements were to contain their own luminous properties. Finally,

human actors will no longer be tolerated . . . Vibrations, luminous forms (produced by electric currents and colored gases) will wriggle and writhe dynamically, and these authentic actor-gases . . . will replace living actors [Futurist Scenography] . . .

In "Futurist Scenic Atmosphere (1924)," Prampolini explained the principle underlying these comments:

I consider the actor as a *useless element* in theatrical action, and moreover, dangerous to the future of theatre. The actor is the element of interpretation that presents the greatest unknowns and the smallest guarantees . . . The appearance of the human element on the stage shatters the mystery of the beyond that must reign in the theatre, the temple of spiritual abstraction.[91]

Here Prampolini's remarks recall the spirit of Gordon Craig's performance theory. But he also articulates the general tendency of abstractionist Expressionist performance, which similarly, if not so radically, conceived of the human form as primarily a scenic element. This was especially the case with both the Sturm-Bühne productions in Hamburg and late Expressionist performance in the Berlin commercial theatres. Unlike Futurism, however, Expressionist abstraction of the actor attempted to render the essence of human life in human, not mechanical, terms. Its icon was Man, not machine. In its insistence on the living presence of the actor, abstract theatrical Expressionism both resembled and differed markedly from the highly conceptual theatre of Futurism. While Futurist performance definitively stressed consciousness of the present, it did not finally locate that sense of presence in the body of the performer but rather in a fragmented, rapid succession of images and sensations instigated by the performer. In a significant way, that is to say, it was predicated on a strategy of disembodiment: the fragmentation, conversion, and dispersion of the expressive self into an environment of variegated sensory and conceptual stimuli. While all modes of Expressionist acting also sought to create a powerful sense of immediacy in the audience, *that* idea of presence was indissolubly bound up in the expressive body and voice of the actor offered as meliorating resources in the present moment of historical exigence. If Futurist performance sought to incite cultural crisis, Expressionist performance was a response to it.

For both movements, however, the function of the performer and the question of his historical materiality were also understood as linguistic problems. The Futurist disembodiment of the performer was only a logical consequence of its dismantling of the syntactical structures of language. The theatrical Expressionists' materialization of the performer likewise began with the attempt to transform him – usually in terms of either long, rhapsodic monologues or intense, desperate "Telegrammstil" utterances – into an incarnation of the expressive revolution they believed to be at the heart of contemporary historical change in Germany. Like Wedekind and dance theorists such as Dalcroze and Laban, Futurism and Expressionism both sought a new language of the body. For the Futurists, the structures of conventional language were the essential form of an obsolete, obstructive past that had to be smashed; for the Expressionists those structures were the materials out of which a new future might be smelted and forged. In both cases, to struggle with language was to grapple with history – as written in the body of the performer and as represented by the audience, the object of the performance, in their role as recipients of linguistic expression. This, of course, was the whole point; this was how theatrical revolution would become socio-political.

The Futurist emphasis on the compressive energy derived from visual and verbal economy went to the heart of abstractionist Expressionism's strategy of cultural revolution. August Stramm, whose dramatic dialogue best exemplifies the staccato "Telegramm-stil" language typical of some Expressionist plays, was greatly influenced by Futurist poetry. Stramm was the Futurists' most ardent Berlin admirer; so much so, writes John Willett, that

when Marinetti's "Technical Manifesto of Futurist Literature" (of May 1912) appeared in *Sturm*, followed by an influential lecture which he gave in Berlin early in 1913, Stramm destroyed all his previous writings and started to work along the principles laid down there; that is, reducing sentences to verbs and nouns, eliminating articles, adjectives and conjunctions, keeping the verbs in the infinitive, doing away with punctuation and introducing an element of noise.[92]

By 1915, Stramm had become the chief literary model for the writers of the Sturm circle. In works such as his *Kräfte* (*Forces*, 1914) and *Geschehen* (*Happening*, 1914), Futurism's influence on one of the most characteristic rhythm patterns of Expressionist dramatic dialogue – and consequently, of Expressionist acting – was deeply felt.

In theatrical terms, the Futurists staged the idea of compression in their "synthetic dramas" or "sintesi." These were mostly short pieces which sought to capture a mood, a sensation, a state of consciousness. One of the most concise was Francesco Canguillo's *Detonation* (1915). Involving simply the momentary rise of a curtain to reveal a deserted road at night, a single gun shot after a few moments' silence, then the fall of the curtain, it anticipated Beckett's *Breath* by a half century. In Marinetti's *Feet* (1915) the curtain rose just high enough to reveal only the performers' feet and lower legs; thus segmented from the rest of their bodies, these appendages bore the entire expressive burden of acting the play's seven disjunctive scenes. As in the *serate*, here again, the idea of the fragmented or disembodied expressive self is central. Like the *serate* performances, the *sintesi* appear to have been most concerned with brevity, discontinuity, abstraction and simultaneity as experiential phenomena in themselves. Similarly, the situation of audience protest itself – rather than the specific merits of either side of an aesthetic argument – was the principal focus of the Futurists. Unlike the Expressionists, the Futurists were not as interested in creating a greater dynamism between performer and audience as in exploring the idea of dynamism itself. As on stage, so in the auditorium: the exploration of anarchy for its own sake, purely as an environment, was prosecuted with calculated determination.[93]

The Expressionists, by contrast, though prepared for vociferously averse audience reaction to their productions, typically strove to inspire rather than merely outrage the spectator. Such performance concepts as brevity, velocity, simultaneity, and discontinuity – to the extent they were employed in Expressionist performance – functioned simply as rhetorical tools used in service of a larger, historical mission: the ecstatic apprehension of the society of the "New Man." Where such apprehension could not be communicated and shared art betrayed its historical calling and integrity. In an open letter to Marinetti after his Sturm lecture, the poet and sometime Expressionist prose writer Alfred Döblin severely took the Futurist leader to task for practicing and advocating just such a solipsistic formalism. After an opening acknowledgement of Marinetti's good intentions in honestly striving for a revolutionary art that is true to the spirit of the modern age, Döblin then decries the Futurists' maniacal obsession with method to the total exclusion of meaning:

But you are most annoying, most dangerous in your monomania – for you are a monomaniac – when you attack syntax in your fondness for pitched battles over form . . . You give to the reader, the listener, short catchwords as substantives . . . You overtax that same listener, reader. You shove onto him your duty to form the substance of the image. Much of your chain of associations remains incomprehensible to me, and why should I care about your chain of associations if you yourself haven't taken the trouble to set them forth intelligibly . . . I'm not interested in hearing fifty times over only "trumb, trumb, tatetereta," etc., which requires no great mastery of speech . . . You seek to condense everything to such an extent that your [chemical] retort in this process of distillation breaks in pieces, at which point you have only the fragments to show us as evidence of your art . . . One achieves plasticity, concentration, and intensity in many ways; your way is certainly not the best, hardly even a good way. Make an effort to learn with us.

Indeed, Döblin had stated at the beginning of his letter, "you are not saying anything new to us; I might say: you declare your allegiance to us."[94] Though Futurist performance had demonstrated effective methods for creating a sense of experiential immediacy, for many Expressionists its dogmatic, elitist formalism stood in the way of societal reconstitution. However, certain Expressionist poets, such as Stramm and his *Sturm* circle colleagues, did employ the method of Futurist condensation in an attempt to forge a new German sensibility based on an imagistic perception of what they believed to be the essential historical situation of contemporary humanity. But as Döblin had said, Marinetti's work was not entirely unprecedented to the German avant-garde. In the theatre, for example – which was the last of the arts appropriated by the Expressionists – the first stirrings of reductivist experimentation in performance had occurred more than three years before Marinetti's 1912 visit to Berlin.

IV. MÖRDER, HOFFNUNG DER FRAUEN

The 1909 Vienna Kunstschau world première of Oskar Kokoschka's *Mörder, Hoffnung der Frauen (Murderer, the Women's Hope)* pioneered an approach to acting which anticipated both the emotional intensity and the evocative abstractionism of later Expressionist performance modes. In both form and content, the play embodied that reductivist impulse which was to become a general feature of Expressionist productions. The action was ritualistic but very brief and cryptic; the diction violent, suggestive and elliptical. In production, the chief performance elements were rhythmic choral lyricism, deliberately provocative stylization of speech and gesture, and above all, extreme physical and emotional commitment. In its savage primitivism, *Mörder* pioneered a definitive aspect of Expressionism not only in the theatre but in painting and literary art as well. Both the visual and linguistic violence of its emotionalism, in fact, presaged developments not consolidated in painting and literature until the period 1910 to 1912.

The *Mörder* "script" was apparently "written" during a single improvisational rehearsal held the night before the production. Kokoschka relates that he "gave the principals and other players an outline of the action and wrote down each of their parts in short key phrases on slips of paper, after first acting out the essentials of the play for them, complete with all the variations of pitch, rhythm and expression." The performance space was a garden which had been set up for open air dance and musical presentations next to a temporary exhibit building of the Vienna Kunstschau. As soon as the Kunstschau committee had given him permission to use this space, Kokoschka immediately designed one of the two famous publicity posters for his play. It depicts the agonized, contorted body of a man, colored blood-red, lying dead in the lap of a ghoulish woman with deathly white skin. Mournfully she clutches the red corpse with a grasp which is at once vicious and tender. Her claw-like hands and arms hold the man's head and left arm, suspending the body in a grotesque inverted *Pietà* position. The overall effect suggests that the man is both icon and victim, object of devotion and prey. "If in art the label 'Expressionism' has a meaning," Kokoschka remarked later, "then this poster was one of its earliest manifestations."[95]

Because the production was twice postponed for scheduling reasons, Kokoschka had time to produce another publicity poster – a self-portrait which resembled his sculpture "The Warrior." The poster is a profile bust with pain-widened eyes and a macabre grimacing smile; a hand points to a breast wound. What is most significant about this poster design, however, is the tracery of veins and nerves on the head, a stroke which Kokoschka duplicated in making up his actors for the play. He costumed the actors, for lack of money, in makeshift designs using rags and such other cloth scraps as could be found on the spur of the moment. Where the rags didn't cover their bodies, Kokoschka painted veins, muscles, nerves, and tendons on the actors' exposed limbs and faces. The inspiration for this idea came from his fascination with South Sea primitive masks he had studied in the local ethnographic museum. "There I learned," Kokoschka recalls,

how primitive peoples, presumably as a reaction to their fear of death, had decorated the skulls of the dead with facial features, with the play of expressions, the lines of laughter and anger, restoring to them the appearance of life. In a similar way I decorated the actors' arms and legs with nerve lines, muscles, and tendons, just as they can be seen in my old drawings.

The actors, mostly young drama students and friends of the playwright,

hurled themselves into their parts, as if acting for dear life. They were not acrobats, but even so they could run, jump, stand and fall better than any of the Burgtheater actors, who often took a quarter of an hour to lie down and die . . . The actors entered into the spirit of the play body and soul, without a trace of false pride or false emotion. In the end some emerged bloodied and bruised.[96]

The audience, too, came prepared with a sense of its part in this event; for its response – catcalling, foot-stamping, scuffling, brandishing chairs – went forth from the house with an intensity which apparently matched that on the stage. Certainly, the première of *Mörder* had triggered the public instinct for bear-baiting, as one anonymous reviewer suggested the next day in the *Neues Wiener Journal*: "The public had a good time, as I said, a very good time, interjecting remarks in the opening scene that were signals for loud laughter" (5 July 1909). Another critic, also anonymous, agreed that

the public took this certainly gaily conceived drama joyfully. The contrived word excesses, the unintelligible yelling, the rolling around of human clumps on the stage, does not strike one as the realization of serious artistic intentions, but rather as a mocking of sound human understanding and of enduring good taste. (*Neue Freie Presse*, 5 July 1909)[97]

What had specifically irritated the audience, Kokoschka felt, was the actor's make-up, with

the nerves drawn outside the figures, on the skin, as though they could in fact be seen . . . The Greeks put masks on their actors, to fix character – sad, passionate, angry, etc. I did the same thing in my own way, by painting on faces, not as decoration, but to underline character . . . All I was after was this enhancement of expression. I treated the members of the cast quite differently. Some of them I gave cross stripes, like a tiger or cat, but I painted the nerves on all of them.[98]

As Kokoschka later reminisced, that his play,

just like each of the pictures of my contemporaries I had painted, called forth hateful and furious opposition had at that time another meaning for me: I was certainly still a foreigner in the world of the adults, in whom was vested the historical judgment of humanity.[99]

Following his first Vienna Kunstschau exhibit the previous year, when his exhibition room had been derided as "the Chamber of Horrors," Kokoschka had been branded by the Viennese press with such epithets as "Der Bürgerschreck" [the bourgeois-baiter] and "Der Oberwildling" [the chief savage]. Hence, he later recalled, the garden theatre "was too small to hold the throng of society, intellectuals, and the merely curious, all of whom had come to see what outrage this bull in the china shop was about to commit."[100] When the action on stage and in the audience had reached its peak, a group of Bosnian soldiers quartered next to the playing space joined in the melee and Kokoschka was whisked away by friends, just in time to prevent him being "beaten to death."[101]

What led up to this free-for-all was a kind of carnival atmosphere established before the production began. The Kunstschau Garden had no theatre space as such, so boards and planks were used as a stage. To its side a crude orchestra pit was dug out by students working with Kokoschka on the production. From here a small band of drums, pipes, clarinet and cymbals – borrowed, along with the audience seats, from the Kunstschau's café – accompanied the performance.[102] Throughout the event the audience was continually prodded by "the harsh, shifting colours of the lighting."[103] From the stage directions – which were actually written out only when *Mörder* was published the following year in *Der Sturm* – we learn much about the kind of acting Kokoschka conceived for his play. Since the written text post-dates the performance, it is likely that it is based, at least roughly, on what the actors actually did on stage. In a brief scenario which is but five pages long on paper, the action is the ritualistic sexual confrontation of a male chorus and its leader with a female chorus and its leader. During an overture of shrill pipes and drum-beating, the two torch-bearing choruses and their leaders entered and confronted one another. Kokoschka directed their subsequent struggle for dominance to be played with violently stylized utterances and movements; first the man is subdued by the woman and then the woman is overcome and killed by the man.

Over the course of this action, the female leader's demeanor was to become progressively more grotesque and animal-like while the male leader metamorphosed from savage brutality to a divine grandeur and expansiveness:

The man in blue armor, white face, kerchief covering a wound . . . woman, red clothes, loose yellow hair, tall . . . the man and the woman meet in front of the gate . . . woman observes him spellbound . . . The man astonished . . . woman, filled with fear and longing . . . the man angry, heated . . . the woman goes up to the man, prowling, cautious . . .

When the man orders his followers to brand the woman with a red-hot iron, the

woman, crying out in terrible pain . . . leaps at him with a knife and strikes a wound in his side. The man falls . . . in convulsions, singing with a bleeding, visible wound . . .

Three masked men then inter the apparently dead man in a cage at the base of a tower with a large red iron grille door. This tower, by the way, is the only set piece called for by the script. Following the interment, the woman,

moaning and revengeful . . . creeps around the cage like a panther. She crawls up to the cage inquisitively, grips the bars lasciviously, inscribes a large white cross on the tower, cries out . . . shakes the bars in despair . . . woman slides her arm through the bars and prods his wound, hissing maliciously, like an adder . . . the man, inside breathing heavily, raises his head with difficulty; later moves one hand; then slowly rises, singing higher and higher, soaring . . . woman, incipient fear . . . once more creeps up the steps, her body trembling, triumphant once more and crying out with a high voice . . . the man has slowly risen, leans against the grille, slowly grows . . . woman weakening, furious . . . trembling . . . man, powerfully . . . woman covers him entirely with her body, separated by the grille, to which she clings high up in the air like a monkey . . . lets go the grille, writhes on the steps like a dying animal, her thighs and muscles convulsed . . . the man stands upright now, pulls open the gate, touches the woman – who rears up stiffly, dead white – with his fingers. She feels that her end is near, highest tension, released in a slowly diminishing scream; she collapses and, as she falls, tears away the torch from the hands of the rising leader. The torch goes out and covers everything in a shower of sparks. He stands on the highest step; men and women who attempt to flee from him run into his way, screaming . . . He walks straight towards them. Kills them like mosquitoes and leaves red behind. From very far away, crowing of cocks.[104]

What the play originally signified for Kokoschka, he recalls in his autobiography *My Life* (1974), was not easily reduced to a stylistic label. Having just encountered the work of Van Gogh, Gauguin, the Fauves, and particularly the Belgian sculptor, Georges Minnes, he had discovered a world of spiritual depth and emphatic spatial contours beneath the decorative mask of *Jugendstil*,

something akin to the tension which, in Gothic art, dominates space and indeed creates it . . . [In] the Gothic age master builders, stonemasons, sculptors, carvers, painters and glaziers worked in accordance with a higher plan. Not content to mirror the tangible, transient world, they sought an image of Eternity, of Space without limits. But in the age of the Industrial Revolution, wherever one looked, the struggle for existence remained superficial . . . The [aesthetic] objective retreated as fast as it was pursued . . . The social situation, similarly, looked progressively dingier . . . In the coffee-houses we read the newspapers and heard, or sensed, political conflict disturbing the air where once one had been able to drink a cup of coffee in peace and quiet. Ideas akin to those of the French revolution were waking again.

Kokoschka then describes the contemporary nightmare world of socio-political upheaval – political assassinations, strikes and demonstrations, violent police reaction – from which he and his small artist fellowship of friends, "all about twenty years old," recoiled. "Though the world we knew was moving towards its end," he writes, "we stood firm against what for most was the compelling slogan of the day: 'Into the streets!'" Reluctant to relinquish a heritage he remembered as the simple, apolitical, suburban home-life and Baroque Catholicism of his youth, he first learned from the Western humanist tradition of Shakespeare and Cervantes, Voltaire and Rousseau, "to stand on my own feet." As he later wrote, however, it was not political so much as sexual agitation that overpowered him at this time:

. . . the erotic advance of the female principle almost at once put my hard-won equilibrium in jeopardy . . . An inner voice tormented me, like a hermit in the wilderness, with imaginings about the female sex.[105]

On the other hand, in his 1935 autobiographical essay, "Vom Erleben," Kokoschka maintains that *Mörder* was actually intended as an attack on "the thoughtlessness of our male-oriented society" in its misogynist acceptance of the "female principle," responsible for all that is evil in human history.[106]

Though he had sought an "enhancement of expression," Kokoschka disavowed any "Expressionist" intent in writing and producing *Mörder, Hoffnung der Frauen*. Indeed, the lofty spiritual goals of Expressionism were yet to be penned by its poets and theorists when this primitivist sketch came screaming to life in the face of the Viennese cultural establishment. Like his posters, Kokoschka's theatre sought to rip away the outer skin of bourgeois sensibility and expose the flesh, nerves and veins throbbing underneath. In an interview some fifty years later, he recalled that he had "wanted, in fact, to turn the figures [of the actors] inside-out, to make the inner man visible, and did exactly the same in the illustrations to the play."[107] Indeed, Kokoschka's theatre was profoundly visual, revealing the same penetrating "eye of God" his friends – notably the architect Adolf Loos and the writer Karl Kraus – had attributed to his powers of insight as a portrait painter.[108] Later, the Expressionist stage would also attempt to make the inner man visible; not merely to outrage its audiences – as, for the most part, did the young Kokoschka – but rather as a graphic strategy of historical typification. Expressionist drama sought to represent not the psyche of an individual protagonist pursuing his particular fate but rather the internal "spiritual" condition of humankind as a whole. To make the "inner man" visible in this sense was to characterize an entire historical situation.

However, there is no evidence that any of the principal figures later associated with the emergence of theatrical Expressionism actually saw the original production of *Mörder, Hoffnung der Frauen*. What they saw, rather, were the graphic illustrations Kokoschka drew for the publication of the script by *Der Sturm* a year later in 1910. It was these shocking images of the primal human being behind the civilized mask that influenced early Expressionist ideas about the theatrical treatment of contemporary German history. In addition to revealing the elemental instincts and impulses at the heart of human social behavior, the illustrations suggested a method for inscribing them in the external body by turning it "inside-out."

The 1909 world première of *Mörder, Hoffnung der Frauen*, together with the illustrations published the following year in *Der Sturm*, had developed a new way of empowering theatrical performance. But it was not until two 1917/1918 restagings of *Mörder* – in a triple-bill which also featured première presentations of *Hiob* (1917) and *Der brennende Dornbusch* (1911) – that its bold gestural strategy directly came clear as a model of theatrical Expressionism. The impact of these productions on audiences of invited guests may be gauged by the intensity of both positive and negative critical responses. Of the latter, that of the Frankfurt critic Bernhard Diebold was perhaps the most extreme. "The word became trivial," Diebold fumed:

scream, play acting, and image predominated. The painter–poet Kokosch-ka wants to be taken for a scenarist. Hence, it is considered essential to the mood: that, perchance, Adam out of paradise appears, with a straw hat, barrel organ, and garbage can; that stage artists perform as eroticized parrots and poodles . . . that naked-legged choruses whine in chorales of lust . . . Everything that undresses itself is about the Eternal-Feminine. A stark naked women runs onto the scene, wearing only a hand muff. The others also haven't much on. Along with this, something symbolic is spoken which now reveals the painter Kokoschka as a poet. But it wasn't poetry, only impudence. Eroticism and erotomania are not exactly the same; any more than health and sickness. The equation tallies only with people who make no distinction between romantic desire and hysteria . . . Under no circumstances will I fall in with those of whom it will be said a hundred years from now that they welcomed the poetic light of Kokoschka as a premonition of paradise regained. No, I am ashamed of such an aberration of "culture" . . . I am ashamed that such anus art found a "hearty welcome" in the loud applause of (apparently) the majority of the audience . . . I even saw a critic who applauded . . . If we go much further this way, we in Germany will be culturally bankrupt.[109]

Diebold's reaction is all the more interesting since by this time he had already become one of the critics who would most labor in print for the next three or four years to distinguish clearly between genuine and false Expressionism. His remarks here reveal the urgent sense of cultural mission – to which I referred in the introduction of this study – that most German theatre critics of this era understood to be their unique calling and responsibility. Indeed, to read the entire text of his lengthy review is to appreciate how much more was at stake, for him at least, than merely an offended sensibility. What was happening on stage was a significant aspect of what was happening to Germany.

While the performance that Diebold decried occurred in April of 1918 in Frankfurt, the première of the Kokoschka triple-bill some ten months earlier in Dresden drew almost equally fervent critical acclamation. In his program notes to this Albert-Theater production,

Paul Kornfeld – whose influential Expressionist script, *Die Verführung* (1913), was soon to première at the Frankfurt Schauspielhaus – lauded the "word-supported pantomime" of Kokoschka's plays:

Kokoschka's human beings express themselves not only in words, but principally through gesture and movement. For the word articulates the verbal form of the content, but the movement speaks its idea; just so in the opera – melody and timbre sing of eternity, the word only of its shadow. We suspect the possibility of a new style, perhaps a new art form, which would most resemble precisely that of the opera: the word-supported pantomime. Not only for the sake of Kokoschka's personality, but also on account of this premonition, these plays should be presented; not only to the public but also to the creative people of our era, in whom the experience of these works perhaps will become seminal and take roots.[110]

Other critics were equally fervent in their advocacy of the kind of performance breakthrough Kokoschka seemed to have found. "In the search to find new possibilities for expression through pantomime guided and supported by the word," exclaimed H. Zehder, "the scenes of Oskar Kokoschka signify the strongest and, up to now, most profound affirmation of this new art form." Zehder also voiced the consensus opinion that Kokoschka's minimalist, symbolic scene design did much to liberate the acting style.[111] From his example, he predicted,

theatre people will one day have learned to achieve striking effects with simple means of stage technology. A couple of backgrounds painted according to sketches by the artist, a few impressive props, light brought to bear in the right place at the right time for clarity and color-music symbolic representation. Nothing for an actor seeking help to cling to or get lost in. The gestures alone determining space and expression.

As a result of these conditions, "Käthe Richter [in the principal female roles] offered a completely extraordinary performance. Without a detour through deep thought, her gestures forced the spectator right into the varying rhythms of her experience and revealed that which got obscured in the dialogue." Another favorable critic, J. von Lücken, argued that "the difficulty . . . in the [production's] rough, peculiar language" – which reminded him of the diction in Kleist's *Penthesilea* – was also the source of its "excellence [in that] each image contained its own unique character and dynamic . . . as though [the dialogue] wanted and had to bore itself into one." These three dramas, which "could in the highest sense be perceived as pantomime," represented the expressive form to which "the new drama is pressing."[112]

For a less sanguine critic such as Emil Faktor, however, "the ambiguous, far-fetched, obscure" diction revealed the three pieces as "pretexts for mimic arrangement." As he saw it, Kokoschka's directing amounted to a "painterly animation . . . of his actors' sound and movement." Stefan Grossman agreed, commenting that "here the painter Kokoschka strongly came to the rescue of the poet [Kokoschka] . . . not only in the decoration . . . but in every movement of the young actors . . . [Kokoschka] offered more to the eye than to the ear." Indeed, what the language lacked in sense it appears to have made up in sheer imagistic stimulation. In particular, Faktor singled out the work of Ernst Deutsch, whose pioneering Expressionist performance in the Dresden première of Hasenclever's *Der Sohn* (1913) had so impressed Germany's theatre critics eight months earlier. With his work in the Kokoschka pieces, Deutsch had "henceforth as an artist of stylization strengthened confidence in his subjectivity." That Deutsch, Richter and the rest of the ensemble "were able to enter into all of [Kokoschka's] intentions," according to an unsigned review in the *Münchner Zeitung*, was the reason that "the audience – all of Dresden was there, and many out-of-town directors and critics . . . summoned the poet and the actors for curtain calls again and again."[113]

However crude its gestural primitivism and elliptical its vocalizations, Kokoschka's vision for revolutionary theatre had finally reached a wide audience in Germany by 1917. Its rough and aggressive performance strategies, as much as Craig's refined formalism and the extremities of Futurist reduction, suggested to the inchoate Expressionist theatre community possibilities for the abstract distillation of stage communication. Inspired by Expressionist poetry and dramatic writing which reflected these influences, the theorists of theatrical Expressionism identified the central performance concept of "ecstasy," by means of which both raw emotion and abstract idea could aspire to transcendent poetic form.

V. THE THEORY OF ECSTASY: POETIC EMOTION AS AN HISTORICAL FORCE

"Our goal," proclaimed Felix Emmel, "is the Ecstatic Theatre." Specifically, "ecstasy," for the actor, involved, in the "ancient Greek sense" a definite stepping outside of oneself. Each actor must stride completely out of his own personality, if he intends to become the embodiment of poetic form. He must, so to speak, transform himself. But this transformation succeeds only through ecstasy, a unique condition in which one is ardently possessed by poetic form.[114]

This statement alludes to a general socio-poetics of performance presented by Emmel throughout his book as governing the emphatically gestural language of body and voice evident to some degree in every Expressionist approach to acting. Whether based on evocative abstractionism or intense emotionalism, Expressionist performance located its historical efficacy in the inspirational power over audiences that allegedly emanated from an ecstatically "possessed" stage. The challenge both to seize and be seized by his medium was possible for the Expressionist actor because of the nature of poetic language itself. As Edschmid described it,

the word becomes an arrow which strikes at the inner nature of an object, and thus inspired, it crystallizes into the true image of the thing. In this way, the word achieves its fullness . . .[115]

Presumably this cryptic statement amounts to the familiar romantic argument that poetic art incarnates reliable images of reality that expose and do away with misrepresentations of truth. In being possessed by this poetic power the actor became a prophet. Once he opened himself to the impact of poetic language, argued the Expressionist theorist/playwright Paul Kornfeld, he could "stretch his arms out wide and with a sense of soaring speak as he has never spoken in life."[116] The objective, as the actress Leontine Sagan later recalled, was that even "the single concentrated word, slung out by the speaker like a stone from a catapult, was to contain a complex of thought and emotion."[117] In the poetic economy of the Expressionist, the symbolic word or gesture was clearly regarded as comprehensive in its historical meanings.

But for stage expression to achieve this kind of impact and profundity the actor had to attempt to become one with his medium, a condition approximating that of the singer or dancer. Hence the critic Walther von Hollander conceived of the Expressionist actor's process as the "quest for the ultimate removal of all corporeal disguises – even the skin – in order to reveal the soul, the only reality." Hollander's position was that the body is the basis of Expressionism. Indeed, no other art, he argued, is better suited to Expressionist ends than that of acting. Only from within and through his body could the actor bear witness ("aussagen") to the spiritual essence of his being, the soul – whose condition, as we have noted, was considered a sign of the times. However, for the spirit to declare itself physically in the art of performance requires that

a great gesture, having towering, momentous effect, must be conceived. This in turn means that a new language of the body must be worked out, if one doesn't evolve of itself; if it does, then it must be thoroughly learned.[118]

As we have seen, this was precisely the objective Wedekind had set for himself as an actor. The spirit of his search for a new "language of the body" runs unmistakably through such theoretical formulations as this one. In so framing Expressionist acting's chief technical problem, Hollander claimed no originality. He needed, he said, only to recall Wedekind's performance interpretation of his own works "in order to mark exactly where the first steps of development" were. Wedekind's plays, he observed, became both intelligible and human when the acting of them, epitomized by Wedekind himself, achieved "a conscious displacement of factual reality by means of a completely alien physicalization."[119] As a praxis of cultural revolution, evidently, the strategy here was not to escape from history but rather to smash its superficial mimetic ("factual") veneer in order to apprehend its essentially "spiritual" determinants. The actor's body became the medium in which this historical mission was worked out. The name given to the rhetorical impact of a successful performance in these terms was "ecstasy." Though this term denoted rapturous abandonment, its more important connotation was that of profound historical consciousness.[120]

Paradoxically, the search for a new language of the body advocated by Hollander presupposed a deliberate alienation from the body – at least in terms of its natural expressive complexity. The Expressionist actor's basic approach to the problem of his own physicality began with a reduction of movement and speech, an economy of gesture and word. Thus, as Lotte Eisner observes, a fundamental principle of Expressionist acting was that gesture and utterance were to be effected without realistic transitional nuances – as Wedekind's acting had first suggested. Typically, Expressionist physicalization involved "abrupt incisive movements, brusquely galvanized and then broken halfway through completion . . . the unfinished gesture seemed particularly important."[121] Consistently, the Expressionist actor avoided Naturalistic complexities of movement in favor of carefully selected gestures which would express, with poetic economy, the truth of the human condition in a simplified, concrete way. As Edschmid once put it, "the suffering of the creature appears, with the compassion of He who created him, in the actor's own suffering."[122] The practical working out of this incarnational objective depended upon an *intuitive* search for the right gesture, a gesture which was somehow truthful in its incompleteness.

For the actors of Expressionist theatre, the issue was not only linguistic sensitivity to the text but also physical sensitivity to the plastic rhythms of the performance space. Movement and vocalization took on and became part of the total poetic form that constituted the staging of Expressionism's sometimes symbolic, sometimes allegorical, but never realistic dramatic world. This, of course, was an inversion of realism where stage space and performance supposedly reflected reality outside the theatre rather than reconstituting it poetically within the theatre. All of the pioneering models of performance experimentation I have been considering originated in the desire to liberate contemporary culture from its mimetic bonds and to offer instead a theatre of empowerment in which contemporary history could be symbolically distilled and critiqued in order to become rhetorically reconstituted.

It was once said of the dancer Mary Wigman, whose work was briefly discussed earlier, that "she felt space as the medium through which she moved in much the same way as the swimmer feels the water . . ."[123] Just so, in theatrical Expressionism the emphatic visual gestures in scene design and lighting – together with the bold strokes and accents of characterization and dialogue, costuming, and make-up – stimulated, indeed forced, the actor to "feel" the performance space and be shaped by its textures and rhythms. Thus aided, Expressionist actors strove to become ecstatically "possessed" on stage. Frequently, the transition into this state culminated in a scream, or *Schrei*. This was the case especially in the first Expressionist dramas whose central figures were typically vitalists seeking to liberate themselves from social and moral constraints. Such characters, however, had been predicated on a mode of acting whose technique had not yet been developed. When the actors and directors began to tackle these early scripts in production, the theme of vitalism was mandated by the texts as the common point of departure. Often, the search for an appropriate expression of this "longing to be fully and irresponsibly alive"[124] eventuated in the ecstatic Schrei. The Schrei, in fact, was to become the single most common feature of ecstatic acting. In early Expressionist performance especially, it typified a primitive purity of expression which was regarded as the vital sign of an historic liberation from the dead past.

CHAPTER 3

Schrei ecstatic performance

I EARLY PROVINCIAL STAGE EXPRESSIONISM: BACKGROUND

The term "Schrei" has a rather narrow semantic range including: "cry, shout, yell, howl, wail, scream, shriek." As applied to Expressionist performance specifically, the significance of the Schrei varied according to the type of script and production it served, but all types appear to have found a use for it. In the première of Ernst Toller's *Die Wandlung*, for example, it occurred thematically as a scripted expression of the horror of war. In Leopold Jessner's staging of *Richard III*, it was a means of summarizing Jessner's demonic idea of Richard's character. In Lothar Schreyer's Kampfbühne productions, it seems to have served primarily a tonal function – as one element in a complex orchestration of sounds. More than any other performance feature, consequently, the Schrei became the hallmark of that breadth of vocal and physical performance capability – and endurance – which was the first standard of excellence in Expressionist acting. However, it seems to have assumed its most comprehensive meaning in certain of the earliest Expressionist dramas, where emotional expression itself was both the subject, and the chief agency, of dramatic action.

Hasenclever's *Der Sohn*, along with Kornfeld's *Die Verführung* (*The Seduction*), and Sorge's *Der Bettler* (*The Beggar*), were all written during 1912–13 and first produced in 1916–17.[1] They were the initial "Expressionist" performance vehicles. Hence, as it initially appears in the present study, the phrase "Schrei Expressionism" is meant to signify *early* stage Expressionism, the development of which occurs first not in Berlin or Vienna but in various progressive provincial theatres, chiefly located in the south-German cities of the Rhein–Main area, as well as Dresden, and Munich. Along with its emotional or socio-philosophical significance, Schrei theatrical Expressionism

for these theatres was also a bold declaration of artistic freedom from
the dominance of both the Naturalist tradition and the shadow of
Max Reinhardt. An appreciation of the "provincial" origins of
Schrei Expressionism, in fact, begins with an understanding of this
basic agenda about creative freedom.

The fact that theatrical Expressionism developed first in certain
progressive provincial theatres is certainly related to the well-established German tradition of subsidized regional theatre dating from
the eighteenth century. When Bismarck united the numerous
German principalities and territories following the Franco-Prussian
War, this tradition continued in force because the various regional
and local theatre administrations were left intact and allowed to
continue. This in itself, of course, did not necessarily result in a   *war*
receptivity to post-Naturalist avant-garde experimentation. Indeed,
many provincial theatres stagnated in their adherence, through
World War I and beyond, to the realist/Naturalist tradition.
However, because they were free to set their own artistic policies,
progressive Intendants and stage directors in certain of the long-
established subsidized theatres of such provincial theatre cities as
Düsseldorf, Frankfurt, Mainz, Darmstadt, Mannheim, Dresden, and
Munich had the opportunity to experiment and seized upon it.

This avant-garde impulse was even more pronouced, of course, in
new private theatres such as the Neues Theater in Frankfurt or the
Kammerspiele in Munich. These were founded in the years just
before the war, roughly at the same time when literary Expressionism, along with the production of Strindberg's "post-Inferno"
plays, was just beginning to revolutionize dramatic composition. In
their support of progressive drama, the private provincial theatres
were following consciously in the "art theatre" tradition inspired by
such theorists as Adolphe Appia and Gordon Craig. Among the most
striking consequences of this theoretical orientation were its architectural expressions. Two of the best-known examples are Appia and
Dalcroze's famous Hellerau theatre outside Dresden built in 1910;
and, before that, the Munich Künstlertheater, conceived theoreti-
cally just after the turn of the century by the Darmstadt architect
Peter Behrens and the theorist/critic Georg Fuchs and built in 1907
by the theatre architect Max Littmann.

Given their reconception of the theatre space itself as something of
a laboratory of artistic experimentation – a studio, in effect, rather
than merely an entertainment venue – it is not surprising that certain

regional theatres attracted innovative playwrights, dramaturges, and actors. The willingness of these artists to forego Naturalism in favor of formalist experimentation was doubtless also linked, as Günther Rühle suggests, to artistic traditions of German idealism which lingered in provincial cities well past the end of the war.[2] By 1900, technological advances resulting from the dramatic development of the German economy in the prior three decades also stimulated avant-garde theatre production by enabling new capabilities in lighting and stage machinery. This greatly facilitated the staging of experimental drama, particularly symbolic plays with their anti-realist conceptions of dramatic space and time. In Berlin and Vienna, of course, it was Max Reinhardt who led the way in taking advantage of new stage technologies. The eclectic stylizations of Reinhardt from the turn of the century until the end of the war doubtless exerted the greatest single influence in the transition from Naturalist to Expressionist staging. Productions by him, Craig and many others of anti-realist dramatists such as Maeterlinck, Wilde, Wedekind, and especially the late Strindberg, established by 1916 a tradition of symbolic staging which provided the basic orientation for directors who subsequently took up Expressionism.

It was Reinhardt's stagings of Strindberg's proto-Expressionist pieces around 1911 that not only caught the imaginations of German directors but virtually pioneered the performance of these dramas in Sweden as well. In Germany, however, what ensued in the next few years was a remarkable Strindberg craze. From 1913 to 1915 twenty-four of his plays received over 1,000 performances in sixty-two German cities.[3] These performances, according to the Austrian dramaturge Otto Zoff, "made so great an impression on us that it would be impossible to describe it."[4] Here, the "us" that Zoff refers to is, in the first instance, avant-garde directors. These directors later applied Expressionist stylization to scripts such as *Der Sohn* and *Die Verführung*, which themselves employ a more or less realistic dramatic structure of action, though language and character, to be sure, are amplified Expressionistically. Given such wide exposure, the impact of pieces like *To Damascus*, *A Dream Play*, and *Ghost Sonata* on the development of early Expressionist production cannot be overestimated. It was this last phase of Strindberg's work – with its dream-like atmosphere, lyrical diction, episodic "station-drama" action, and abstract characterizations – that filled German stages with the symbolic imagery of psycho-spiritual anguish and social alienation that seemed to capture so perfectly the young Expressionist generation's sense of their own historical situation.

Strindberg's anti-realist dramaturgy was particularly influential on German avant-garde theatre through its revolutionary conceptions of dramatic space. Its cinema-like fluidity of spatio-temporal transformations inspired directors, as well as playwrights, to experiment with a variety of spatial premises for staging anti-realist drama. Strindberg, like Appia and Craig, had sought to develop spatial ideas for staging an essentially inner, spiritual drama. But as Klaus van den Berg has noted, Strindberg:

created a richly representational version of kinetic space that contrasted with the abstract solutions of Appia and Craig. His complex dramatic visualizations, consisting of fragmented spaces, symbolic rooms, simultaneous representations of interiors and exteriors, metaphoric images, and distorted empirical reality, represented an interior subjective space that was very different from Appia's and Craig's.

In Strindberg's strategy for staging subjective experience, argues van den Berg, space and time become primary dramatic agents rather than mere backdrops. Perceptually, the resulting "half-reality" of plays like *Ghost Sonata* and *A Dream Play* reveals a dialectic between an inner or "deep" perspective and an outwardly realistic "wide" perspective. The latter often uses the street as a central spatial metaphor connecting sequentially a wide range of images, while simultaneously the former involves a structuring of scenes which lead the audience into and then back out of the psyche whose perceptual experience is the main subject of the play.[5] The presentation of dramatic space as a sequence of continually transforming spatial images, or tableaux, amounts, then, to dramatizing the temporal process of perception. This resembles the reading of a modern abstract painting, as the eye moves over the canvas continually refocusing on different elements in the non-representational abstract design. The spatial subject of the painting, in effect, is the temporal process of reading it. Strindberg's emphasis on the fluid, though (with reference to realistic convention) illogical, transitions between stage images constitutes a "spatial representation of the temporal process of perception." In fact, concludes van den Berg, a governing principle in Strindberg's post-Inferno dramaturgy is the Swedenborgian idea that "all states of mind are in fact places."[6]

If Strindberg's conception of inner, or "spiritual," dramatic space revolutionized German avant-garde dramaturgy, directors such as

Otto Falckenberg and Ludwig Bernauer led the way in developing the necessary practical techniques for staging the new drama. In 1915, Falckenberg's successful production of *Ghost Sonata* (Kammerspiele, Munich) caught the attention of many producers and directors because it was seen not only during its long run in Munich, but in brief guest performances in Frankfurt, Mannheim and several other provincial cities. Bernauer's 1916 Theater in der Königgrätzerstraße staging of *A Dream Play* in Berlin became, according to van den Berg, "a point of reference for most critics, and even for directors such as Max Reinhardt, throughout the remainder of the decade."[7] It was in this same year that Expressionist drama itself was first professionally staged in widely influential productions mounted not in Berlin but in the provincial theatres.

What this period in modern German theatre history signaled, in short, was an unprecedented freedom and opportunity for directorial conceptualization and visualization of scripts. Along with challenging directors to break free of realist assumptions about the stage as a domain of spatio-temporal representation, mountings of the proto-Expressionist plays in the wide-spread wave of Strindberg productions also helped to develop a specific, if comparatively small, national audience for avant-garde theatrical experimentation. By opening both the creative thinking of directors and the aesthetic expectations of audiences, these stagings set a precedent that broke significant ground for the more radical demands, on both the artists and the public, of Expressionist scripts soon to follow.

Related to these circumstances, another reason that stage Expressionism developed first in the provincial theatres was that directors there felt relatively free of comparison to the Reinhardt tradition of eclectic brilliance. Reinhardt dominated the first two decades of twentieth-century German theatre to such a degree that many regional and municipal theatres by and large simply imitated his work. However, several provincial Intendants and directors resolutely resisted identification with the Reinhardt legacy. Hence, that Expressionism should have developed away from Berlin, as Günther Rühle has observed, meant particularly that it was free to develop "away from Reinhardt." By 1917, as Rühle stresses,

what in the provinces was released with new power, happened consciously apart from Berlin. As [Otto] Zoff affirmed: at that time one no longer troubled oneself about Berlin. The polemics of [Richard] Weichert reiterated again and again the desire to be free from Berlin. Each success was regarded as proof of self-sufficiency. For a decade already, the Berlin critics, above all [Herbert] Ihering, had upbraided the Berlin theatre with the artistic depth of the provinces: as a model of accountability, of artistic development; as a paradigm of integrity in the work.[8]

This sense of independence in some provincial theatres came relatively late and rather suddenly, while in others it developed well before the war years. In the case of a self-conscious art-theatre venture like that conducted by Louise Dumont and Gustav Lindemann at the Düsseldorf Schauspielhaus, the search for alternatives to Naturalism dates from as early as 1905.

Though Reinhardt continued to dominate the two principal theatres centers, Berlin and Vienna, there was a great deal of innovative work and much influential traffic of creative talent and new ideas in the regional theatre system between these two poles. In 1917 at Dresden's Albert-Theater, Kokoschka restaged *Mörder, Hoffnung der Frauen* in a triple bill which also premièred his Expressionist dramas *Hiob* and *Der brennende Dornbusch*. This production featured an ensemble that included Ernst Deutsch, Käthe Richter, and the young Heinrich George in the lead roles. A year earlier, Richard Weichert's directing at the Mannheim Hoftheater had already reoriented its repertoire toward the new anti-realist/symbolic production styles. In Frankfurt, the progressive Intendant Arthur Hellmer encouraged Georg Kaiser and other emergent authors by making the stages under his control available for the development of their new plays. Carl Zeiss came from Dresden to Frankfurt in 1917 and, with his Regisseur Gustav Hartung, introduced Expressionism to both theatre and opera production at the Schauspielhaus there. The convergence of Expressionist authors such as Hasenclever, Kornfeld, Unruh, Zoff, Döblin, and Bronnen completed the transformation of Frankfurt into one of the most vital provincial centers of development for theatrical Expressionism. Subsequently, Hartung took Expressionism to the Darmstadt Landestheater and Weichert assumed control at Frankfurt. In Munich the Kammerspiel had been staging progressive drama under Erich Ziegel's leadership since 1913. From 1917 onward, Otto Falckenberg – whose avant-garde reputation had become established with the 1915 Kammerspiel staging of *Ghost Sonata* just mentioned – assumed leadership from Ziegel and produced a wide array of Expressionist works by Kaiser, Sorge, Kornfeld, Essig, Goering, and even Brecht's early, quasi-Expressionist piece *Trommeln in der Nacht*. Ziegel, in turn, opened the

Hamburg Kammerspiel with a program devoted to Wedekind's works and his subsequent repertoire included Kaiser, Kornfeld and Barlach.[9]

During this era, Heinrich George referred to Frankfurt as his "motherland"; and, indeed, between 1916 and 1919 it was in acting ensembles at Frankfurt, Dresden, Hamburg, Mannheim, Darmstadt, and Munich that most of the great names of the Expressionist stage – Kortner, Deutsch, George, Elisabeth Bergner, Erwin Kalser – first explored their way into the innovative conceptions of performance required by the new drama. They did so, however, not only in response to Expressionist dramaturgy but also with reference to how their own training and experience had been shaped by divergent and longstanding traditions of acting. This generation of young actors grew up amidst a conflict between classical declamation or its neo-romantic variant, on the one hand, and the Naturalist version of realism, on the other.

From the early eighteenth century onward, in fact, two opposing ideas of acting had vied for dominance on the German stage. One was the formal, declamatory style based originally on the French classical tradition, championed first by the Neubers, and later developed by Goethe at Weimar according to his concepts of "harmony" and "beauty." The other was the so-called realist school that emerged from the Hamburg National Theatre in the mid eighteenth century. In this tradition the ideal of a technically perfected mimetic performance, articulated by Lessing in his *Hamburg Dramaturgy*, had been most influentially exemplified in the work of Friedrich Schroeder. This, of course, was not a psychological, emotion-based realism, but rather an artificial realism of the kind advocated by Diderot around the same time in France.[10] It was in reaction to such artificiality – both of the "classical" and the "realist" sorts – that Naturalist theatre developed in Germany. To be sure, Naturalist dramaturgy in Scandinavia and Naturalist production in France had led the way. But Otto Brahm's advocacy of naturalistic acting was also a stylistic argument against prevailing traditions of technique and artificiality:

We don't want to be anything else but human beings who find the emotions of the character to be represented from within and who express these with a simple, natural voice – regardless of whether that voice is beautiful and resonant, regardless of whether the accompanying gesture is gracious or not, and regardless of whether it fits in with the conception of stock types.[11]

Notwithstanding the success of naturalistic acting in Naturalist plays, however, productions of the classics attempted by Brahm suffered from stylistic disunity because the older poetic drama facilitated the grand manner of declamation and resisted the new approach. By the turn of the century, both declamation and strict naturalistic acting were becoming outmoded. *naxualtinm ouse of date?*

Indeed, it seemed clear that a single style would no longer do for the diversity of dramatic literature then finding its way on to the German stage. In the wake of enthusiasm over Strindberg, provincial Intendants – if not yet those in Berlin – were gradually persuaded to try the more daring experiments of early Expressionism, building as it did on the successful anti-realist innovations of dramas like *To Damascus*, *Ghost Sonata*, and *A Dream Play*. Since the turn of the century, Reinhardt's work had argued persuasively that each distinct style of dramatic composition called forth its own specific directorial strategy. Certainly directors of Expressionist drama during and after the war would find this to be the case, particularly where the play culminated in so strong a moment as the ecstatic Schrei.

II. THE SCHREI: THEORETICAL BASIS

Though it is unlikely that the actors and directors of these early productions thought of their work categorically as "Schrei Expressionism," the rubric is nonetheless useful for an understanding of early ecstatic acting. In the first instance, I employ the term to designate certain Expressionist scripts which called for extraordinarily intense and protracted vocal outbursts of emotion. However, the original inspiration for this conception was probably more visual than aural. When thinking of the Schrei, of course, one immediately calls to mind Munch's famous 1893 lithograph.[12] Along with this, the emphatic accents in certain works of Gauguin and Van Gogh together with the vivid palette of the Fauves profoundly influenced the Dresden circle of avant-garde painters who called themselves "Die Brücke," as well as a parallel circle in Munich known as "Neue Künstlervereinigung". These groups were not merely loose associations but tightly knit artists' communes which sought a new model of social living as well as a new artistic vision. Inspired not only by the examples of the painters just mentioned, their fellowship also included reading and discussion of such literary figures as Whitman, Nietzsche, Wedekind, and, again, Strindberg.[13] Yet it was not until artists connected with both groups began to illustrate Expressionist literary art in periodicals such as *Der Sturm* that the violently emotional angularity and distortion typically associated with Expressionist visual art became generally evident.

Between 1910 and 1912 graphic artists such as Max Pechstein, Emil Nolde and Cesar Klein, associated with Die Brücke, responded in periodical illustrations and woodcut imprints to the vivid imagery of the verse and prose being written by members of Expressionist literary associations such as the Neopathetisches Cabaret, Sturm, and Aktion. During this period, as noted earlier, Kokoschka was illustrating his own and others' literary work in the pages of *Der Sturm*. Kandinsky, a founding member of Neue Künstlervereinigung, published the *Blaue Reiter* Almanac along with Franz Marc in 1912; this in conjunction with an exhibition of paintings under the same title in December 1911 by them, Delaunay, the composer Arnold Schönberg, and August Macke among others.[14] Among publishers, Kurt Wolff was particularly responsible for facilitating exchange between Expressionist artists, poets and dramatists.

The principal stylistic result of this extended interaction between visual and literary artists was a vivid, often violent imagistic visualization of emotion as the alienated young artist recoiled from his experience of the city, the machine, the institutions of official culture, and the patriarchal family. Kaiser's *Von morgens bis mitternachts* and the poems of Ernst Blass and Gottfried Benn expressed this with a mixture of visceral imagery and ironic distance, while the Cubist/Abstractionist work of painters like Kandinsky and Marc by 1912 registered a dynamic, forceful angularity. At the same time, the "Oh Mensch!" poetry of Franz Werfel expressed not revulsion but an equally intense embracing of "Mankind" in a passionate call for "Universal Brotherhood." Both outrage at the deadening effects of bourgeois culture and empathy for all human suffering had, at their core, the vitalist desire to be intensely alive. This was the basic meaning of the Schrei in Expressionist art before 1914. By the end of the war, the desire for life, of course, had taken on a grotesquely new significance, and the Expressionist Schrei assumed the much more sharply defined function of expressing battle trauma. Indeed, in his 1918 anti-war drama *Seeschlacht*, Reinhard Goering stipulates that "the play begins with a scream." In the early Expressionist dramas to be considered in this chapter, however, the vitalist cry of and for life is embodied not in traumatized soldiers but in the typical figure of the artist of "lean face and burning eyes," as Kurt Pinthus described the young Hasenclever when he read his new play *Der Sohn* at the literary cabaret Das Gnu in early 1914.[15] In these plays, the Schrei arises out of a cultural, rather than military, battle of life against death. In the struggle of son against father it is conceived as the cry not of isolated individuals but of a whole generation.

Indeed, the Schrei appears to have embodied for the Expressionists something of an ultimate common denominator of human existence. It was the primal democratic gesture; the badge of humanity both at its most primitively animalistic and its most spiritually sublime. The epigraph Bernhard Diebold chooses for his study of the various Expressionist dramatic models illustrates the common spirit underlying them all. He quotes Pascal:

It is dangerous to show man too much of his resemblance to the animals without showing him his greatness. It is dangerous to allow him to see too much of his greatness apart from his baseness . . . Man may not believe that he is like the animals; he may not believe he resembles the angels. He cannot ignore one and not the other; he must know both.[16]

The Schrei was at once the experience and the expression of this dual self-knowledge. Diebold's citation of Pascal's opposition of animal and angel, body and spirit, is telling. It reveals that "baroque tension" in which, as I noted in the last chapter, Kasimir Edschmid recognized the "fanatic ardor" of "the true German national tradition in acting."[17] The synthesis of these oppositions, according to Felix Emmel, was the "ecstatic gesture," which was the embodiment of "the internal transformation of the private man in the poetic form . . . that religious condition of being possessed by the act of poetic creation."[18]

For the Expressionists, as Günther Rühle notes, "the center of Man was now [i.e., with the emergence of the new performance art] experienced as energy; in expression, one perceived the internal thrust."[19] This energy the Expressionists most often denoted with the term "Gefühl", by which they meant something like "instinctively creative emotion." For Edschmid, the breaking point of creative emotion was the Schrei. It was at once a breakthrough in emotive expression and emotive cognition: both release and insight. "The climax of Gefühl," he explains, "so burdens the creating spirit that darkly desiring the immeasurable, it begins to cry out the unprecedented" [das Unerhörte].[20]

Rhetorical oppositions such as "animal" and "angel" are typical of the bi-polar thinking which runs throughout Expressionist performance theory. Emmel, for example, argued that art embraces two levels: the "peripheral" and the "central." Peripheral art has to do with the physical senses [Kunst der Nerven]; central art involves the spiritual faculty [Kunst des Blutes] (28). For Emmel, Albert Basserman was a "nerve actor," while Friedrich Kayssler was a "blood actor." Basserman produced a "masterful psychological mosaic, a consciously worked out, intellectually perceived, characteristic illusion of mankind."

His ability to transform himself is astonishing. Kayssler, by contrast, plays only himself; however, he doesn't give the illusion of mankind, but is mankind himself. His rhythm and his inner melody come, unconsciously, right out of the blood. (35)

The "blood actor," Emmel elaborates, creates "instinctively, within his role." He is driven to "internal transformation"; whereas the "nerve actor" seeks "external transformation" (36). The difference is between a performance that rationally explains and emphasizes, and one that creates a "spiritual song." More to the point, "nerve" acting allows for no real unity of word and gesture, no truly integrated expression; word and gesture cleverly cooperate by illustrating one another, but they never become one. Such unification is possible only through the instinctual creativity of "blood" acting in which expression is induced in a "poetically spellbound" condition, and in that way becomes the ecstatic unification of word and gesture (40–41). Thus ecstatic acting is "a strange mixture of the conscious and the unconscious" – a "dream-vision consciousness" in which, as the "blood" actor Kayssler observed, "it is the soul that acts."[21]

The two actors whom Emmel most praises are Fritz Kortner and Werner Krauss. "Kortner," he says, "is a master speaker [Meistersprecher] among us."

He shows us what it means to speak fatefully. He concentrates Destiny into a single word, or he can allow it to drive through his phrases. He builds an overwhelming word gesture before us, which captures in word-rhythms the Destiny of the character he is playing. (39)

If Kortner was the "Meistersprecher," Krauss's acting, by contrast, was the epitome of ecstatic physicalization [Gebärdenekstase]. "Almost every one of his characters," says Emmel, "signifies a physically ecstatic metamorphosis." Yet neither virtuosity, by itself, fully achieves the Expressionist performance ideal. Rather, "what we strive for in the ideal actor is an inner unity of Krauss's ecstatic physicalization and Kortner's verbal dynamic force" (41).

Julius Bab, in his comprehensive gallery of actor portraits, *Schauspieler und Schauspielkunst* (1926), used the same method of epitomizing and contrast that Emmel employed. His essay on Krauss and Kortner, for example, is entitled "Krauss and Kortner, or figure and voice" [Gestalt und Stimme]. Like Emmel, Bab saw the two actors as total opposites in terms of their respective virtuosities, but what united them as "Expressionists" was both "the sense of enormous scale" and "the courage for a certain rhythmic simplification" which they shared.[22] This premium on simplification was also expressed by Gustav Hartung in his essay "On the Essence of Directing":

For this is [the director's] task: to find the performance and scenic expression for the linguistic form which the poet has given to his experience: and the simpler the means by which this expression is achieved, the greater is the art of the director.[23]

We know that such simplification for the Expressionist actor involved the reduction of physical movement to a minimum. The idea was that when a gesture did occur it would be symbolically comprehensive, not psychologically illustrative. The reduction of speech in Telegrammstil dialogue aimed at a similar essentialization of expression. At the same time, the physical and verbal restraint in this strategy of reduction, as applied to Schrei acting, was intended to create an enormous emotional pressure which would eventually explode in expansive gestures and long passionate monologues. Words and gestures were fired like bullets or came rushing forth in resounding aural and visual avalanches. This pattern of compressive reduction and explosive expansion, in fact, was the essential rhythm of Schrei ecstatic acting. Hence, the "Schrei" was much more than a literal scream; rather, it was an enormous release of emotional pressure which fused movement and speech into "ecstatic gestures." In theory, at least, speech became visual and movement became aural.

III. SCHREI PERFORMANCE PARADIGMS: KORTNER, KRAUSS, AND DEUTSCH

In Bab's portrait gallery, Kortner, Krauss and Ernst Deutsch are the best representatives of "Expressionist" acting; on the other hand, none of the three are regarded solely as "Expressionist actors." In the essay on Kortner and Krauss, Bab echoes Emmel's distinction between the two actors by locating Kortner's power in his voice and Krauss's in his ecstatic physicalization of character. Bab spends most of his time discussing Krauss, which suggests a priority of physicalization over voice in his view of the essence of Expressionist performance. Yet he also emphasizes the importance of Krauss's voice, which while not the basis of his characterizations, was nonetheless a "suitable support and illustration of the prevailing mood which his 'spatial images' establish."[24]

However, for Bab,

the experience of Krauss begins in space, culminates in the contour of his physical characterization, remains for my sensibility always on the surface. I see his magnificent, fully convincing, living characters . . . as portraits [*Bilder*]. And certainly never as oil paintings with colors glowing out of profound depth, but rather as pastels, colorful chalk drawings, very sharp in stroke, very well defined . . . The imagination of this actor grasps the physical contour of a character with quite astonishing energy. (133)

It was this last quality, energy, in fact, which made Krauss the bridge between Wedekind and the young actors of 1920, according to Günther Rühle. Early in his career, Krauss had performed with Wedekind. The chief result of this experience was that he had taken up in himself Wedekind's "passion, his obsession with truth [*Wahrheitsbesessenheit*], and united it with his own magical power of metamorphosis." Hence, Krauss acted with "unprecedented spiritual energy" and became the "prototype of the new actor."[25] Though he began acting at a very early age, he was never formally trained. In 1913 his performance in a production of *Peer Gynt* attracted the attention of Alexander Moissi, upon whose recommendation Reinhardt hired Krauss at the Deutsches Theater. Moissi, of course, was also a colleague of Wedekind's, having first performed with him under Reinhardt's auspices in the 1906 Kammerspiele première of *Frühlings Erwachen.* Krauss's work with the playwright/actor took place principally during the 1913–14 season with Reinhardt's company when he acted several Wedekind roles. Kurt Wallstab, in his monograph chronicling the roles of Werner Krauss, draws a specific connection between these Wedekind performances and Krauss's definitive work on the Expressionist stage. His acting of the role of the fourth sailor in Reinhardt's 1918 Deutsches Theater production of Reinhard Goering's *Seeschlacht,* for example, "exactly corresponded to the [performance] conceptions of the Expressionist dramatists." But this "exemplary manner of playing . . . had already been evident five years earlier in his Wedekind characters" (Schigolch/*Erdgeist*, Launhart/*Hidalla*, Professor Dühring/*Der Stein der Weisen*, Konsul Kasimir/*Marquis von Keith*) at the end of his first season with Reinhardt.[26]

Krauss's work at the Deutsches Theater contrasted with the psychological approach of other actors in Reinhardt's company in that he kept his characters "at a distance, like an artist in the process of sculpting a work."[27] Yet this manipulative distance apparently was no impediment to Krauss's total involvement in his work. Herbert Ihering, commenting on his performance as the fourth sailor in *Seeschlacht*, remarked that he acted "with exchanged senses." That is, Krauss had become so "possessed by his inner experience" that

the word was not accompanied by gesture, not amplified by movement: the word was gesture, the word became flesh . . . It [was] as though he saw sounds and heard gestures.

This image of fusion recalls Emmel's ideal actor, who is a combination of the opposed qualities of Kortner's dynamic voice and Krauss's ecstatic physicalization. Krauss's acting was of a kind, says Ihering, which

opposes stage direction and thus stimulates it productively in that he fulfills that which he has only attempted fragmentarily: he abridges instead of completing. If Expressionism ultimately is concentration, here is an Expressionist actor.[28]

The technique of abridgement to which Ihering refers, while the opposite of naturalistic "completion," was nonetheless undertaken with the idea of "fulfilment." Its execution, however, was elusive and often susceptible of misunderstanding or outright failure. The critic Fritz Engel, for example, panned Krauss's performance of the role of the "Other" in the 1919 Kammerspiele production of Strindberg's *Advent* as merely a

showcase display of the new style. What capering and fawning; suddenly speaking rapidly, suddenly slowing down: all only in order to indulge himself "expressionistically!" I question whether here the actor "acted" anything; whether the sense and intention of the poetry was not completely obscured.[29]

Vocally, the Expressionist goal of building a performance out of the power of the poetic word could backfire into a ridiculous obfuscation of the poet's language – either through arbitrary rhythms of enunciation or turgid bombast. In terms of physical movement, abrupt changes of tempo often seemed only mechanical, not essentially efficient. Thus the Expressionist ecstatic actor sometimes took on the qualities of a puppet, "stepping with primitive, abrupt gesture into the midst of the spectators," as Rudolf Frank put it.[30] Yet such abruptness, properly controlled, served to focus expression rather than obscure it.

It is clear that the strategy of physical and vocal reduction required not only great concentration and intensity, but also a fine precision in gesture and utterance. In Krauss's acting Bab found a "ghostly, marionette-like exactness in each movement."[31] His voice was somewhat rough and melancholy, lacking in melody. For this reason, he typically shaped the rhythmic contours of his speech not with great bold strokes but with "spasmodic punctuation" – a kind of natural Telegrammstil tendency. Yet such was Krauss's control of his staccato vocal style, according to Bab, that he could turn a character's derisive laughter – or even his death rattle – into a "ghostly melody." This precise control was accompanied by a great physical and vocal range which Krauss could traverse with lightning suddenness: from "melancholy, hoarse single tones up to the sudden, raw scream of a bird of prey"; from the "most concise, punctuating movements of fingers stretched, as though pushed from within the wrists, to the sudden leap" of the entire body.[32] Apparently, it would have been as impossible to separate the vocal element from the physical element of his acting as it is to distinguish between the sensation of a wild predator's shriek from that of its physical leap-to-the-kill. We don't really hear, as much as see, the animal scream, so absorbed is the aural into the more dominant visual image. Yet in that visual image, the savage scream pierces one's heart all the more frightfully.[33] It was precisely this absorption of sound into sight in the Schrei acting of Werner Krauss that enabled him, as Bab said, to be "one of the few in Germany [at that time] who [could be] truly creative in the cinema."[34]

If Krauss's ecstatic physicalization had an augmented visual impact upon the spectator, Kortner's voice, according to Bab, could manifest his physical presence on stage even before he had made his entrance. As Gessler in Jessner's production of *Wilhelm Tell* (Berlin, Staatstheater, 1919), Kortner, while yet backstage, thrilled the audience with his driving, raging, blood-surfeited voice vibrating in wrath . . . And a certain dread, a fear-instilling paralysis confronts our hearts. Then, indeed, he enters, like a red, piercing flame . . .

But even though his physical appearance as this demonic character was impressive,

what holds us fast in his spell, what takes our breath away, what fills us with almost physical fear, as long as he stands on the stage, is first and foremost the voice, which crackles like a flash of lightning (138).[35]

In this description, as in the preceding account of Krauss's work, the characteristic perception is that of a sudden burst of energy. Yet the difference between Krauss's degree of focus and that of Kortner "is the difference between a dagger and a cudgel." The art of the former was the "sharply dissecting" work of the "brain"; it yielded the "fervently defined concreteness of a portrait." The art of the latter was a "swelling stream, a shattering blow" impelled from the "blood"; it produced the "ever inconceivable, soaring magic of a voice" (139).

Krauss's acting was galvanized by the energy of sudden transition; Kortner's performances appear to have been driven by an energy of momentum. Here we see the opposite ends of the rhythmic spectrum of Schrei ecstatic performance: Schrei as expressive burst and Schrei as cumulative crescendo. In this latter rhythmic sense, Kortner was a verbal architect. "His Othello," as Felix Emmel recalls it, "allowed an exorbitantly credulous love to grow up into a word-cathedral."[36] If Krauss was Wedekind's heir, Kortner – whose verbal tectonics hearken back to the Storm and Stress tradition of declamatory art – took his inspiration from the great turn-of-the-century Austrian actor, Josef Kainz. In his autobiography Kortner recalls that, as a youth, he lacked any sense of vocation until

one night, for the first time, I saw Josef Kainz as Franz Moor on the stage of the Burgtheater . . . The age of electricity had begun, and Josef Kainz was its son, and through him we flowed into and were swept along in the main current of the era. His equanimity itself was electrically charged; his spirit transmitted scintillating energy; his speech was a strong current. At times it took on the rapidity of the speed of sound, when Kainz angrily, rebelliously, passionately, exultantly discharged himself and propelled his voice up to unprecedented heights. Here a genius sang a new melody, pulsing throughout with the rhythm of an age which was dawning before we were yet conscious of it.[37]

Kainz had been among the original Deutsches Theater company

formed by Adolf L'Arronge in 1883 to preserve the staging traditions
of the Meiningen troupe. Yet his style of acting recalled the Weimar
ideals of "harmony and beauty," a style which ill suited the goals of
the Naturalist program later introduced at the Deutsches Theater by
Brahm in 1894. Hence, the grand gestures and magnificent voice of
this actor of the "older school" would become a theatrical model for
the revolt against Naturalism long before "Expressionism" took
shape as a theatrical movement. What Kortner brought to the
Expressionist stage was precisely the lyrical performance aesthetic he
so ardently admired in Kainz. That aesthetic was essentially musical
in nature. Kainz once remarked in his diary that

the movements of the actor's body are the expression of the Psyche, the
external signs of what is happening within . . . His acting must always be
music . . . He must become neither a restrained God from Olympus nor a
mere beast who surrenders himself to his instincts . . . He must know the
limits and scale of his instrument . . . He must have a light and sensitive
touch for every stage of transition from piano to forte . . . His words and
movements must appear from the front as if coming instinctively in
harmonious accord.[38]

This theory of performance was one by-product of the on-going
struggle between the ideals of Weimar and the Hamburg realist
tradition mentioned earlier.

From its beginning, the Weimar tradition itself was built on the
conflict between Goethe's preference for "classical restraint" and
Schiller's taste for flamboyance. What united the two poets was their
belief in ideal beauty and their common view of acting as a matter of
musical declamation and orchestrated effects. Indeed, it was this
musical model for staging that Felix Emmel regarded as the earliest
forbear of Expressionist ecstatic performance.[39] The violent lyricism
of early nineteenth-century Romantic drama distended and stretched
the range of the Weimar musical idea of performance without
destroying its essential view of the actor as instrument. This view had
been consistently opposed by the Hamburg tradition with its concept
of the actor as real person. During the middle part of the century,
the school of romantic realism – that which produced actors like
Kainz – attempted to synthesize these classical and realist ideas of
performance. It continued to stress the instrumental nature of the
actor's body and voice while allowing for the individual motivation
which Goethe had steadfastly disregarded. The Naturalist insistence
on mimetic performance based on materialist determinism attempted

to destroy this compromise, but the instrumental tradition in acting was not so easily set aside. Brahm's Naturalistic productions of the classics, for example, failed for lack of unity in performance style because, while younger actors played naturalistically, Kainz persisted in performing in the traditional flamboyant manner.[40]

It was this neo-romantic tradition which Kortner embraced when he first experienced Kainz's work at the Burgtheater. Whatever the extremes to which Expressionist ecstatic acting was impelled by the inspiration of performers like Wedekind and by the demands of the scripts themselves, such acting began with the neo-romantic approach to the actor as instrument. Here another of Reinhardt's contributions to the development of Expressionist performance is evident: he trained actors like Kortner in choral performance on the grand scale. This style was necessary for huge staging areas such as that used in *Oedipus Rex* when it toured Russia in 1911. As a chorus leader, Kortner recalls,

it was my responsibility to lead my choral group vocally. My solo passages I was to characterize effortlessly as an old man with full voice in charismatically ["*gezogen*"] rhythmic, singing tones. This delivery, ever fanatically soaring higher, signaled the climax of the drama. The smaller passages I had to speak from within the choral group. For my aria I was permitted to go up one step on the high staircase leading to the palace of Oedipus. Supported by a cane, wearing a long gray beard on my youthful face, I was then to turn myself around, facing the public, and fire away.[41]

These "arias," says Kortner, required "great breath" (169); and in performing them he first learned to support the powerful voice which would later rock the Expressionist stage. If Expressionist playwrights sought to exploit the raw emotional material in actors, the traditions of Kainz and Reinhardt provided the core of formal principles upon which those actors depended for expressive control. Schrei Expressionist playwriting, in short, did not call forth a new form of acting as much as it inspired the rejuvenation and adaptation of an old one.

The technical virtuosity required for this kind of acting, however, had its limits in terms of expressive satisfaction for the actor. Kortner soon grew cynical about his ability,

with my unique vocal virtuosity, to achieve effects according to proven patterns, to intensify a speech, to shout louder than others, to seize the stage at the conclusion of the act, to aim for applause at the curtain. I had abandoned myself to vocal delivery and had no time to really learn, much less to shape, the role, to get in touch with its corresponding mimic effect.

Much as I wanted to, I could not find the way from solely vocal to bodily expression. I had not yet seen Chaplin.

The war years were, for Kortner, the "pre-Chaplin era," during which he had attempted to learn mime from his observation of the "silent expression of faces, of the bodies of animals, of children." The work of Albert Basserman, the great naturalistic actor who was somewhat "hindered of voice," according to Kortner, was also a model of gestural expression. But the

magic of the expressive silence which could even dispense with speech I did not yet know. It required time for it to occur to me that forehead, eyes, eyelashes, brows, pupils, lips, corners of the mouth, chin, back of the head, nape of the neck, arm, leg, wrist, finger, backbone, throat, hairline, trunk and pelvis had to take part in order to communicate the secrets of humanity as I later saw for the first time with Chaplin . . . I realized that gesture rules speech, indeed creates it. Through my later experience of Chaplin this recognition finally persuaded me that bodily and facial expression liberates true vocal expression . . . When, with a gifted actor, the sound is false, then the source of the failure lies generally in the face, in the physical demeanor, often in the legs, many times in the gesture.(276–77).

It is not clear from Kortner's autobiography how long after the war he actually saw Chaplin's work. Most likely, this influence post-dated Kortner's Expressionist stage work and coincided with his silent film acting in the later Republican era. In any case, he claims that this view of the relation between physical and vocal expression had been "percolating in me for a long time" (277).[42]

The distinction between true and false expression which Kortner draws upon refers to aesthetic consistency and harmony, not mimesis. Its basis was the philosophical tradition of Schiller's aesthetics. Schiller's formulation of the principle of expressive unity, as I argued earlier, was that "form does away with content" – which is to say that meaning and its formal expression become one. In the Expressionist era this principle became the idea that expression itself is content, as much as are the ideas being expressed. Hence, the unification of expressive means served the goal of its own aesthetic integrity, as well as the social or spiritual thematic objectives of the playwright.

Whereas Kainz had argued for the *appearance* of instinctual harmonious accord between word and gesture, the Expressionist performers strove for the *actuality* of such a synthesis. Given the technical capacity, the energy needed to produce that Schrei fusion of voice and body was – in apparently all but the rarest cases, such as Krauss, Kortner, and Deutsch – beyond the resources of the individual personality of the actor. For Ernst Deutsch it was a question of openness to the energy of other artists – in particular, the director. Deutsch wrote that

> even the greatest genius among actors falls short in his personality alone, of all the suggestive power he needs . . . No matter how ambitious and enthusiastic he may be, he feels that he needs help to attain the top. And the day comes when he sees the helping hand. He faces one who is so rich that he can afford to be a spendthrift. The nature of this wealth is nothing but the immense suggestive power which he communicates to the actor, thus enhancing to a phenomenal degree the latter's means of expression – suggestion.[43]

Here Deutsch is referring to the effect Reinhardt's direction had upon him as an actor. Like the anecdote which Kortner tells of his chance meeting with Wedekind, recounted in the last chapter, this statement is indicative of the extraordinary vulnerability of the Expressionist actor. These were artists who cultivated, to an unusual degree, a sensitivity to their performance environment – to other actors in the ensemble, to the director, to the scenery, to the text above all. Indeed, they looked to each other – and the critics looked to them – for inspiration in performance.

The primary channel of this inspiration was the ability to "feel." Known as *ein Liebhaber*, the actor who could infuse the audience and his fellows on stage with the experience of his passion was typically an intense young man. The general prominence of such a performer in German theatrical tradition, as well as his specific centrality on the Expressionist stage, was noted somewhat ironically by Julius Bab:

> But is there no contemporary Liebhaber? We would long since have been dead, completely decayed and without hope, if we no longer had this youth, for whom the boiling up of great erotic passion is typical – one who believes, who is rapturous [*schwärmen*], and above everything else, who can feel . . . The movement of "Expressionism," of course, wanted to re-establish instinctive feeling [*Gefühl*] as the ruling force in the world . . . And the first-born of Expressionism, in no way accidentally, have sought to connect with Schiller and have made abundant use of the tradition of youthful pathos . . . Ernst Deutsch played [Hasenclever's] "Son" in the 1916 Dresden première, and the success of the actor was almost greater than that of the piece. A new portrayer of the young man had been found, a "youthful Liebhaber," an ecstatic modern type . . .[44]

Interestingly, while Kortner regarded Kainz as his seminal inspiration, Bab saw Deutsch as the true heir – amongst "a hundred imitators" – of Kainzian technique. The essence of this technique was an "explosive accentuation," in which the "rigidity [*Starrheit*] of the Schillerian hero was released – muscle energy was transformed into nervous energy" (174). In this regard, Deutsch was the quintessential Schrei ecstatic actor, for his power on stage resembled "electric energy" which "erupted with lightning surprise" (173). This image of sudden expressiveness also recalls the technique of Krauss, described above. The difference is that the explosiveness in Krauss's acting appears to have been more calculated than that in the work of Deutsch, which reportedly proceeded from his own "vibratingly spasmodic" temperament.

Such descriptions, to be sure, are the rhetorical stock in trade of critics such as Bab; and Kortner assures us that "no one suspected, behind those melancholy eyes, the wit and joyous delight which the private Deutsch possessed in full." The two actors first met at Dresden in 1916 while both were employed at the Neues Theater. They quickly became the kind of fast friends who could keep each other laughing through the grimness of an experience like the war. "Slim and dark-skinned, with long fingers," Kortner recalls, "he had the characteristics of an ascetic."[45] Deutsch apparently learned to focus a good deal of expressive energy in his hands, a quality which Karl-Heinz Martin exploited with close-up shots in his 1920 film version of *Von morgens bis mitternachts*. This localization of physical expression was also one of the characteristics in Deutsch's work that remined Bab of Kainz:

Deutsch has once again the nervous groping and parrying play of slender fingers. Again we see the bitter, sorrowful twitches of disdain about the lip. Admittedly, it is with him a harsher nuance. And this, to be sure, is the difference of the thirty years which lie between his youth and that of Josef Kainz.[46]

Despite the innocuous quality of his private life, Deutsch, like Wedekind, quickly developed a sensational public image that had a life of its own. In physical appearance alone, even his intimate friend Kortner regarded Deutsch as "a model for the graphic illustrator of the expressionist-ecstatic period."

Older actors such as Paul Wegener and Gertrud Eysoldt brought their own exotic physical presences to bear in the Expressionist character roles they played. But they, like Kortner and Krauss, had developed their essential performance identities before the Expressionist era. Like most Reinhardt actors, Kortner recalls, they weren't attractive according to conventional standards. Rather these faces were beautiful because they captured the essence of their time. "There is something like a 'new' face," he explains; "every era has its face, not only in the figurative but also in the literal sense . . ."[47] In this way, Deutsch's countenance epitomized the central figure in early Expressionist drama – the rebellious son who is a visionary poet. He was a versatile and accomplished character actor. But, according to Bab, "in between playing old men and cold devils [he] never ceased playing boys and youths." He had a wide range of moods at his command but "his beauty appeared more naturally related to suffering" than anything else. It was Deutsch, prior to Kortner and Krauss, who established the paradigm of Schrei ecstatic performance. In creating the title role of Hasenclever's *Der Sohn* he infused the traditional Kainzian *Liebhaber* with a new, more abrasive, combination of "vibrating nervousness, intellectual sharpness, and spasmodic wildness."[48]

The early Expressionist scripts I am concerned with at this point – Hasenclever's *Der Sohn* (1913), Kornfeld's *Die Verführung* (1913), and Sorge's *Der Bettler* (1912) – do concern themselves with how someone becomes the new *Liebhaber* that Bab describes; but they go about it quite differently from a later Expressionist play such as Toller's *Die Wandlung*. Rather than depicting the emergence of the *Liebhaber* out of a radical transformation in the central figure's identity and values, these earlier pieces tend to assume his essential existence at the outset of the play. *Der Sohn*, *Die Verführung*, and *Der Bettler* are not Stationendramen like Toller's *Die Wandlung*, where the central figure develops through a "journey of the soul." Rather, the playing of their central figures is more a matter of expressively expanding a character who, from the first, is already the playwright's ideal. The Son in *Der Sohn* doesn't have to learn how to become a charismatic leader, he just is one. Bitterlich in *Die Verführung* does not have to work up the courage to strangle Marie's fiancé, his Nietzschean lust for experience simply prompts him to the crime on impulse. The Poet in *Der Bettler* knows early in the first act that he "will be able to unite work and fulfilment. I have the call, and hence I can accomplish what I must do."[49]

Der Sohn, *Die Verführung*, and *Der Bettler* all call for a small, intense performance ensemble. It was in this small ensemble context that

Schrei ecstatic performance was first envisioned and developed. There were, I would argue, three basic tendencies: in *Der Sohn* the primary Schrei mode is two-person confrontational dialogue; in *Die Verführung* the Schrei emerges out of operatic verbal duet; and the predominant method of *Der Bettler* is the Schrei monologue. The distinction between what I am calling "confrontational dialogue" and "verbal duet" is structural. The former builds to the Schrei climax for one of the actors through a pattern of numerous give and take utterances with another actor, much like realistic dialogue though in a more exaggerated manner. The latter involves a pattern of fewer, more lengthy speeches with less of an action–reaction structure to the dialogue. One actor delivers a long passionate speech while the other listens to this verbal aria as passionately enthralled as is the speaker. Then the second actor performs his or her own aria, not so much as a reaction, but as a complement to the first aria. Indeed, the operatic Schrei model is repeatedly suggested in reviews of *Die Verführung* which speak of the actors as "singing" their parts.

IV. DEUTSCH, WEICHERT, AND *DER SOHN*

It is not surprising that the first attempts at staging *Der Sohn* – at Prague (Deutsches Landestheater/Demetz) and Dresden (Albert-Theater/Licho) in 1916 – "left much to be desired." Elaborating this judgment in his review of Weichert's 1918 Mannheim production, Ernst Leopold Stahl recalled that

in Dresden the drama was played realistically in the essentials, emphasizing of necessity its weak side and illustrating its dependence on a model: Wedekind. In Mannheim they played it purely symbolically. Hasenclever's basic idea . . . was also the directorial concept.[50]

The problem with the play's première in Dresden was really two-fold. The script itself, while revolutionary in content, was conventional in form. Its theme of youthful expressive rebellion drew upon the Wedekind of *Frühlings Erwachen*.[51] Formally, then, the play was more a part of the transitional bridge between Naturalism and Expressionism than a full-fledged Expressionist drama. The opening description of the Son's room in the parental house reveals Hasenclever's original conception of the physical context for his play:

The Son's room in the parental house. In the center wall a large window

with a view of the park; in the distance, the silhouettes of the city: houses, a factory chimney. In the room the moderate elegance of a respectable middle-class home. A study furnished in oakwood: bookshelves, desk, chairs, a map. Doors right and left. The hour before twilight.
The Son. The Private Tutor.[52]

These stage directions, with the exception of the silhouettes, describe the kind of setting detail typically found in a Naturalistic play. Moreover, within each act *Der Sohn* observes the unities tightly; and scene transitions, more often than not, are signaled by announced entrances of new characters. The opening scene, true to well-made-play format, is a two-person expository one.

The second problem with the Dresden première was that the director, Adolf Licho, was a Berlin Regisseur imported for the occasion. "Rooted in the school of Brahm," observed the reviewer Camill Hoffmann, "he squeezed Sturm und Drang into an Ibsen tempo."[53] Indeed, the difficulty of breaking free of Berlin realism was evident again two years later in the Das junge Deutschland production of the play, directed by Felix Hollaender under the auspices of Max Reinhardt.[54] Given the bias in Berlin toward realism, and the Naturalistic form of the script itself, it is understandable that Licho mistook *Der Sohn* as merely another "Familiendrama," as Hoffmann termed it. The key to the revolutionary nature of this piece, however, is in the idea of character embedded in its realistic dialogue. Here the Expressionist spirit of *Der Sohn* is evident from the start.

In the opening exposition scene, the Son confesses to his sympathetic tutor his complete alienation from the educational system which perpetuates the philistine culture of his father's generation. He then announces that he has decided to forego the graduation exams:

THE PRIVATE TUTOR: What will you do now?
THE SON: Perhaps perform a monologue. I must express myself within myself. This mode is commonly despised, you know. But I have never found it disgraceful to kneel before my own pathos, for I know how bitter is my joy and my pain. Since my earliest childhood I have learned to inspire myself in loneliness until it spoke to me in tones . . . Do you not know that feeling?
THE PRIVATE TUTOR: (unpretentiously) We live on a stage.
THE SON: When they cheer and one must bow with a carnation in his buttonhole . . .
THE PRIVATE TUTOR: Who cheers?
THE SON: The people who are not there! Comprehend it, man: one only

lives in ecstasy; reality would make for confusion. How beautiful it is to experience, again and again, that oneself is the most essential in the world. (103)

While such a sentiment revealed the egocentric form of the whole play to Kurt Pinthus as early as 1914, and merely outraged Siegfried Jacobsohn as late as 1918, its implication for acting was apparently first grasped in 1916 by the actor who created the title role, Ernst Deutsch. Notwithstanding Licho's realistic direction, Deutsch, according to Hoffmann,

moved through the play as if in a trance, the paradigm of Ecstatic man, hollow-eyed, passionately aglow, led by higher will.[55]

It was in this role, in fact, that Deutsch first began to discover and develop the art of expressive gesture appropriate to the new drama.[56] Along with the idea of egocentrism set forth repeatedly in scenes such as the one cited above, the most frequent performance stage direction is "he staggers." Otherwise, Hasenclever's stage directions seem to expect from the actor nothing other than the sort of focused dramatic intensity one might find in a play by Zola or Tolstoi. Aside from the limited use of monologue – of the five in the script, only two are spoken by the Son – it is only the conception of ecstatic character which distinguishes *Der Sohn*, formally, from the Naturalistic drama.

In practical terms, Deutsch's playing of the role in a trance-like fashion must have facilitated the openness to suggestion which, as we saw, he came to view as central to his art. The script of *Der Sohn* certainly requires this kind of vulnerability because of the Son's relationship to the Friend. This is most clearly illustrated in the Son's soul-baring autobiographical speech, which inspires his lecture hall audience to a spirit of rebellion against "the fathers." The scene is not played on stage; rather, it is cleverly inverted so that the setting and the actual audience are backstage of the lecture hall and the audience in the play. The Son's performance is described from backstage of the lecture hall curtain by one of the leaders of the pseudo-liberal "Club for the Preservation of Joy" which has sponsored the evening:

VON TUCHMEYER: He tears the mask away. His eyes still haven't focused. He speaks of his childhood. Many can't understand him . . . there, he's speaking louder. One stands up and comes near him.
THE FRIEND: (clenching his hands): Is he moving his hands?

VON TUCHMEYER: No. Yes – now –

THE FRIEND: (opening his arms): – Is he stretching them out: like this?

VON TUCHMEYER: He is uncertain! He says –: He takes the torment of early childhood from all of us onto himself!

· ·

THE FRIEND: (bending forward with all his muscles tensed): The spirits stand by him! (He moves his limbs and the features of his face with magic force): Now! Say it! (A fearful Will is in him to force the speaker under the control of his thoughts.)

VON TUCHMEYER: This is disastrous!!! He says: the fathers who beat us, should be brought to justice! The audience is frantic – (Colossal tumult in the hall.)

· ·

VON TUCHMEYER: He tears the clothes from his body. He bares his breast. He shows the stripes which his father beat into him – his scars! Now I can't see him any more, so many are around him. Now – they grasp his hands – they shout for joy with him –

THE FRIEND: (in triumph): Now has he conquered! Now has he accomplished it!

Von Tuchmeyer might well have been describing the extremities to which Deutsch, and other Expressionist actors, would go in the next four or five years on the German stage. But in this play what we see is not such histrionics but rather the spiritual control of the Friend over the Son. In fact, the Son's charismatic power over other men is dependent on his own vulnerability to the suggestive power of others over him. This is the quintessential Schrei performance situation in the early Expressionist theatre – characters powerfully influencing one another in a small ensemble context. In *Der Sohn* the vehicle of Schrei acting is not principally the monologue, but the dialogue. The most powerful Schrei moment in the script, for example, rises out of the dialogue in Act IV, sc. ii, where the Friend convinces the Son that he must kill his father. Here is the climactic moment:

THE FRIEND: (following after him): What will you do? Where will you go?

THE SON: (pressed against the wall): You are fearful. – There's nothing left of me – (screaming) parricide!!!!

Clearly the actor playing the Friend must have the same degree of mesmerizing expressive power as the one who plays the Son; and the role of the father is equally demanding. Felix Hollaender's Deutsches Theater production marshalled the combined forces of Deutsch,

Werner Krauss as the Friend, and Paul Wegener, who played the
Father. For Siegfried Jacobsohn, these actors were the production's
saving grace. Krauss was especially notable in that "when he entered
as the Friend, he didn't merely come on, rather, he appeared; his
exits weren't simply departures, he vanished."[57] Perhaps it was the
"inclination for playing in profile," noticed by Emil Faktor, that
helped to create the apparitional effect in Krauss's performance.
This strategy, said Faktor, "sharpened the demonic contours
[*Umrisse*] of his chimerical acting" to the degree that "he was the
most fascinating apparition of the evening."[58]

Deutsch did not play the title role in Richard Weichert's Mannheim production (Nationaltheater, 1918) because Reinhardt had
already wooed him to Berlin in the wake of his sensational performance at Dresden. But his interpretation of the Son anticipated the
seminal production concept Weichert would use, and it established,
as Pinthus noted, the paradigm of Expressionist acting "for the next
ten years."[59] Initially, Hasenclever himself apparently failed to
recognize the revolutionary performance implications in the dialogue
he had written. There is no evidence of his dissatisfaction with
Licho's naturalistic directing. Two years later, however, when the
play was again directed naturalistically by Hollaender, Hasenclever
was so disappointed with the result that he refused to take the
customary playwright's curtain call on opening night.[60] What had
happened in between was Weichert's Mannheim production, of
which the playwright remarked:

The idea, the spiritual content was evident . . . For me, it was as though I
were in the theatre for the first time ever . . . The complete realization of the
word on the stage was no vacuous illusion; here was absolute theatre . . .[61]

According to Pinthus, Hasenclever in fact regarded Weichert's
production as a "decisive turning point" in his career as a playwright.

The central feature of Weichert's production was the placement
of Fritz Odemar, who played the title role, in the middle of the
stage under a glaring overhead spotlight. Actors playing the other
roles apparently remained consistently on the periphery of the
spot's circumference, "appearing and disappearing more or less in
the twilight," as the reviewer Fritz Droop put it.[62] Presumably in
the scenes not involving the Son, these actors continued to play
in the shadows, although this is not explicitly mentioned in any of
the available reviews. Stahl merely notes that the Son, though

absent, "towered over" ["*beherrschen*" – which more literally means "to dominate," or "to control"] these scenes. Perhaps Odemar looked on from the shadows while other players stepped into the light at these points in the production. In any case, the Mannheim production apparently did not suffer from the stylistic inconsistency for which Jacobsohn faulted Hollaender in the Das junge Deutschland staging.[63] Stahl does mention that the scene between the Son's father and the more sympathetic police commissar – who, also a father, argues for an understanding, compassionate view of the Son's behavior – is both thematically and technically out of step with the rest of the play.[64] But this is a criticism of the script, not of Weichert's production.

The overall feel of the Mannheim production's style, according to Stahl, was one of "the most extreme austerity." Utilizing a deliberately restricted black and white color scheme, Ludwig Sievert's set consisted only of black background curtains, much less furniture than called for in Hasenclever's stage directions, and doors and windows represented merely by their outlines. This "open decoration," as Stahl called it, surrounded the central cone of light and made for a broad playing space in which it was possible to enter almost accidentally, "as if out of the realm of chance." The problem with the setting was that its openness created acoustic difficulties, especially for the actors playing in shadow. Weichert directed his ensemble to amplify their words with large movements which came in fits and starts. Stahl complained, however, that at times speeches got lost in the shadows anyway (109). In the title role, Odemar appeared "charmingly blond and boyish, with dreamy, grief-stricken eyes"; his acting was characterized by "emphatically completed, far-projecting, angular and awkward" gestures. These "exaggerated movements described the entire playing circle" defined by the cone of light (110). As Rudolf Frank described the general visual effect, "the objects on the stage lay like white streaks, before which the actors stood without make-up in their timeless costumes, like chalk ghosts."[65] For Weichert himself, the result of the images that he and Sievert created was that "some of the pictures [were] like Munch's visions."[66]

Just weeks before the Mannheim *Der Sohn*, Reinhardt had used sectional lighting in his Das junge Deutschland world première of Sorge's *Der Bettler*. But, as John Willett remarks, "if his use of spotlights in *Der Bettler* seemed more expressive [i.e., than heretofore] this was only as prescribed in the author's stage directions."[67] For his part, Weichert, in what might be an implicit reference to Reinhardt's penchant for technical innovation, later wrote that

it is not revolving stages, the pit, the lighting, the technical aspects, the magical effects of the machinery that must prevail, but the words, the text.[68]

According to Stahl, Weichert's production concept was gradually developed over long weeks of close textual analysis which resulted in an interpretation based on the "style of the poetry" (108). His scenic realization of *Der Sohn* thus grew out of his sense of the play's "internal rhythms." This rhythmic approach, according to Stahl, paid its greatest dividends in the acting, which was characterized by a "subtle development [*Ausarbeitung* – which also means "completion" and "elaboration"] of word and gesture" (109). Though it seems odd to describe the fitful, angular movements used by the actors in this production as "subtle," there apparently was subtlety in the way they grew out of the rhythms of the text. Here is an instance of Wedekind's "new language of the body" concept at work. Word and gesture had become ecstatically unified. It was for this reason, not mere technical innovation, that Weichert's *Lichtregie* ["light-directing"] showed Hasenclever "an absolute theatre" he had never before seen in his play. This was why, for the critic Stefan Grossmann, the Mannheim *Der Sohn* was "the only Expressionist staging based on a new idea."[69]

The importance of Weichert's work for the development of Expressionist performance was that he was the first producer to approach the new drama on the basis of something deeper than mere stylistic fascination. He *believed* in the drama at its thematic level. Whereas Reinhardt was a brilliant stylist, Weichert was a committed visionary. Weichert's pioneering interpretive work at Mannheim paralleled, on the ensemble level, the individual performance breakthrough of Deutsch at Dresden. Perhaps this was due to a naive provincial enthusiasm, as the contemporary reviewer Stahl suggested (108). Certainly Weichert and Deutsch both demonstrated the fruit of whole-hearted commitment to the new drama. The chief result of their work was that a stylistic purity, derived from a belief in the spirit of the text, was achieved in these early Expressionist performances. As Stahl observed, Weichert's *Der Sohn* was the play's spiritual, if not its chronological, première (108). But whereas

Hasenclever himself did not, at first, realize what kind of acting his script required, Paul Kornfeld clearly wrote *Die Verführung* with the "new" actor in mind.

V. *DIE VERFÜHRUNG*: SCHREI AS OPERATIC DUET

At first glance, the two most striking features of the script of *Die Verführung* are its length and its absolute dearth of stage directions. Although the script contains dramatic events – including a murder, a prison-break, and a suicide – the preponderance of its action occurs in speech. With a typical running-time of over four hours, *Die Verführung*'s prolixity made Shavian demands on the performers. It is therefore no surprise that Kornfeld, like Shaw, counseled his actors to

think of opera, in which the singer, as he is dying, still rings out a high C and with the sweetness of his melody says more about death than if he were to crawl and writhe.[70]

In *Die Verführung*, as in traditional grand opera, plot is really secondary to expression, or, in Aristotle's terms, "melos." What the audience experiences primarily is not the tension of character in relation to character but that of performer in relation to his or her medium. When characters do engage each other in this script the result is not fourth-wall realistic confrontation between characters, but a presentational operatic duet. As Kasimir Edschmid put it,

In Strindberg, people shoot at one another. In Kornfeld they sing arias to the sky beside one another. This is not humanity any more, this is feeling. Gramophones behind the scenes would give the same effect.[71]

More often than not the duet becomes a duel, a fateful struggle between two virtuosos to subdue one another by out-performing one another. This is clearly the dynamic of the play's title scene. Ruth Vogelfrei,[72] a youthful temptress somewhat resembling Ibsen's Hilda Wangel, "seduces" the play's cynical hero, who bears the allegorical name Bitterlich, to escape from his ascetic contentment in prison to a life of vitalist adventure (III, i). When he later persuades Ruth's brother Wilhelm to kill himself over his disgrace at his sister's wayward conduct, it is again clear that language, in the world of this play, is the elemental power (V, i). Whoever wields it with the most passionate inspiration will impose his or her will thereby, and triumph. Language in fact even has incarnational power, as when

Bitterlich, musing over the women in his life, is immediately – and quite improbably – visited by them in prison (II, iii). This Faustian faith in the power of language to create reality is the most "Expressionist" aspect of the script, and it suggests why Kornfeld's notion of stage direction amounts to little more than indicating that a character enters or exits. Speech is the script's movement and action; the actor – voice primarily, and body secondarily – is the only clearly established physical context. Unlike in Hasenclever's play, there is no description of setting in *Die Verführung*, as one reads through the play characters seem to appear or disappear or reappear from no clear point of spatial reference. The script thus almost demands a "dream-state" approach, as in the 1920 Hamburg Kammerspiele production, during which, according to one anonymous reviewer, "the spectator had the continual impression of a dream, the impression that everything grew out of the soul of the hero."[73]

Yet *Die Verführung* is clearly not intended by Kornfeld as pure lyrical ego projection; the characters of Ruth, the seductress, and of Frau Bitterlich, the obsessively devoted mother, are as fully realized as that of the hero himself. Indeed, the remarkable thing about this script is that all of its passionate prolixity is compressed into a small principal ensemble playing within the thematic context of the Wilhelmine family. Even more than in *Der Sohn*, a sense of great emotional pressure is thus built up to the point of explosion. Both plays also utilize a group of secondary characters in one or two scenes; and like Hasenclever's play, *Die Verführung* contains a scene in which the protagonist, having escaped from confinement, engages the world outside (IV, i). But the journey of self-discovery in these early Schrei dramas does not occupy a large portion of the script. Rather, the playwright appears more concerned with what the protagonist will do, assuming self-realization has occurred at the outset.

Hence in both *Der Sohn* and *Die Verführung* the actual journey of self-discovery is treated briefly, in a scene or two. The balance of the script is a demonstration of how the newly liberated hero explodes the claustrophobic family situation. In both plays the action returns to the principal ensemble and concludes in the domestic prison from whence it only temporarily departed. It is true that the comparatively brief final scene in *Die Verführung* is set "outside," in the precincts of a convent where Ruth and Bitterlich have gone to die. But the fates of these two nihilistic vitalists are sealed within the confines of Ruth's home, where both are poisoned. Even during the long third act, set in Bitterlich's jail cell, the continual, hovering presence of Frau Bitterlich maintains the sense of domestic imprisonment. Bitterlich, moreover, is not the play's sole vehicle of Schrei expression. The seduction scene with Ruth (III, i), the suicide scene of her brother Wilhelm (V, i), the family scenes between Wilhelm and his father (III, iii; IV, ii), and the prison scene between Bitterlich and his mother (III, i) all provide Schrei opportunities for the actors involved. Unlike *Der Sohn*, however, these Schrei moments are structured not as dialogue but as operatic duet, where characters deliver long passionate speeches by turns. As in operatic performance, the playing of such scenes requires an equal energy of stage presence for the characters who are not speaking as for the one who is; all must sustain the presentational tension of the scene.

Like Hasenclever's Son, Ruth's charismatic power is simply innate, not learned; it is a capacity for experience defined in terms of expression. She herself actually does nothing; rather, like Ibsen's Hilda, she draws her life's blood out of others by exciting them to action. Ruth is the vitalist stimulant for Bitterlich just as the Friend is for the title character in *Der Sohn*. Bitterlich in turn is defined by his complementary capacity to be thus stimulated. This innate capacity for stimulation in him is expressed, for example, in his impulsive murder of his cousin's fiancé, Josef. "My hand understood before my reason," he says, "what my heart desired" (57–58). This statement is a good summary of the condition to which Schrei actors aspired on stage. It implies the existence of a kind of physical cognition which enables direct experience and expression of the will. Here is the Schopenhauerean element in the physicalization of Schrei ecstatic performance: "action" not as representational pursuit of a goal but rather as the incarnation of the very principle of human will itself. In this play, however, the murder is not performed physically on stage, but rather vocally back stage, after Josef and Bitterlich have struggled their way off:

BITTERLICH (behind the scenery): Now I will never release you! How long have I wished to get someone in my hands! – Fellow, what do you think of immortality? – Finally my body expresses my frenzy! – You have come to the Hell of stupidity! – Do you feel safe in the world? What do you think of Napoleon? – Oh, you – ! – To Hell! To Hell! So – ! Ah! – Now? What do you say now?! Ah, you – ! You have made me tired! Ah, finally! How liberated I feel! (36–37)

The challenge to the actor is formidable: he must realize this intensely visual event solely in vocal terms.

In *Die Verführung* speech is the continuum both of physical action and of its sublimation into spiritual experience. This is evident in the language of Bitterlich's rhapsodic meditation on what the murder signifies in his life. This speech immediately follows the killing, almost flowing out of the deed as a part of it; it aesthetically completes the murder:

MARIE   What have you done?
BITTERLICH   I believe I have strangled him. Don't scream! Don't merely
     scream! How long have I wished for this, precisely this! I would like to
     do it daily! Don't scream! Why this noise? – I had to strangle someone!
     Don't lament! There is no cause for that! You really don't know how
     liberated I feel! I almost feel fortunate!. . . I thank God – it was me!
     And I feel relieved and liberated! (37)

As in operatic characterization, Bitterlich's deed is not fully incorporated into his identity until he, in effect, sings about it.

According to Günther Rühle, Gustav Hartung's 1917 première of *Die Verführung* inaugurated "the Expressionist phase" of the Frankfurt Schauspielhaus. Having moved from his native Prague to Frankfurt in 1916, the play's author, Kornfeld, established close contact with Carl Zeiss, who had newly been appointed Intendant at the Schauspielhaus. These two, along with Hartung, Arnold Bronnen, Hasenclever, Fritz von Unruh, and Otto Zoff, formed a union of young theatre artists at Frankfurt. During the time of this association, production at the Schauspielhaus was exclusively determined by Expressionist aesthetic principles. In the context of this commitment, Hartung's production of *Die Verführung* appears to have pioneered operatic Schrei ensemble acting. It is clear from the reviews, in any case, that the play's "melos" was the determining performance factor.

Of the script Bernhard Diebold remarked that

everyday speech yields to the melody of the most highly intensified utterance; the emphatic expression of the lovers, in tone and gesture, becomes an operatic duet – not merely people, but souls burst into jubilation.[74]

As Diebold saw it, Hartung was faced with "the difficult task of creating, in application and scope, a new kind of performance art." Diebold felt that either the most refined skill of the realistic actor or the practiced art of the court actor would only hinder a successful performance of this kind of text. In fact, he argued, the performance of one Fräulein Brod as Ruth proved that a script like *Die Verführung* was better served by the "musical and sensitive amateur." Because of her uncommon "style-instinct" for mimic and musical rhythm, Brod's acting was thrilling in its state of excitement, if somewhat self-conscious for lack of experience. This idea that "style" is more a matter of instinct than training was especially prominent in the provincial Expressionist theatre circles. Composed substantially of university students and talented amateurs, the ensembles in Mannheim, Frankfurt, Dresden and Munich drew heavily upon the enthusiasm and spontaneity of their typically youthful actors. As we saw in the last chapter, Kokoschka was among the first Expressionist theatre artists to use such an ensemble. His actors "hurled themselves into their roles," as he put it, producing a result which, for one critic, amounted merely to so much "unintelligible yelling [and] rolling around of human clumps on the stage." But the instinctual energy of Hartung's *Die Verführung* was much more formally shaped. Jacob Feldhammer, for example,

as Bitterlich, offered a perfect model of Expressionist technique. Turned out to the audience with his arms at his sides (while at the same time remaining lyrically compressed within himself), he restrained his gestures during his gradually intensifying speeches up until his expression reached its climactic scream in tone and movement together.[75]

Edschmid, in his *Vossische Zeitung* review of the production, stated flatly that "Feldhammer sang his entire role."[76]

Aside from the performers' enthusiastic, if unpolished, vocal commitment to their parts, both Diebold and Edschmid specifically noted the predominance of the "pose of crucifixion." This was utilized repeatedly by most of the principal players over the four-hour course of the production. Often specified in later Expressionist scripts, this physical image was to become a hallmark of Expressionist performance. Kornfeld's text, however, provides no stage direction for the crucifixion posture. Its use by Hartung suggests a spiritual attitude in the acting which was apparently carried further in John Gottowt's Neue Wiener Bühne production, mounted two months after Hartung's. The critic Alfred Polgar commented that

the actors behaved in a subdued priestly manner; they sought for the intersection of theatre and worship; and acted with Destiny, as if it came very near to them.

In its musicality, says Polgar, it was as though the production was striving "to develop a fourth dimension on the stage, which would enable the simultaneous apprehension of several spiritual entireties at once."[77]

Movement in these productions of *Die Verführung* appears to have been a matter of symbolic posturing. Such poses as that of the crucifixion, or the arms raised high, or arms held at the side, were not merely arbitrarily chosen signs, as Annalisa Viviani argues in her analysis of Kornfeld's concept of the ecstatic or "great" gesture.[78] They were the physical means of throwing vocal expression into relief by establishing a physical tension of expressive contrast with the voice. While the actor waxed eloquent for two or three pages he apparently would assume a pose and hold it. In such moments, Expressionist physicalization became literally sculptural. Hartung's *Die Verführung* was one of the first Expressionist productions to explore this tension between verbal dynamism and physical stasis. As we shall see in Chapter Five, Jessner took the experiment to its greatest extreme. Kornfeld developed this baroque contrast of expressive means by operatically emphasizing language and refusing to supply movement direction. On the other hand, Sorge, in the stage directions of *Der Bettler*, explored the power of language to stretch poetically the physical dimensions of gesture and stage setting. His use of the monologue as the primary Schrei vehicle depended on the concept of Gothic "steepness."

VI.   *DER BETTLER* AND THE PRINCIPLE OF GOTHIC STEEPNESS

Friedrich Michael, in a 1919 essay on Expressionist semantics, identified the adjectival idea of the "steep" [*steil*] as central to a cluster of terms used by contemporary artists to denote the nature of ideal expression. The centrality of this concept of steepness, argued Michael, illustrated the essentially Gothic spirit of the new expressive art, in which "the instinctive emotive insight [*Gefühl*], the will of the poet, soars steeply upward like Gothic buildings."[79] Likewise, Wolfgang Paulsen characterized Expressionist sensibility as that of an "unmediated yearning," in the dramatic expression of which

again and again the word "Sehnsucht" is directly articulated, paraphrased and embodied. "Yearning forces onward," Reinhard Sorge has his Bettler say . . . That is, the way which is here traversed is the way upward . . . For the man of ardor [*Pathos*] is the extended [*gestreckte*] man. This ardor of speech and gesture remains pure and unencumbered. It is instinctive emotive insight; it is not earthbound, does not exhaust itself in thought, but pursues itself with ever new power into the heights. This man therefore is extended, as only the Gothic can be extended.[80]

Viviani goes so far as to claim that "this immense, heaven-striving, 'steep' gesture is the axis about which the whole of Expressionist dramatic art turns" (118). It is most often indicated in Expressionist scripts, she notes, by the stage direction adjectives "ecstatic" or "visionary" or "great." The Expressionist "great gesture," she argues,

claims to commune with the cosmos, with heaven and hell. It attempts to lay hold of the total stage space, to structure it, to agitate it, to stretch it, to make it burst forth. It functions by giving form to the ecstatic Expressionist word; it acts as a mediator between space and word. The Expressionist flow of gesture moves in hectic transition from stiffness to explosion, from explosion to stiffness. (117)

Whether or not the ecstatic "great gesture" is realized according to this description in most Expressionist scripts as Viviani claims, it certainly explodes upward into Gothic steepness in *Der Bettler*. Unlike *Der Sohn* and *Die Verführung*, where stage directions are chiefly realistic or non-existent, Sorge's script carefully specifies an essentially vertical grammar of expression. Most prominently, the playwright calls for the use of spotlighting from high, steep angles. Consider, for example, this stage direction:

The curtain separates again. Now the right half of the stage is dark and deserted. From somewhere high at the left, a floodlight falls slantwise across the left half of the stage, illuminating the prostitutes . . . Their voices emphasize the shrill and bare impression made by the floodlight.[81]

Or this:

They rush toward the girls. Noise, screeching, pushing, embraces, shrill laughter. Wild commotion of the group swaying back and forth in the white beam of the floodlight. (36)

In effect, what Sorge's lighting direction does in these crowd scenes is collapse space into a vertical shaft, abstracting the group movements into a unified choral gesture. The back and forth swaying movement creates a tension based on the clash of horizontal and vertical lines. The group images of unenlightened humanity work horizontally against the heaven-reaching possibility of the vertical light shaft, expressing obliviousness to that human potential.

Elsewhere in the lengthy coffee-house scene which comprises Act I, however, Sorge directs that when the light from an "invisible" source darkens on The Girl sitting in the alcove, "the rest of the proscenium turns bright . . . [with] The Poet, beginning to speak almost simultaneously with the brightening of the proscenium" (37–38). In the course of this scene with The Patron the dialogue is suddenly interrupted by "The Poet, abruptly bursting forth" into a long rhapsodic monologue (40). At the end of the speech "the light upstage [i.e. on The Poet] goes out immediately after The Poet's last word" (42). The light then dimly identifies another area of the stage for the choral scene of the Five Fliers. What Sorge is doing with this light play is helping the actors to structure their playing space expressively. Whereas the light on the group of prostitutes is a horizontal slice of human obliviousness, on the Poet it becomes the stairway to heaven itself. It almost seems to pull him from his seated conversational position to an upright, arm-raised posture. Although Sorge does not here specify this, the following excerpt suggests such direction:

My work! My work! My work alone was master!
How best to say it. . . I want to show you images
Of coming things which have in me arisen
In all splendor, visions that led me on
To where I am today, and neither love nor lust
Has hitherto been able to displace them
Or even for one instant make them dim! . . .
Just listen now: this will become the heart of all art: from all the
    continents,
To this source of health, people will stream
To be restored and saved, not just a tiny esoteric
Group! . . . Masses of workmen will be swept
By intimations of a higher life
In mighty waves . . . To lofty birth let a highborn but in many ways
    corrupted age
Advance toward me!   (41–42)

Further on in the script Sorge does specify the vertical gesture repeatedly, and not just for the Poet. Consider the following sample of stage directions: "Fourth Flier, with gesture. 'His longing lifts high our hands.'" (44); "The Father, growing in stature as he revels in his vision" (56); "the Father tries to raise himself again; twitches with the effort" (63); "the Youth [Poet] raises himself gazing" (66); "The

Youth . . . He stirs on his seat, rises, bends over backward, staring up toward the sky . . . Raising his head and trunk high, erect . . . The Girl tenses her body and gazes steadily up at the Youth . . . The Youth, uttering the first verses bent down over the Girl, the last ones erect, gazing to the sky" (71–72); "The Father . . . He works himself up gradually into an ever-intensifying state of rapture" (85). Invariably, the vertical gesture occurs either in the vertical shaft of light; or in the context of its linguistic equivalent, the ecstatic monologue; or both. Both spotlight and ecstatic monologue have the same Gothic steepness which defines the characteristic Schrei form of *Der Bettler*. As distinct from the outward direction of *Die Verführung*'s operatic Schrei, and the centripetal thrust of Schrei dialogue in the Mannheim *Der Sohn*, the basic spatial orientation of this Schrei model is upward.

Yet that upward consciousness in Sorge's characters is not essentially one of humility but one of aspiration. If there is any "Ur-theme" in the Expressionist scripts we are considering in this chapter it is the idea of the complete expression of one's will or desire, for its own sake. This Ur-theme underlies the Father's insistence on his authority, the Son's rebellious defiance, and the Friend's persistent vitalist provocation of the Son in *Der Sohn*. It flows beneath Bitterlich's caustic elitism, his mother's obsessive protectiveness of him, Ruth's vicarious vitalism, and Wilhelm's determination to avenge what he considers to be his sister's disgrace at the hands of Bitterlich in *Die Verführung*. It drives both the Poet's messianic visions and his Father's insane technological fantasies in *Der Bettler*. When, in *Die Verführung*, Ruth is questioned by the prison director about why she insists on visiting Bitterlich in his cell, she replies:

RUTH I simply must!!
DIRECTOR That's certainly no reason!
RUTH What! – That's not a reason? That's the strongest reason! In the whole world I couldn't find a better one than that I must! I simply must! (49)

Ruth articulates the motivation of all the characters mentioned above. All are facets of a Nietzschean personalization of what Schopenhauer called the "Will," which fundamentally exists to express itself, to insist that its desires be effected without mediation or negotiation. The distinction between this principle and the Freudian Id is seen in its character of conscious, language-mediated, rational self-assertion. Where the Id subsides in pre-linguistic, symbolic expressions of desire at the level of animal instinct, Expressionist self-actualization strives from within the historically determined structures of culture, grappling with their ideological, ethical, and aesthetic limitations. Unlike Dada, which simply denied institutional cultural structures, theatrical Expressionism powerfully seized upon and reworked the spatial and temporal limits of Wilhelmine stage Naturalism. Just as Gothic architecture demonstrates the enormity of that spiritual power which effortlessly hurtles the materiality of the earth aloft into graceful spires of praise to itself, so the Expressionist assertion of the human will sought no less than to reshape the materials of cultural representation in the image of its desire.

It is the homogeneous attempt to experience and demonstrate this expressive power which distinguishes the Schrei group performance from the subtly differentiated ensemble playing of psychological realism. The primitive gestures developed by Expressionist actors illustrate their efforts both to summon up and to submit to the energy of untrammeled human will. These performers realized that the body can kinetically discover the Ur-forms of human desire, an insight which Michael Chekhov later corroborated in his work with the "Psychological Gesture." In early Expressionist productions the Schrei was the most common expressive vehicle of those Ur-forms. Again, "Schrei" is to be understood here not simply as the scream outburst, but as a culminating moment of ecstatic speech and movement whose expression signals the occurrence of decisive historical insight. In the pioneering Expressionist scripts considered thus far that breakthrough in cultural consciousness focused on the principal institutions of Wilhelmine authoritarianism, the educational system and the family. The Schrei thus became an assertion of historical empowerment: a revolutionary gesture of insight expressed in defiance of traditional Wilhelmine academic and domestic power structures. Hence, in *Der Sohn* the Schrei is largely centered in the Son's escape to freedom over his father's corpse – Schrei as the release of pent-up domestic rage. In *Die Verführung* it is the cry of Nietzschean vitalism – Schrei as Dionysian aria, as pure self-expression in the face of the so-called "slave morality" of familial duty and Christian piety. In *Der Bettler* it is the ecstatic augmentation of a developed poetic vision – Schrei as rhapsodic, intellectual hymn transcending philistine attitudes and habits of thought.

In this third Schrei mode, the actor must possess not only emotional intensity but mature verse-craft as well. Emil Faktor found Ernst Deutsch lacking in this quality as the "young poet figure." Though he had successfully played similar "restless spirits [*Rumorgeister*]" in scripts by Hasenclever and Wildgans (*Liebe*, 1916),

for the more demanding lyricism of Sorge his vocal art seemed to me not yet sufficiently developed. His voice, lacking richness of modulation, gasped with too much difficulty in delivering the verse. Also, he acted, for the most part, purely with the head. This was noticeable when he turned away from the audience and his voice then seemed to come from somewhere else.[82]

For Fritz Engel, Sorge was a "neo-Romantic" whose "mixing" of prose and verse revealed the "cathedral tendency characteristic of Romanticism generally." The challenge for the actor was to master "prose which, written for higher sensibilities who crave the musical, begins to surpass the music of the organ itself."[83]

The première of *Der Bettler* was the first in a series of Expressionist productions offered by Das junge Deutschland from 1917 to 1920 at Max Reinhardt's Deutsches Theater. However, John Styan's remark that "the generally adopted style of acting for Expressionist drama was also established in these productions of Das junge Deutschland" must be understood to mean that Expressionist acting methods were not developed but rather popularized here.[84] I have already noted the work of Ernst Deutsch at Dresden and of Richard Weichert at Mannheim. Along with the powerful influence of Wedekind over a whole generation of young actors – most notably Kortner and Krauss – the insights of Deutsch and Weichert had already broken much fertile ground in the development of Schrei ecstatic acting. The chief contributions of Das junge Deutschland in the history of Expressionist performance were twofold. First, it developed the large audience for the new drama that the smaller provincial theatres, which had spawned Expressionism's Schrei production style, had been unable to command. Secondly, it created a huge community of artists, critics, theoreticians, and publishers around the new drama.[85] In this way Das junge Deutschland did much to establish Expressionism as a bona fide movement in the theatre by promoting the work of its young, mostly unknown artists.

Though he never became actively involved in Das junge Deutschland, Reinhardt did agree to direct *Der Bettler*, perhaps because of his general appreciation for experimental theatre. Styan, quoting from Reinhardt's Regiebuch for *Der Bettler,* describes how Ernst Deutsch was directed in the Poet's first monologue, a portion of which we have already noted above. He was to begin "vehemently, but not loudly," with a suggestion of "bitterness," searching for words "out of the depth" of his soul. As the monologue built, Deutsch was to become successively "elated," "more passionate," "filled with emotion," "possessed," "vehement" and ultimately "radiant." "When the Poet's feelings soar," Styan notes, "his voice rises and he lifts his head nobly." At the close of Act I, Reinhardt had Deutsch prepare for the curtain speech as follows: he "rises slowly, stands still, runs a hand through his hair, lifts up his head and speaks quietly but with elation." In the course of the speech he has "straightened himself defiantly"; "looking into the distance" he utters the final words with "assurance," "imposingly." During the rhapsodic monologues in Act I, Reinhardt coordinated the vertical movements of The Girl with those of The Poet: "she rises involuntarily, more and more fascinated, moving up a step and staring at the speaker fixedly." At The Poet's lines: "Let woman excel in allegiance to man! / Let his aim be: graciously to yield to her!,"[86] Reinhardt's marginal note reads, "Girl transfixed."[87]

Reinhardt's production of *Der Bettler* expanded the limits of Expressionist performance in part because of the particularly cinematic quality of the script itself. The spot, falling from numerous overhead angles onto different stage areas, created a magic fluidity of spatial transition and afforded a kind of spatial freedom similar to that produced by shot editing in film production. In effect, the use of sectional lighting created what film editors call "jump cuts" in *Der Bettler*'s flow of action. In specifying the use of the spotlight, Sorge emphasized his play's episodic structure to a degree that Kaiser, for example, did not in his equally episodic *Von morgens bis mitternachts*. Because of its marked discontinuity of action, *Der Bettler* presented the actors with a performance problem similar to that posed by cinematic acting: namely, sustaining the necessary performance intensity across the structural interruptions of episodic staging. The continuity of scripts such as *Der Sohn*, by contrast, assisted the actor in this regard. Under actual cinematic conditions, however, the degree of structural disruption that Schrei ensemble performance could tolerate was first tested in Robert Wiene's film *The Cabinet of Dr. Caligari* (1919).

VII. "CALIGARISM"

The filming of *Caligari* is stagey, the camera for the most part shooting the actors full front in tableau groupings. The principal ensemble players listen intently to whichever of them is speaking, while often staring, trance-like, outward somewhere beyond the camera. Here Felix Emmel's dictum that an ecstatic actor "must speak with the body . . . even if he is only listening" is fulfilled.[88] The actors "listen" with their whole bodies bound up in a dynamic tension, a performance task no doubt complicated by the disruptions to temporal and spatial continuity in the shooting process. Not only did they have to sustain their performances through repeated takes of the same shot, they also had to conform their acting to the particular visual features of the settings. As a result, the Schrei ecstatic acting of the film developed what some critics have called a "painterly" dimension. Artists such as Kokoschka, in his posters for *Mörder, Hoffnung der Frauen*, and Munch, in his lithograph *Der Schrei*, had long since foreseen the Schrei in graphic terms. But in *Caligari* the notion that painting was an element of performance had developed into its reverse, for performance had virtually become an element of painting. Frank Witford has aptly described the relationship between the film's actors and its set:

The brickwork, flagstones, windows, even the shadows cast by the buildings, actors and furniture have been painted onto the sets with more concern for their vitality as forms as such than for any approximation to reality. It is as though the actors are walking around in an enormous Expressionist painting . . . The girl's bedroom is decorated with soft, yielding patterns, and her acting style is comparatively graceful and rhythmic. This is in marked contrast to the cramped and crazily-angled police office, where two officials are perched on impossibly high chairs, and to the claustrophobic prison cell where the man, wrongly imprisoned for the murder, sits trapped in the centre of a large, sharp, claw-like cluster of black shadows. The composition of each scene in terms of lights, darks and patterns on the set mirrors the tone and predominant feeling of each stage of the action . . . Even the make-up is exaggerated; the expressions of Caligari himself and of the somnambulist were applied line for line and shadow for shadow as though they are painted caricatures.[89]

Such performance conditions produced, literally, "moving-picture" acting. That is, actors became kinetic pictorial elements; they were part of a continuously moving Expressionist painting. In her well-known study of early German cinema, *The Haunted Screen*,

Lotte Eisner argues that setting stylization in *Caligari* in fact *dictates* acting stylization. Of the performances of Werner Krauss, as Caligari, and Conrad Veidt, as the somnambulist killer, she observes that

> through a reduction of gesture they attain movements which are almost linear and which – despite a few curves that slip in – remain brusque, like the broken angles of the sets; and these movements from point to point never go beyond the limits of a given geometric plane. (25)

By incorporating the actors as pictorial elements the setting engulfs their performances in its design of distorted shapes and jagged lines. If Mel Gordon's claim that "the *Schrei* directors and actors freely borrowed from the contemporary middle-European . . . painters" is accurate,[90] *Caligari* illustrates the danger of such derivation when it becomes immoderate. For here the Schrei has become so entangled in its graphic reflections in the set designs that it loses something of its human-centered emotional power, in spite of the intensity of the performance ensemble.

Though the Expressionist theatre is remembered for its conscious theatricality, Schrei acting steadfastly shunned artificial emotionalism. Indeed, the intensity of feeling required in the scripts mandated no less than a complete physical and vocal commitment by the actor if the performance was to escape the ridiculously bathetic. Without such a level of credible personal risk on stage, Schrei Expressionism could not hope to compel the commensurate level of audience involvement that was its goal. This was a level of experience which the producers of *Caligari* apparently feared. Presumably attributing as great an emotional impact to the celluloid image on the screen as to the live theatrical situation, they worried about averse box-office reaction to the insane spirit and style of the main narrative. For this reason they added a harness of psychological realism around the ecstatic acting of the principal characters – Francis, the protagonist; his friend, Alan; Caligari; and the Somnambulist. Using the convention of the flashback, they reduced Francis's narrative to the paranoid ravings of a madman by framing his story of the mad Caligari with an introduction which he delivers to a fellow patient as they sit in the realistic garden setting of an insane asylum. In the film's final shot, the director of the asylum looks into the camera as he puts on his glasses and immediately bears a haunting resemblance to the mad Caligari in Francis's allegedly true story. It is such psychological ambiguities which have occasioned the

charge that because *Caligari*'s narrative is thus parenthetically qualified it is not truly an Expressionist film.

I would agree with this criticism but even more so because
Caligari's conscious artificiality reduces Schrei acting to mere stylization. The problem is obviously compounded because the acting is
directed at a camera rather than a live audience. What is lost for the
actors performing under such conditions is the powerful presence of
a living human being on stage pushed to his or her expressive limits.
In *Caligari*, actor physicalization reveals the same characteristic
reduction and abruptness as performances in earlier Schrei stage
productions. But those characteristics no longer materialize the
presence of a "great gesture" which comes from within an actor
performing in a spare, symbolic stage setting. Rather, they are the
function of a graphic design externally imposed on the actor. The
chief performance value of those spare settings in Weichert's *Der
Sohn*, Hartung's *Die Verführung*, and Reinhardt's *Der Bettler* was that
they forced the actors to concentrate on the poetic language of the
scripts. The extremities of diction and image in the text, then – more
than the graphic exaggerations of the designs – became the impetus
to that totality of physical and vocal gesture by which Expressionist
directors and actors sought to overwhelm their audiences.

The purpose of all this, of course, was to create a theatre of
historical consequence, a theatre that mattered. Here we return to
the fact, noted at the outset of this chapter, that revolutionary plays
written in 1912 and 1913 were not produced until 1916, at the earliest.
The pre-war genesis of all these scripts was a praxis of *literary*
revolution; in the theatre itself, at this time, Naturalism still held
sway. It was only as the war plodded toward its chaotic end for
Germany that Expressionist dramatic art became a *theatrical* revolution. Perhaps the explanation is to be found in the uniquely public
nature of the stage. The state of German culture by 1916 was no
longer simply an individual problem for alienated young artists and
intellectuals; rather, it was a rapidly developing catastrophe for
German society at large. It would seem that by 1916 history had left
the Wilhelmine theatre public no choice but to consider alternatives
to the reassuring positivism of the Naturalist stage. Life simply did
not make that much sense anymore. The drastic accents and urgent
tone of Schrei Expressionist staging resonated historically even as, in
many cases, they offended aesthetically.

This early phase of Expressionist performance represents a good-faith, if at times crude, attempt to redeem German culture and to forge a new historical identity. Its mode of theatrical praxis – what I have been calling Schrei performance – was inscribed upon the actor in powerful distentions of body and voice. In this way, both the oppressive effect on humanity of the contemporary German cultural situation and an expressive response of appropriate dimension were demonstrated. The force of history acting upon the actor's body was met purportedly with an equal or greater force of emotion from within that body. Thus, in ecstatic "great gestures" of voice and body – across a wide range of emphatic, often frenetic, rhythmic and tonal patterns – the Schrei actor became the incarnation, the site of the revolutionary struggle for which the play was written. The actor, in short, was the object demonstration of the play's themes, the walking text of its conflicting cultural forces.

What "Caligarism" signals, however, is a development away from the whole-hearted aesthetic and social commitment of these early Schrei productions toward a newly fashionable and opportunist abstractionism. Yet for some Expressionist theatre artists abstractionist performance strategies were not at all a symptom of compromise but rather an alternate path to stylistic integrity. This was the case with Lothar Schreyer and his Kampfbühne ensemble, whose actors sought to enact symbolic events in a theatre where ecstasy was a matter of spiritual evocation rather than emotional eruption, and contemporary German history was met with archetypal myths and images.

CHAPTER 4

An "Expressionist Solution to the Problem of Theatre": Geist Abstraction in Performance

I. SPIRITUAL THEATRICALITY: THE DISTINCTIVENESS OF GEIST EXPRESSIONISM

Even as the Schrei productions I have just discussed were being mounted, another kind of "Expressionist" performance was developing under the auspices of Herwarth Walden's *Sturm* circle in Berlin. Directed by Lothar Schreyer, the "Sturm-Bühne" ensemble – later renamed the "Kampfbühne" – created its *Bühnenkunstwerke* ["stage works of art"] based on plays such as those of August Stramm. These abstractionist scripts experimented radically with language and deliberately avoided the use of conventional characterization and narrative plot structure. However, the most comprehensive source of information about how they were produced by the Sturm-Bühne/Kampfbühne ensemble is Schreyer's own elaborate polemical account published in 1948 under the title *Expressionistisches Theater.*[1] Despite the subjectivity of this memoir, written at three decades' distance from the fact, the theoretical principles Schreyer sets forth therein as the basis of his work with Sturm-Bühne/Kampfbühne actors are worth examining. One reason is that they bear close relationship to the writings of Vassily Kandinsky, of all the artists associated with the *Sturm* circle the most significant early theorist of Expressionist abstractionism.

Whether Schreyer was successful in realizing the performance principles he derived from Kandinsky's theoretical work is questionable. The one disinterested account of a Sturm-Bühne production that I have been able to find, Herbert Ihering's review of a mounting of Stramm's *Sancta Susanna*, is highly critical both of the performance and of Schreyer's theoretical remarks preceding the performance. Ihering's report of Schreyer's introductory comments, however, establishes the fact that the theoretical principles described by

139

Schreyer in contemporaneous *Der Sturm* essays and later writings were attempted to be practiced, at least on this occasion. This is the second reason for examining Schreyer's theoretical writings on performance. My assumption is that what Schreyer had to say to the *Sancta Susanna* audience about "Expressionist" performance is consistent with his direction of the actors in rehearsal. Given the coterie nature of Schreyer's ensemble, it seems likely that the concepts of rehearsal and performance he describes generally in his later writings were those to which his actors actually subscribed. Indeed, Schreyer acknowledges, those actors who could not accept his performance principles did not long remain a part of the ensemble. In general, those principles define a spiritualized type of Expressionist acting in which the elements of performance were synthesized in the art of "sound-speaking."

Schreyer's Bühnenkunstwerk performances, he maintains, stressed not the power of individual feeling but the purity of communal spirituality, a condition dependent upon what Kandinsky called "spiritual harmony." Here the impetus to theatrical performance was not the explosive expansion of individual personality as in Schrei performance, but its dissolution and subsumption into a collective "Geist." This term resists a narrow English rendering because its rich semantic range includes the ideas of: mind, intellect, wit, imagination, genius, soul, morale, essence, spirit and apparition. The Expressionist use of the word "Geist" requires that we keep most of its connotations in mind all the time. As its sense of the apparitional suggests, Geist performance was concerned with rendering a kind of disembodied human consciousness. The type of "action" in which the actor engaged had little or no mimetic purpose. In Geist performance both the actor's human body and his emotional resources were stripped of their individual identity in order to become elements in an evocative theatrical environment. The objective was to unite actors and audience in purely spiritual communion. In the context of this goal, Schreyer claimed that the work of his ensemble was the only true theatrical Expressionism.[2]

The "New Man" of Schrei Expressionism, such as Hasenclever's Son or the Poet in *Der Bettler*, was a uniquely gifted leader whose mission was artistically to inspire other men to heightened consciousness. For Geist Expressionists, on the other hand, every man – to different degrees, albeit – had the capacity for artistically creative work.[3] In 1912, Kandinsky, in his *Blaue Reiter* essay "On Stage

Composition," stated what was to become the Geist view of the relationship between artist and audience this way:

There is no man who does not respond to art. Each work and each method of work causes in every man without exception a vibration fundamentally identical to that felt by the artist.[4]

Of all the modes of Expressionist performance, Geist acting was the most inclusive of the audience. Indeed, its entire concept of theatre is based on the idea of "expression" as a communion, a sharing between actors and audience. At the same time, it deliberately cultivated a customized audience. Like many Schrei productions, Geist performances were "private." However the members of a Geist audience were "invited" not as a ploy for avoiding censorship but because of their willingness to be open to an experience of the performance on its own terms. Moreover, members of the press were welcome at Schreyer's productions, he says, but only on condition that they not review them (*Expressionistisches Theater*, 201).[5]

Geist performance was mystical, its process meditative. Its rebellion against Wilhelmine culture was more of a formal than a thematic matter. Here the Kantean and Schillerian elements of the philosophical tradition I traced in the first chapter of this study are relevant. In Kant's doctrine of the "aesthetic idea" we saw that intuition replaced reason as the cognitive mode. Equally important were Schiller's concept of artistic totality as an "organism" and his dictum that "form does away with the content." These principles had been evident in the work of Poe, Maeterlinck and the French Symbolists. Their tradition and legacy clearly carry through in the symbolic strategies used by abstractionist theatrical Expressionists in their renunciation of the aesthetics of mimesis.[6] The basic aesthetic goal in Geist productions was to present a *unified* work in which all performance elements were truly fused, not merely juxtaposed. In this regard, Schreyer acknowledged Kandinsky's critique of the Wagnerian "Gesamtkunstwerk."

Wagner attempted to connect organically the various elements of performance – music, movement, speech, costume, scenic design – by causing them to reinforce one another representationally. He would musically illustrate the hissing of glowing iron in water, for example, or highlight a character's entrances with leitmotifs. But this was merely an "external," additive method of "mechanical reproductions," argued Kandinsky, not a truly organic "universal" art.

Such illustrative use of the arts obscured their "inner sense, the purely artistic inner meaning . . ." ("Stage Composition," 195–96). Geist theatrical Expressionism was the result of the application of this concept of "purely artistic inner meaning" to dramatic performance. It located the tension upon which drama depends in the rhythmic interaction of elements in a non-representational aesthetic design rather than in the conflicting psychological objectives of a narrative plot. Dramatic tension was not confrontational but "harmonic"; for this reason, acting was conceived primarily in terms of musical sound.

Such an esoteric conception of performance rendered the "communal" idea of Geist theatre problematic; and Schreyer was well aware of the danger of being misunderstood, as his forbiddance of critical reviews at the Kampfbühne demonstrates. In contrast to the confessional and demonstrative nature of Schrei acting, Geist Expressionism's self-consciously spiritual theatre of pure abstraction was produced in determined retreat from publicity, politics, and commercial exploitation. Schreyer says that by the end of the war he had come to feel that the integrity of Expressionism in the theatre had become corrupted. He associated this deterioration with the social chaos following upon the revolution as much as commercial enterprise. For these reasons, he claims, he and his pupils left Berlin in 1919 in order to continue their performance work in the more peaceful setting of his home in Hamburg (*Expressionistisches Theater*, 198).[7] A more pressing motive for Schreyer's departure, however, may have been that Walden had run out of funds for the support of the Sturm-Bühne by 1919.[8] Given the harsh critical reception of the Sturm-Bühne *Sancta Susanna*, it is also likely that Schreyer wanted to avoid further embarrassments at the hands of Berlin theatre critics.[9]

So it was that the essential social posture of the Sturm-Bühne/ Kampfbühne's version of theatrical Expressionism was one of withdrawal, a position decidedly the opposite of activist Expressionists like Toller, who sat out the entire movement in a Bavarian jail as a result of his involvement in the short-lived Bavarian Socialist Republic. To be sure, by the mid-twenties, Walden would also make a radical conversion to Socialism. But throughout the preceding decade his dogmatically formalist conception of "true" Expressionism occupied all of his attention and all of the resources of *Der Sturm*. As the leading journalistic champion of the "new" art, he functioned as an aesthetic rather than a political agitator. Indeed,

Walden's concern over aesthetic debates led to an astonishing lack of acknowledgment of current events in *Der Sturm* during the war years.[10] For him, as for Schreyer and other close associates such as the actor and elocution teacher Rudolf Blümner, "true Expressionism" revealed the proper arena of cultural struggle to be aesthetic not political.[11] Such a position was all the more congenial to Schreyer because of his life-long inclination toward a mystical sense of the relationship between art and society.[12] Together, these abstract formalist and mystical agendas produced an a-political, intellectually elitist Expressionism on the stage whose idea of cultural revolution ultimately amounted merely to a process of coterie initiation.

It is probably because of its deliberately isolationist profile that Geist performance has received little attention from theatre historians.[13] Yet an account of Expressionist performance is incomplete if the Kampfbühne's own particular version of theatrical Expressionism is neglected. This is because the Sturm-Bühne/Kampfbühne represents the only systematic attempt to apply to the stage an abstractionist aesthetic embraced by a large community of Expressionist artists – painters, sculptors, musicians, poets – whose formative work was initially fostered by the *Sturm* Association. Artists such as Kokoschka, Chagall, and Kandinsky – whose work would become internationally definitive aspects of Modernism – were first promoted by means of Walden's abstractionist polemics. Though Schreyer was the chief proponent of Geist Expressionist performance, however, Kandinsky was its theoretical progenitor. Its seminal idea of a "unified" art is as dependent on his concept of "spiritual harmony" as its expressive theory is on his principle of "inner necessity." Accordingly, I begin with a look at Kandinsky's essays on dramatic art and his "stage composition," *The Yellow Sound.*

II. KANDINSKY: "INNER NECESSITY" AND THE CONCEPT OF SPIRITUAL HARMONY

In his influential treatise, *Concerning the Spiritual in Art* (1912), Kandinsky was one of the first Expressionist artists to discuss the spiritual impact of the nineteenth-century revolution in science and philosophy:

When religion, science and morality are shaken (the last by the strong hand of Nietzsche) and when outer supports threaten to fall, man withdraws his gaze from externals and turns it inwards. Literature, music and art are the

most sensitive spheres in which this spiritual revolution makes itself felt . . .
they turn away from the soulless life of the present toward those substances
and ideas that give free scope to the non-material strivings of the soul.[14]

This withdrawal Kandinsky viewed positively, not negatively. He
argued that to recognize the insubstantiality of empirical reality was
an act of courage, and he praised those "men of learning who test
matter again and again, who tremble before no problem, and who
finally cast doubt on that very matter which was yesterday the
foundation of everything . . ." (31–32).

For Kandinsky, the art of Maeterlinck was prophetic of this
courageous turning away from the material to the spiritual. From
Maeterlinck's work he deduced in dramatic art the principle of the
"inner sound" and its "corresponding vibration":

Maeterlinck's principal technical weapon is words. The word is an inner
sound. It springs partly, perhaps principally, from the object denoted. But if
the object is not seen, but only its name heard, the mind of the hearer
receives an abstract impression only of the object dematerialized, and a
corresponding vibration is immediately set up in the "heart."

The chief technique he identified in Maeterlinck's process was simple
word repetition, which "deprives the word of its external reference
. . . and only the sound is retained." The result is a "pure sound"
which, even if only unconsciously perceived, "exercises a direct
impression on the soul" (34). This technique became part of a
general abstractionist strategy of reduction which was later most
developed in the "Telegrammstil" dramatic works of Schreyer and
August Stramm.

We have previously noted a tendency in Schrei acting towards
reduction of movement for the purpose of intensifying its explosive
power. In Geist performance reduction was frequently carried to the
radical extreme of stripping away all "external" reference – that is,
narrative significance – from speech as well as movement. While the
purpose of Schrei reduction was more forceful expression, the
function of Geist reduction was the opposite: greater receptive
sensitivity to "the spirit, the inner sound, in all things."[15] Indeed,
"the inner sound increases in intensity," argued Kandinsky, "if we
remove its stifling, external, practical meaning" (174). This concept
of "sound" was not primarily physical, although physical sounds –
along with objects, colors, light, and movement – had, for Kandinsky, an "inner" sound. The kind of "sound" of which he speaks
was not perceived as waves striking the eardrum but as vibrations

striking the soul. The rhetorical advantage of this discourse of the spiritual is that it allows Kandinsky to define individual subjective intuition as the universal principle of social formation. For, though "each art has its own language . . . its own methods," nonetheless,

> *in their innermost core* these methods are wholly identical: their final goal obliterates external differences and reveals their inner identity. The *final* goal (knowledge) is reached through delicate vibrations of the human soul. These delicate vibrations are ultimately identical . . . When the artist finds the appropriate means, it is a material form of his soul's vibration, which he is forced to express. If the method is appropriate, it causes an almost identical vibration in the soul of the audience.[16]

Implicit in this statement are the two key principles of Geist theatrical Expressionism: the possibility of harmonic spiritual relationship between actor and audience; and the law of "inner necessity."

These two principles reflect Kandinsky's preoccupation with the mystical doctrines of theosophy. In this regard, the writings of Rudolf Steiner, as much as the poetic art of Maeterlinck, influenced his ideas of spiritual harmony and inner necessity. Kandinsky was particularly inspired by Steiner's theosophical reading of Goethe's aesthetic philosophy. In the words of the art historian Sixten Ringbom:

> Goethe's dictum that works of art, like works of nature, are produced according to the divine necessity of true and natural laws is by Steiner regarded as an epoch-making discovery . . . Steiner lays great emphasis on Goethe's assertion that "the Beautiful is a manifestation of secret laws of nature which otherwise would have remained hidden forever" . . . By conforming to the "necessity" and "secret laws" governing nature, art is capable of surpassing nature in essential truth . . . Steiner concludes his essay on Goethe's aesthetics with an appeal for a new theory based on this principle . . . Steiner's appeal can be said to have been answered by the theory proposed in *Über das Geistige in der Kunst*.[17]

Ringbom speculates that Kandinsky first encountered the work of Steiner in the course of his own research on Goethe's color theory and aesthetics. In any case, it is well documented that Kandinsky attended many of Steiner's over 2,000 theosophy lectures throughout the period 1902–13. "During the early 'twenties," adds Ringbom, "Kandinsky still referred to the theosophical impressions which he had received during the first decade of the twentieth century" (394). On the basis of its doctrine that art, religion and science are interdependently developing toward the unifying goal of spiritual "Knowledge," theosophy gave Kandinsky a conception of art as mankind's primary means of spiritual insight and progress.

Kandinsky, however, did not consider himself a theosophist. Rather, he saw an analogy between the theosophical process of mystical gnosis and the revelation of spiritual laws through art. Both kinds of spiritual cognition depended upon a kind of perceptual sensitivity which, as Steiner put it, "penetrates through the surface of things, reaching their secrets."[18] As we have noted, Kandinsky characterized this faculty as a susceptibility to "finer vibrations." According to Ringbom, the idea of "vibration" is the key concept in theosophy's mystical approach to color and form (399). One of the ways in which Kandinsky appropriated this principle was in his theory of the pure "sound" [*Klang*] of words which directly affects the soul by inducing it into a state of "objectless vibration" [*gegenstandlose Vibration*].[19] Since all artistic media – music, color and form, as well as words – generate such objectless vibrations, he argued, the essential method of the various arts is identical, and synaesthetic perception is possible. Furthermore, the experience of art is inevitably communal because the spiritual vibration from an artistic stimulus is identical for artist and audience. For this reason such vibrations are not at all subjective but rather objective in nature. But because few individuals are sensitized to such a fine level of perception, Kandinsky argued, the social goal of art is to lead them to this cognitive ability. Mankind, he believed, was entering the "Epoch of the Great Spiritual," and therefore the time had come to make esoteric knowledge perceptible to everyone.

For Kandinsky, the communal nature of artistic experience was not something directly experienced in the five physical senses as a composite material image, like Wagner's "Gesamtkunstwerk." Rather, even though distinct arts be functioning in external isolation from one another in a stage composition, their several "inner sounds" were nonetheless internally unified in harmonic fusion. Selected movements, spoken tones, color or light forms would be isolated and explored in terms of various rhythmic patterns. Even if these elements were in dissonant relationship superficially, their resonating inner sounds would, as Peter Jelavich puts it, "awaken . . . the mystic sensation of the essential unity of all worldly opposites."[20] In fact, argued Kandinsky, harmony today rests chiefly on the principle of contrast, which has for all time been one of the most important principles of art . . . The strife of colors, the sense of balance we have lost . . . antitheses and contradictions – these make up our harmony.[21]

Such dissonant "harmony," he maintained, was necessary to penetrate deeply to the spiritual level of the audience. In its synthesis of dissonant elements this kind of harmony required what Kandinsky termed a "constructional" technique, which was not an arbitrary procedure but a method of "reasoned and conscious composition" (77).

Indeed, the choice of form, color, and object rested "ultimately on purposive playing upon the human soul"; and Kandinsky likened the achievement of spiritual harmony in these choices to playing the piano. "Color," for example,

is the keyboard, the eyes are the hammers, the soul is the piano with many strings. The artist is the hand that plays, touching one key or another purposively, to cause vibrations in the soul (45).

Note that color is treated *objectively* here, its selection and resultant "sound" being as precise and predictable as striking a middle "C" on the piano. The same procedure obtains in the choice of form and in the choice of the object which is defined by the chosen colors and forms. The effect of an artistic composition is a function of these three elements: "the action of the color of the object, of its form, and of the object *per se*, independent of either color or form" (50). This was the kind of action which occurred in theatrical performance, as Kandinsky defined it. Stage composition, in fact, was "the first form" of an art of spiritual harmony. It consisted of the elements of "musical movement," "pictorial movement" and "dance movement."

For Kandinsky, and for the Geist Expressionists whom he influenced, the idea of "movement" was as critical and unique as that of "sound." The verb they used in connection with their concept of movement was *bewegen*, which is a word for the kind of "movement" which directly *influences* people. This term can refer both to *affective* influence which agitates one to a particular state of feeling, and to *inductive* influence which draws one into that state. In Geist performance all elements of stage composition – sound, light, visual image in the decoration and costuming, and human presence – were to be infused with this sense of a movement that both stirs and induces.

Such movement, says Kandinsky, "affects us . . . as pure harmony, when its actual purpose is not revealed." Unmotivated movement, he explains, is "dramatically in default of explanation" and therefore fraught with "unlimited possibilities." But where the utilitarian motive in action is evident movement loses its mystery because

the functional meaning of an action negates its abstract meaning. From this premise the "new dance" is being evolved, that is to say, as the only medium in terms of time and space expressing the interior meaning of motion . . . (71–72).

Kandinsky explored the practical implications of his dramatic theory in four "stage compositions" – *The Yellow Sound, The Green Sound, Black and White,* and *Violet* – written between 1909 and 1914. None of these works was ever produced during the Expressionist era. However, the earliest and most influential of them, *The Yellow Sound,* was included in the *Blaue Reiter Almanac* (1912) as an illustration of the application of Kandinsky's aesthetic principles to performance. In addition to the three movement elements – musical sound, "physical-psychical sound," and colored tone,

the word, independent or in sentences, was used to create a certain "atmosphere" that frees the soul and makes it receptive. The sound of the human voice was also used pure, i.e., without being obscured by words, or the meaning of words.[22]

Indeed, *The Yellow Sound* contains no dialogue, and only two occurrences of a scripted utterance. Rather, it is written as a descriptive scenario which is divided into six "pictures." The text is composed of prose descriptions of elaborate lighting, musical, and setting effects and changes, along with specific instructions for actor movement and demeanor. As such, *The Yellow Sound* reads like one long stage direction whose proto-surrealistic flights of fancy were far beyond the technical resources of theatre at the time of its composition. Consider the following excerpt from Picture 2:

At the rear a completely round hill, intensely green and as large as possible. The backdrop is purple, rather bright. The music is shrill, stormy, with A and B and A-flat frequently repeated . . . the backdrop suddenly turns dirty brown. The hill becomes dirty green. And exactly in the center of the hill an undefined black spot forms, which appears to be sometimes distinct, sometimes blurred. At each change the dazzling white light by jerks becomes progressively grayer. On the left side of the hill a *huge* yellow flower suddenly appears. It remotely resembles a large crooked cucumber, and it becomes more and more vivid. (216–17)

Or this from Picture 1:

From right to left five intensely yellow giants (as large as possible) slide forth (as if gliding over the stage) . . . the giants' *very* deep singing without words becomes audible (pianissimo), and the giants approach the footlights *very* slowly. Quickly from left to right fly vague red creatures, *somewhat* suggesting birds, with large heads that are remotely similar to human heads. This flight is reflected by the music. (214)

In *The Yellow Sound*, Kandinsky conceives of actors as agents for shaping the rhythmic patterns and dynamics of the visual and aural events. In Picture 2, for example, a chorus of actors rush on stage wearing flowing, monocolored robes. Standing in a group tightly pressed together, they recite a chant

first together as if in ecstasy (very distinctly). Then they repeat the lines individually, to each other and into the distance – alto, bass, and soprano . . . Occasionally the voices become hoarse. Now and then one screams as if possessed. Here and there the voices become nasal, sometimes speaking slowly, at other times extremely fast. (217)

During this recitation extreme light changes and harsh instrumental notes occur at specified points in the chant. Finally, the orchestra crescendos, overwhelming the voices. Physical movement assumes rhythmic control at the end of the Picture when

the people move slowly to the front of the stage as if in a trance and gradually move farther away from each other. As the music fades, the same recitative is heard (Half a sentence is spoken in unison; at the end of a sentence one voice very indistinct. Changing frequently). Soon they stop as if enraptured and turn around . . . [they] turn away and take a few quick steps to the front of the stage; they stop and turn again, and remain motionless as if chained (these movements have to be executed sharply as if on command). Finally . . . forcibly casting off their immobility, they run to the front of the stage, close to each other. They look back frequently. Suddenly it becomes dark. (218)

The combined sensual effect of all this movement in sound, light, and human form presumably might turn out to be something like an orchestra tuning up before the start of a concert – an oddly euphonious cacophony.

For all of its apparent arbitrariness, however, Kandinsky insisted that the method of *The Yellow Sound* was the furthest thing from capricious. Rather, as we noted earlier, his stage composition was a product of "reasoned and conscious" creation.[23] Among theatrical Expressionists, it was Lothar Schreyer who most devoted himself to fulfilling Kandinsky's confidence in the dawning of an "age of conscious creation . . . *an epoch of great spirituality*,"[24] in which "the drama finally consists of the complex of inner experiences (soul = vibrations) of the audience."[25] Schreyer, in fact, built a whole theory of performance on the expressive process first suggested in *The Yellow Sound*.

III. SCHREYER, THE *STURM* CIRCLE, AND THE KAMPFBÜHNE

When Schreyer joined Herwarth Walden's *Sturm* circle of Expressionist artists, he had for some time already been writing paratactic, "Telegrammstil" plays and poems in the manner of the circle's most accomplished playwright, August Stramm. In late 1914, he became aware of the group and its periodical, *Der Sturm*, and he submitted his play *Die Nacht*, which was immediately accepted and subsequently published in the July 1916 issue. Within a year of Schreyer's addition to the *Sturm* circle, the kind of Expressionist theatre that Walden had been calling for since February 1915 came into being.[26] Walden's vision for drama may well have grown out of his association with Hugo Ball, dating from July 1914. As I noted in Chapter One, Ball was among the first to conceive of an "Expressionistic" theatre. His plan for a September 1914 *Sturm* exhibition – thwarted by the outbreak of war – had provided for a performance which integrated painting, music, dance and poetry. He finally realized this project in his "Galerie Dada" series of *Sturm* exhibitions of 1917, the same year that Schreyer, under Walden's auspices, established the Sturm-Schule for "instruction and training in Expressionist Art."[27] In September 1917 the Sturm-Bühne was established for the experimental practice of Expressionist drama. While it survived for only four years, the Sturm-Schule continued to function until 1932 when it closed along with the parent journal, *Der Sturm*.

The school offered instruction in painting, poetry, music and dramatic performance. In this last department – which was the school's most prominent – Schreyer, along with Rudolf Blümner,[28] was initially responsible for teaching acting and recitation. But the Sturm-Bühne produced only one script in Berlin, Stramm's *Sancta Susanna* (16 October 1918), before Schreyer relocated his ensemble to Hamburg. There he founded the Kampfbühne Association which mounted a total of eight productions from 1919 through 1920 including: Schreyer's *Kindsterben* [*Child Death*], *Mann* [*Man*], and *Kreuzigung* [*Crucifixion*]; Stramm's *Die Heidebraut* [*The Bride of the Moor*] and *Kräfte* [*Forces*]; Walden's *Sünde* [*Transgression*]; Hölderlin's *Der Tod des Empedokles* [*The Death of Empedocles*]; and a sixteenth-century nativity play. The first members of his ensemble at Berlin were his acting students, but later, at Hamburg, this group was augmented with equally ardent performers from the working classes. Most of these amateur actors, he says, were "laborers, primary school teachers, shop-keeper's helpers," and most came out of the "Youth Movement." All worked out of devotion to the Kampfbühne goals of "human growth" and "unity of life," not for personal gain. Each production was performed only three times because it was regarded as only a step toward these goals. As people joined the ensemble, says Schreyer, they quickly realized the radical alternative to traditional stage acting his "new Expressionist stage art" presented them; and some left to pursue traditional, representational performance training.[29]

The fundamental premise of Schreyer's theatrical work was the communal context of performance. For his actors, true Expressionism, as opposed to "pseudo-Expressionism," was not merely a production style, but a way of life (126). As a matter of principle, Schreyer worked only with amateur actors, who would be able to "live in community with the other actors" (179). This was impossible for professional actors, in Schreyer's view, because such performers had learned their craft as a self-serving business (204). Kampfbühne audiences, for their part, also had to be prepared specifically to receive the performance in order for it to be considered "successful." Although Schreyer never goes into much detail about the nature of such preparation, it appears that audience and actors shared in common at least the philosophical portion of Kampfbühne performance training. This "coterie" aspect of the Kampfbühne theatre's work somewhat resembles that of later avant-garde groups such as Jerzy Grotowski's Polish Lab Theatre, Richard Schechner's Performance Group, and Robert Wilson's "Byrd Hoffman School of Byrds."[30]

Having founded the Kampfbühne Association in 1919 with his Sturm-Bühne ensemble, Schreyer gathered about him a group of approximately two-hundred "friends of Expressionism." In the course of the following year, approximately one-hundred more joined them. The basic idea of the Association was "to train a

consistent and receptive circle of listeners for our performances"
(198). Among other things, this specially prepared audience was
required to maintain the integrity of the physical circle in which it
was placed around the actors. Schreyer says that he stopped the
first performance of Stramm's *Kräfte* when a number of the "dis-
satisfied" and "merely curious" broke the circle by leaving prema-
turely. The result, however, was that shortly no one was attending
Kampfbühne productions with inappropriate expectations, and "we
had the joy," Schreyer recalls, "of performing in a circle of true
friends" (201).[31] In this way, the Kampfbühne Association sought to
indemnify Kandinsky's faith that "each work is correctly understood
in the course of time."[32] In Geist Expressionism, the audience was
considered part of the creative community. The actor, argued
Schreyer, did not appear "before" the spectators, nor did he speak
"to" them, but rather he was the "expression – word and effect – of
those who are beholding." For this reason the Kampfbühne playing
space was known as the "circle of the beholding" [*Kreis der
Schauenden*] (181–82).

Schreyer sharply differentiated between *status-quo* theatre production and his own productions, which, as I noted earlier, he called
Bühnenkunstwerke. These were "stage compositions" – detailed
performance scenarios, in the manner of Kandinsky's The Yellow
Sound. They were created by the *Bühnenkünstler* and his ensemble on
the basis of his own or another's poetic dramatic texts, known as
Wortkunstwerke ["word works of art"]. The process of composing the
Bühnenkunstwerke resulted in *Spielgängen* ["performance scenarios"]
or *Partituren* ["full musical scores"]. The Spielgang most resembled a
musical score, with its various parts orchestrated into a unified
whole; but Schreyer clearly distinguished this method of "fixing" a
performance from that of the "Regiebuch," the use of which he
consistently renounced. Apparently, the difference was that the
Spielgang, though equally "fixed," i.e., "set down," was more
concise and symbolic, like a musical score or choreographic nota-
tion. This was to allow the director and actor more creative
freedom of interpretation – of the sort a musical score affords a
conductor and an orchestra – than does the Regiebuch. Schreyer
stressed that the Spielgang should be "written with simplicity" so as
to be "easily readable,"[33] and he regarded it as an indispensable
tool for all concerned: Bühnenkünstler, Spielleiter [director], actors
and designers.

IV. PRINCIPLES OF "SOUND" IN GEIST PERFORMANCE

The most critical issue in Geist performance was formal unity. This, it was thought, could only be realized in terms of non-referential expression, for which music was the paradigm. The principal means of unification, Schreyer argues, is cultivation of "the rhythmic."[34] As applied to the Bühnenkunstwerk, this principle, he explains, has little to do with tempo or metre, but rather refers to a word's "richness of relationship to other words and to all words." This nexus of words, however, has its substance in sound more than semantics. Every word has a particular "sound value" based on its structure of consonants and vowels; in this regard, then, each word is "composed."[35] The spoken sound of a word is comprised of the "tone" [*Klang*] of vowels and "noise" [Geräusch] of consonants; together they determine the unique "word-tone" of every word. Each word, each sentence, has its unique rhythmic properties; the rhythmic succession of words in drama is a rhythmic succession of sounds.[36] For this reason, "every word-based work has its rhythmic law." Rhythm, in fact, is "the logic of art."[37]

To be sure, all this talk of logic and law was Schreyer's way of reifying what is, after all, an extremely subjective matter. Yet it must be taken seriously if one wishes to understand the creative process and rehearsal methods of the Geist actor. This particular type of Expressionist theatre artist was trained to learn, and to study the effects of, the "fundamental forms of movement, sound, color, and form." In this way, art would again be "taught and learned as a craft." Out of these fundamental elements the Bühnenkunstwerk was created by an intuitive process in which the rhythmic shaping power of each element upon the other elements was explored by the Bühnenkünstler, his performance ensemble, and his designers. Herein, according to Schreyer, lay the key to the unity of the Bühnenkunstwerk and its superiority to Wagner's Gesamtkunstwerk. Instead of words and music illustrating one another, and decoration illustrating both, the materials of the Bühnenkunstwerk, he says, actually shape each other.

Admittedly, it is difficult to imagine exactly how this process was actualized in rehearsal. The key, I think, is to be found in the word *bewegen*, which is the term Schreyer uses most frequently, both as a verb and (in past participle form) as an adjective, in his theoretical writings on the Bühnenkunstwerk. As we noted earlier, one meaning of *bewegen* is "to induce." Quite often Schreyer will speak, for example, of the "induced sound-form" [*die bewegte Tongestalt*] or "the induced movement-form" [*die bewegte Bewegungsgestalt*] or "the induced color-form" [*die bewegte Farbformgestalt*]. The process of creating a Bühnen-kunstwerk, apparently, was thoroughly synaesthetic. According to Schreyer,

> the fundamental forms stand in intimate relationship. There is no form without color. There is no color without form. The color induces [*bewegt*] the form. The form induces the color. The movement colors the form. The movement forms the color. The sound induces the color-form. The induced color-form produces sound.[38]

As vague and whimsical as this language seems, I suspect that the very circularity of its almost mantra-like rhetoric was a typical means by which Schreyer drew the Kampfbühne ensemble into his abstract aesthetic principles. At any rate, the rehearsal process itself bore striking resemblance to mantra-based meditation in that the actor's participation in the process began and was based on his work with the "Expressionist Wortkunstwerk."[39]

At the time of Schreyer's submission of his play *Die Nacht* to *Der Sturm*, Walden and his colleagues had already developed the theory and practice of what they called the "Wortkunstwerk". This kind of poetic writing sought to communicate "directly" with the reader by presenting images unfettered by the logical constraints of grammar and syntax. The two primary structural devices it employed were "concentration" and "decentration." "Concentration" was a matter of using a single word instead of several to convey not the poet's thoughts or feelings, but "the intelligence of revelation" [*Kunde einer Offenbarung*], presumably based on the isolated word in itself. The omission of articles and declensional endings intensified this compres-sion of form and content. "Decentration" involved the repetition of words or groups of words and the use of parallelisms, word associa-tions and inversions of word order.[40] Through these devices, Schreyer maintains, isolated words were liberated and enabled to shape each other into a synthetic unity of poetic expression. The work of August Stramm was the *Sturm* circle's paradigm and inspiration for the Wortkunstwerk. Schreyer highly praised Stramm's ability to capture the word in its *Urbedeutung*, its archetypal meaning.[41] He and his ensemble regarded the process of the Wortkunstwerk as an invaluable model in their own efforts to capture the archetypal source of acting:

As in all areas of life, we too sought to attain the origin, the source out of which the art of acting, as a proclamation of spiritual reality, could flow and give to the actor the appropriate human form. (125)

The Wortkunstwerk, in fact, was more than an inspiring model; it was the raw material for the creation of the Bühnenkunstwerk. However, Schreyer believed that his actors needed to undergo a period of personal artistic preparation before effective work with the Wortkunstwerk could begin. Accordingly, he says, the rehearsal process at the Kampfbühne began with finding the "inner" or "fundamental" sound [der Grundton] for each actor. Each individual, Schreyer explains, is by nature

a sound-form [eine Tongestalt], that is to say, he has been created from a creative word, from a divine word, whose echo and harmonic answering word this particular individual is. Each person, so to speak, is a sound-figure, a specific sound in the symphony of creation which must ring out in purity. (153)

The process of finding the fundamental sound

was thoroughly meditative . . . The practice of concentration in which the sound speech was awakened stripped one of one's individual will. In that way one could only perceive the inner voice – one's fundamental sound. (200)

The result was an "internal perception" [inneres Vernehmen] which was at once both an active and a passive event. It was active insofar as it began with a conscious self-detachment from all "external impressions and influences," and ended with the return to consciousness through the execution of a "sound creation" [eine Lautbildung]. It was passive in that the fundamental sound itself was not the one produced at the end of the meditation, but was rather an exclusively internal perception which was "received" (154).

Schreyer is not at all specific on the exact relationship between the fundamental sound and the sound which the actor actually produced. Presumably, the fundamental sound itself remained in the realm of the ineffable, while the "sound creation" which ended the meditative process was either regarded as an echo of the fundamental sound or as merely a physical procedure for facilitating the return to consciousness. In any case, this personal artistic self-exploration was the starting point for "the art of sound-speaking" which was the basis of Geist performance. Having undergone this process, individual "sound-speakers" then learned to create a "rhythmically harmonized" ensemble, known as a "speech-choir."

The fundamental sound, which resonated "out of the soul of man to the soul of man," recalls Kandinsky's theory of "fine vibrations" which resonate between the "soul" of the artist and that of his audience. The fundamental sound was the spiritual glue of the Geist ensemble; the article of artistic faith which fostered the performance unity of the actors. In practical terms, the fundamental sound in Geist performance, like the heightened emotion of Schrei acting, appears to have been one of those means of focusing by which the Expressionist actor passed outside of himself into a state of performance ecstasy. Unlike the individualized and demonstrative Schrei which signaled the ecstatic transformation in Schrei acting, the fundamental sound appears to have pulled the Geist actor outside of himself in a communal and quietly meditative manner. Geist ecstasy, however, may have been more of a rehearsal than a performance phenomenon since the fundamental sound appears to have been explored only in rehearsal, not in performance. On the other hand, the distinction between rehearsal and performance seems to have been less clear in Geist acting than in other Expressionist modes.[42]

In rehearsal, the fundamental sound was used by Schreyer as a touchstone for the "sound-structure" of a given word. Since the scripts used by the Kampfbühne ensemble were never more than a few pages long and were always comprised of a series of single-word or short-phrase utterances, Schreyer and his actors enjoyed the leisure of working in detail at the level of the single word. The sound-structure of a word was established according to the word's rhythmic character, its pitch, and its volume or degree of metrical stress. The result was "sound-speech" – an utterance quite distinct from either sung lyrics or the sound of everyday speech. The "middle range" of this utterance corresponded to the specific fundamental sound of the given actor performing the word's sound structure. Having thus found the audible form of the fundamental sound for the performance of the word in question,

the actor develops at any given time musical pitches which are suitable for him: high, very high, deep, very deep . . . The tone can have differing volumes and herein most closely approximates musical form as double pianissimo, pianissimo, mezzoforte, forte, double forte. Musically, sound-speaking is related to the recitative . . . (194)

One practical foundation of Geist performance, then, was the idea, and the exploration, of sound. The word, once freed from its syntactic fetters, became pure sound; and only as such could language, for Schreyer as for Kandinsky, become a medium of revelation. This is because the word functioning as pure sound could "resonate," as Kandinsky put it, in musical ways which break down the barriers between the physical and the spiritual, the intellectual and the mystical. What one lost in rational clarity one apparently gained in intuitive stimulation. In this regard, Geist performance represents the most radical idea of theatre to emerge from the Expressionist era. Its ideas of communication and performance were based on the expressive possibilities of single words or phrases. In Wortkunstwerk dramas like Stramm's, for example, the text did not admit of reading, interpreting, or completing meaning "between the lines"; rather the playwright's intent, as Rudolf Blümner put it, was that "words were to play to one another, nothing else."[43] It was the Geist actor's job to be the medium of this dramatic interplay of words, as they rhythmically encountered one another in all dimensions of their significance – musical tone, sound, and sense. In conventional realistic drama the actor is the agent and words are the agency; in Geist performance the actor sought to reverse this principle of dramatic action by becoming the agency through which the word could be effective as an agent. In this way, a range of significance was discovered, Geist Expressionists argued, which "radiated" well beyond the semantic dimension of the word.

Kenneth Burke's gloss of Aristotle's theory of "entelechy" is useful for understanding the Geist actor's creative process. For Aristotle, Burke observes, the formal principles which govern a work of art are evident in the completed or "actualized" work, but they existed "potentially," before the work was ever begun. Thus though they follow the work temporally, they are prior to it causally. In Aristotle's view of causality, Burke explains,

Everything that comes into existence moves towards an end. This end is the principle of its existence; and it comes into existence for the sake of this end. This state of completion is its full actuality . . . Since an action contains some ingredient of purpose, or end, Aristotle uses the term "entelechy" ("having its end within itself") as a synonym for "actuality" . . .[44]

For the Geist actor, all fundamental forms – sound, movement, color, form – took their particular concrete character from the completed work, but they already existed, *in principle*, and were simply waiting to be discovered and actualized in that work. The idea here is something like the sculptor "liberating" the sculpture from the block of stone. Thus Geist rehearsal didn't "build" a performance – as in psychological realism – but rather uncovered or disclosed it; performance wasn't communication, it was revelation. The Geist actor's job was to discover his place in the structure of the ensemble performance as it was being revealed in rehearsal.[45]

Such an approach to acting may sound impossibly arbitrary, but for the Kampfbühne ensemble it was really quite practical. The word, resonating with the actor's inner or fundamental sound, was the impetus to discovering the fundamental forms which would govern the performance. "The optical images," Schreyer explains, "are given in the content of the words, the acoustic images in the sound of words, the movement images in the rhythm of the words" (104). Optical images – embodying the fundamental structures of color and form – were as much the concern of the Geist actor as the fundamental structures of movement and sound. In this regard, Schreyer recalls the importance of the mask in performance. "The human form," he notes, "usually was simultaneously a mask form . . ." (153). Along with its power to sculpt the human form, the mask was also explored kinetically by the actors for what it could teach them about "the drama of movement."

V. PRINCIPLES OF MOVEMENT IN GEIST PERFORMANCE

Like Kandinsky, Schreyer saw in abstract human movement a self-contained dramatic event. Kandinsky had arrived at this perception through his study of popular culture, in the course of which, as Peter Jelavich says, he became convinced that only popular art forms "took full account of the contradictions that infused human existence: life and death, love and hate, humor and tragedy, secular and sacred."[46] In this regard, his view of popular entertainments such as circus and vaudeville was quite similar to Wedekind's. For Kandinsky, as for Wedekind, these kinds of amusements celebrated abstractly the joy of sound and movement as non-referential ends in themselves. Like Wedekind and Kandinsky, Schreyer found stimulation in the sheer physicality of the circus. Where Wedekind was inspired by the *élan vital* and the "physical morality" of the circus act, Schreyer appreciated the way such performances enhanced his formal awareness of movement as a phenomenon in itself. Like

Kandinsky – and unlike Wedekind – Schreyer found a profound spiritual significance in this awareness. He recalls that the trapeze performer especially

revealed to us the necessity of inner equilibrium – spiritual and physical – as well as the swinging of movement about the center of gravity. We saw how it was possible to displace the center of gravity, which is a spiritual / physical phenomenon, and thereby to make movement an event and finally an action. This movement action – the drama of movement – we recognized as one of the fundamental prerequisites of Expressionist stage art.[47]

The mask became the Kampfbühne actor's trapeze: a vehicle for exploring the "drama of movement" as an abstract spiritual event. It was especially useful, says Schreyer, in clarifying the *fundamental form* of actor movement [*die Bewegungsgestalt*]:

The more the human form is a mobile mask, and therefore the more the actor is solely the bearer and mover of his mask, the more clearly can the movement gestalt – in its type and in its fulfilment through the Spielgang – be fixed. (195)

Although two members of the ensemble were regarded as "principal mask-builders" (it is not clear whether they also performed), the other actors apparently created their own masks as well. Each production, Schreyer recalls, required weeks of late-night mask building sessions in his home. He stresses the importance of these sessions as part of the rehearsal process because they were a "joyful respite from the intense concentration demanded for the awakening of sound-speaking." Many of the masks built by the ensemble members were oversized, some covering the performer's entire body. In the Bühnenkunstwerk of Herwarth Walden's *Sünde*, for example, the masks were some three meters high (199–200). Working with the mask – both as a design project and a rehearsal object – also revealed the fundamental form of movement in connection with the actor's fundamental sound. All other movements were then derived from the fundamental one in the realization of the Bühnenkunstwerk's movement gestalt.

The mask was a means by which the Kampfbühne actor could become the point of intersection for the dimensions of color, form, sound and movement. It revealed the form of movement to him because within it he could best sense how this dimension of performance shaped, and was shaped by, the others. This process, Schreyer insisted, was simultaneously aesthetic and spiritual. The mask was not merely a physical disguise but a vehicle of spiritual transformation as well. In its ability to stimulate the actor's rhythmic intuition, argued Schreyer, it retained the primitive power to spiritualize dramatic art.

I noted earlier the Kampfbühne ensemble's search for "the source out of which the art of acting, as a proclamation of spiritual reality, could flow and give to the actor the appropriate human form" (125). In this context the ensemble studied the primitive theatre's use of masks as a means of *Wandlung*, or "transformation." Primitive Man, observes Schreyer,

beholds the forces of nature and makes himself one with those forces. He transforms himself within the forces of nature. The rhythms of his movement allow him to flow right into these forces. He clothes himself with the symbols of natural force, masks himself with the symbols. The magic sign of the mask is a means of metamorphosis [*Verwandlung*]. (129)

In primitive cultures, the person becomes the mask, "opening man up to both the demonic and the holy dimensions of life forces conjured up through the use of the mask." Thus the mask serves as a powerful channel between the physical and spiritual dimensions of life because it can be manipulated, in ritual, to open that channel at will. Schreyer specifically noted the ensemble's interest in the Javanese "mask/shadow-play," in which the actor is completely hidden behind the mask:

The mask here has a characteristic life of lines, apart from the man. It is borne only by the characteristic tones of Javanese music and the word-tones of the hidden actor who proclaims the unchanging text of the great sagas with simple and with baroque tone-creations . . . .. The body in this theatre is transformed into a pure vessel of the spirit. (131)

In such *Ganzmasken*, or "total masks," the Kampfbühne ensemble discovered the structures of color and form which revealed the "principles of the color-form gestalt" – along with the appropriate movement patterns – for a given Bühnenkunstwerk (89).

For Schreyer, movement based on natural goal orientation had to become transformed into movement having "a solely artistic objective." This was more easily accomplished with marionettes, he acknowledged, than with the human body (196). This view, of course, had been espoused earlier both by Craig in his "Übermarionette" theory of acting, and by Maeterlinck, who wrote his plays with the assumption that they could only be performed correctly by puppets.

Schreyer says that his study of non-goal-oriented bodily movement lead him "necessarily" to the marionette. He cites as inspirational the challenge of weaving together in performance "the mechanical and the mysterious" aspects of the puppet, identified by Kleist in his famous essay "On the Marionette Theater."[48] Schreyer claims that he and Oskar Schlemmer – independent of one another – were the first German Expressionists to arrive at the solution of the "Über-marionette, as our form was called, not by us, but by others."[49] That solution, quite simply, was to make the marionette actor simultaneously the bearer of the marionette:

He now bore the marionette as a total mask, which completely covered him; or as others said, he became involved in the mask, in the marionette. He danced in it and with it; performed the movement play in and with the mask. He himself was now the marionette's center of gravity. The mask could now move itself only in the movement-forms, in the mask-forms, which were mechanically possible for a marionette. (52)

Schlemmer indeed developed a similar technique in his *Triadic Ballet* of 1922. However, he did not share Schreyer's quasi-religious view of stage work. Rather, his abstractionist productions were created as visual essays on what, for him, was the fundamental problem of the stage: "Man, the human organism, stands in the cubical, abstract space of the stage . . . Each has different laws of order. Whose shall prevail?"[50] Schlemmer's answer was to use the human body as one means of visually exploring the abstract laws of the theatre. In the *Triadic Ballet*, performers, whose bodies were transformed into three-dimensional abstract forms with costuming, danced in geometric patterns:

Thus, for instance, a dance moves only from downstage to the footlights along a straight line. Then the diagonal or the circle, the ellipse and so on. There were no underlying definite "intellectual" considerations. Rather it was the inventive esthetic joy of fusing contrasts into form, color, and movement.[51]

Schreyer's work with the Kampfbühne ensemble also led him to identify as "fundamental movements" certain geometrical patterns underlying the specific movement forms developed for each Bühnenkunstwerk: circling, rotating and revolving movements; the straight line movement; and broken movement.[52] But for him these physical movements were "simultaneously images of 'inner movements' in the spiritual-conceptual realm." Accordingly, each fundamental type of movement form was the repository of a correspondingly fundamental category of symbolic significance. It was equally important to recognize, moreover, that "for each natural creation – plant, animal, man – the artistic structure seeks to recognize the force lines and to develop out of them the organic form" (87). Schreyer here uses the word "force" [*Kraft*] to signify not only the spatial vectors implicit in form, but the emotional / spiritual effect of color as well.[53] In this way, the concept of "force lines" became one of the unifying principles of Geist performance because it united in the actor the kinetic dimension of movement with the structural dimensions of color and form. Most importantly,

all dimensions of the material world are included in the dimensions of man – the mineral, plant and animal form structures as well as the form structures of the extraterrestrial cosmos. The human form therefore stands in closest relation to the fundamental shapes of form – to the sphere, cube, pyramid. The cosmic character of man indeed becomes visible in that all his forms are variations of the sphere, circle and pyramid. (89)

Seeking not to portray man, but rather to become "animated and resounding color-form,"[54] the Geist actor explored the suggestions of movement in color and form just he as felt for the form and color of certain movements and sounds. In this process, the "lines of force" concept was a bridge, a principle of correspondence, between the color and form contexts and the movement and sound patterns of the Bühnenkunstwerk. However, Schreyer acknowledged that a geometric approach to the principles of theatrical movement tended toward "undisguised constructivism," and he cautioned that

the more mechanical the movement play became, the more unavoidable was this development. It led finally to the "shells" of Expressionism, which were so significant as signs of the times, indeed, of the lack of actual artistic life in favor of the Monster-Technicalism which overpowers the senses.[55]

Theatre historians who call the work of Schreyer and his Kampf-bühne ensemble "Cubist Expressionism" overlook the spiritual intent of their formalism. Annalisa Viviani, for example, groups together the theatre artists of the Sturm circle and the Kampfbühne with those of the Bauhaus as "Cubist Expressionists," for whom "the world behind things" is a "continuous system of mathematical or mechanical references to order." While this description may be true of Schlemmer's purely geometrical experiments at the Bauhaus, it indicates precisely what Schreyer sought to avoid at the Kampfbühne. Viviani remarks that "the real force in the drama of Cubist Expressionism is not man, but the space, which, since Naturalism, has

increasingly emancipated itself from the word."[56] In the self-consciously experimental formalism of the Bauhaus's Stage Workshop, it
is true that the word exerted little formative influence. The degree to
which language was an afterthought for Schlemmer is evident in this
self-assessment following four years of experimentation:

For the time being, we must be content with the silent play of gesture and
motion – that is, with pantomime – firmly believing that one day the word
will develop automatically from it.[57]

By contrast, the formalist performance work of the Kampfbühne was
based, in the first instance, on the actor's improvisational encounter
with the Wortkunstwerk. Indeed, the "real force" in Geist Expressionism was not man but the poetic word, with reference to which
the elements of form, movement, sound, and color shaped each
other in the human presence on stage.

I noted in the last chapter that the essential challenge posed to the
Expressionist actor was that of becoming poetic material. In Schrei
performance this was accomplished by an extreme emotional intensity
which ecstatically transformed the actor. The voice and body of the Geist
actor, on the other hand, became the *formal* materials of poetry. If the
Schrei actor represented the explosive pressure of sheer emotional
content, the Geist actor sought to incarnate poetic form as an absolute
fusion of symbol and performer. Both modes of Expressionist acting were
concerned with embodying the essence of humanity; both subscribed to
Schreyer's dictum that on the Expressionist stage "humanity" stands in
the place of "personality."[58] Whereas the Schrei actor rendered this
essence by transcending his personality in heightened emotion, the Geist
actor sought the same goal by abstracting his human "person-ness" into
pure form. Thus these two modes of Expressionist performance produced
two opposite, and complementary, images of "essential Man" – feeling
and form. Most importantly, the principle which synthesized this opposition was the actor's belief in the poetic theatrical process to which he had
submitted himself. The touchstone of this commitment, either in terms of
feeling or form, was the actor's capability for ecstatic self-abandonment.

VI. COMMITMENT VERSUS STYLE: SCHREYER'S *SANCTA SUSANNA* AND REINHARDT'S *FORCES*

The ecstasy of the Geist actor, according to Schreyer, arose from his
status as artistic instrument, for

the artist is the man who is put outside himself, the ecstatic man. The ecstatic man is the instrument [*Werkzeug*] prepared for creation by the necessity of vision . . . The artist is gifted. Through this endowment he is not man, but instrument.[59]

As I noted in Chapter Three, this instrumental view of the actor grew out of a tradition dating to Goethe and Weimar Classicism. In Schreyer's extreme version of that view, acting was not "performance" [*Aufführung*] but rather "execution" [*Ausführung*] of the Spielgang, and was therefore more correctly designated as "playing." The quality which distinguished different "playings" of the same Bühnenkunstwerk was "the intensity of execution."[60] The Geist ecstasy of "intense execution" was first displayed in the première of Schreyer's first Bühnenkunstwerk, Stramm's *Sancta Susanna* (Sturm-Bühne, Berlin, 1918).

In comparison with Stramm's later work, this early script has a recognizable narrative structure. The stage directions include frequent performance instruction in terms of mimetic actions. However, the "action" does not develop a plot but rather evokes an atmosphere whose general tone is one of subconscious longings and fears, reminiscent of the plays of Maeterlinck. The actors do not embody abstract forms; they play characters which are recognizably human, if somewhat ethereal and bizarre in what they say and do. Outlining a generally familiar theme, the dialogue suggests a story of moral conflict between sensual desire and the religious discipline of chastity. The action ends in a standoff between the church establishment and the rebellious nun Susanna.

The script appears to have been a transitional bridge for both Stramm and Schreyer's Sturm-Bühne ensemble. Stramm's dramatic oeuvre is comprised of ten plays, some of which are lost or only partially preserved. In fact, Stramm himself was on the verge of destroying his writings when he was discovered by Walden, who immediately began to publish both his poetry and drama in *Der Sturm*. The plays indicate a development from Naturalism (*Die Unfruchtbaren* [*The Sterile Ones*], c. 1910; *Rudimentär* [*Rudimentary*], 1912–14) through a mystical-erotic period (*Sancta Susanna*, 1911; *Die Heidebraut* [*The Bride of the Moor*], 1913), to abstract, "Telegrammstil" Expressionism (*Erwachen* [*Awakening*], Spring 1914; *Kräfte*, Summer 1914; *Geschehen* [*Happening*], c. 1914).[61] Overall, they become progressively more elliptical and abstract in character and action, and thus more typical of the Wortkunstwerk style of writing for which Stramm was revered in the Sturm circle. Yet interestingly, Schreyer selected not one of these later, more paratactic plays but the mystical, Maeterlinckian *Sancta Susanna* for his first public Bühnenkunstwerk.

Perhaps this choice indicates just how revolutionary Stramm's later plays were. Schreyer, the radical director, apparently wished to ease into his revolutionary dramatic program at the Sturm-Bühne with a piece written in the more familiar symbolist style. Yet, as we shall see, he and his ensemble considerably refashioned the play according to their musical "sound-speaking" model of acting. The players, by the way, were students from Schreyer's Sturm-Schule acting classes who were specially trained for this performance for more than a year. Music for the piece was composed by Herwarth Walden, although Paul Hindemith had previously written a score for *Sancta Susanna*. The title role was played by one of Schreyer's first pupils, Lavinia Schultz, whom he describes as "a highly gifted person of wild passion, which could only be tamed by the discipline of art." Apparently, she responded boldly to the challenge of the production's concept as "a play of naked man." According to Schreyer, she performed a portion of the role in the nude as the audience looked on "with breathless perseverance, perhaps horror." Near the end of the performance he recalls the audience erupting into two camps, one applauding in a frenzy, the other protesting wildly. The press "thoroughly denounced the piece and its performance."[62]

This last recollection is accurate only in part, at least in relation to Herbert Ihering's review of the première. Ihering certainly disapproved of Schreyer's production, but he was not unsympathetic toward Stramm's play. What he said, rather, was that both author and script ought to be protected from treatments like that of Schreyer's. Before delivering this evaluation, however, he described what he saw and heard:

Before a gaudy black, yellow, green and red wall stands a woman [Clementia], to the left, in profile. Wearing a facial mask and a dress which mimics the background, her arms are stretched forth as she speaks, sings, sounds [*blasen*] a litany. Cowering on the ground with her back to the audience, a second woman [Susanna] answers in a shrill, whistling, giddily high voice. The antiphony continues on in harsh dissonances until the woman who is lying on the ground begins to sing a coloratura aria. She glides with sighs and words down over a gradation of tones and, at another time, she clambers back up again. A girl enters, bows before Susanna, pushes and shoves clumsy word-clusters from herself. A slave appears in a barbaric, shaggy garment . . . slave and girl exit. The acoustic signals of

Clementia and Susanna . . . are again exchanged. Now there are trombone flourishes; then later, whistles. One time, muffled thuds; another time, clinking glasses. The bodies move like marionettes. Anything dropped to the ground is supposed to be inwardly composed sound, and a nude scene is supposed to be austerely rhythmic. Behind the scenery, Negro drums complete and intensify the orchestration.[63]

If we compare this description with the text and stage directions of *Sancta Susanna*, it would seem that Schreyer took considerable liberty with the script, particularly the stage directions. However, he never pretended that his Bühnenkunstwerke were mountings of plays, but rather he insisted that they were autonomous stage compositions inspired by plays. Nonetheless, Ihering protested, the results were not worthy of the name Expressionism. For one thing, he argued, true Expressionist stage art masters language through selectivity and rhythmical shaping; it does not abrogate the laws of language and then claim to invent them anew (81–82). The production had also failed to achieve its arrogated "ultimate unity" in terms of sound, color and gesture "because the arbitrary had superseded the necessary" in Schreyer's directing:

For intensification, Herr Schreyer offered dissolution; for concentration, tearing to pieces; for compactness, dilation . . . [He] denied any ulterior meaning to the events, and he created no symbolically expressive signs through his extinguishing of reality . . . Herr Schreyer was intentionally affected and boring. His primitive screaming wild west art had no character, no sensation, no fanaticism. It only howled. (82)

Schreyer had evidently alienated Ihering, even before the performance began, with his introductory remarks. He claimed a "decisive breakthrough" in stage art, Ihering reports, and he rejected "everything natural and lifelike" in favor of an exclusive commitment to "intonation, rhythm and concentration." Such talk, which would purport to "tear down the laws of the theatre," Ihering dismissed as "the most serious enemy of any revolution because it remained unoriginal and soporific" (80).

Ihering's review, however, reveals the shortcomings of the production in terms of his own prejudices toward a more realistic and sensational stage Expressionism. The performance model he proposes that the Sturm-Bühne adopt in place of Schreyer's is that exemplified in "the burning creations . . . the splendid characters of Werner Krauss" (82). His paradigm for genuine "Expressionist" theatre appears to be the detailed character acting of Max

Reinhardt's Deutsches Theater ensemble, in which Krauss was one of the stars. Schreyer cites Josef Kainz as his own performance paradigm. "A true art of acting," he argues, "originated when the actor, like Josef Kainz perhaps, abandoned the 'as-if acting' prescribed by Hamlet." Interestingly, Kainz, as I mentioned in the last chapter, was also the revered model of Fritz Kortner, another Reinhardt luminary. It is, to be sure, an impressive testimonial to his artistic stature that Kainz should have been the inspiration for both an essentially representational character actor, like Kortner, and a militantly non-representational director, like Schreyer. In this regard, however, what unites these two distinct schools of "Expressionist" acting is their emphasis on the vocal dimension, and it is in this context that both cite the inspirational work of Kainz. For Kortner, Kainz was "a genius [who] sang a new melody" in speech, the "strong current" of which pulsated with the rhythmic speed and power of the dawning age of electricity. Schreyer saw in Kainz an actor who "created an unpsychological word-sound movement play."[64]

Reviews such as Ihering's, according to Schreyer, were common during the brief run of *Sancta Susanna* which inaugurated the Sturm-Bühne. But he also recalls the response of Max Reinhardt to his work. In May 1920 Herwarth Walden arranged a production of Schreyer's play *Mann* at the Kammerspiele.[65] Schreyer remembers that "Max Reinhardt took care to respectfully acknowledge our play as 'a great achievement, but he himself would probably never do anything similar; he would have neither the desire nor the ability for anything similar.' "[66] This response, of course, was nothing more than mere polite condescension. Yet interestingly, a year later we find Reinhardt directing a play very much like *Mann*, Stramm's *Forces* [*Kräfte*], at the Kammerspiele (première 12 April 1921). Günther Rühle remarks that this staging achieved for Stramm – albeit posthumously – his greatest success as a playwright. It was also "Reinhardt's last contribution to Expressionism; or better, his last attempt to humanize expressive texts through the employment of realistic style, to transform sound and movement rhythmicism into living representation."[67] But Alfred Kerr, in his review of the production, recognized the problem implicit in Reinhardt's approach:

Reinhardt has chosen a middle-of-the-road treatment; not fully characteristic of Stramm; only a compromise work. He wished not to disappoint. Thus he has certainly *played* August Stramm . . . but not played August

Stramm . . . Reinhardt produced flesh where Stramm would have wanted lines . . . And he muddled two styles together. First: realistic drama (only played in dumbshow). Second: Expressionist drama – this however was evident only in [Agnes] Straub. Stramm's stylistic chaos has nothing to do with Reinhardt's stylistic chaos.[68]

What was chaotic by design in Stramm's play became confusion by default in Reinhardt's production because the director could not fully subject himself to the playwright's sensibility. The Kammerspiele mounting of *Forces* demonstrated the uncompromising nature of Geist dramatic material: more than any other type of Expressionist script, it demanded to be directed on its own terms. Like *Sancta Susanna, Forces* is a mystic-erotic ode. Its complementary themes of adultery and revenge, however, are more powerfully concentrated in Telegrammstil utterances and brutal action. The characters are generically designated as "She," "He," "her friend," and "his friend." The central figure, "She," played in the Kammerspiele première by Agnes Straub, is a woman whose husband is having an affair with a friend of hers. In a jealous rage Straub's character causes her husband's death at the hands of a friend of his whom she has falsely claimed as her own paramour in order to instigate a duel between the two. She then forces her friend, the consort of her husband, to lie on his corpse and kiss his dead lips before strangling her. Finally she kills herself with a draught of poison.[69] This, the "realistic" side of the action is performed primarily in dumbshow, while the accompanying utterances of the characters are nothing more than brief "keywords" to be performed "Expressionistically."

Whereas Stramm meant only to suggest actions with his paratactic dialogue, Reinhardt felt he had to illustrate the words with psychologically detailed business. But his stage pictures, according to Emil Faktor, "through their unmysterious clarity, stood in the way of the play's mysticism, and thereby directly caused some confusion."[70] In a realistically detailed setting which created the "milieu of an aristocratic comedy," the actors were placed in "stiff groups" and spoke "in musical round." Posh manners – such as deep formal bows and the kissing of the women's hands in greeting and leave-taking – were suddenly, brutally undercut by the violent actions just described.[71] In fairness to Reinhardt, we should note that the details of the violence at the end of the play are dictated in Stramm's stage directions. However, the stage directions are otherwise quite unspecifically related to the utterances of the characters. Predictably, the audience, which had sustained a suspenseful expectation throughout, was left in bewilderment at the conclusion of the performance. "Instead of appropriately thunderous applause for the performance, at the very least," recalls Faktor,

silent embarrassment prevailed. And as a result of their inward rejection of Strammish "Forces," the spectators had an easy time of it acknowledging the force of the leading actress, Agnes Straub (305).

Though not for Reinhardt, this production was universally regarded as a triumph for Frau Straub, and won her acclaim as the leading Expressionist actress of the day.[72] Her performance was characterized by sudden transitions from wildly passionate outburst to a composed calm in which all bodily agitation immediately ceased. She had about her the quality of "a German she-wolf," according to Kerr (302); and Siegfried Jacobsohn observed that her acting "was a bold advance on the graphic beginnings of [Gertrud] Eysoldt and [Tilla] Durieux" (307). Interestingly, the "Expressionist" passion and physical dynamism of Straub's performance were derived from enacting the role of sexual beast. They were not inspired by some more lofty spiritual or political sentiment, as is usually the case with the male principal figures in Expressionist plays. Notwithstanding Stramm's misogynist conception of his principal character, however, what the critics recognized in Straub's performance was the tradition of dangerous sexuality established two decades earlier by actresses performing in the cabaret and the Kammerspiele settings. Straub's intention may simply have been to create a specific character; but, as they had with Eysoldt and Durieux, these male critics saw a persona that transcended the script.

Jacobsohn's comparison of Straub with Eysoldt is telling, for it illustrates how the personality of the performer had been allowed – indeed, had been relied on – to define the text in this case. As Reinhardt had exploited the unique personal qualities of Eysoldt for his demonic realization of the title character in Wilde's *Salomé* (Kleines Theater, 1902), so here the force of Straub's individual artistic temperament was really what this production of *Forces* was about. Powerful individual character acting, of course, is expected in the theatre of psychological realism. As applied to Wortkunstwerk dramas like *Forces*, however, such methods, as Kerr observed, could lead only to *playing* Stramm, not to playing *Stramm*. It is significant that this judgment, by one of the critics who often mocked the Sturm circle and their productions, was shared by theatre artists within the circle, such as Schreyer and Rudolf Blümner. Reinhardt's production of *Forces*, acknowledged Blümner, was "the best of the realistic-psychological style . . . [to which] the drama itself was sacrificed."[73] This agreement bespeaks a general recognition of the necessity for a radical new form of production which would grow out of the intense linguistic compression of plays like Stramm's. Though members of the Sturm circle and members of the press disagreed about what that new form should be, they concurred that Reinhardt had merely engrafted an old form, not discovered the new one.

Reinhardt's theatre was one of personalities, his own predominating above all. His approach to Expressionist scripts "from above," and that of much less gifted dilettantes and commercial opportunists "from below," drew fire both from the movement's ideologues and from the press. Kasimir Edschmid, whose performance theories can be associated most nearly with Schrei Expressionism, as well as Schreyer, the champion of the Geist school, complained about unprincipled imitators. And Alfred Kerr cynically observed in reference to *Forces* that Reinhardt,

who just wanted to demonstrate that he also could do Expressionism and to show how easy it was, proved it strikingly. He, the master-Impressionist, simply transformed Expressionism into Impressionism. In the same way, Jessner, the new master-Expressionist, had developed [Barlach's] *The True Sedemunds* (Staatliches Schauspielhaus, 1 April 1921) not out of its style but out of his own.[74]

Arguably, Schreyer's Bühnenkunstwerke were similarly egoistic. However, the degree of artistic control itself is here not the issue, but rather what it was that these directors were seeking through the exercise of that authority. For Reinhardt, Expressionism was simply another style over which to demonstrate his mastery. Jessner built his career on large-scale productions to which he applied his own uniquely monumental aesthetic. In Schreyer's view, however, there was something of the priestly in his relationship to the performance ensemble. Indeed, he argued, the priest and the artist perform the same spiritual functions:

Both partake of vision, of revelation. Both proclaim their vision to their faithful. The ecstatic artist, like the enraptured priest, is no longer human. Only one who is transformed transcends himself for the contemplation of the spiritual. The work of the artist, like the work of the priest, transforms the community into believers.[75]

Here again, the coterie nature of the Kampfbühne Association is evident. The "community" to which the director/priest ministered included actors as well as audience. The theory of the "fundamental sound" and the appropriately resonant "fundamental forms of sound, movement, color and form" was a performance grammar that made sense to them. Though we have only Schreyer's account to substantiate this point, there are the facts that a group of individuals did for a brief time associate themselves with him in Hamburg and that they took part in a number of private productions under his direction. Whether or not Schreyer's rhetoric of a resultant spiritual harmony seems fanciful, its reality, for the Kampfbühne coterie of actors and audience, appears to have been tantamount to a litany of faith.

In this sense, the Geist performances of the Kampfbühne ensemble attempted to implement, more seriously and thoroughly than any other mode of theatrical Expressionism, the goal of human spiritual renewal espoused by all Expressionists before the war. But perhaps what Schreyer's theatre demonstrates most clearly is that the spiritual power of art is "real" only in the society which it fabricates. The Kampfbühne commune at Hamburg was such a society – audience and actors alike, an artifice created by Schreyer. When he left for the Bauhaus in 1921, it vanished like a forgotten dream. Indeed, it would appear that Geist Expressionist theatre was virtually a one-man show. The Sturm-Bühne, which was the only other Geist vehicle, lapsed into a nominal existence after Schreyer's removal to Hamburg following the armistice. In addition to the 1920 Kammerspiele staging of Schreyer's *Mann*, it produced only one other play (also in 1920), Stramm's *Die Heidebraut*, after its 1918 première of *Sancta Susanna*.

Yet, while working with his Kampfbühne in Hamburg, Schreyer always strove to maintain close connections with Walden in Berlin.[76] More importantly, the Sturm-Bühne and Kampfbühne in the last analysis must be seen as outgrowths of the much higher-profile "*Sturm*-Abende" [*Storm*-Evenings], produced by Walden since the founding of the Association in 1910. According to one *Sturm* historian, these performances exceeded over 1,000 throughout Germany, some 350 of them occurring in Berlin alone over the twenty-two year life span of the *Sturm* Association.[77] It was in the context of this performance venue that both Futurist poetics and Stramm's revolutionary poems and plays were given their first public exposure.

Working with this sort of material, the *Sturm*-Abende performances functioned as a kind of laboratory for the development of the "Wortkunst" theories on which both the curriculum of Schreyer's drama section of the Sturm-Schule and the performances of the Sturm-Bühne and Kampfbühne were based. Thus, the *Sturm*-Abende, together with the long-lived Sturm-Schule – which, as I noted earlier, remained active until 1932 – enjoyed a highly visible profile during the Expressionist era. Accordingly, the *Sturm* Association's ideas concerning the nature and means of performing Expressionist stage art – which were the very foundation of the Sturm-Bühne and Kampfbühne productions – were quite well known, despite Schreyer's withdrawal from public dramatic performances.[78]

Schreyer characterized his "Expressionist solution" to the problem of the theatre, the Bühnenkunstwerk, as a unique event in German theatre history. He was convinced that he had "planted a seed" which would one day blossom into a new form of theatre. Not an imitation but an outgrowth of the Bühnenkunstwerk, this theatre of "a future generation" would "fulfill the promise of the spiritual unification of mankind, not simply a small circle of friends."[79] However, Schreyer's "seed" – planted almost secretly in Hamburg – never bore fruit suitable for the turbulent post-war Berlin theatre market. On the contrary, in the great metropolis politics and commercialism shaped the Expressionist actor quite differently into an emblematic image of alienation.

CHAPTER 5

Late Expressionist performance in Berlin: The Emblematic mode

I. THE EMBLEMATIC ACTOR

The acting of Expressionist performers such as those in Schreyer's Kampfbühne ensemble resembled the evocative art of the French Symbolists. It created images which signaled such a multiplicity of possible meanings that audience reading of the performances was unavoidably idiosyncratic. For the purposes of this final chapter, therefore, I should like to draw a theoretical distinction between this kind of Expressionist performance and yet a third type which I shall call "emblematic stage Expressionism." The typically *denotative* imagery mobilized in this mode drastically curtailed ambiguity by reinforcing a single dominant idea. Denotative signification is most clearly operative in allegorical representation. The actors in the medieval morality play *Everyman*, for instance, do not play characters but rather abstract moral ideas. Assuming a production which stresses the play's allegorical quality, the actors must create images which denote those ideas. The images thus created become emblems of these ideas; and the aggregate of such images becomes a macro-emblem of the whole production – the composite emblem, that is, of the production's dominant idea. In *Everyman*, the embodiment of the title character himself could most readily function as the macro-emblem, into which all the other emblematic significations – such as those denoting the Seven Deadly Sins, Death, and so forth – are subsumed.

The abstractionism of the late Expressionist theatre in Berlin utilized this allegorical method of reinforcing a predominant idea through the emphatic coordination of all production elements. In Jessner's *Richard III*, for example, the red costumes and the red lighting were denotative images of blood which cooperated with other production elements to reinforce the idea of political assassination. Such was the predominance of the color red in this production that it could be viewed as its macro-emblem. This method of coordinating the emblematic significations of the various productions elements – setting, lighting, costumes, acting – produced the simplified but overwhelming effect sought by such directors as Jessner, Karl-Heinz Martin, and Jürgen Fehling. Each director, as we shall see, had his characteristic approach to emblematic emphasis. Jessner, of course, did much with his staircase setting and with color imagery in lighting and costuming. Martin exploited the dramatic tension between sharply focused light and surrounding darkness. Fehling molded dynamic plastic imagery with a chorus of ecstatic actors. My concern is to describe how these directors incorporated actors into an emblematic approach to dramatic texts. In all three cases, the actor's expressive resources were treated as design elements to be unified with the rest of the production components for the purpose of clarifying the controlling idea. Ideally, every movement or utterance was to reinforce – that is, be emblematic of – this idea.

Of course, a unified production in any theatrical style has a controlling idea. In a Naturalistic production, the idea of environmental influence on the characters is subtly suggested through detailed settings which reproduce an ostensibly "real-life" social milieu. But the aesthetics of realism require that the production concept be hidden from the audience's awareness by the fourth wall effect. What distinguishes the emblematic work of the late Expressionist directors is the extraordinary degree of control they allowed the dominant idea to exercise. Their goal was the opposite of Naturalism: namely, to present the idea rather than represent it.

Theatrical signification, to be sure, is highly elaborate; it is never purely symbolic, emblematic, or mimetic. What characterizes a production is the predominance of one type of signification over others which may also be involved. The same may be said of the individual elements of a production, such as acting. In late Expressionist acting the signification of idea was developed primarily in ensemble, as distinct from individual, performance. This was a function of the scripts. The plays of Georg Kaiser and Ernst Toller, as well as the classics of Schiller and Shakespeare, were the basis for some of the most famous late Expressionist productions. These scripts generally specify more supernumerary actors – more of a choral element – than typically do the pre-war dramas of Sorge, Kornfeld, Hasenclever and Stramm. On the other hand, Toller's plays, and those of Kaiser which are Expressionist, often call for a central ecstatic figure set apart from a chorus, which abstractly reflects the hero's spiritual condition. Hence these plays are sometimes called *ich* ("I" or "ego") dramas. However, the application of this rubric to late Expressionist *acting* of such scripts is superficial and inadequate for conveying the nature of the emblematic performance methods that were employed.

The label "*ich* performance" is misconceived in this context because it places an incorrect emphasis on the central figure. For Martin, Jessner and Fehling, the choral actors were the primary focus of their scenic approach to Expressionist performance. What was really innovative about late Expressionist productions in Berlin was not the performance of the individual ecstatic actor as much as that of the abstractionist ensemble. Typically, while the central figure remained distinct as a character he nonetheless was incorporated into the ensemble's emblematic playing style. In this way his or her isolation was intensified by the position of being both a part of the ensemble stylistically and yet apart from the ensemble structurally.

The basic function of the ensemble actor in late Expressionist productions was to *embody* the idea of a human spiritual condition rather than to play a mimetic image which exemplified that condition. For the vocal approach to this goal, Expressionist directors generally agreed that the actor's speech had to become musical. That is, it had to emphasize the rhythmic and tonal qualities of language. In this way, the actor could attempt to render musically an abstraction such as "oppression" or "disillusionment," for example, by way of shaping the rhythms and tones of speech in support of the verbal significance of lines which refer to such ideas. The effectiveness of such a performance strategy is suggested by the fact that critics of late Expressionist productions often praised this musical quality in the acting. Also, the actor's gestures and posturing had to approximate the plastic properties of dance and sculpture in order to express physically an abstract idea. These expressive translations of speech into music and gesture into dance and sculpture, in fact, illustrate the characteristic semiotic process in emblematic performance: "sign transformability."

This principle depends on what Keir Elam calls the "semantic versatility" of the stage sign, which may be operative "not only at the connotative level but also, on occasion, at the denotative [level] – the same stage item stands for different signifieds depending on the context in which it appears . . ."[1] Emblematic Expressionist production, however, is a reverse instance of denotative signification in this sense where several different sign vehicles stand for the same signified, as in the red costumes and red lighting of Jessner's *Richard III*. Moreover, as Elam notes, "the mobility [of the sign] . . . is dependent not only on the interchangeability of stage elements, but still more on the reciprocal substitution of sign-systems or codes." This he terms the process of "transcodification," evident where a given type of signified is conveyed in a code materially distinct from it – a physical object such as a wall, say, is indicated by elements from a gestural rather than an architectural repertoire of sign vehicles.[2] By synthesizing selected acoustic, kinetic, and pictorial elements of music, dance and sculpture into sign-vehicles, emblematic Expressionist actors sought to "perform" ideas. Jessner, in fact, characterized this process as one of turning actors into "transcendental sculpture."[3] Amplified by ensemble presentation, such synthetic acting was powerfully evident in his *Richard III*, Martin's *Die Wandlung*, and Fehling's *Masse Mensch*, all three of which I shall presently examine in this regard.

The emblematic presentation of ideas such as "political oppression" or "the horror of war" had a significance which spoke powerfully to newly politicized post-Wilhelmine audiences in Berlin. Indeed, the growing social impact of post-armistice politics transformed early Expressionist spirituality into late Expressionist activism in the theatre and mandated an inescapably editorial role for the emblematic actor. To be sure, it was precisely the connection between the overt theatricality of stylized ensemble statement and the urgencies of political agenda which caught the attention of directors like Piscator and Brecht in the early 1920s. The Expressionist approach to political commentary remained essentially hortatory, however; and this non-dialectical aspect of their "activism" was flatly rejected by Brecht. But the alleged heavy-handedness for which the critics castigated Expressionist directors like Jessner was nonetheless, for Brecht's political purposes, one of Expressionism's most important breakthroughs. The power for activist agitation in emblematic stylization is well illustrated, for example, in Jessner's 1919 Berlin staging of *Wilhelm Tell*, a discussion of which will conclude this chapter.

The two primary influences on late Expressionist performance, emblematic scenic formalism and socio-economic turmoil, came together on the post-war Berlin stage in the person of the emblematic ensemble actor. This kind of Expressionist performer was first conceived, however, not in a postwar script but in Georg Kaiser's 1912 drama *Von morgens bis mitternachts* (*From Morning to Midnight*). It is true that Reinhard Sorge used abstract choral figures in *Der Bettler*, also written in 1912; but he did so only sparingly, at the beginning of the play. The major portion of that script, as I indicated earlier, involves only the more developed characters of the Poet and his family. Kaiser, in *Von morgens bis mitternachts*, was the first Expressionist playwright to employ the emblematic ensemble consistently in a script. He was also the first to incorporate an ecstatic central figure into the abstractionist style of characterization which he had conceived for the ensemble. I begin therefore by considering this play on stage and in Karl-Heinz Martin's film version, which affords by far the most detailed visual record available of an individual ecstatic abstractionist performance, that of Ernst Deutsch as the Cashier.

II. KAISER AND THE THEATRE OF TWO DIMENSIONS: *VON MORGENS BIS MITTERNACHTS*

Von morgens bis mitternachts was one of the most frequently produced scripts during the Expressionist era. The central role of the Bank Cashier, who one day impulsively steals 60,000 Marks and abandons his life of bourgeois tedium in a vitalist quest for self-fulfilment, became one of the great challenges for the leading actors of the Expressionist era. The heart of this challenge lies in the fact that Kaiser compresses what, in reality, would be a much more protracted journey of self-discovery into one frantic and ultimately fatal day. Arguably, the degree of intensity and the expressive range which the role demands is unparalleled in Expressionist drama. Additionally, the script calls for a large cast of supernumeraries whose function is to represent abstractly the contexts and reflect the stages of the Cashier's development.

Though it is contemporaneous with *Der Sohn*, *Die Verführung* and *Der Bettler*, *Von morgens bis mitternachts* is dramaturgically quite different from them. Not the least of its distinctive qualities is the way in which its abstractionist dramaturgy anticipates the course of late Expressionist performance. In the figure of the Cashier, Kaiser embodied the central problem of emblematic acting: namely, how to synthesize the two-dimensional semiotic "flatness" of emblematic denotation with an emotional depth in the playing of the central role. Kaiser conceives of the Cashier as both a generic and an individualized figure, and the actor playing the role therefore was to share the ensemble's abstract style of acting while remaining distinct as a psychologized character. He had to alternate between an economical stylization, characterized by rapidly abrupt movements and bursts of Telegrammstil utterance, and an expansive lyricism conveyed in long, ecstatic monologues. The Cashier's final speech, in fact, is an ecstatic monologue composed of Telegrammstil phrases. It illustrates how his development proceeds not in subtle realistic detail but rather in sudden epiphanic leaps, as though Kaiser were attempting to approximate the rhythms and speed of thought itself. Hence, as Michael Patterson has observed, the actor must maintain the anti-realistic style even in the play's more realistic scenes, in order to "shift from the ecstatic to the grotesque, from emotional climax to cartoon-like comedy."[4]

In Victor Barnowsky's 1921 Lessing-Theater production, Alexander Granach was considered to have achieved the greatest success as the Cashier. The key to his performance was his sense of pace. This involved not only the ability to deliver clipped Telegrammstil passages rapidly but also to shift tempo with sudden energy. For the reviewer Alfred Klaar, the result was that Granach's Cashier was like "an unleashed wild animal."[5] In terms of physical and vocal qualities, according to Franz Servaes, "a drawn, haggard face with hollow eyes, emaciated hands with spidery fingers, and a shabby ill-fitting coat characterized the external appearance. But from within a hoarse and hungry despair cried out with hard jerky sounds."[6] Apparently Granach's characterization achieved a consistency of balance between the ecstatic and the grotesque which was lacking in Max Pallenberg's creation of the role for the 1919 Berlin première at the Deutsches Theater. The combination of comic grotesqueness and intense line delivery in his performance impressed Fritz Engel with the "forcefulness with which Pallenberg throws himself on each word and each thought." But Emil Faktor complained that the actor was unable to sustain the "tragic mania" when he shifted to the grotesque. Alfred Kerr felt that "he often restrained himself in order not to make fun of himself . . ." For Alfred Polgar, Pallenberg had created a "melancholy clown, a depressive eccentric."[7]

This last comment suggests the oddly un-Expressionist, tragi-comic feel of the role. Indeed the script itself ironically undercuts the ecstatic solemnity of the final moment when the Cashier shoots himself:

POLICEMAN: Switch the light on again.
(Girl does so. At that moment all the bulbs explode.)
(CASHIER: has fallen back with outstretched arms against the Cross sewn onto the curtain. His dying cough sounds like an 'Ecce' – his expiring breath like a whispered 'Homo'.)
POLICEMAN: There must have been a short circuit.
(It is quite dark.)[8]

In this way, Kaiser invites the audience not to get emotionally involved with the Cashier but rather to sit back and "behold the man" as an emblem of an ironically reduced, vitalist idea of the Christ figure. But emblematic acting, as employed by the great directors of late Expressionism, was intended not to promote critical distance in the audience – Brecht adapted emblematic performance to that purpose. Rather, the Expressionist emblematic actor was to convey the essential idea of his character with great emotional power directly to the audience. The whole point of the style was to maximize thereby the spectator's receptivity to the idea of the human condition which that character signified.

To this end, the play was well suited for adaptation to the cinema, given that medium's power to magnify. Karl-Heinz Martin's film version of the play, with Ernst Deutsch in the leading role, achieved a forceful synthesis of the grotesque and the ecstatic, the emblematic and the emotive. Herman Scheffauer calls the film a "light-play," noting that

here space is not treated as something concrete and plastic but as something abstract – diffused – immaterial. Light and shadow are not massed, but broken and dissolved. The original settings are not constructed in the round and in color, but are suggested in the flat in different tones of black and white. Space does not obtrude; the world becomes a background, vague, inchoate, nebulous . . . In such surroundings the actor no longer feels the support of active space and a living environment, but is flung back upon his own resources. He even loses much of his own corporeality and relief and becomes two-dimensional, an actual picture.[9]

The film, as preserved on video cassette at the Stiftung Deutsche Kinemathek in Berlin, actually begins with a preview section showing several images and scenes to come. We first see Deutsch in medium close-up staring at the camera in wide-eyed grimace with his hands, held like claws, to his head. The effect is intensified by the Expressionistically exaggerated facial make-up, including darkened eye sockets and garish, white accents on the nose, cheek bones, and forehead.[10] The rest of the ensemble, to varying degrees, wear similarly stylized make-up, and the claw gesture is ubiquitous throughout the film. As in *The Cabinet of Dr. Caligari*, the actors' bodies are strongly textualized after the manner of primitivist Expressionist painting.

Unlike *Caligari*, however, Martin's film attempts some Expressionist cinematography in complement to the acting. Following the preview, the first scene opens with a blurred focus which clears to reveal the bank where Deutsch as the Cashier sits hunched over (with few exceptions, his characteristic posture throughout) in a teller's booth constructed to look like a cage of chicken wire. This initial scene first establishes the deadly tedium and machine-like rhythm of the Cashier's work and then shows his transformation as a beautiful, exotic female client approaches his booth to do business. During this segment of the film Martin repeatedly features extreme close-ups of the Cashier's hands rapidly counting money, the lady's hands and arms sensually gesturing to the Cashier, and the Cashier staring forward. This imagistic fragmentation of the actors' bodies, readily available even in early cinematic art, here makes a deeply felt psychological impression. Throughout *Von morgens bis mitternachts*, Martin returns to close-ups on the Cashier's hands and particularly on female arms and legs. This, together with superimposed body images – the faces of several women the Cashier encounters suddenly turn into skulls, the prone torso of the exotic lady momentarily becomes naked after she has fainted – create a striking effect of abstract, imagistic emphasis cinematographically, quite apart from the acting.[11]

Yet Deutsch's acting also exploits the cinematography, particularly the close-ups. At moments of particular emotional intensity, his facial expressions go as far as rolling eyes and bared teeth. It is almost as though the actor is exploring the individual components of his physical expression by concentrating all of his emotional energy in them separately. Dennis Calandra notes in particular

a remarkable ability to communicate with the fingers alone . . . When the Cashier first appears, his hands are tensed before him, the fingers pinched together in the gesture of a man counting out bills . . . after he decides to steal the money, the fingers become talons as they hover above and then clutch at the notes; plagued by visions of impending death and by violent feelings of guilt, the Cashier then tries to claw at his own face . . .

This expressive ability is also evident in several scenes where his entire body assumes an abstract pose. After he has met the exotic lady, for example, he expresses his instantaneous sexual desire and determination to pursue its fulfilment by extending his hands and arms through the window of the teller's cage in an intense grasping gesture. In a later scene showing the Cashier in his oppressive bourgeois household, he and his family – an emphatically homely wife, mother-in-law and two daughters – confront one another with hands held claw-like down at their sides and wide grimacing stares.[12] At the end, in the Salvation Army scene, Deutsch assumes the crucifix pose against a backdrop of a cross painted in the cubist style just after he shoots himself. Such poses illustrate the general sculptural tendency in late Expressionist acting. Along with the dance-like quality noted earlier in this study, it establishes the generally plastic nature of Expressionist physicalization on stage.[13] Thus the subject of a given shot of Deutsch turns out not to be the emotional content of the moment as much as the gestural sign, or emblem, of that content. Yet the intensity of Deutsch's characterization is emotionally gripping precisely because of his abstractionist exaggeration.[14]

The stylization of ensemble gesture and movement, evident in the domestic and Salvation Army scenes, is particularly emphatic during a middle segment of the film where the Cashier, having decked himself in fine clothes following his bank theft, attends a six-day bicycle race and offers exorbitant wagers to various contestants and spectators. Here, by means of costuming, the crowd of onlookers is clearly differentiated by social class. Though the costuming codes are utilized in a basically realistic manner, however, the movements of actors playing the various classes is markedly stylized: the upper class figures sit perfectly still in the bleachers, the middle class engage in occasional movements, while the working-class spectators are characterized by constant vigorous movement. To counterpoint this, Martin uses a roving follow-spot to track the Cashier as he sways to and fro within the crowd. The back and forth movement of the spot against the various rhythms of stasis and movement in the ensemble creates a disturbingly effective impression of disorientation, meant to signify abstractly the Cashier's heightened state of vitalist intoxication.

Both before and after this point in the Cashier's development, the general movement pattern of Deutsch's body is abrupt and irregular, characterized particularly by spasms of sudden rigidity and jerks of the head. Such a moment occurs, for example, when the seductive lady who will trigger his transformation enters the bank; Deutsch suddenly sits bolt upright and jerks his head toward the doorway. Later, after being brushed off by the lady, in pursuit of whom he has embezzled the 60,000 marks, he stands outside his house staring into the camera as his eyes widen, expressing his realization of the enormity of his crime. Suddenly he turns his back to the camera and rushes into the house.

The key to the success of the performance appears to be a combination of Deutsch's intensity, Martin's close-ups and editing, and the larger-than-life movie screen itself upon which the idea of a person such as the Cashier is automatically writ large. Emblematic stage productions of the play, of course, lacked the benefit of these last two performance factors. Although a spotlight on stage could isolate a figure, the expansive abstracting focus of the film close-up simply was not possible. It would seem, however, that the large supporting chorus could be used to broaden the dimensions of a scene. For example, during the testimonial scene in the Salvation Army hall at the end of the play, Kaiser specifies that first one man in the crowd, then many, and finally all are worked into a frenzy of confessing their sins. With the Cashier's concluding confession thus prepared for, one imagines a staging with the penitents grouped in some mass pose of attentive concentration on him. When he confesses his crime he then flings the stolen money away prompting a riot of the "penitents" who scramble for the strewn bills. In this way, Kaiser shatters the emblematic group image, abstractly reflecting the Cashier's final disillusionment with mankind which leads to his suicide.

It would appear, however, that such abstractionist ensemble possibilities went largely unrealized in stage productions of *Von morgens bis mitternachts*, at least during the Expressionist era itself. The reviews of the Munich Kammerspiele première either make no mention of ensemble performance at all or they dismiss the choral actors as "supernumerary figures . . . who are only ornamental."[15] As one critic put it, "of the actors only Herr Kalser [who played the Cashier] need be mentioned since all the other roles are unimportant."[16] Stylistic inconsistency apparently plagued the Deutsches Theater production, with the scenes in the Cashier's home and at the six-day bicycle race being stylized and the rest presented more or less realistically.[17] Of Felix Hollaender's direction, Herbert Ihering complained that "despite all of his twitching and bouncing his conception is always somehow softened by Naturalism – or rather dulled and turned grey by it."[18] César Klein's settings for Barnowsky's Lessing-Theater production seem to have come closest to establishing an abstract playing space. However, there is no indication in the extant review sources that Barnowsky did anything with the choral actors to complement Pallenberg's grotesque pathos as the Cashier.

Kaiser once remarked that "to write a drama is to think an idea through to the end."[19] In practical terms this led him to an abstract, symmetrical dramaturgy in his early Expressionist plays. The "idea" in *Von morgens bis mitternachts*, however, is not a polemical one as in the Shavian drama of ideas; rather, it is essentially emblematic, visually and aurally. Kaiser has no specific argument to offer about human beings with longings and frustrations such as those of the Cashier. He simply wants us to behold the idea of such a man. This calls for a heightened visual approach to acting the play which the tradition of Berlin realism persistently impeded during the Expressionist era. The impeding bias is typified in a comment by the reviewer Richard Specht, concerning Pallenberg's grotesque Cashier, that "one has the feeling that Reinhardt would not have permitted the role to be played thus."[20] It was the particular contribution of directors such as Karl Heinz Martin, Jürgen Fehling and Leopold Jessner to challenge this tradition of Reinhardt realism with a scenic approach to acting which allowed for an ensemble emblematically to play an idea through to its end.

III. SCENIC ENSEMBLE ACTING: MARTIN'S *DIE WANDLUNG* AND FEHLING'S *MASSE MENSCH*

From 1916 through 1918, the experiments of both Weichert at Mannheim and Schreyer at Hamburg retained a stylistic homogeneity. This reflected a kind of solipsism at the provincial theatres, where Expressionist performance was primarily about itself; that is, about the question of expression. But when, in 1919, Expressionist theatre came to prominence in Berlin it quickly became the tool of post-war political activism. Moreover, as Günther Rühle observes, it was not the Das junge Deutschland productions of 1918 at Reinhardt's Kammerspiele but the "curtainless podium stage" of Karl-Heinz Martin's Tribüne Theater that typified "Berlin Expressionism" in drama.[21] Among actors, Fritz Kortner, who played the leading roles in several of the major late Expressionist premières, became the prototypical ecstatic emblematic figure.

Kortner's Berlin career began in association with Martin at the Tribüne [i.e., "platform, rostrum"] Theater. As the name of Martin's theatre suggests, this kind of Expressionist performance took on a specifically rhetorical dimension which shifted the focus of actors and audience away from the question of theatrical self-expression to that of theatrical persuasion, and its socio-political applications. Unlike *Der Sohn, Die Verführung, Der Bettler*, and the plays of Stramm, the script which crowned the inaugural season of the Tribüne, Ernst Toller's *Die Wandlung (Transfiguration,* 1918), was a product of the war.[22] Yet the play was not simply an anti-war statement; rather it used the image of war to dramatize Toller's sense of the sickness and death of the human spirit in general. What it sought to "express," was not simply the transcending of individual alienation – as in pre-war Expressionist drama – but rather the idea of the redemption of all humanity from every condition of wretchedness. The means of this redemption in the play is the inspired, ecstatic monologue. In the final monologue, the hero, Friedrich, purports to lift his on-stage auditors rhetorically out of their individual sense of misery and unite them in a communal consciousness of faith in the dignity and potential of "humanity." What Toller posits is nothing short of the spiritual regeneration of mankind through oratory, right before his audience's eyes. Though such a premise may today seem ludicrous, it was received in its own day with the greatest enthusiasm.[23]

The Tribüne under Martin was a decidedly leftist theatre, and so it is quite unlikely that the audience at the première of *Die Wandlung* included many right-wing ideologues. But its receptivity to powerful, dramatic oratory nonetheless typified a society which would soon demonstrate the lengths to which it could be persuaded by moving rhetoric. The script thus contained a prophetic irony in its premise about the power of exhortation; an irony all the more grim for the fact that the orator–hero of *Die Wandlung* is a Jew. I noted in Chapter One that many Expressionists' sense of alienation was compounded by their Jewish identity. For Fritz Kortner, whose playing of Toller's orator–hero made him the toast of the Berlin theatre world over-night, creating the role of Friedrich was a particularly personal experience. "What I played at that time," he recalls, "was myself, a young German Jew and rebel in conflict with the world about me."[24] For Martin, on the other hand, there was great intellectual, though not autobiographical, significance to Toller's play. Sent to him scene by scene as it was completed by the playwright from his prison cell in Munich (341), *Die Wandlung* was the perfect vehicle for launching the activist Expressionist theatrical program upon which the Tribüne was founded.

Martin and Kortner had first become associated in Hamburg at Erich Ziegel's Kammerspiele, a struggling avant-garde theatre which was "meagerly funded but rich in talent" (285). According to Kortner, it was at the Kammerspiele that the two conceived of the idea of the Tribüne (297). He implies further that the concept grew out of their mutual sense of exclusion from important theatrical opportunities which only the "Hauptstadt," Berlin, could offer. This nose-thumbing attitude was apparently as much behind the Tribüne's revolutionary spirit as any purely ideal devotion to Expressionist social philosophy. In any case, it was Martin and Rudolf Leonard, "a good Marxist and a bad playwright" (293), who actually founded the Tribüne, just eighteen days prior to the première of *Die Wandlung*.[25]

Martin maintained that his production of *Die Wandlung* was an attempt to unify actor and audience by revolutionizing the playing space:

> The irresistible and necessary revolution in the theatre must begin with a transformation of the playing space. Out of the unnatural separation of stage and auditorium must evolve an organically unified artistic space which will unite all who are involved in the creative process. We do not want an audience, but a community within a uniform space . . . not a stage, but a pulpit . . .[26]

To this end, the Tribüne Theatre was housed in a small auditorium, seating approximately three-hundred. The stage was a shallow raised platform with three upstage entrances which were hidden by a green curtain. This playing space was separated from the house only by a small three-step staircase. Martin used no footlights, proscenium curtain, full-stage scenery, prompt box or stage-effects machinery. Scenes were played in front of Robert Neppach's primitivistically painted movable screens; and sharply focused front light carved a small acting area out of the surrounding darkness. The radical transitions in time and place required by Toller's "Stationendrama" structure were easily effected by changing the screens during blackouts.[27] During scene changes, the playing of a single violin haunted the darkness, according to Alfred Kerr, with as great an effect as "half an orchestra."[28] By thus suspending the action in a void,

Martin was able to create both the dream/nightmare effects required throughout the stations of the hero's spiritual journey and the visionary atmosphere for the "People's Assembly" redemption scene. In the latter case, he positioned the ensemble so that only the actors closest to Friedrich were in the light while the rest listened to his monologue in the shadowy fringe of the acting area, suggesting the huge multitude required for the scene.

As in Weichert's *Der Sohn*, lighting here seems the most dominant and "Expressionist" design element of the production. The sharply delimited playing space which it defined provided both the lyric isolation and the centripetal focus required for Friedrich's dual function as suffering comrade and inspirational leader. As we noted a moment ago, Martin desired a theatre which would "unite all the participants in the act of creation." It is significant that he should conceive of the physical context of this communal expression in terms of such an isolated spatial image as a pulpit. This apparent contradiction in the production concept of *Die Wandlung* suggests the basic assumption about "expression" held by many Expressionists: namely, its messianic power. The inspired leader envisioned by Toller, though an extraordinary individual quite distinct from the masses, nonetheless intuitively understood and shared their essential condition. He thus entered into a representative relation with them both in terms of his own experience and in terms of his expressive response to that experience. Like the Son in Hasenclever's play, he could both share the suffering of the masses and rescue them from it by means of his ability to feel and speak with inspiration. This, in short, is the elitist idea of an historically empowering rhetoric offered by the play: the orator–hero empowers through expression, the masses are empowered through their receptivity to that expression.

But more than Toller's messianic vision it was Martin's interpretation of the script, as influenced by its subtitle "The struggle of a man," which shaped the première of *Die Wandlung*. In Hamburg, Martin had developed an "expressionist" approach to directing the method of which was "to take a play as an *organic unity* independent of its author, to place it under the dominant aspect of its *central idea* and so to arrive at a conception for the production."[29] Though there is no extant prompt book, the reviews of this première indicate that the script was edited so that Toller's final scene of mass regeneration was given a penultimate position. An earlier scene, in which the birth of the orator–hero's illegitimate child symbolizes the individual birth of the New Man, actually concluded the production. Martin's concept of theatre as pulpit was certainly appropriate for Toller's script; but it was the director's "central idea" of the struggle of a man, not the playwright's theme of mass regeneration, which that concept principally served. The result was that the production was generally heralded for its revolutionary staging techniques depicting Friedrich's personal odyssey through the horror of war, rather than its revolutionary content which proclaimed the spiritual regeneration of all mankind.

Both director Martin and principal actor Kortner identified with the revolutionary spirit of this script, but their approaches to the play's "Expressionism" appear to have been divergent from the start. Martin located the play's expressive core in its scenic potential and the startling rhythmic changes of its Stationendrama structure. He appears to have been more concerned with incorporating his actors into his scenic ideas than with helping them to individual realizations of their roles.[30] He was most celebrated for his ensemble work in this production, but he was not an individual actor's director like Reinhardt, who personally demonstrated and exhaustively rehearsed even the smallest roles in crowd scenes. Kortner, on the other hand, used his identification with the central character as a trigger for his own personal Expressionist release. According to Herbert Ihering, he "rebelled against script and director" in his effort to make the role of Friedrich his own.[31]

Martin, says Kortner, was

urgently concerned about an external, visual style. Expressionism made its entrance on the stage through distorted doorways, usually without walls. The scene of the action, which was only suggested, was bizarrely lighted. The word remained unilluminated if the actor himself did not shed light on it.[32]

Yet had Martin provided the direction which Kortner implies was lacking, Kortner probably would have rejected it anyway. A fiercely independent artist throughout his career, he frequently quarreled with directors, especially those who, because of commercial pressures, took short-cuts in the rehearsal process.

Already as a provincial beginner I rebelled against the bustling lack of understanding which was to cause so much dissension later in my career ... From that time on I have struggled with the commercial theatre, hoping, hoping against hope, for the extraordinary theatre which will break through the routine. I struggle even now in the closing phase of my career.

Now, when it has become a matter of simply going out there every night, my eyes are fixed upon the stage in love for its vocation . . . (155–56).

Expressionism, as Kortner encountered it with Martin in *Die Wandlung*, was a very important phase of his artistic development because he saw it as basically an actor's, not a director's, challenge.[33] Of his performance in *Die Wandlung*, Ihering observed that he seemed to succeed as Friedrich only where he was able to wrest the character out of Toller's autobiographical mold. For Ihering, whose judgment commanded the greatest respect in the Berlin theatre community,[34] this came in the long ecstatic monologue of the People's Assembly scene near the end of the production. Though no detailed description of Kortner's work in this scene survives, Julius Bab's recollection of his general effect in *Die Wandlung* is suggestive:

The commanding voice of Fritz Kortner was introduced. Along with a bear-like physical ponderousness and powerful thrusting movements, he possessed a voice which had the shattering strength of a trumpet. And he knew how to make it effective in steep curves, rapidly soaring and suddenly falling.[35]

As discussed in Chapter Three, Kortner developed the techniques required for this dynamic vocal variation in his days as a chorus leader in Reinhardt's ensemble. Having at that time learned to think of monologues as "arias," he may have used a similarly operatic approach for his ecstatic address in the People's Assembly scene. In any case, Ihering recalls that this speech bore the personal stamp of neither playwright nor director but of the actor: "Kortner played not transfiguration, but defiance."[36]

Martin apparently was not one of those compromising, cost-conscious directors about whom Kortner complained, although financial difficulties were in fact severe enough to close the Tribüne just three months after the première of *Die Wandlung*.[37] There is no indication that he deprived Kortner of the time he needed to develop the role of Friedrich, only the suggestion that he was not of much help because his concerns were more scenic than textual. Left to his own devices, Kortner developed a powerful, if uneven performance. At the beginning, according to Ihering, he seemed to be feeling his way along in reserved tones and movement. As the performance progressed and his passion mounted, the strength of his acting, though gripping, frequently overstepped the dimensions of the production in terms of the performance level of the rest of the ensemble. As Ihering put it, Kortner "went beyond the limits of the stage and exploded the space around him" (159).

Emil Faktor described his performance as that of an "actor still in a developing stage whose forms of expression fluctuate between fervent, inflammable pathos and nervous, flickering sensuality." However, he was struck by the hospital scene where Kortner, reacting to the pathetic speeches of the war wounded, "captures feverish moments . . . in which his arms make the swinging movements of a mower. He individualizes states of agitation through a passionate turning about his own axis. He has gestures which explore the meaning of words."[38] This swinging movement is another example of the Expressionist actor's tendency to search for the elements of dance in his performance, not for the sake of mere variety, but as a way of exploring "the meaning of words." In other words, movement in emblematic performance was not merely a matter of gestural illustration but, beyond that, a means of conceptual development.

Faktor also hailed the hospital scene as a triumph for Martin. It was one of several ensemble moments in which his masterful work with choral actors "burned into one's consciousness with ardent symbolism the incomprehensible tragedy of world war" (162). The setting of a military hospital was rendered simply with three sick beds,

upon which, in pairs, lay victims of the war's fury: languishing, half delirious, maimed, crippled humanity, ravaged by grievous physical agony. Each individual spoke of his martyrdom, all cried out for salvation. It was a masterstroke how each affliction distinguished itself from the others, how bed after bed revealed its tragedy. In spite of all the dreadfulness, it was not the impression of horror but of something holy which predominantly bestowed its magic on the scene. Here the ear of the director found wonderful nuances. (161)

Apparently, Martin directed his actors to find subtle variations of cadence and tone in their individual testimonies. After these were delivered, the wounded lined up one by one in a pathetic troop inspection during which one of them was continually shaken by uncontrollable seizures. The scene then culminated in a unison lamentation by the six battle victims, which was echoed by the sympathetic moaning of attendant hospital nurses.[39] This is an example of Martin's directorial manipulation. According to Toller's stage direction, it was the nurses, not the wounded soldiers, who were to "raise their heads, shape their lips to a shattering cry, [and] collapse,"[40] following the individual accounts of suffering. In any case, Martin's ensemble vocal technique here was one of

many unison utterances [which] had a novel excitement. The multiplicity of voices was so sharply and tightly compressed together that cries seemed to spring out of a single throat (Faktor 160).

In general, Martin's directing of actors had a striking unity of design, most evident in his work with group scenes. Ihering remarked that Robert Neppach's "abridged" and "compact" settings called forth a correspondingly abridged, compact type of playing:

Words formed into clusters rhythmically and broke apart. Screams rose up and died away. Movement pushed forward and back. Here was no psychology and development, but compression and impulse. Not illustration but punctuation. Not demeanor but force . . . (158)

Faktor praised the simplicity of Martin's suggestive method in the People's Assembly scene:

Even before their cue comes, figures are poised on the sides of the stage grouping themselves in corners where they appear as lifelike statues. The idea of the world beyond the stage is represented, so to speak, by emissaries who prepare the audience for the play's points of climax. At the decisive moment, their life streams out of the corners and nooks in flowing lines. It seems to me a very pure means of awakening the spirit of movement in drama. (162)

Here is another instance of the sculptural quality in emblematic acting which I noted earlier in reference to Ernst Deutsch's performance as the Cashier in *Von morgens bis mitternachts*. Its effect on individual actors in the ensemble was noted by Ihering who observed that

A student (in the People's Assembly scene) had such intensity of listening and involvement in her forehead, chin, eyes and hands, that her spoken lines were of secondary significance. (158)

The actress was not playing the realistic *action* of listening as much as embodying the emblematic *idea* of rapt attention. Moreover, though her words seemed secondary to Ihering, such individual physical concentration, according to Faktor, helped to build not only a physical, but also a powerfully vocal, unity in the whole ensemble. The result was that "sentences flow[ed] together in a uniformly accentuated relationship."

In the No-man's Land scene, Martin developed a rich texture of visual, as well as aural, effects. The lights came up to reveal actors wearing black leotards painted with white skeleton designs. They were positioned in grotesque hanging poses about barbed-wire trestles. As the actors spoke in "diabolical falsetto voices," they moved, at first slowly, then with increasingly jerky emphasis. The scene culminated in a macabre dance of death, which the actors performed while clattering real bones which they held in their hands. Martin accomplished all of this, according to Faktor, "without offensive shrillness, irritating overtness, or mood-disrupting exaggeration" (160). Although Ihering, at the time, credited Martin with creating both "concentrated stillness and harsh outburst" in the production as a whole,[41] he later remembered only the latter:

Expressionism, like any artistic movement, was at first recognizable through its excesses: in the theatre it came to light with the performance of Toller's "Wandlung" . . . In the Tribüne everything was interpretation and accent . . . Martin has shaped revolutionary Expressionism – the scream, the exaltation – with fundamental precision . . . But Expressionism is more. If he wants to come out right in the end, he must also adapt the moving power of stillness to his expression . . . The solution demands a deeper relationship with the artistic requirements of the era than a devotion to outburst and scream.[42]

The charge of heavy-handedness is one which plagued many Expressionist directors and actors. Kortner was quite sensitive about this kind of critical reaction to the risks he took on the Expressionist stage. He stressed the distinction between his work with Martin and Jessner and what he sarcastically termed "the good old Expressionism." Such acting, he said, was characterized by

a fortissimo in the voice which caused the swelling of varicose veins in the calves . . . [and it] trampled sense, content, and interpretation underfoot in a shrieking pointlessness of voice and hand expression.[43]

Ihering himself, however, acknowledged that Martin's direction of *Die Wandlung*, even if heavy-handed at times, had a definitive function. In its brief life-span of three months, the Tribüne managed to generate a high-profile revolutionary image. As a result, its première of Toller's play had a great deal to with national and international impressions of the characteristic features of stage Expressionism. Toller's script and Martin's directing were considered so innovative that for one contemporary American critic "scenes never before risked upon a stage were presented as matters of course in this torrential play."[44]

Aside from the fact that Martin's *Die Wandlung* catapulted Kortner and him to fame in Berlin, it also occasioned the advent of several influential critics. Kortner recalls that

The première evening was considered an event: a new piece, written in prison, was given its first performance, a new director and a new principal actor were offered to the Berlin public. And in the orchestra sat the new critic of the *Berliner Tageblatt*, Alfred Kerr, who up until then had written only for *Der Tag*, and who was taking up his new position with his review of this première. Also in the orchestra was Herbert Ihering, formerly director of the Vienna Volksbühne, and next to him sat Emil Faktor, the young, extremely modern critic of the *Berliner Börsen-Courier*.

In fact, the beginnings of a new theatrical community whose influence would long outlive the Expressionist movement came together on that première evening. The transitory existence of the Tribüne was symptomatic of the momentary but profound impact that the Expressionist movement as a whole brought to bear upon the German theatre. Though *Die Wandlung* was the Tribüne's only successful production, it was nonetheless "one of three key premières (along with Weichert's staging of *Der Sohn* and Jessner's *Wilhelm Tell*) for the coming decade in the theatre."[45]

For the development of Expressionist performance itself, Martin's primary achievement lay in his emphatic stylization of ensemble acting. In the process, more importantly, he created a kind of composite character out of the ensemble which took on a life of its own. This dynamically shaped mass personality also functioned as one of his principal design elements. Actors became a kinetic scenic environment of sound and movement. In the cinema, Fritz Lang was to take this kind of ensemble work to unprecedented visual levels of geometric abstraction in his 1926 film, *Metropolis*. On the Expressionist stage, however, kinetic ensemble scenography reached its culmination in Jürgen Fehling's 1921 Berlin première of Toller's *Masse Mensch* (Volksbühne, 29 September).

The ambiguity in the title of this script – which might be rendered, variously, as "Mass Humanity" or "Man and the Masses" – suggests that in this second play of Toller's the ensemble had in fact become the principal character. Although both *Die Wandlung* and *Masse Mensch* (1920) superficially exhibit the same character relationship of central figure and anonymous chorus, the dynamics of that relationship have significantly changed. In *Die Wandlung*, Friedrich emerges as the charismatic leader who inspires and directs revolutionary energy in the masses. In *Masse Mensch*, the heroine, Sonia Irene L. – a woman who abandons her middle-class background in order to promote non-violent resistance among the masses – is finally engulfed by a directionless mob anarchy. Humanity thus governed by its worst instincts is personified in a protean character who is an emblem of the proletariat and whom Toller calls simply, The Nameless One. Whereas Friedrich's long ecstatic exhortation is a controlled force which triumphs at the end of *Die Wandlung,* Sonia's power of speech, by the conclusion of *Masse Mensch,* is reduced to futile expressions of horror at the violence of the revolutionary mob. Her martyr's death is but a flickering exemplary light within the pitched battle between the government monolith and the mass of oppressed humanity. This diminution of the central figure's rhetorical power is reflected in the fact that the reviews of the première largely neglected the performance of this role and concentrated instead on the ensemble acting.

Toller used the The Nameless One to represent abstractly the face of the masses as, variously, "Might," "Madness," "God," "Destiny," and "Guilt." But Fehling concentrated on shaping the visual image of Mass Man out of the ensemble of actors who actually portrayed the proletariat. In terms of their physical appearance, according to the eye-witness account of Herman Scheffauer,

the characters were crassly realistic in their dress – bald, commonplace, negligent garb, without the slightest concession to the theatrical . . . These were the rough, untidy garments of the proletariat – they spoke, they sobbed of grime and use, the dull, drab husks of prisons, real prisons and symbolic, those of the soul and of the body and of civilization. The actors . . . seemed devoid of all make-up, seemed scooped up out of some metropolitan mob slum, factory serfs with grim, hard-bitten, suffering faces, fanatic eyes, faces shining with sweat or with oil, the sweat of machines. Their speech was feverish, hoarse, ejaculatory – the speech of men and women who were being chewed between the jaws of Crisis and Catastrophe.[46]

Here the realistic costuming might be considered a symptom of the impending decline of Expressionist stylization, but Fehling used it not for individual verisimilitude but for composite visual effect. When he shaped this multitude into a moving ensemble, the individual figures of wretchedness were united into one powerful kinetic emblem of desperation. In the workers' strike meeting scene,

an orotund chorus comes swelling into the theatre, as from vast distances . . . A high pyramid of human forms and faces becomes visible, piled thickly

together like a segment of an amphitheatre high above a small platform . . .
Speeches, violent, brutal, demanding the imperative of force, or soft and full
of pacifistic persuasiveness, go shuttling to and fro. The Crowd is lashed into
pitching rapids, to wild outcries, then stricken to silent lumps of slag. (237)

Fehling became famous for visionary choral scenes such as that
required by Toller in Picture Four. Scheffauer recalls his rendering
of it as a

phantasmagoric sketch in sanguine and bitumen of humanity's great prison.
A catastrophic, evil murk. Great rocks – or are they walls? – lean top-heavily
from the sides, like forbidding presences, watching. In the centre on the
ground there is a bluish-greenish light, smoldering like something submarine
or phosphorescent. A man with shorn head, in loose purple garb stands on a
low flat box of black which contains the lantern. His attitude is grotesque
and strained, an accordion hangs loose between his outstretched hands. A
doleful chorus, a ribald lamentation, a kind of jailbird's *De Profundis* resounds
slowly – a grim, almost majestic chorale. The concertina squeaks and
belches. Shadows in prison dress arise, chains rattle – an abominable dance
of wrenched joints and stiffened limbs begins. The music grows slimy and
lascivious, then ponderous and plodding, then whips itself into drunkenness
and fury . . . Parti-colored light from above falls segmentally upon the
writhing mass, like the ribs of a many-colored revolving fan, lashing them
on, spinning them round, round, round. (238–39)

What is significant about Fehling's use of actors in this visionary
scene is that it does not differ essentially from the more realistic
scenes, such as the one described above, or the climactic Revolution
scene:

A broad flight of steps, as in the hall or lobby of a public building, steps
leading nowhere, cut off by curtains. Fighting in the streets – barricades.
Sonia and the Nameless One. Man is slaughtering Man – Sonia's voice is
uplifted in terrible protest . . . Suddenly an avalanche of revolutionaries in
flight, men and women, drab and dingy but with blazing eyes and streaming
hair, bursts into the hall and floods up the steps. They press close to one
another, then turn like harried animals at bay . . . With convulsed, ecstatic
faces, with out-stretched hands and heads, the human pyramid thunders
forth the "Internationale" with its devastating music of the "Marseillaise"
. . . (240)

In both kinds of scenes, the ensemble actor's job approaches that
of the ensemble dancer, whose body is kinetic material in the
molding and re-molding of visual imagery. This process, aside from
any narrative interest, is really what the performance is about. In the
realistic crowd scenes of Fehling's *Masse Mensch*, humanity grouped

in ecstatically vibrant pyramids is just as "phantasmagoric" as any of the ensemble work in the dream scenes. Fortunately Fehling's visionary style suited Toller's dramaturgic strategy. "You have acted according to my intention," he remarked in a letter to the director. "What can be real in a drama like *Masse Mensch*? Only the spiritual, the immaterial breath."[47] As Siegfried Jacobsohn observed,

Since Toller has not made it possible to separate dream and reality, Fehling has not at all attempted to do so. He presents the "back room of a working class pub," the "great hall," the "prison cell," all in the visionary world of dream. To cater to the eye and ear in this manner uninterruptedly requires an imaginative richness which is all the more astonishing the less it has the possibility to replenish itself out of the subject matter.[48]

As in Martin's staging of *Die Wandlung*, the rhythmic coordination of lighting, movement and utterance here was carefully executed. Jacobsohn noted how ensemble actors spoke in a slow tempo and apathetic rhythms by way of symbolizing the uniformity of their oppressive existence. Suddenly an agitator would break out of their midst "with a wildly distorted voice," and a glaring spotlight would illuminate him. The "cold, automatic laughter" of a prison guard "froze one's blood"; an upstage curtain was opened and closed at regular intervals revealing the silhouette of a caricatured stock exchange; screaming voices "dr[e]w near from a distance in a rhythm fraught with danger" (326). The high point of this "musical director's" texturing of sound in the production came in the Revolution scene. Here the masses sang their battle song, the Internationale, in rhythmic counterpoint to the gunfire of government troops as "volleys of song answer[ed] the hammering machine-guns."[49] Through it all, remarks Jacobsohn, "one doesn't understand a syllable, one doesn't need to understand" (326). As in the visual imagery, Fehling used his ensemble to shape aural images to render not the play but his expression of its "central idea." With the ascendance of this abstractionist tendency in late Expressionist directing, the actor's humanity became more and more subordinate to his function as a stylized scenic element.

IV. MONUMENTALISM AND POLITICS: JESSNER'S *RICHARD III* AND *WILHELM TELL*

Scenic Expressionism and, with it, emblematic acting, reached its culmination in Leopold Jessner's 1919–20 stagings of Schiller's

Wilhelm Tell and Shakespeare's *Richard III.* In the following discussion, I have chosen to examine the two productions in reverse chronology. This is because Jessner's *Richard III* best typifies his monumental emblematic aesthetic as such, while his staging of *Wilhelm Tell* serves as the clearest illustration of its political implications near the end of the Expressionist era. Hence, the earlier production, more than the later, aptly conveys the furthest reach of this study's argument concerning theatrical Expressionism. That is, its historical character – its strengths and weaknesses as a rhetoric of social empowerment – is most evident where Expressionist discourse concerning the role of theatre in contemporary German history actually confronted the forces of the contemporary historical situation. In these terms, *Richard III,* though chronologically later, actually can be seen as somewhat regressive in terms of theatrical political activism. As I shall show at the end of this discussion, in fact, it represents the beginning of a pattern of withdrawal from politically confrontative Expressionism into a more private spiritual/mythical aesthetic the vehicle of which was Jessner's own personal *"Expressivität."* For him, the Expressionist understanding of political conflict as spiritual conflict increasingly meant that its effective representation could occur only in symbolic terms.

Perhaps the two most characteristic features of Jessner's work were the dominance of abstractionist sets in his productions and his tendency to stage Expressionist versions of the classics rather than Expressionist dramas themselves. In the work of Fehling, scenic formalism found its agency in the dynamically moving ensemble; space was shaped out of the fluid energy of mass humanity. With Jessner, a similar formalism expressed itself in an architectural stasis: the images of both isolated man and man in community were subjected to the geometry of monumental stage setting. Here the term "monumental" refers to a kind of abstractionism the dimensions of which are massive in terms of setting and larger than life in the acting. Jessner's consistent use of the stage center staircase, for example, compelled a statuesque type of performance in which actors, as we noted earlier, were to become "transcendental sculpture." To this end, Jessner established the convention that an actor could move and gesture only when speaking his own lines. Anyone else on stage was to remain frozen in his pose and not react naturalistically to what was being said or done.[50] When an actor's cue released him from the frozen pose, according to Günther Rühle, his movements were typically concise and tense. "The type of actor developed by Jessner," he explains, "was the austere, precise, cold dramatic worker with mythic or political contours."[51]

Though he often paid lip service to the importance of the actor's individuality, Jessner's actual use of actors clearly reflects his pronouncement that "directing today primarily means subjecting the individuality of the actor to strong guidance."[52] According to Fritz Kortner, Jessner so stubbornly adhered to his scenic method of staircase directing, that his "guidance" finally became coercive. Ironically – if Kortner's account be reliable – the famous "Jessner-treppen," which first appeared in *Richard III* (1920, Staatstheater, Berlin), were originally his, not Jessner's, idea:

> Jessner had accepted for *Richard III* the fundamental concept which I had of this piece. In my boyhood fantasies, I had always imagined a career as an action of climbing up over many steps – right up into the dizzying heights . . . So it was that for the first time in my life I made a scenic sketch. Since I was unable to draw in perspective I was helped by Erich Engel, who had come to Berlin as a director. The fortunes and end of Richard would be played in ascending and descending movement on stairs.[53]

Others, among them the contemporary critic Julius Bab, have argued that Jessner was merely executing the scenic discoveries of Appia and Craig.[54] In any case, Jessner seized upon the idea, Kortner continues, and subjected every other production value to the concept of the will to power which the staircase image captured for him.

Although the use of a staircase as a central set piece dates back to ancient Greece, Jessner's innovation was to use it as a concrete method of allegorizing character presentation. In this way, he sought to help his actors "to play only the idea of the piece, not the extensive development of its story."[55] Kortner was able to use the steps to help him play the idea of his character in *Richard III* because their vertical simplicity corresponded with the simplicity of the action where "in raging forward movement, Richard leaves behind himself whatever gets in his way, including the supporting cast."[56] The resulting characterization was a masterful physical and vocal caricature of the idea of lust for power.

Physically, Kortner developed such a grotesque image that Siegfried Jacobsohn marveled at how "with broad visage and flattened nose he resemble[d] a swollen monster." His "stocky" figure clambered up and down the steps with "the out-reaching movements of a belly-swollen spider." When he

allows an arm to dangle along his body while striking its clenched fist with the other hand; when he stretches the right thumb wide and supports the left hand in it while bracing the right arm on his hip; when he suddenly turns round or bends – then has he captured the altogether thrilling, suggestive energy which hardly requires the commentary of words.[57]

Kortner generally moved rapidly, in accordance with "the driving tempo" Jessner had established for the production as a whole; his entrances were effected either by jumping or running onto the stage (262). But in the famous "A horse, a horse" segment of the battle scene, Kortner, naked from the waist up and waving his crown in his hand "like a decapitated head" slowly hopped down the stairs.[58] This movement, executed with legs spread wide as though straddling a horse, reminded Alfred Polgar of an "Indian war dance."[59] Ironically, Kortner's emblematic rendering of Richard's maniacal desperation for a horse became the horse which carried him into the midst of Richmond's troops, who were arranged at the bottom of the staircase in an open semi-circle. Here Richard was killed with rhythmically stylized blows which never actually touched his body (Ihering, 64). For Polgar, the most striking thing about Kortner's acting in this scene was how the idea of the horse was expressed through his stylized movements: "the steed was absorbed by the rider" (71). Kortner himself recalls that, while collapsed in exhausted slumber at the opening night cast party,

my knees, so they told me, continued to perform in sleep the movements with which I had suggested the panic-stricken Richard's desire to escape from the stage as he cried, "A horse, a horse." (369)

The actual utterance of this line, in contrast to the broadly stylized movement which accompanied it, was a masterpiece of subtlety. "Strictly speaking," Jacobsohn reports, "he sang it. Always differently. Not constantly harsh, but always more hopelessly yielding to destiny" (262). In the measured repetition of the line, Alfred Kerr heard "an act of raging despair. . . the rhythm of madness, a babbling cry for deliverance."[60] His voice in this moment was one of "broken ecstasy," though generally his vocal delivery had "a cutting, metallic sound."[61] Typically, Kortner delivered his lines in a "raging tempo, in galloping speech which rode under pangs of conscience, people, obstacles" (369). This accelerated line delivery, like the rapid

movement pattern, was in keeping with Jessner's "wonderful tempo
. . . In every moment, dashing and flashing words radiated all their
contours; one wanted to take them all in, but they stormed by"
(Kerr, 258). Yet Kortner's ability to vary that tempo achieved the
greatest effect:

With him a retardation of tempo caresses; an acceleration of tempo whips
the nerves of the listener. As though he intended to especially excite by this
means, he stormed right over all those passages which one knows by heart
. . . (Jacobsohn, 264)

At the moment of Richard's coronation, Kortner's screaming
"Amen" was "an almost painful cry of fulfilment" (Kerr, 259). It was
not acted "circumstantially, but like a bolt of lightning, a flash of
genius which illuminated retrospectively the entire path he had
traversed to the throne" (Jacobsohn, 264).

In contrast to Kortner's variety of tempi in speech and movement,
the performance tempo of the remainder of the ensemble appears to
have been regulated in a stylized manner by Jessner from scene to
scene. Their positioning in groups on stage had "the stiffness and
symmetry of primitive effigies. They strove for the effect of a relief"
(Polgar, 69). For this reason they often appeared "like figures out of a
chronicle" (Kerr, 259). Fehling also used the staircase setting, but he
flooded it with waves of ecstatic human movement, thus calling
attention to the ensemble rather than the steps. Jessner, on the other
hand, emphasized the staircase tableau by precisely restricting actor
movement on its levels. Some staircase group scenes, in fact,
appeared chiefly to serve the purpose of presenting Jessner's varied
color palette:

From below left, a group is arranged transversely upwards to the central
apex: blue, green, yellow, black. Next to black stands lilac and then the
group is completed transversely down to the right: violet, brown and again
blue . . . (Jacobsohn, 261)

The spectator only became conscious of this statuesque color
pattern, however, when a figure violated staging style by moving
quickly through the ensemble, as Old Queen Margaret did in her
first scene.[62]

Jessner's monumental blocking along the levels of the staircase
helped both to stylize and to project the actor's speech and movement. Artur Michel noted how the "voices were harmonized on a
certain tone and the gestures coordinated on a fixed tempo and

direction for whole scenes" (265). Buckingham's movements, in particular, according to Herman Scheffauer,

were strangely conventionalized and were dominated by a restrained athletic grace and a statuesque immobility. Now his gestures became hieratic as when offering Richard the crown, now he made steps that seemed part of a solemn dance. (212)

The messengers reporting to Richard on the changing tide of battle were symmetrically divided on the stage. The murderers "shot forth from behind the central door curtain and assumed twisted postures in the playing space." The townspeople who offered the throne to Richard awaited his appearance as a group on bended knee. While Richard mounted the staircase at his coronation, "the nobles of his realm, to his left and right on the steps, bowed with their faces to the ground in all too Oriental obsequiousness" (Michel, 265). At the final battle, Richard's army, represented by four actors, set to marching in a manner which suggested that they were riding. The stylization of Richard's killing by Richmond's army, as well as the entire battle scene, were accompanied by the rhythmic throb of tympany and drums (Jacobsohn, 262; Ihering, 64).

This rhythmic repetition was anticipated verbally by actors throughout the production wherever the text permitted such emphasis. The most controversial use of verbal repetition came in the "Despair and die!" nightmare sequence where Richard's victims haunt and curse him on the eve of the battle. Jessner rendered the ghosts solely by off-stage speech, which was "only a murmur, a buzzing; a whisper, swelling, ebbing away, threatening, laden with menace" (Kerr, 259). Scheffauer described the "spookish symphony" which Jessner created:

Richard, shimmering in armor, slumbers in an eerie dimness upon the dark-red expanse of [the] steps, as in bed . . . Through this haunted gloom there comes a low moaning, a whispering, a groaning, a gibbering, a whirring and a squeaking; cries, ejaculations, curses, direful oracular voices rolling out of another world; clanging chains, heavy footfalls, crashing, plangent, as of some doom advancing nearer and nearer . . . (214).

Scheffauer raved about the originality of the scene because it dispensed with "the usual procession of haggard ghastlinesses, the memorial train of phantoms defiling in the crass, fluttering limelight" (214). Kerr applauded Jessner for avoiding a "spook comedy" by assuring that the spectator "need not worry about a spotlight failing or ghosts disappearing at the right time" (259). This was the one scene, however, in which Jacobsohn felt that Jessner depended too much on the power of speech alone. The actors were unable to "chisel out the words in such a way that the tents, the situation, and the future of both camps would appear before our eyes" (262).

Indeed, Jessner's success was not unqualified. Both Scheffauer and Michel felt that the coronation scene was inappropriately "Oriental"; and Michel damned the "expressionist stylization" of the battle scene, with its half-naked Richard, as "an unprecedented rape of Shakespeare's text" (266). Jacobsohn, however, simply puzzled over the enigma

that this Kortner was not thoroughly embarrassed at setting up a billboard monster, at snarling through his teeth, at shooting devilish looks and laughing diabolically – and that he in spite of this, in every word and characteristic, is our brother and fellow-sufferer. The technical execution is more easily explainable than the artistic-human effect. (263)

In the uncanny human appeal of both its breakneck pace and its caricature stylization, Jessner's *Richard III* brought to the mind of more than one critic the ideas of commedia and farce. For Ihering, Jessner was "the essential comedian when at the end of the production he [made] Richard into a red devil" (64). Here, of course, Ihering is not thinking of the comedic in terms of laughter, although Polgar felt that Jessner had taken the principles of conciseness and precision to laughable excess. In the scene where Richard woos Lady Anne, for instance, the symmetrical positioning of pallbearers at the upstage wall with their backs to the audience for several minutes "made it appear as though they were relieving themselves" (69). What Ihering is getting at, rather, is the kind of comedic excess or exaggeration which captures the essence of character and situation.

In Kortner's acting in particular, the broadness of stylization in movement and speech appears to have grown out of the same strategy of typification developed in the antics of such medieval theatrical figures as the Vice. Some critics have argued that Shakespeare's Richard is indeed a version of the medieval Vice.[63] But for Jacobsohn, Kortner's Richard was "the latest in the line of primitive farceurs, of irrepressible stage charmers" (264). An important aspect of that charm is the unique kind of vulnerability such overreaching figures possess. When they finally get their just deserts, we somehow sympathize with them while simultaneously applauding their punishment. We are attracted to the Vice because he is so skillful at his craft; yet he moves our pity at some level because he seems a prisoner of his type, with no choice but to act out the idea which he embodies. As Kerr put it, this Richard was "no mere monster, but an impassioned creature come too short, cut off from greatness; not only a cynical manipulator, but a sacrificial animal" (259). Jacobsohn also felt a poignancy in Kortner's emblematic acting of the will-to-power idea (263). This kind of performance employs the techniques of caricature as a way of getting at the spiritual core of human nature; it operates on an allegorical level of significance. Though it is non-representational and overtly conceptional, it never allows the spectator to distance himself completely. The ideas of human nature it enacts are broad enough to encompass everyone, to some degree, in the community of self-recognition. Kortner's Richard, as the emblem of unchecked self-assertion, arguably touched a basic human fantasy.

On the other hand, allegorical art never allows the spectator to get fully involved emotionally. Jessner's staircase provided an allegorical setting. On its steps every movement and gesture were magnified in order to focus the production's central idea ever more sharply. One result of this emphasis on idea was that humanity itself became more of an idea than an experience. As Polgar put it,

> the achievement of such directing is purity; rigor; sharpening of every dramatic line . . .; transparency; spareness; economy of time and means. What is lost is the Shakespearian fullness, roundness and variety; warmth; color; the exciting oscillation and flow of organic life; all magic of the ordinary theatre . . . everything was very beautiful and fascinating but also very cold and abstract. (69)

Jessner's staircase, unlike the thrust stage, didn't bring the central character experientially closer to the audience; rather it revealed that character in three-dimensional analysis. Believing that mimetic impersonation could reveal only psychology, not the soul, Jessner directed his actors to play the allegorical idea of character in order to lay bare the spiritual level of character.

In such ways, late Expressionist performance appears to have pulled back from the emotional directness of early Expressionist Schrei acting. This was not a repudiation of ecstatic performance as much as it was an effort to perceive it abstractly, with an attitude that anticipated a new spirit of "objectivity" that would characterize German cultural production in the mid twenties. Notwithstanding its emblematic excesses, Jessner's staircase directing in *Richard III*, in its visually analytical attitude, marks an early point of transition between Expressionism and the rise of New Objectivity aesthetics.[64] His three-dimensional strategy for tempering experience with comprehension, emotionalism with rationality – like Fehling's use of actors as kinetic scenery – found a more developed parallel a few years later in Fritz Lang's film *Metropolis*. Jessner moved his actors up and down the staircase to give the audience a variety of angles – points of view – by which they could understand the characters' progressions or regressions. In *Metropolis*, Lang, with the freedom of radical camera angles and editing, moved his *audience* up, down and around his central characters and mass ensemble. The progression of the relationships of these characters could thus be studied in purely visual, geometric terms.

Jessner's "idea directing" and the emblematic acting it produced, however, were not *primarily* exercises in monumental abstractionism, like Lang's film. As Rühle notes,

Reinhardt had always staged his productions for a festive evening in the theatre. Jessner had a new, political idea of theatre . . . For Jessner, the age of theatre as enchantment was past. He argued that the cinema had liberated the theatre from enchantment. He staged a "program," he attempted a new aesthetic which was developed out of spiritual intentions. "The theatre," [Jessner argued], "has become an object of conflict for all parties and social classes."[65]

Though emblematic performance was shaped by a monumental aesthetic in *Richard III*, it also proceeded from Jessner's idea of political conflict first expressed in his Berlin staging of Schiller's *Wilhelm Tell*. This production, which Jessner called "a cry for freedom," catapulted him into the limelight as the leading Expressionist director of the day. However, Rühle draws a valuable distinction between the theatrical features of the Expressionist movement in Berlin and Jessner's personal expressiveness [*Expressivität*]. Jessner, he argues, was too old and too laden with a tragic sensibility to have come of age with the Expressionist generation and its vision of world renewal. Yet he shared the Expressionist view of political conflict, typified in the early plays of Toller, as an essentially spiritual matter. As Rühle put it, "he was fascinated by political conflict which could intensify itself to the level of the symbolic."[66]

The basis of his spiritual expressiveness, however, was an austere, disciplined formalism, not passionate, visionary formlessness. He stressed that his own style of directing had "nothing in common with that lawlessness which proclaims itself as the Expressionist mode of speech."[67] He sought rather to express "the hypnotic world of the inner self" by essentializing word and gesture in a highly regulated abstractionist aesthetic. But the application of this aesthetic to the political themes of *Wilhelm Tell* produced shocking results, both for the director and actors, and for their audience. As Francis Servaes had written in response to a 1918 Volksbühne staging of the play, "No piece of a modern writer has articulated with such inflammatory force the contemporary mood."[68] Indeed, no production better illustrated that mood, and its effect on late Expressionist performance, than Jessner's *Tell*.

Kortner, who played the villain oppressor, Gessler, describes the political context as follows:

> We of the theatre were shocked and outraged when Karl Liebknecht and Rosa Luxemburg were murdered and thrown into the Landwehr Canal. The murderers were officers of the radical right. We theatre people, with few exceptions, were against the murderers. But had radical right-wing officers been murdered, we would certainly have been in favor of the murderers. We began thus to take cognizance of political murder and to adjust our consciences to the application of two standards: for assassinations as a symbol of our political persuasion, and against them in practice. We knew so little at that time, we beginners in this struggle to the death. The theatre comported itself toward the left as the right-wing clandestinely prepared its conquest. Out of this chaotic upheaval grew Jessner's staging of *Wilhelm Tell* . . . In the course of the [première] evening, Tell, the recluse, the ingenuous one, became the celebrated political assassin. (351–52)

It appears, however, that Jessner and his company were not as yet in touch with the grim realities behind this irony. Indeed, such was the political isolation of the actors of the Berlin Expressionist theatre community that, for example, when Kortner and Ernst Deutsch found themselves caught in the cross-fire of streetfighting during the Kapp Putsch attempt just three months after the première of Jessner's *Tell*,

> Deutsch pulled his coat-collar up high as a way of protecting himself. In spite of the danger and my fear, I had to laugh. Then we threw ourselves, along with others passing by, into the mud in the street. There I laughed still more because Deutsch was wearing a new coat. Finally he laughed with me. We didn't believe in a life-threatening danger, not there on the ground and not even later. We didn't really know who was shooting at whom. Political disputes were not yet of concern to me at that time, much less to Deutsch. And ones like this, which degenerated into shootouts, appeared to

play themselves out completely outside the circle of our lives. In this instance we were physically incorporated in such a ludicrous, Chaplinesque way, it was as though we had stumbled unawares into a film shooting. Street battles, threatening masses, shooting soldiers are only scenes for us who work in theatre and film. (363–64)

Along with political *naïvete*, an atmosphere of political extremism also affected the actors of late Expressionist performance in Berlin. As Kortner observed of the recently discharged soldier whom he had retained as a valet, "he was a refractory radical. Whether he was left-wing or right, he didn't yet know" (365). This attitude of indiscriminate activism had grown in Berlin since the armistice.[69] It appears to have been the basis of the opening night uproar over Jessner's *Wilhelm Tell*. Virtually every critic present at the première either declined to discuss the audience disturbances at all or passed them off as merely aesthetic reactions of offended sensibility. However, the deepest nerve which the production struck was, in fact, a political one. Or, stated from another perspective, Jessner's *Tell* illustrates how questions of aesthetic taste, including those raised by Expressionist theatrical performance, had become politicized by 1919 in Berlin.

Elements of the radical left and the radical right were both represented at the première of *Tell*, and they began to skirmish verbally from the moment the lights came up. Instead of the traditional realistic setting of Swiss Alpine grandeur, the audience beheld Emil Pirchan's abstractionist assault on those expectations. Placed upstage at a quarter-turned angle, the set was a permanent framework of stairs, bridges, and ramps in grey and green hues, backed by dark side curtains and an abstract mountain range on a white cyclorama. In the open playing space immediately downstage a variety of different locales were suggested through the use of simple movable abstract set pieces. This method of staging is now commonplace, but on that evening it provoked audible murmurs of protest from a reactionary faction in the audience. As Paul Fechter recalled the developing response,

There was already in the first act, during a pause, a *sotto-voce* discussion in one of the upper galleries. When the hut scene began with Friesshardt and Leuthold keeping watch in shining green robes at the foot of the flagpole, a call from above rang out: "Caricatures!" The audience energetically demanded quiet and got it. The play continued undisturbed, but at the conclusion of almost every scene a soft struggle between hissing and applause sprang up.[70]

By the time Kortner arrived at the theatre – his entrance as Gessler was near the end of the third act – "the noise of protest in the auditorium, and of the actors on stage struggling against it by roaring out their text more and more wildly, made a conversation impossible." The "conversation" to which he here refers amounted to a set of farcical exchanges between a panic-stricken Jessner, shouting orders for the fall of the curtain and the cancellation of the performance, and one Albert Florath, his stage manager, who had gotten tipsy earlier that evening and was equally determined that the performance should go forth at all costs. Jessner advised Kortner not to bother getting into costume. Florath issued the opposite order, after which, "like a watchful herd-hound," he chased other actors who were attempting to abandon the stage back out again. Meanwhile, "the noise became as loud as a hurricane" (Kortner, 353). Having finally gotten the curtain down, Jessner tried to persuade Kortner to abandon the performance by inviting him to observe the uproar in the audience through the curtain's peephole. As Kortner, Jessner, and Florath vied for turns at the peephole, they observed

a show more wild and fantastic than any I have ever again experienced. Siegfried Jacobsohn, the publisher and theatre critic of the journal *Die Weltbühne* (until 1918 *Schaubühne*) stood on his seat in the orchestra and had a crescendoing argument with the wild, malicious faction in the gallery. This group simultaneously launched forth into a screaming insult-orgy with other gallery patrons who were enthusiastic about the performance. The fortissimo, howling exchange of opinions raged from gallery to gallery, down to the orchestra and back again, to and fro in all directions. Julius Bab also jumped on his seat and shouted along. [Alfred] Kerr held his ears shut while the critic of a right-wing newspaper screamed at him. Whoever of us was lord of the peephole at the moment reported in the dramatic cadences of a sports broadcaster at the microphone. All about us the half circle of the curious grew ever larger: actors, stagehands, dramaturges, lighting technicians, wardrobe workers . . . Florath had slipped away and on his own authority had the curtain raised. The unexpectedness of this coup produced a moment of stillness. The audience on the stage, surprised by the sudden rising of the curtain, scattered apart and, to the amusement of the auditorium audience, fled in all directions from the stage.[71]

Of course, none of the above-named critics mentioned anything in their reviews about their own involvement in the disturbance. Kerr only remarked discreetly that he did not stay until the end of the performance. He did, however, serve notice to any among his readership that may have sympathized with the protesters that Jessner's *Wilhelm Tell* marked the emergence of a new "important" theatre which "you cannot shout down."[72] Fechter issued a similar appeal to his readers to "whistle afterwards all you wish, but during the performance behave yourselves, at least halfway, as Europeans" (195). Jacobsohn, after praising the production for allowing one to "suddenly hope again," observed that "now if we only had an audience instead of rabble-rousing racketeers, we could have a German theatre, in spite of the sad course of world events."[73]

In these remarks one senses a reluctance to acknowledge the *Wilhelm Tell* protests as something more than mere aesthetic dissatisfaction. Yet, as Günther Rühle observes, "the tumults during the performance were the accompanying noise of change; they suggested the political forces with which the Intendant Jessner had to reckon."[74] The obvious implication – and the reason that I have chosen to describe this première-evening audience disruption in detail – is that the actors also had to reckon with these political forces. Clearly, the ugly facts of post-armistice political life in Berlin were more formidable than Jessner had ever dreamed of as a response to his "cry of freedom." Kortner, admittedly writing with the wisdom of hindsight, claims to have had no doubt about the motives of the disrupters:

I believe they were a voluntary vanguard of self-inciting vandals, the first pack of hounds which were let loose on those who think and behave differently, on "foreigners." The Brown Beast, in the sheepskin of the indignant theatre patron, had made his entrance. (358)

When Albert Bassermann, walking down Pirchan's abstract ravine setting of the assassination scene (IV, iii), began Tell's famous monologue "Through this pass must he come," Paul Fechter recalled scattered mocking laughter and someone calling out "Idiocy!" from the audience (194). Kortner however – who, like Jessner and Bassermann, was a Jew – remembers a cry of "Jewish swindle!", which swelled up into a choral chant and then erupted into the kind of full-blown altercation described above (359).

Yet apparently the protests which intimidated the director had precisely the opposite effect on his principal actors, Bassermann and Kortner. As he listened backstage to the noise in the audience, having just arrived at the theatre, says Kortner, "I felt the gamecock rousing up in me" (353). When he later returned to the wings for his entrance as Gessler, his costume and make-up were a caricature of repressive authority:

The completely unraveled Jessner looked at me wide-eyed: "When people see you that will be the last straw."[75] That was a reference to my drastic costume and my face painted rage-red. I had hung practically every branch of the military somewhere on my Gessler. Medals dangled on him like a presentiment of Göring. "At least take the medals off," exclaimed Jessner, who was always prepared to compromise, even when he wasn't desperate. I held my hands over the medals protectively. Jessner cried out something else, which was drowned out by the trumpet signals which evoked memories of the motor horn on the former Kaiser's auto. These trumpet signals touched off an ear-splitting scandal with those who were loyal to the exiled Kaiser. Counter-demonstrations ensued. Exceedingly provoked, excited by all possible passions, fully armed, medal-decorated, cracking my riding whip, I raged onto the stage roaring "Drive them apart!" (355–56)

In his role as emblem of repressive authority, Kortner apparently played Gessler in this moment not to the on-stage crowd but to the unruly real-life mob in the audience. He strode to the edge of the ramp repeatedly bellowing his entrance line "Drive them apart!" and cracking his whip, until the protesters finally quieted down. Bassermann then played the apple-shooting scene with such emotional truth that the production was again halted, this time by a long storm of applause (356–57).

   The triumph was short-lived, however, as the opposition renewed its disruptive activities more vehemently than ever. Bassermann, whose voice had become grizzled with advancing age, at first abandoned the stage, then stormed back on with the command "Throw these hired louts out!" ringing forth in strong, clear tones from his lips (357–58). Fechter adds that on his crowd-shocking re-entrance, he carried with him Tell's triumphant cross-bow (195). At this point the police arrived, ushered the hecklers away, and the performance resumed without further disturbance. Bassermann left the stage to the sound of thunderous applause and bravos, but the victory for him was different from that supposed by the audience. As Kortner recalls,

Bassermann came to me, who had witnessed, backstage, his manly protestation in front of the curtain. He was happy. Not, as I presumed, however, about his admirable demeanor, but over the sound of the voice with which he had projected the words into the audience. "Did you hear how clear my voice was," said the one who was always hoarse. "That's what did it, nothing else!" In the highest indignation he had still been attentive to the sound of his voice. That's how we are! (358)

It would appear, then, both from the reviews and from Kortner's backstage account of the première of *Wilhelm Tell*, that factors apart from Jessner's emblematic idea directing – and quite beyond his control – affected the acting of the piece. Yet even the direction itself seemed to flirt with chaos by employing, or tolerating, a variety of distinct performance methods. Fechter complained about a lack of stylistic unity in Jessner's staging, which he felt wavered "between a monumental *Tell* and an adventurous [*bewegt*] one" (196). The production "embraced acting performances from the collected styles of thirty years: Naturalism, Hoftheater, Ekstase, everything" (195– 96). Jacobsohn described the utterances of the three boy actors in the play's lyrical prelude as "solemn declamation," while their movements were "stiffly hieratic" (192). Alongside of this, Bassermann's realistic playing of Tell was "simple, almost childlike, guileless." Yet in a given moment, such as the assassination scene, he could be "fearsome . . . full of fire and manly rage . . ." Kortner's Gessler, however, "in red coat, sinister, with hard-bitten face, is entirely a devil, a sharp-taloned vampire of tyranny."[76] Not one sentence, Jacobsohn recalls, "hissed out of the toad's stomach of this fairy-tale figure which did not flicker about with sulphurous flames. It is really worth it to see how the riding whip held in the hand becomes, in the fist, a daggerknife, a sword, a scourge" (192).

But what unified the work of the Naturalistic "Brahm-actor," Bassermann, with that of the "new actor," Kortner, was the emblematic significance which each actor, in his respective style, brought to the idea he embodied. Bassermann's Tell, dressed in white and bathed in white light, presented a figure which "took on something of the mythical," a Tell who was "more of a legend than a Schillerian hero" (Falk, 197). Indeed, such was the allegorical power of both Bassermann's and Kortner's performance that "Leopold Jessner and his actors were celebrated as though, on this memorable evening for the first time, the [Nationalist] danger so unmistakably articulated had conclusively been overcome by us" (Kortner, 359). For the audience, any problem of stylistic disunity was subsumed by the production's powerful emblematic unity.

As Julius Bab saw it, the work of Jessner represented the point of greatest possible development for stage Expressionism; beyond this limit it ceased to have integrity and degenerated into unsuccessful stylizations.[77] Günther Rühle has argued that the modal purity with which Expressionist performance evolved in the provinces had depended primarily on the stability of the German Idealist tradition in those regions. In Berlin, by contrast, that tradition had been quickly eroded after 1918 by the pace of political and cultural change. Idealistic Expressionism, Rühle explains,

> remained foreign to Berlin. Criticisms against the pieces which it presented were much more harsh than in the provinces. It was not accepted as a style, nor as a phenomenon of expression, nor for its themes. What counted was the great acting performances which bound themselves to it.[78]

However, actors such as Kortner became unwilling to bind themselves indefinitely and unconditionally to Expressionist stylization. Jessner had become so taken with the staircase setting, for example, that he insisted on using it in production after production. Kortner drew the line at Jessner's staging of *Macbeth* (1922, Staatliches Schauspielhaus, Berlin), or rather, he drew the line after it had failed:

> *The Marquis of Keith* and *Richard* had both become parade pieces of Expressionist theatre. Shakespeare's *Macbeth* is of another kind. I realized that this mist-shrouded piece wanted no steps, no harsh lighting, no sharp outlines. But Jessner would not relinquish the staircase. It was to express his Weltanschauung, he had explained in an interview; therefore he had to stand by it, and I had to clamber up over it. Jessner, offended by rumors that I had influenced his directing, barricaded himself against me. We merely copied ourselves – and we failed. (370)

The interview to which Kortner refers was probably the one published in the periodical *Die Szene* in 1928, where Jessner had described the staircase setting as the primary tool in his "Thematic Theatre" [*das motivische Theater*]. On this occasion, according to Günther Rühle, Jessner in fact had cautioned critics against regarding the staircase as merely a stylistic signature. Rather, it was simply the most effective setting for playing the "mythic events" which comprise the "idea" of a play.[79] Though the critics appreciated the fact that Jessner varied the size of the staircase from production to production, they nonetheless came to regard its consistent use after *Richard III* as more a matter of style than substance. Alfred Kerr agreed with Kortner's charge that the staircase in *Macbeth* was a mistake:

Jessner no longer has a need for steps as a distinctive characteristic. To be sure these stairs have shrunk . . . but still [they] become at times a hindrance, an interruption of the emotion; a withdrawal from the world of the soul to the world of the stage.[80]

Even a critic who liked the staircase in *Macbeth*, such as Ludwig Sternaux, saw its use a stylistic inevitability: "A *Macbeth* by Jessner. Therefore the stairs are not missing."[81] For Kerr, the staircase had become a cliché of Expressionist staging in general a year before Jessner's *Macbeth*. Fehling's *Masse Mensch*, he quipped, featured "the steps of the Expressionists, of course. Their symbolic effect is false."[82]

Kortner, perhaps unfairly, attributes Jessner's insistence on the staircase setting to the stubbornness of wounded pride. However, it appears that this striking design feature and the abstractionist approach to Expressionist staging it typified eventually became ends in themselves. For the Expressionist actor, the consequence of this was that ecstatic individualism lost the battle with abstractionist ensemble de-personalization. In this regard, Jessner's work with actors at this time became the fulfillment of Gordon Craig's "Über-marionette" theory. In his Moscow Art Theatre production of *Hamlet*, according to Edward Braun, Craig had sought to present the play as "a 'monodrama', with all the action viewed through Hamlet's eyes, ideally with Hamlet himself on stage throughout." His abstractionist approach, as might be expected, discounted the individual contributions of Stanislavsky's actors and their psychological approach to performance. In the designs, however, Craig forged emblems of "the idea of this play," which he saw as "the struggle between spirit and material – the impossibility of their union, the isolation of spirit in material". The opening court scene (Act I, Scene 2), for example, was costumed so that the individual figures of Hamlet, Claudius, Gertrude and their retinue would "merge into one generalized background of gold . . . and [could not] be perceived to have individual faces." As one of the actresses in the scene recalls, the actors were arranged on platforms of varying levels so as to give "the impression of a monolithic golden pyramid," an emblem of the feudal hierarchy.[83]

Here the scenographic generation of emblem would have completely subsumed the actors and obviated their work had not Stanislavsky finally intervened. Similarly, by 1922, Jessner's enthusiasm for the scenic element of production – epitomized in the staircase setting

– threatened to reduce the art of the actor to empty stylization. This in turn compromised the whole emblematic enterprise of presenting the "idea" of the play by depriving that presentation of its vital element – the actor's personal commitment. Just as the acting of the Moscow Art Theatre *Hamlet*, in its insistent realism, inevitably clashed with the abstractionism of the other production elements, so the depersonalized abstractionist acting of the late Expressionist theatre finally exhausted the patience of its actors.

Expressionist acting had never been based on the psychology of personality. But from Hasenclever's Son to Toller's Friedrich, the playing of the central figure in Expressionist productions had always involved the ecstatic creation of a human character. As Friedrich in Martin's production of *Die Wandlung*, Kortner had played a person of great vulnerability, passion and spiritual vision. The Expressionist "ecstatifying" of these traditional "Liebhaber" qualities, as I noted earlier, was pioneered in Ernst Deutsch's portrayal of the Son. However, by 1920, Deutsch's Cashier in the film version of *Von morgens bis mitternachts* was not so much an alienated bank clerk as he was a two-dimensional, rhetorical figure of Alienation itself. Similarly, in Jessner's productions of *Wilhelm Tell* and *Richard III*, Kortner played not a man but a monstrous idea. But during the 1922 Jessner staging of *Macbeth*, Kortner recalls,

I, the one who had always stormed forward with broad blinders, suddenly held myself in. It gradually dawned on me that what Expressionism did away with was indispensable in *Macbeth*; that behind the sentences of this piece lay things in twilight, which had to be grasped . . . I learned much at that time through our failure. I had to pull back, to retrieve, if I wanted to make use of the victory which my recognition had won over my acting methods. Speech cannot exist for itself alone. As it was for the ideas of the author, so, through re-creation on the stage, must speech again become supplementary expression for the actor. (370–71)

This would appear to be Kortner's version of Hamlet's "suit the action to the word and the word to the action." Perhaps it was also his way of justifying his personal failure to perform up to expectation. Nonetheless, this statement reveals the actor, not the Expressionist, as the guiding spirit in his work. For Kortner, the issue of staircase acting was a matter of facilitating the performance, as much as clarifying the idea, of the text. In *Richard III*, the steps were an appropriate metaphor for the director's production idea and a useful tool for the actor attempting to embody that idea. The production process here appears to have been much more actor-sensitive than it was for *Macbeth*. Before Jessner's Expressionism had been reduced to a style it apparently had had great inspirational power for his actors. Kortner recalls an "incessant rehearsal" process for *Richard III* which often continued all night long in his apartment, after regular rehearsal hours. But without such a full commitment to Jessner's style, Kortner's *Macbeth* was plagued by "a certain monotony" and lack of vocal precision: "in softness too soft, in loudness too loud; thus many words were lost for the sake of gestures" (Sternaux, 414). Kortner performed "a role without any extension into a nature." Hence, "the more his voice vaulted in the high ranges, the more the form lost its basis. A rabid temperament foamed so excessively that all contours were blurred beyond recognition."[84] Because "one sees Kortner in terms of the ear," Herbert Ihering remarked, "and because his speech yesterday was unsuggestive, he remained dull of facial expression as well. A verbally and physically unexciting, uncertain performance."[85]

Ironically, the actor whose career had been launched, and who had won so much critical acclaim, on the Expressionist stage attributed his success to the tradition of realism in which he had trained:

No protagonist of Jessner's theatre would have been able to survive the Berlin press – and a demanding public who were accustomed to the Brahm-Reinhardt performances – if this actor were not able, in spite of the Expressionist flatness of trajectory, to allow the intonations of human intimacy and the revelations of ordinary physicality to resonate. That we were in a position to do so, we thank Brahm and Reinhardt; that this realism, albeit intensified to a furioso level, survived, was the merit of Leopold Jessner. His style, under the current circumstances, was short-lived. Significantly, he could only use for his stylized productions the actors who came from Realism. The ones who "only speak," the "declamation fellows" with dagger looks and stage-center voices, he pushed away. (53–4)

Yet, it is even more ironic that the press would not tolerate on the Expressionist stage the kind of realistic strategy of pulling back with which Kortner approached *Macbeth*. By this time, Expressionist performance, especially in Jessner's productions, had become conventional. The critics apparently were expecting an "Expressionist" *Macbeth*, à la Jessner. What they got was the performance of an erstwhile Expressionist actor in transition. Thus it was not only the politics of the inchoate Weimar Republic that cut across Jessner's emblematic, monumental art, but also the yearning of his principal actor to perform with psychological veracity rather than programmatic discipline.

The motto of provincial Expressionist directors such as Richard Weichert had been "freedom from Berlin." As Rühle observes, "freedom from Berlin, between 1917 and 1919, meant freedom from Reinhardt." Moreover, in spite of their critical success the Das junge Deutschland productions – with which Reinhardt was only briefly involved as a director – always remained overshadowed by the "Reinhardt art of detail." Berlin Realism, explains Rühle, "remained the basis of Berlin theatre during the entire Republican era. Even Karl-Heinz Martin adapted himself to it when he took Reinhardt's place [directing at the Deutsches Theater and Großes Schauspielhaus in 1920], though he still comported himself expressively from time to time."[86]

Reinhardt's "realism" was a matter of actor-centered directing, not a style of staging which he imposed indiscriminately on every production. His staging method was an eclectic one which allowed the script to suggest an appropriate production style. In the same way, Reinhardt encouraged actors to bring their own unique expressive resources to whatever style the play required. It is this actor-centered "realism" to which Kortner refers above. During his Expressionist years, the Reinhardt tradition was both Kortner's touchstone of artistic integrity and his chief strategy for professional survival. He was never quite able to turn his back on this tradition, just as he could not ignore the developing contemporary political situation and its disturbing anti-Semitic tone. Along with his sense of artistic integrity, it was a growing sense of political urgency which finally drew him away from Expressionist stylization in search of a more socially effective application of his performing talent.

Jessner's *Richard III* opened at the Staatstheater on 5 November 1920. During the run of the production, Kortner began to experience racial antipathy from some of the Staatstheater employees. In one case, the newly elected Reichspräsident Ebert had been denied access to the Kaiser's box by an attendant who was a loyalist. Kortner's refusal to perform unless the president was seated in the Kaiser's box brought about the desired result, but "the incident was later exploited as an instance of Jewish domination." Some of the theatrical staff, in turn, were suspected of membership in the Sturmabteilung ["Stormtroopers," "Brownshirts," or simply, the

"S.A."]; and two of the actors were already active in the National Socialist German Worker's Party ["N.S.D.A.P."]. This situation, along with the increasing appearance of *Mein Kampf* in the bookstores, says Kortner, led him to accept eagerly the role of Czar Paul in Alfred Neumann's *Der Patriot* at the Lessing-Theater. His intention was to portray a despot as such a negative example that it would make "a small contribution to the anti-Hitler movement" (382).

Indeed, the political climate was forcing other Expressionist actors to consider their art as a polemical weapon which had to be aimed in one direction or the other. While Kortner was playing a despot in *Der Patriot*, Werner Krauss was being celebrated for his work in the nationalist box office hit, *Gneisenau*. Krauss went on to win favor during the Nazi era for his anti-Semitic character acting.[87] As Jessner came under increasing right-wing attack, according to Kortner, Krauss left the Staatstheater while Kortner returned to show solidarity with the beleaguered director. As a result, "it was declared in the Prussian provincial diet that the Staatstheater was becoming 'Jewified' through my influence" (383).

Jessner, however, apparently tried to appease his critics on the right with his 1923 re-staging of *Wilhelm Tell*. Kortner, who did not appear in this production, later characterized it "as an obeisance to the increasing reactionary element in cultural life." For example, Jessner still used the staircase setting but he covered the steps with grass-like carpeting to give them more of a realistic mountain hillside look.[88] Attinghausen's line "Embrace the fatherland, embrace the beloved," which had been struck out in the 1919 staging, was not only restored, but the actor playing Attinghausen was placed on a pedestal in full spotlight for the line. The revolutionary theme of the piece this time was not the struggle against oppression in general but simply against a foreign army of occupation in the land. "Gessler," says Kortner, "was no longer the tormentor of the farmers, but only the brutal deputy of a foreign military power. The farmers had become patriots" (361).

The distinction which Kortner draws here illustrates the difference between emblematic acting of the idea of oppression and realistic portrayal of a character in a narrative about oppression. In the former, Kortner used the technique of caricature to confront the audience directly with the idea of the will to power, challenging them to contemplate it in terms of the chaotic socio-political situation in which they all were inescapably involved. The latter approach to the character permitted the audience to distance itself from that challenge by limiting Gessler to the role of "bad guy" in the narrative. The former approach is in the democratic spirit of self-criticism; the latter serves nicely the scapegoating spirit of nationalism. Indeed, so powerfully was Jessner's nationalist interpretation of *Wilhelm Tell* conveyed in the 1923 restaging that at the end of the première performance the audience rose to its feet singing "Deutschland, Deutschland" (Kortner, 362).

Jessner may have been a political ostrich, as Kortner alleges. But his ability to utilize the resources of the theatre to stimulate a political response in his audience was unique among Expressionist directors. However, the inability of the Expressionist theatre to develop an ultimately effective political discourse revealed the inadequacy of its vague, spiritualized political activism. Jessner, as I noted earlier, shared that spiritual view of politics. While Brecht rejected this view, he very much appreciated the political value of Jessner's emblematic directing, with its power to turn the actor into a captivating flesh and blood *idea*. One of Brecht's great contributions was to develop the art of the dramatized political parable into a theatre of dialectics. Only in this way, he argued, could performance become the effective agent of social change which the Expressionists had hoped it would be. In place of Expressionism's hortatory, rhetorical idea of activist empowerment, Brecht proposed an analytical, politicized grammar of performance applied not to achieving a final utopian vision but to developing a day-to-day critical method for understanding and coming to terms with the social realities of ideological struggle.

The principal directors of Berlin stage Expressionism, Jessner, Fehling, Martin – together with such significant figures of the provincial Expressionist theatre as Schreyer and Weichert – were auteurs. For these directors, the Expressionist actor appears to have functioned essentially as an operative. There is scant record, aside from Kortner's memoir, of how the actors themselves felt about what it was that the directors, as well as the theorists and the critics, expected them to accomplish. Yet all were bound up, as I suggested earlier, in a new theatrical community constituted by the fundamental assumption that prepared the way for the Weimar Republic: namely, that everything – politics, aesthetics, every cultural institution – was open to question. Everything, in short, became politicized. By 1922, this process of cultural re-evaluation had outstripped the emblematic theatre of late Expressionism. Though his personal philosophy may have tended to socialism, a director like Jessner was an aesthetic formalist in his theatrical work. His emblematic approach addressed politics in a vaguely spiritual way which did not interfere with his stylistic goals. In the 1919 *Wilhelm Tell* particularly, Jessner challenged the *status quo* without fully realizing the political implications of that challenge or the intensity of the response it would generate. The actors, like Deutsch and Kortner on that morning they stumbled into the Kapp Putsch streetfighting, were simply caught in the cross-fire.

Concluding observations

THE NATURE OF EXPRESSIONIST PERFORMANCE

At the beginning of this study I argued that theatrical Expressionism was shaped by a newly historical consciousness in German society. This awareness was one of historical crisis, broadly understood as the matrix of tensions and pressures experienced by a people as they attempt to keep pace with, or as they resist, rapid and substantial cultural change. This was the German situation from the turn of the century through World War I; and, of course, it continued throughout the Weimar era until the advent of the Nazi monolith quelled all debate. In the first instance, however, the crisis in Germany was that of its relatively late consolidation into nationhood and emergence as a modern state. The problem, as I noted, was that German society had developed much more rapidly in economic and technological terms than it had politically and culturally in the time between the Prussian victory in 1870 and the outbreak of world war forty-four years later. In attempting to mediate this discrepancy, the artistic avant-garde in Germany drew markedly upon international aesthetic ideas and influences as it critiqued contemporary German culture. The German avant-garde's initial form of cultural resistance was to reject the strictures of traditional German values and nationalist identity in favor of assuming an internationalist cultural posture. Hence, what Expressionism first sought to address was the general crisis of Modernism itself. This was basically the subject, for example, of Sorge's *Der Bettler*, one of the earliest Expressionist plays.

The writings of Marx, Nietzsche, and Freud; the plays of Strindberg, Wedekind, Kaiser and Sorge; the paintings of the Fauves, Kokoschka, Kandinsky – these are but a few representatives of the new era whose work revealed economics, philosophy, psychology, and the arts to be intercultural sites of crisis. As it impacted traditional German culture through the German avant-garde, however, international Modernism clarified and amplified philosophical, economic, and sociological crises specific to Germany as well. Within a year or two of each other, Kornfeld's *Die Verführung* (1913) dramatized the impact of vitalist philosophy on traditional ideas of the German family and family relationships, Kaiser's *Von morgens bis mitternachts* (1912) depicted the fragmentation of German middle-class identity in the context of capitalist alienation, and Hasenclever's *Der Sohn* (1913) savagely critiqued Wilhelmine patriarchy and the social relevance of traditional German education. After the outbreak of war, Toller's *Die Wandlung* was but one expression of how German nationalism had become a crisis for the whole society. Along with *Die Wandlung*, other Expressionist plays, such as Reinhard Goering's *Seeschlacht* [*Naval Encounter*, 1917] and Fritz von Unruh's *Ein Geschlecht* [*One Race*, 1918], attempted to enact directly the horror of the war experience itself.[1]

In the revolutionary period immediately following the armistice, the crisis of reordering a devastated society with its attendant dangers of political extremism inspired Jessner's emblematic stagings of Shakespeare and Schiller. This in turn precipitated a vehement aesthetic controversy in regard to the relationship between theatre production style, the dramatic canon as bastion of traditional culture, and politics. The sweeping administrative changes in government and cultural institutions alike wrought by the new moderately left-wing Republic were not the least sites of contention, prompting reactionary stirrings and fueling anti-Semitic attitudes which erupted early on in the Kapp Putsch of 1920.[2]

These were some of the principal cultural crises which theatrical Expressionism sought to negotiate performatively. Having considered three of the most distinct performance strategies in pursuit of this goal, I should now like to conclude by offering an argument for synthesizing them in a general theory of the Expressionist "performance of cultural crisis." For this purpose, I find very helpful the work of Jean Alter in a recent study entitled *A Sociosemiotic Theory of Theatre* (1990). In non-realistic kinds of theatre, actors, observes Alter,

are needed to release the meaning of symbolic stage signs that subvert iconicity: slabs manage to stand for beds or chairs only when actors lie or sit on them . . . gestures can produce signs out of nothing . . . [Thus,] actors on the stage not only produce themselves as signs but also, as actor/signs, produce or modify other signs around them.[3]

Here Alter draws upon the principles of "sign-transformability" and "transcodification" which I discussed briefly in Chapter Five. The agency of the actor in mobilizing these semiotic functions is particularly evident in all three modes of Expressionist performance identified in the present study. Going well beyond naturalistic vivification of a stage environment, the Expressionist actor infused the spare, symbolic settings in which he or she performed with a high degree of energy to which theorists gave the name "Ekstase." Jessner's staircase, for example, or Weichert's cone of light, were not only concretized as stage signs but amplified as well by the actors.

However, what Alter says of theatrical performance in general — that it fulfills both a referential and a "performant" function — is especially relevant to Expressionist acting. "Reference" in acting, of course, is the familiar process of conveying information from the stage about the relationship between the real world of the audience and the dramatic world being presented in the production. By contrast, the "performant" function simply satisfies "our natural desire to achieve or witness something extraordinary." Performances, in this sense, are well illustrated in sporting events or the circus. They

are not communicated with signs; they are experienced directly; they fall outside the operations of semiosis. However . . . the performant function coexists with the referential function, and interacts with it . . .

Because of this duality, moreover, audience attention is actually bifurcated in such a way that it "constantly moves from the stage, which we perceive to be real, to the story space, which we concretize in our mind."[4]

Whether the performant function generally "falls outside the operations of semiosis," in Expressionist performance specifically, quite to the contrary, it constitutes the most central field of semiotic activity. The distinction between reference and performance, in fact, particularly illuminates Expressionist acting because the performant function is so markedly foregrounded in the productions, at least as they were reported in the reviews. Indeed, the rhetoric of critics in describing actors like Kortner, Krauss, Deutsch, and Straub on the Expressionist stage often stressed the sheer performative impact more than the referential truth of their characterizations. Superlatives that described Kortner's shattering voice, Krauss's gestural power, Deutsch's explosive nervous energy, Straub's wild passion, and so forth, called attention to the skills of these performers as athletic phenomena in themselves, aside from their metaphorical aptness to the characters being played. Characterization, in fact, seems in many instances to have been merely the occasion of performance rather than its objective. Typically speaking in the editorial "we," these critics constructed images of Expressionist theatre audiences as subject to an expressive power that often exceeded the dimensions both of stage and script. Represented thus in the reviews, Expressionist performance was not as much about the plays and their themes as about the demonstration of expressive power itself. In a different way, Schreyer represented his acting ensemble as having an athletic ability for creative concentration; and certainly Geist performance was about this kind of performative virtuosity as a spiritual phenomenon in its own right, not about the realization of a given script.

Thus, theatrical Expressionism foregrounded actors as an extraordinary cultural type, whose "ecstasy" on stage – quite apart from any actual personal state of transcendence – was the metaphorical name for the overpowering performant effect they generated in the theatre. The state of ecstasy was a performative mode specifically derived from Expressionist drama's discourse of cultural crisis and transformation. In this way, the actor's body became semiotized as a text for articulating the process of contemporary historical change. Together with its referential function as the vehicle of ethical critique and exhortation, Expressionist acting advanced the performant argument that powerful expression was in itself a kind of symbolic action with historical consequences. Erika Fischer-Lichte's characterization of the anti-realist approach to acting in the early modern avant-garde as a whole is particularly apt for understanding this kind of historical action in German Expressionist performance:

The body of the actor was no longer considered and exploited as a natural sign pointing exclusively to psychic states and processes of an individual but [rather] as an arbitrary sign . . . By means of the increasing semiotization of his body, the actor produced movements in the modern theatre which pointed to the total integration of the once-natural human organism into a nonhuman, non-natural "superior" order: either into a world of technique . . . or into a metaphysical order formed by transindividual, rather mysterious forces. That is to say, the treatment of the human body by the avant-gardists was marked by ambiguity. On the one hand, they employed the actor's body as raw material, as a precise and easily moldable instrument . . . On the other hand, by remaking (and defamiliarizing) the actor's body, the avant-gardists aimed at creating a "new man" beyond the limits of contemporary Western civilization: man as "producer of new meanings" (Meyerhold) or "man in harmony with the universe" (Artaud).[5]

Just so, in Expressionist performance the actor's expressive power – to the extent that it actually corresponded to what the critics reconstructed in their reviews – created an extraordinary experiential space for the audience to occupy; a phenomenological, transhistorical space from which "new meanings" could be signaled into the historical moment of the production.

Wedekind, it may be recalled, talked in these terms about the circus, arguing that it drew spectators into a liberating dimension of "wonderful virtuosity" where it was possible to explore the "good" and "true" relationship between body and spirit apart from its alienating, everyday historical determinants. The resulting "moral" insights, in turn, injected a regenerating sensual energy into one's experience of day-to-day life. Indeed, Expressionist drama took its characters and its audiences through just such a body-centered exploration of cultural values. Whether as the physical text of a vitalist quest, of a spiritual meditation, or of a socio-political protest, the body of the actor was deliberately "defamiliarized" by means of ecstatic energy shaped in musical speech, dance-like movement, and so forth. In this way it was constituted synthetically on stage as a performant site whereupon the crises of contemporary German life could be inscribed abstractly and enacted with "wonderful virtuosity." Hasenclever's character of the Son, as representative of an entire generation in rebellion against the culture of father and Fatherland, reshaped Ernst Deutsch's body into "the paradigm of Ecstatic man, hollow-eyed, passionately aglow, led by a higher will."[6] Kortner's political usurper in *Richard III* clambered up and down Jessner's steps with "the out-reaching movements of a belly-swollen spider," while in the "A horse, a horse" scene he virtually sang this repeated utterance in "a rhythm of madness, a babbling cry for deliverance."[7]

The performant function of these images conveyed them with an extraordinary intensity that was in excess of their referential requirements in the scripts. In this way, Deutsch's scream of "Parricide!," when the Son is confronted with the action necessary for his liberation in the 1916 *Der Sohn*, paralleled Kortner's screaming

"Amen!" as his Richard was crowned four years later. Both moments carried a sensory impact, a force of sheer stimulation, that went beyond the clarification of character behavior. This "supplement of expression," so to speak, had the potential of literally spilling over the boundaries of stage and script into the contemporary historical moment. Clearly, Hasenclever envisioned this and built it into his play where von Tuchmeyer narrates the incendiary effect of the Son's oratory (Act III, Scene 5).[8] And Kortner's subduing of the 1919 *Wilhelm Tell* audience disruptions with his commanding repetition of Gessler's line "Drive them apart!" is an instance where the supplement actually, if momentarily, entered the realm of political action. Despite the superlative rhetoric of the scripts, however, it is not at all clear that the audiences of Expressionist theatre were actually inspired to new consciousness or otherwise empowered for social action. Rather, the extraordinary performant effect of Expressionist acting, unlike the power of Hitler's oratory some ten years later, seems to have remained merely phenomenal; it finally was unable to become the kind of symbolic action that significantly influences the social behavior of many individuals.[9]

As Günther Rühle observed of late Expressionist performance, Jessner and his Staatstheater company were the only significant disruption to the inertia of the realist tradition in Berlin; and "only for a short time" did they present a truly alternative theatre.[10] Moreover, Jessner himself disavowed any inspiration from Expressionist performance theorists, claiming his own "Expressivität" as the source of his distinctive production style. The staircase, of course, was the principal image of Jessner's monumental aesthetic, whose reduction of politics to a set of overpowering allegorical images adumbrated the central strategy of Nazi aesthetics. The staircase setting of the Jewish director, Jessner, ironically anticipated the centripetal structuring of performance space at Nazi rallies, where phalanxes of enrapt automatons gazed up at their Führer, who stood at the apex of a monumental flight of stairs. From atop this mythical setting, Hitler – as much an orator hero as the Expressionist "New Man" – fashioned German society into a totalitarian monolith primarily through the power of impassioned rhetoric.

Expressionism launched Kortner's Berlin career, though his training had come from the Brahm–Reinhardt tradition of realism to which he returned in his post-Expressionist development as an actor.

After 1922, both he and Jessner turned their backs on what they had never fully embraced in the first place. Herein, they are most representative of the artists whose task it was to perform what the Expressionist playwrights and theorists had envisioned. Aside from the Kampfbühne community – and in that case we have only Schreyer's word to go on – there is little evidence that many of the actors of Expressionist plays drew inspiration from the movement's spiritual rhetoric or its philosophical principles.

It is true that Erwin Kalser, who played the Cashier in *Von morgens bis mitternachts* (Kammerspiele, Munich, 1918) talked of "removing the obstinacy of the body" in order "to make it completely and totally the organ to the soul."[11] Also, the actor Friedrich Kayssler had once written that "it is the soul that plays the roles, not the body. The body is an instrument . . . means of expression, tool."[12] But the fact remains that that instrument was very complex and required a good deal of technical mastery for the demands of Expressionist performance, in any of its modes. In fact, *because* of the instrumental view of the actor's body and voice in the Expressionist era, it is all the more likely that Expressionist actors spent their rehearsal time on technical strategies, not philosophy. Even Schreyer's meditative process at the Kampfbühne was a technique to be mastered, as much as a philosophy to be contemplated. In any case, I have found little substantiation for Christopher Innes's remark that "the actors themselves believed [that] they achieved . . . 'tremendous spiritual ecstasies' . . . when they were able to reach a semi-conscious dream state in performance."[13] The abundance of Expressionist theoretical work which employed this kind of rhetoric and the relative dearth of descriptive material on actual performances makes such generalizations tempting. But there is no compelling evidence that they are accurate summaries either of the technique or of the on-stage experience of most Expressionist actors.

There were points of congruence between Expressionist acting and Expressionist ideology, as the comments of Kalser and Kayssler indicate. There is even some indication of actor involvement in Expressionist theoretical circles: Ernst Deutsch, for a brief time, was a member of the Das junge Deutschland association at the Reinhardt theatre complex. But sooner or later the actors of the Expressionist theatre seemed to experience a sense of alienation, both from the movement and, as Kortner's account of his involvement in Jessner's *Macbeth* illustrates, from their own creative identities. I noted in

Chapter Four that several of the actors who came to work with Schreyer at Hamburg left disillusioned. Leontine Sagan, one of Expressionism's less-renowned performers, expressed her sense of frustration this way:

the actor remained what he was, tied up to his own bodily naturalism, restrained by the century-old tradition of his means of expression. We actors had a hard job at that time. The new style of theatrical art excited our imagination. We struggled honestly and desperately for a new method of expression. We started to behave "expressionistically"; we reduced our gestures to the minimum of active movement. In our ambition to become abstract, we went to the extreme and became as stiff as sticks.[14]

It seems reasonable to assume that the alienation of the actor increased as Expressionist staging tended more toward the depersonalization of abstractionism. Yet it was in abstract performance that the Expressionist actor's achievement and the nature of his art were most clearly revealed.

Latter-day critics often describe Expressionist acting as deliberately "artificial." But the uniqueness, as well as the accomplishment, of this kind of performance was in its power to synthesize itself out of the expressive properties of related arts such as music, dance, mime, sculpture and painting. We have seen throughout this study, for example, how reviewers repeatedly noted the musicality of speech – whether it be in Jacob Feldhammer's portrayal of Bitterlich in *Die Verführung*, Lavinia Schultz's Susanna in the Kampfbühne *Sancta Susanna*, or Kortner's beleaguered usurper at the conclusion of Jessner's *Richard III*. The musical model of performance was also paramount in the writings of performance theorists as distinct as Kandinsky and Kornfeld. As Schopenhauer's epitome of absolute art, it was a principal element of the philosophical tradition underlying Expressionist performance aesthetics generally.

The plastic nature of Expressionist acting was evident both kinetically, in its dance-like movement patterns, and statically, in the sculptural qualities of the motionless actor, especially in the emblematic productions of Martin, Fehling and Jessner. The dance tendency, first suggested in the trance-like movements of Deutsch in the 1916 première of *Der Sohn*, became progressively accentuated. Two years later, in the Hospital and No-Man's Land sections of Martin's *Die Wandlung*, Kortner and the actors playing the wounded soldiers and the skeletons virtually danced these scenes. The sculptural tendency, of course, was most developed in Jessner's work, but it was envisioned by Kaiser as early as 1912 in *Von morgens bis mitternachts* where he called for the crucifixion pose at the final curtain. Arguably, it came to the fore in Expressionist performance as Fritz Odemar stared into the audience from under the glare of Weichert's overhead spot in the 1918 Mannheim *Der Sohn*.

The painterly dimension of Expressionist acting is most obvious in *The Cabinet of Dr. Caligari*. But the work of Schreyer's Kampfbühne actors in designing and performing with masks, and especially the nerve-painted bodies of Kokoschka's actors in the première of *Mörder, Hoffnung der Frauen*, represent earlier explorations of the graphic possibilities in Expressionist performance.

Yet none of these related arts so predominated as to subsume completely the human element on stage; indeed, as Sagan stresses, its historical materiality stubbornly resisted total abstraction to the last. However, instead of being a mimetic agent, the actor strove to become the synthetic "agency" of expression. Rather than playing an action, he or she sought to become an expressive instrument who could be played by the director. What Expressionist theorists termed "ecstasy" was that condition wherein the actor indeed had to transcend him- or herself; but in practice what this actually meant was complete submission to the director's agenda.

The actor's forfeiture of his traditional function as mimetic agent in order to become the synthetic agency of directorial expression was the common and fundamental element among three quite distinct modes of Expressionist performance. Aside from the ecstatic commitment of individual actors, however, the success of those performances was a function of the particular historical moment in which they emerged. The era of theatrical Expressionism in Germany was one in which a series of drastic cultural changes – not only during the war but in its immediate "revolutionary" aftermath – radically, if temporarily, altered the conventions of traditional realistic representation in the theatre. During that time, the Expressionist actor was a synthetic medium through which contemporary crises of historical change were powerfully registered on the stage. Beyond its referential appeal to future social visions and human possibilities, or its critique of the cultural past, the Expressionist performance of crisis sought to enable audiences by demonstrating the power of expression in the historical present. An allegorical face and body, a symbolic demeanor, a typifying rhythmic pattern of movement, an evocative voice – to name the historical moment in this way, to embody its chaotic spirit, was hopefully to acquire some measure of control over it. Such naming, in fact, was a version of the myth-making strategy for survival by which human beings since the dawn of time have negotiated not only social relations but, even more, anxieties about the ultimate meanings and purposes of life itself.

However, by 1921 the interlude of interest in "humanity" and its regeneration was past, engulfed by the socio-economic and political complexities of the emerging Republic. For a year or two longer Expressionism would struggle to remain a marketable commodity; but the new era was one which nurtured a less lofty renewal, the revitalization of the German mark. Yet what would emerge as the "New Objectivity" in the mid 1920s was not simply a reaction against Expressionism. As John Willett observes, the New Objectivity should be viewed as

an offshoot of German Expressionism as well as a reaction against it; in other words . . . what had changed was not so much the principles and formal innovations arrived at from 1910 onwards as the spirit in which they were applied. The movement had run down; the ideological pressures driving it had fallen with the establishment of the Weimar Republic; its financial stimulus went with the end of inflation . . .[15]

With the coming of relative social stability in the mid twenties such a drastic theatrical language as Expressionism was no longer historically alive. As early as 1922, all that remained was the stylistic shell of what for a brief time had served as a more or less credible discourse of social empowerment.

THE LEGACIES OF THEATRICAL EXPRESSIONISM

Expressionism, wrote Ivan Goll in 1921,

was the name not of an artistic form but of an *attitude of mind*. Not so much the object of an artistic impulse as the meaning of a particular outlook on the world . . . Challenge. Manifesto. Appeal. Accusation. Entreaty. Ecstasy. Struggle . . . Expressionism was a fine, good, great, cause . . . But the result alas, by no fault of the Expressionists, is the German Republic 1920.[16]

By this time, Expressionism had indeed become merely the name of an artistic form. Any vestige of an Expressionist "attitude of mind," in Goll's sense, had simply been crushed by the political, social and economic realities of post-Versailles Treaty Germany:[17] the disastrous fortunes of war and the interlude of revolutionary chaos that followed; the humiliatingly punitive treaty; the impossible

reparation payments, which, along with German "passive resistance" to the French Ruhr occupation, finally triggered a runaway
inflation that nearly destroyed the economy; political and racial
violence, at times amounting to a *de facto* state of civil war. Such
circumstances, by 1923, had long rendered the Expressionist
"outlook on the world," together with the kind of vague strategies
for implementing it enumerated by Goll, ludicrously inadequate. As
Kortner summarized the situation in his memoir, Expressionism
had been "a breakthrough, an explosion and a pointer. But it [was]
no more a form of theatre than a revolution is a form of state."[18]
Yet, if Expressionism had proven illusory as sociology and impotent
as political rhetoric, it had at least revived the question of how and
to what degree theatrical formations can influence larger socio-
cultural formations.[19]

But whether and how the stage could help simply to steady, let
alone to shape, the progress of Weimar culture must have seemed an
impossibly convoluted problem in the first years of the Republic.
Even with the advent of currency stabilization in 1924 and a
resurgence of prosperity thereafter, both Germany's economic recovery and her emergence from political isolation were rather more
illusory than real. Recovery was heavily dependent on foreign
investment, which in turn was always tied to negotiations with the
Allies over such persistently vexing issues as the Ruhr occupation,
reparations payments, rearmament, and international peace treaties
such as the Kellogg–Briand Pact. Republican domestic political
strategies of conciliation and consensus negotiating were so ineffec-
tual at mediating partisan conflicts that by mid 1928 no less than
fifteen cabinets had failed.[20] Up to this point, as Peter Gay has
summarized this impossible situation,

the Communists continued to refuse cooperation with the "Social Fascists"
– that is, the Social Democrats. The new army retained its old ideas: it
wanted political influence, nationalist policies, and secret rearmament. And
right-wing fanatics never weakened in their determination to overthrow a
regime that was being almost suicidally indulgent with them.[21]

By early 1929, a world economic crisis was clearly looming. German
unemployment was rising and tax revenues were falling at an
alarming rate; and in October the Wall Street crash signaled, among
other things, the beginning of the end for the Weimar Republic.
Early on in this era of frightening insecurity the response of the

artistic community was to start searching for some new aesthetic program of cultural stabilization. Beginning with the visual arts around 1919, what the New Objectivity came to mean in practice was a turning away from visionary idealism and lyrical expression toward a more moderate discourse of social utility. Now the goal was simply to acknowledge and analyze contemporary socio-economic conditions. Kornfeld, for example, had once declared "Long live chaos!"; but in 1924, writing now as a decidedly former Expressionist, he advised his colleagues to

be modest and direct our attention to other and smaller things. Let us meditate on a human being, upon a soul or a fool. Let us play a little, look round a little and, if we can, laugh or smile a little!

Hasenclever, for his part, felt that the Expressionist generation had simply matured beyond thundering "the storm of freedom. We were youngsters. Now we are men. . . . Step into line!"[22] In the theatre, this new pragmatism was evident in several ways. Around 1919, satirical variety cabaret resurfaced, notably in the Reinhardt revival of Schall und Rauch. As in the pre-war Wilhelmine era, so now, cabaret offered both a sobering sense of honesty about the present cultural situation and a much-needed opportunity to escape from it temporarily in laughter. During the winter of 1922–23, Berlin actors staged a strike in response to abysmal employment conditions in the theatre. At the same time, several groups of them formed small alternative theatre companies – such as Berthold Viertel's Die Truppe – in an attempt to create opportunities for themselves in whatever performing space they could find. These and such organizations as Moritz Seeler's private theatre club Junge Bühne were among the leaders in the search for a new drama and production aesthetic. What exactly the times required remained uncertain: restagings of earlier Expressionist successes such as Kaiser's *Von morgens bis mitternachts*; experiments like Brecht's *Trommeln in der Nacht*; revivals of the classical and recent modern repertoires; new foreign imports such as Pirandello and O'Neill – all these yielded inconclusive results.

Though Expressionism itself was moribund, however, its legacies – particularly in this context of a deliberate search for a theatre of social relevance – were already evident in Erwin Piscator's initial experiments with political theatre. Piscator's aim of creating a theatre that would instill political consciousness in its audience grew

out of the same sort of front line war trauma that so many
Expressionist artists had suffered. In response, some among them,
such as Toller, had turned to a vaguely Socialist-inspired utopian
idealism. But the war experience radicalized Piscator in a different
way, and by 1918 he was committed specifically to Marxism. In the
light of this conversion, his 1919 staging of several Expressionist plays
in Königsberg revealed to him the inability of Expressionism to
articulate a concretely political representation of the contemporary
German situation. Yet the paradox of his relationship to Expressionist theatre from 1920 onward is that its emotional orientation toward
activism and certain of its specific stylistic features continued to
characterize his subsequent production work.

Piscator wanted to substitute a rationally enlightened collectivist
stage for the visionary theatre of ecstatic individualism. In pursuit
of this goal, he sought a style of acting that I would call "abstract
realism": by thoroughly absorbing the production's political ideas,
the actor's characterization was expected to be realistic, but in
such a way that it transcended individual psychology and instead
represented collective historical experience with "naturalness."[23]
Practically, this seems to have meant that actor performances were
subordinated to Piscator's main concern with creating powerful
documentary scenic images. The performer, however accomplished, was simply one element in a total emotional experience by
means of which this director hoped to induce audiences to become
involved in the production's political themes. Thus, the position of
the actor in Piscator's theatre took on something of the same
ambiguity as can be seen in the relation of an actor like Kortner
to a director like Jessner. Notwithstanding his status as a star of
the Berlin commercial theatre by 1919, Kortner's personality was
subsumed in emblematic political roles such as his "belly-swollen"
spider-like Richard III. Just so, a star like Alexander Granach, at
Piscator's insistence, was made-up to look like Lenin for his
portrayal of the fifteenth-century revolutionary character Asmus in
Piscator's production of Ehm Welk's *Storm Over Gothland* (Volksbühne, Berlin, 1927). Here the Expressionist legacy is evident in
the penchant for stylized semiotization of the actor's body: by this
method both directors forcefully clarified the message they intended their productions to deliver.[24] In general, Piscator's actors
were as subordinate to his staging concepts – the pervasive film
projections and other technical effects of his documentary style –

as Expressionist actors were to the scenic agendas of the directors who so strongly shaped their work.

In 1920, moreover, Piscator had opened the Second Proletarian Theatre with a speech that showed how indebted to the Expressionist idiom his political rhetoric was: "Comrades! The soul of the Revolution, the soul of the classless society to come and of the culture of the community is our revolutionary feeling." Thirty years later, he still spoke of the "confessional" nature of his particular kind of political theatre.[25] In short, the effect of his productions was to perpetuate the Expressionist idea of political consciousness as more a matter of strong feeling than one of dialectical thinking. Accordingly, he assumed the necessity of an hortatory theatrical language for mobilizing his audiences, as had the Expressionists before him. Perhaps this was because Piscator – like Jessner, whose stirring political adaptations of the classics he greatly admired – was principally a director concerned with immediate production results. Unlike Brecht, he was not in that uniquely dialectical position of being a director who is also the playwright developing his script.

To be sure, Piscator employed dialectical staging strategies. Beginning with the 1924 Volksbühne production of Alfons Paquet's *Fahnen*, he achieved striking representations of contradictions, for example, by contrasting live stage action with film and slide projections. By such means, he did much in the 1920s – along with directors like Martin, Fehling and Jessner – to demonstrate the stage's power of representing contemporary political events with clarity and emotional force. On the other hand, it could be argued that his dialectical stagings, like Eisenstein's films of the mid twenties, were readily resolved in affective political statements. By contrast, the less easily synthesized contradictions of Brechtian dramaturgy define a different sort of dialectical procedure which produces a more ironic, less declarative mode of political theatre.

Expressionism's most committed dramatist, Ernst Toller, continued to write political plays; however, he never completely forsook the Expressionist idiom in diction and characterization. His 1927 *Hoppla, wir leben!*, written specifically for Piscator's proletarian theatre, was severely edited by Piscator to rid the language of its "Expressionist lyricism" and to de-emphasize the bourgeois individuality of the protagonist as Toller had conceived him. Among other playwrights who had held the stage during the Expressionist era, however, the versatile Georg Kaiser particularly seemed to catch the new pragmatic tone of social analysis. His *Nebeneinander* (1923), a cynical study of contemporary inflation-era Berlin, was staged in November 1923 by Viertel's Die Truppe with sets by the graphic satirist George Grosz. Kaiser, of course, had written successfully in a wide variety of dramatic genres, from the rather straight-forwardly tragic *Die Bürger von Calais* (1914) to satirical comedies such as *Europa* (1915) and *Kolportage* (1924). But the ironic tone that runs through many of his plays, not least *Von morgens bis mitternachts*, distinguished the intensity of his Expressionism from that of other dramatists by its balancing sense of analytical distance from his protagonists. Brecht's assessment of this objectivity in Kaiser's work is evident in a fragment from a 1928 radio interview with Herbert Ihering. In response to Ihering's question as to who Brecht considered "the most recent example" of developmental tendencies in German literature of the preceding fifteen years which "lead right up to Epic drama" Brecht names Kaiser. While clearly distinguishing Kaiser's "individualist" drama from the "collectivist" content of his own plays, he remarks that "there is something in Kaiser's technique that is not suited to individualism, and therefore is apt for my concerns . . . Kaiser, after all, appeals to what is rational."[26]

For Brecht, what specifically set Kaiser apart from the "manic one-sidedness of Expressionist drama"[27] in general was a set of techniques that broke the continuity of dramatic representation into discrete components which could be set in dialectical relation. The episodic Stationendrama structure and the clipped, disjointed rhythms of "telegraphese" dialogue in a play like *Von morgens bis mitternachts* modeled an interruptive dramaturgy that facilitated precisely that juxtaposition of contradictory images and ideas that would become the heart of Brechtian dramaturgical method.[28] At the same time, episodic structure foregrounded the element of narrative – an emphasis typical of much Expressionist drama. Its subordination of psychological characterization, by means of abstract typification, to the interests of clear narration would become one of the Epic theatre's definitive strategies. Further, although the lyric excesses of "ecstasy" in Expressionist drama disgusted him, Brecht did admire – particularly in Kaiser's work – the sheer force with which words were mobilized in Expressionist diction. As early as 1921, he observed in reference to the Neue Bühne production of *Von morgens bis mitternachts* that "Kaiser, by means of his astonishing emphasis of word, doubtless represents the ultimate and most extreme exertion of the word that can be attained – that which film has attained *without* the word."[29] Just as gestures had a verbal significance in silent film, so Kaiser's words apparently had a virtually physical impact on Brecht in this performance.

The remarks just cited are those of a young Brecht, the cynical, nihilist poet of *Baal*; nonetheless, throughout his career Brecht strove for just such a physicality in the vivid diction of his own plays. But whereas word and gesture in most Expressionist drama combined forces to work for a total, overwhelming effect, Brecht typically set them in dialectical tension. In accordance with this objective, he developed his fundamental performance concept of the "Gestus." With this principle Brecht theorized the theatrical representation of contradictions in gestural and spatial, as well as verbal, terms; gestic performance being a matter, quite literally, of actor/characters taking contradictory "positions" in a scene. What Brecht admired about Expressionist stylization, where he judged it successful in a production, was its clarity of gestural statement. The theatricality of Expressionism frankly acknowledged the situation of actors and audience confronting one another in a theatre. Moreover, it presented the body and voice of the actor as rhetorical images and acting as, essentially, argumentation. Out of these specific legacies of Expressionist performance, Brecht began to develop what he considered an historically relevant theatrical language; one which reflected a different reading of Marx than that which produced Socialist Realism. Through stylized emphasis of word and gesture, the Expressionist actor's body had been a text for the inscription of historical argument in the declarative mode. In his development of gestic theatre strategies, Brecht redirected this praxis of stylization into the analytic mode, transforming a rhetoric of pronouncement into a performative language of interrogation. Thus not only historical conditions but also their means of theatrical representation came under scrutiny in gestic performance.

As Brecht appreciated the dialectical capabilities of episodic structure and disjunctive dialogue, he also valued an indexical grammar of acting that clearly illustrated ideas. In accordance with this it is perhaps not surprising that he drew as well upon the Expressionist tradition of abstract reduction in set design. Of course, he was not interested in filling the stage with symbols. Rather, from the symbolic selectivity of detail in Expressionist settings Brecht derived a design principle of synecdochic selectivity. The idea here was that a well-chosen realistic prop, such as Mother Courage's wagon, could suggest, more or less, a larger historical situation. As with acting, however, design was intended to be active, gestic – clarity of intention rather than suggestion of naturalistic detail was the final objective. Relatively early in his career, Brecht remarked that:

It's more important nowadays for the set to tell the spectator he's in a theatre than to tell him he's in, say, Aulis. The theatre must acquire *qua* theatre the same fascinating reality as a sporting arena during a boxing match. . . . If the set represents a town it must look like a town that has been built to last precisely two hours. . . . Everything must be provisional yet polite. A place need only have the credibility of a place glimpsed in a dream. The set needs to spring from the rehearsal of groupings, so in effect it must be a fellow actor.[30]

The Expressionist theatre, as I have argued, sought to foster the same productive interdependence between actor and set; so much so as sometimes to yield a reverse result where the actors became kinetic scenery. But even in a comparatively static production like Weichert's Mannheim *Der Sohn* the immovable cone of light from the overhead spot took on something of a performative character. Certainly one of the best-recognized principles of Expressionist performance was the way in which setting exerted a shaping influence on actor movement and gesture. Jessner's staircase, the exploding angular designs of *Caligari*, and Schreyer's ten-foot-tall masks are clear examples. Brecht's particular appropriation of this dynamic actor–set relationship is evident in a description of Caspar Neher's set design methods that Brecht wrote in 1951 near the end of his career:

With what care he selects a chair, and with what thought he places it! And it all helps the playing. One chair will have short legs, and the height of the accompanying table will also be calculated, so that whoever eats at it has to take up a quite specific attitude, and the conversation of these people as they bend more than usual when eating takes on a particular character, which makes the episode clearer.[31]

Where the dominant traditions of Naturalism and the classical repertoire had sought to mask the nature of theatrical art mimetically, Expressionism forced people to *see* the actor, the set, the stage, the theatre. Brecht took this basic strategy a step further and insisted that audiences *think* about what it was they were impelled to see so that they could really see it. Among other results, Brecht argued, this would also help them to realize what they were not shown but might have been and hence also make them aware of the resources of theatrical art as tools for constructing and revising representations of social reality. Where Expressionism proclaimed an inevitable link between revolutionary theatrical aesthetics and social progress, Brecht developed a dialectical art in which such mutual influence was possible but not automatic. Expressionism attempted to revolutionize people's lives for them within the theatre; Brecht simply sought to prod audiences into assuming this responsibility for themselves once they had left the theatre. The Expressionist theatre had demonstrated the sheer motive power of words chosen in poetic economy and forcefully delivered. By calling attention to the various ways a given social situation might be articulated, Brecht attempted to show that the power of words was simply a function of the power of choice itself. Expressionism imparted a vision; Brecht taught a critical method. Indeed, Brecht's principal transformation of the Expressionist legacy was his stylized demonstration that choice, rather than notions of inspiration or revelation, was the source and end of theatrical art; that historical contingency rather than historical inevitability were the realities it had to convey.

The legacies of theatrical Expressionism that have most influenced later generations, in fact, are those which Brecht appropriated and adapted. The result became a political theatre tradition of major influence to the present day. Its tactics have influenced playwriting, directing, acting, and scene design throughout Europe and America in every generation since World War II. Most recently, they are evident in the deconstructionist dramaturgy and staging methods of various activist theatres – such as those of feminist, ethnic minority, and third-world movements – of the last twenty years. The basic argument of this tradition is that theatre performance can specifically affect the processes of historical change. In general, this is accomplished by applying the critical method of dialectical materialism to questions of social reality and its truthful representation in theatre. Specifically, this "didactic" goal is pursued by means of such strategies of stylization as: subverting the identification of actor and character, textualizing performance through stylized clarity of statement in acting and set design, and dialectical exploitation of episodic structure and disjunctive action.

The other principal conduit of Expressionist influence passes, quite indirectly of course, through Artaud. The legacy here is the idea of what Peter Brook and others have called "holy theatre"; and it chiefly involves the gestural, ritualistic, and visionary aspects of Expressionism's "ecstatic" performance traditions. Though Artaud probably encountered productions bearing the influence of Piscator during his 1932 visit to Berlin,[32] he clearly could have had no direct contact with Expressionism itself in its heyday. The closest link would have come via the nihilistic cultural protests of the Dada stage. This nay-saying tradition of mockery – which cabaret, Futurism and Expressionism, in varying degrees, had also fostered – was kept alive briefly after the war by Dada performances in Germany and France. Through his association as an actor with Lugné-Poë's Théâtre de l'Oeuvre, Artaud may well have witnessed the Spring 1920 Théâtre de l'Oeuvre presentation of a series of Dadaist programs. Notably, these featured Tristan Tzara, the Romanian poet who had co-founded Dadaism and authored several of its theoretical manifestoes, and the future Surrealist movement founder, André Breton. Artaud's relationship with Breton and their disagreement over the application of Surrealist principles to theatre, of course, was the initial context in which Artaud began to develop his own revolutionary notions of performance. However Dada may have influenced Artaud, he clearly identified with the spirit of its prototypical figure in his founding of the Théâtre Alfred Jarry in 1927.

Of greater relevance to specific traditions of ecstatic performance carried forward in Artaud's work, however, were his experience in silent film acting during the twenties and his eventual encounter with Balinese dance-drama in 1931. From these he learned a great deal about the possibilities of gesture and movement as physical languages in themselves. Like the Expressionists, Artaud sought a grammar of expression whose physical and verbal dimensions would propel each other to an ecstatic level of efficacy. One year after seeing the Balinese dancers, and in the early stages of articulating his concept of a "Theatre of Cruelty," he wrote to a friend:

I have added another language to speech and am attempting to restore its ancient magic effectiveness, its spellbinding effectiveness, integral with speech, and whose mysterious potential is now forgotten. . . . I will not act plays based on writing or words: rather, in the shows I intend to put on, the predominant part will be physical and could not be determined or written in normal word language.[33]

Artaud's "[addition of] another language to speech," of course, was nothing new. The experience of the circus and the silent cinema in these terms had long fascinated the theatrical avant-garde throughout Europe. Brecht, for instance, had been greatly influenced by the precise physical art of performers such as Charlie Chaplin and Karl Valentin. But whereas he admired this precision as an analytical resource, Artaud thought of the actor's body as a kind of dynamo in itself which, if sufficiently stimulated, would generate a shattering urgency in performance comparable to nothing less than a martyr at the stake "signaling through the flames."[34]

This was precisely the kind of intensity for which ecstatic Expressionist actors had striven, and Artaud revealed how fundamentally transformed a conception of acting it assumed. As I noted at the beginning of this study, I have used the term "performance" to stress how the Expressionist expectation of efficacy on stage replaced the traditional mimetic idea of acting. For them it was an art with power to affect real life beyond the confines of the theatrical frame. In very different terms, Brecht too conceived of acting as historically efficacious. For him, the actor's body was a dialectical text of specific historical contradictions; but for the Expressionists and, even more so, Artaud, it was a symbolic text of the crises of civilization as a whole. The Brechtian actor is a polemicist; the Artaudian actor a shaman. If Brecht admired the rationality of episodic dramaturgy in an Expressionist like Kaiser, Artaud developed the praxis of ecstatic irrationality into a theatre of virtual exorcism.[35] Hence, his visionary writings – though largely unrealized in his practical work – propounded an idea of "acting" that has stimulated and troubled all who have since needed the theatre to matter as much as he said it did. In the modern era, this urgent expectation of stage performance had originated with Expressionism. Through Artaud, it was further amplified in rhetoric which proclaimed the goal of theatre to be the draining of "civilization's abscesses" by means of a kind of acting which had the purgative effect of a "plague."

When one thinks of Artaud's theories, one immediately thinks of Grotowski's early achievements. However, through Grotowski pass Brechtian as well as Artaudian variations on the Expressionist performance legacy. Grotowski's work with his Polish Laboratory Theatre employs the exorcizing, totalist idea of acting celebrated by Artaud and first introduced in ecstatic theatrical Expressionism. But it also contains elements of the dialectical, gestic conception derived by Brecht from the episodic theatricality he admired in dramatists like Shakespeare, Büchner, Wedekind, and Kaiser.[36] Both traditions

– Brecht's "scientific" idea of theatre as experimental laboratory and Artaud's shamanistic model of theatre as sanctuary for ritual – come together in Grotowski's central concept of a "poor theatre." In this conception, performance, stripped of all non-essentials, is radical in its search for human truth both in terms of mythic roots and of gestic clarity. This is particularly evident in the way Grotowski focuses so intensively yet systematically on the body of the actor: on breathing, on kinesic analysis, on the concentration of specific energies in the anatomy. His principle of the "via negativa" pursues the same methodical reduction of performance to a state of elemental clarity and power as that which defined the Expressionist performance legacy. The idea of theatrical "poverty," the Expressionist principle of "ecstasy," Brecht's terminology for describing the Verfremdung-seffekt, Artaud's invocation of the imagery of plague – all partake of the same rhetorical search for a theatre empowered through a radical transformation of its procedural metaphors.

In the nuclear aftermath of World War II this objective acquired an enlarged significance. Expressionist reduction and explosion, Brechtian dialectics, Artaudian prophecy – all had been attempts to find a specifically theatrical way of dealing with a civilization whose institutional power to alienate, oppress, exploit, and outright destroy human life was continuing to expand. The brutality of trench warfare had been nothing compared to the systematic horror of the Holocaust, which in turn was dwarfed by the bomb and the magnitude of the threat it posed to the entire planet. It was in this context that the absurdist playwrights sought yet a new theatrical language with which to address the kind of anxiety and alienation specific to the nuclear age. Here the Expressionist legacy of performing crisis as a rhetorical strategy for containing crisis is evident. In Beckett's *Waiting for Godot*, for example, characters who are abstract typifications of humanity ritualistically act out the crisis of their existence. The scope of the play, like many Expressionist dramas, is not simply social or cultural but ultimately spiritual, metaphysical. The belief that drama can be efficacious on such a scale, of course, is as old as Aeschylus; but its twentieth-century reappearance happens first in the Expressionist theatre. Like the dramas of Expressionism, Beckett's subject is "humankind," represented in the most comprehensive terms possible. The disjunctive structure of *Godot* is held together not by an epic element of narrative but rather by a series of minimalist rituals; here, all specific stories of individual or collective humanity are distilled ritualistically into one essential predication of existence – we wait.

This kind of absurdist drama, in contrast to the philosophical plays of Sartre or Camus, works by demonstrating rather than discussing its ideas. The acting of *Godot* depends a great deal on physical performance skills, which in part are used to show the limitations of language in the face of the problem the play is attempting to address. In ritualistic physical interactions (e.g., the Pozzo–Lucky relationship, the hat routine of Act II) and obsessive physical self-preoccupation (e.g., Vladimir and his hat, Estragon's feet) the Expressionist episodic quest for meaning and purpose is abstracted to an even more fundamental question: is there any significance at all in the fact of human existence? The Expressionist legacy is further evident here in that the problem is explored primarily in terms of the physical body; more than the mind, it is the body that becomes the site of existential inquiry. As in Expressionist theatre so in Beckett's plays: the human body becomes the plastic material in which dramatic themes are embodied and action is worked out. Beckett adopts the Expressionist technique of subjecting the body to the ravages of the play's dramatic argument.[37] In plays written after *Godot* he carries this technique much further: two characters appear in a trash can, another is buried up to her head in sand, elsewhere characters are nothing but body parts, and finally, in the vignette *Breath*, the body has altogether disappeared.

Our own age of information saturation and virtual technology is one in which some aspects of the physical substance of human identity, as it is clarified in face-to-face human interaction, have electronically disappeared. One result of this is that the particular tradition from Expressionism through Beckett I have just mentioned has emerged in the present time as what I would call the problem of "presence." The most characteristic theatrical expression of this problem is to be seen in performance art. Like some Expressionist dramas and, of Beckett's works, *Godot* most prominently, performance art often conveys autobiographical significance in the way its exploration of the history and the present condition of one's identity is worked through, written in, the human body. The live presence of the performance artist is not simply taken for granted as a transparent vehicle of entertainment; rather it confronts audiences "opaquely" with the physical and emotional facts of its own existential process. Often, moreover, this performance of presence is intended to be representative of the audience, or a portion of it, as well. Thus, in one of her pieces the performance artist Karen Finley defaces her nude body with food as a means of performing both autobiographical issues of feminine identity and political statements concerning sexist representation of women in patriarchal culture.

As a modern performance tradition, of course, the inscription of conceptual images and abstract forms on the performing human body is as old as Dada, Futurism, and earlier, the theatre of French symbolism. But in the Expressionist version of this tradition such textualization of the body is linked to issues of human identity, not simply to aesthetic/sensory formal explorations or the tactics of cultural protest. In this way, the Expressionist/vitalist "journey of the soul," the groping of *Godot*'s tramps for a sense of their existence, and autobiographical performance art all perform a fiction about the physical appropriation of identity in the present moment of self-awareness. Such performances, as distinct from the moment-to-moment experience of real life, are rhetorical statements about the possibility – or, in the case of *Waiting for Godot*, the impossibility – of self-determination through self-definition. The Expressionist hero journeys from life-changing epiphany to life-changing epiphany in a station drama structure of action. Beckett's tramps engage in a series of time-killing games which pitilessly confirm, rather than redeem, their impressions of existential desolation.[38] A performance artist like Finley extemporizes on the reality of the moment by way of performing herself, as she would have it, in "real time."[39] The legacy of Expressionism here is the vitalist idea – both literary theme and principle of performance – that to be fully alive is to be fully present to one's self. The pathos of Vladimir and Estragon's situation is that, recalling no past and hoping vainly for a future that never arrives, they are trapped in a present in which presence is unbearable and therefore impossible. Their appearance in the play's dramatic world, in fact, concretizes not presence but "absence." The beatings that Estragon tries to recall but is not sure he received are perhaps the play's clearest instance of how Beckett renders the numbness of existential absence as a physical experience.

In twentieth-century theatre, two predominant methods have arisen for staging an exploration of the problem of presence. One is to use the stage as a confessional; the other is to make it into a sanctuary. The legacy of Expressionism eventuating in performance art follows the first path. The bold, defiant theatricality of a performance piece like the one Finley performs in the nude employs, to be sure, a Brechtian "distancing" technique: the artist subverts voyeuristic pleasure as she smears food on her body. But this piece also creates a specific kind of emotional environment in which feelings associated with being sexually objectified draw audience members, particularly women, together with the performer in a community of shared experience. The result is a kind of "confessional presence" which takes on a very specific historical meaning for artist and audience alike. In the modern era, of course, the art of lyrical communion dates from Romanticism, whose artists – and after them, the French Symbolists – projected the lyrical experience into some natural, historical, or visionary locale in order to infuse artistic form with a sense of "atmosphere." With theatrical Expressionism, however, this lyrical energy turned itself violently back upon the body and voice of the actor. The dynamic stage presence of the actor himself became the locus of that particular emotional environment in which some Expressionists sought to establish the community of the "New Man." For this reason, as I have argued, ecstatic Expressionism attributed historical power to the performance of the actor willing to make himself totally available and vulnerable to the expressive life of his character. This willingness to bare all for the sake of the performance constituted the confessional element in Expressionist acting.

Although the Expressionist rhetoric of "ecstasy" may have passed away, the tradition of uncompromising confession as an act of social, not merely personal, relevance is a legacy of theatrical Expressionism that lives on in the performance work of artists like Finley as well as the dance/drama creations of Pina Bausch. Like the interdisciplinary Expressionist stage tradition, Bausch's productions combine elements of dance, singing, and dramatic speech. But instead of scripted dramas, Bausch stages performance texts typically comprised of disjunctive vignettes, dance pieces, and songs. These are not usually related in a continuous plot action but rather they are simply juxtaposed to constitute specific emotional environments – what the Expressionist's would have called "soul states." The Expressionist legacy of confession is particularly evident in Bausch's focus on exploring darker emotional conditions: anxieties, obsessions, phobias. In her 1983 dance/drama *Carnations*, for example, actors in a collage of song, dance, and dramatic scenes confronted the audience with intimate confessional statements about their own emotional lives. Like ecstatic Expressionist productions, although not with their explosive level of intensity, the social effect of such performances is to create an emotional continuum in which audience members can be induced to feel as their own reality the effects of the culture's destructive psycho-social, ideological, political, and economic patterns. Here again, presence – being alive in the moment – is specified as a matter of a strongly felt emotional communion similar to that upon which the efficacy of ecstatic Expressionism was predicated.

On a more expansive scale, Robert Wilson has used the same disjunctive strategy of collage to immerse his audiences in experiential environments. Often these performances in their duration or spatial logistics have aspired to exhaustive totalizing effect.[40] Along with the prodigious dimensions of his production vision, Wilson recalls the Expressionist legacy in his subordination of actors to the striking visual effects of his scenic designs. As often in Expressionist productions, figure movement in Wilson's stage creations is carefully coordinated with lighting dynamics in precise visual compositions. Where exploration of human social conditions happens in his work, however, it does so not in an emotional environment of confessional utterance but rather in something like a surrealist landscape of imagery. Audience awareness develops with the freedom from spatial/temporal and logical constraints characteristic of the dream state. Yet there is a resulting depersonalization of theatrical representation in Wilson's celebration of the image which bears comparison not to the ecstatic Expressionist legacy but rather to the Geist Expressionist productions of Lothar Schreyer.

Wilson's stage imagery is typically less abstract and more referential than was Schreyer's; but his strategy of turning the actor into a medium for symbolic signification is essentially the same. Like Schreyer, with his "Bühnenkunstwerke," Wilson stages not scripted dramas but stage creations of his own in which the actor's body and voice are but elements in a larger symbolic design of images deployed in specific rhythmic patterns on the stage. Here the other twentieth-century tradition for addressing the problem of presence in the theatre, making the stage into a self-contained sanctuary for its own ritual purposes, is evident. In this tradition the problem of human presence also centers upon the body of the actor, but it is treated as a formal, rather than an existential, problem. Admittedly, the idea of acting as ritual performance calls to mind figures such as Artaud,

Grotowski, and Richard Schechner more readily than Wilson. But a definitive aspect of ritual, both within the theatrical frame and in other contexts, is the way its performers are transformed into symbols and deployed in overtly formal patterns of symbolic action. This property places Wilson squarely in a ritualistic staging tradition that runs from French Symbolism, Geist Expressionism, and the school of Artaud to the present.

Notwithstanding the rhetoric of mysticism or magic in this tradition – particularly in the theoretical writings of Schreyer, Artaud, and Grotowski – a spiritual attitude is not really at the heart of its practice. Though it certainly requires this attitude in the context of religious worship, the patterning of ritual behavior within the theatrical frame is finally an aesthetic and rhetorical concern. However much its rhythmic and structural patterns may resemble or even deliberately imitate the features of religious ritual, the action of ritual performance within the theatrical frame is theatrical, not sacramental, action.[41] Its mode is rhetorical, not liturgical. Sacramental action references and stimulates belief in a metaphysical power through and beyond its own symbolic structure; ritual performance in the theatre locates its power precisely in the physical substance – the imagery fashioned in body, voice, costume, props, set design, lighting – and the rhythmic expression of that symbolic structure itself. Sacramental action, for the believer, is spiritually real and direct; but the action of theatrical ritual, though metaphorically indirect, strives for no less genuine an impact as rhetoric. Underlying the specific imagery and themes of any particular ritualistic stage production, in fact, is an implied rhetorical comparison between the effect of that kind of theatrical performance on an audience and the comprehensive meaning and efficacy of religious ritual for the community of those who believe. Ritualistic theatre is recognizable where the actor's task is to bear an image in a symbolic structure of actions whose ultimate meaning is believed to arise mysteriously out of the overtly formalized pattern of its presentation.

A good illustration of this is to be found in a recent work by the exiled Iranian stage auteur Reza Abdoh. His 1992 Los Angeles Theatre Center production, *Bogeyman*, according to journalist Richard Stayton, featured the following actions:

A chorus of nine naked males clog dance to bouncy rhythms of "The Boogie Woogie Bugle Boy of Company B." A boy with green hair is immersed upside down in a fish tank and whipped, his nude body sparkling with rings through his tongue, nipples, stomach and genitals. Somebody's Fairy Godmother is carried onstage: a four-foot-high physically handicapped half-man, half-woman. All join in a chorus of "Take Me Out to the Ball Game" – but not until a black man is castrated with a chainsaw and his severed organ ritually devoured.[42]

Performed simultaneously in a horizontally and vertically sectioned stage reminiscent of the concept Piscator used for his 1927 production of *Hoppla, wir leben!,* these events clearly aspire to an Artaudian effect. But in their use of actors they differ little from *Mörder, Hoffnung der Frauen,* where Kokoschka painted blood vessels and nerves on his archetypal male and female figures, or those productions of Schreyer's where actors' bodies were partially or completely covered with masks. In all of these cases, movement, gesture, and vocalization are determined by the task of bearing the image and performatively actualizing its mysterious meanings within the formal symbolic structure of which it is a part. Abdoh's actors are not mimetic human images but rather symbolic texts. Upon their bodies his abstract version of the psycho-social conflict between the liberation and the regulation of sexual freedom is inscribed. Although the violence and extremity of his methods are far from the quasi-mystical evocations of Schreyer's Kampfbühne stagings, Abdoh's strategy depends upon the same conception of the actor as image bearer, whether of an archetype or a pop culture icon.

Here the Expressionist legacy of transforming the human body into an abstract medium for purposes of ritualized symbolic performance is also evident in terms of its totalizing rhetorical purpose. Schreyer sought to transcend the cultural catastrophe of World War I by creating a spiritualized world apart from it on his stage. Just so, Abdoh – a gay activist who is himself HIV-positive – attempts to conjure a differently spiritual, Artaudian realm on stage by way of negotiating the cultural alienation of the AIDS generation. For that generation, tragically, Artaud's metaphor of "plague" has become all-encompassing reality. As Stayton remarks,

In a decade oppressed by economics and *safe* "choices," Abdoh adheres to the experimental tradition of 1960s collectives like the Living Theatre. He's gathered a permanent ensemble of performers eager to stretch their limits of endurance (as well as an audience's tolerance). His style is that of an outraged and outrageous born-again Artaud. . . . Just as Artaud ordered, Abdoh insists theatre artists *must* rage as if they're burning at the stake, signalling through the flames.[43]

Moreover, as Schreyer realized, such a totalizing and extreme rhetorical agenda requires not only the freedom from mimesis afforded by abstract symbolic form but also the collective support of a faithful band of believers. His Kampfbühne ensemble were among the earliest pioneers of the modern coterie tradition of anti-realist alternative theatre that became the working model of such later ensembles as Grotowski's Polish Laboratory Theatre, Schechner's Performance Group, and Beck's Living Theatre. What distinguished the Kampfbühne from groups such as the Futurists and the Dadaists was the homogeneity of its members' belief in and commitment to the collective. The performances of Futurism and Dada acted out an idea of theatre based on radical individualism; the Kampfbühne acting tradition performed the idea of a radical community. This tradition is an Expressionist legacy that remains viable, as the case of Abdoh's ensemble suggests, to the present day.

The range of twentieth-century theatrical experimentation bearing some affinity – either through direct influence, some sort of mediated exposure, or simply by analogy – with German Expressionist performance is impressive. Taken together, the achievements of the European and American theatrical avant-garde, from Piscator and Brecht to the present Postmodern era, suggest that the most significant legacy of theatrical Expressionism is its discovery of a means whereby contemporary cultural themes and images could be made to converge with rhetorical power upon the body of the actor. In this tradition, the living presence of the actor on stage is foregrounded as problematic, to be sure; but it is a problem particularly rich in rhetorical possibilities. Even the "realist" Brecht embraced these possibilities, so much so that a significant number of post-World War II German dramatists turned away from what they saw as an excessive dependence on theatricality in his political dramaturgy.[44] For the Expressionists, the presence of the actor on stage constituted a specific rhetorical domain within which cultural crisis could be acted out and thereby addressed in a way not otherwise possible. As they saw it, this defined the theatre's unique role in the course of Weimar culture's historical development. Artaud expanded this conception of the actor's presence to the metaphysical level. For him, the actor embodied not only an historical argument about a culture's ethical malaise, but also the sacrificial offering for its cure. Though this extreme, visionary position stands in polar opposition to the rationality of Brechtian theatre, the two share the same view of the actor as a rhetorical medium. First developed by theatrical Expressionism, this idea of performance conceives the body and voice of the actor as tools for demonstrating, playing out, a given cultural situation.

The best of what Expressionism had to offer is what passed through the filter of Brechtian dialectics and the fire of Artaudian rhetoric. Apart from this, Expressionist theatre, simply as a stylistic novelty, certainly had its own impact. The Expressionist legacy in scene design is well recognized, for example, in early twentieth-century avant-garde commercial theatre experiments. These were mostly due to the influence of Expressionist stage productions and films on designers and directors like Robert Edmond Jones and Orson Welles. In the context of my concluding remarks to the present study, however, there is no concern for this sort of superficial, purely stylistic influence. Rather, my aim has been to identify the legacies of German theatrical Expressionism as a set of recurrent problems in theatrical representation; problems specific to the twentieth century's unique patterns of historical crisis. It is in this sense that the heritage of Expressionism can most profitably be appreciated. The continuity of that heritage is not to be seen principally as a matter of direct stylistic influence affecting generation after generation of theatre artists. Rather, it is evident in a particular sort of demand upon theatre recurring throughout most of this century from the era of World War I to our own time. Theatre in every age is more or less responsive to history, and cultural crises are certainly not unique to our era. War, revolution, plague, famine, economic or natural disasters – such historical forces have affected theatre in many epochs. What differs in our time is not the kind but the degree of impact such events have registered in the theatre.

Expressionism is a cultural heritage whose central theme is the experience of life as historical crisis. To the Expressionist generation World War I demonstrated in unprecedented scope and horror the human capacity for destruction of life. Yet the extent of this impression prepared no one for the Holocaust or the bomb; nor does it approach the dimensions of our own musings on World War III or the prognosis of the AIDS epidemic. The speed and efficiency of communication, of course, has kept pace with these developments. Indeed, the rate both of ideological change and of technological development that so distinguishes the modern epoch is the principal reason that perceptions of crisis have affected theatre in the twentieth century so uniquely. Never before has the theatre been so frequently challenged to participate in ideological revolutions. Concomitantly, the unprecedented rate of technological development over the past century has expanded both our ability to enhance or destroy life and our ability to imagine and represent in the theatre that enhancement or destruction. As a consequence, what I would call an "Expressionist attitude" toward the theatrical representation of life is a significantly recurring feature of twentieth-century theatre. Despite the persistence of realist impulses such as the New Objectivity, this general attitude – as distinct from any specific stylistic tradition expressive of it – has repeatedly surfaced and required the theatre to develop performative rhetorics of drastic cultural change.

In these terms, a playwright like Büchner should be regarded as more of an historical visionary than a theatrical reformer. His *Woyzeck* anticipated, nearly a century before its time, the violence that history would inflict upon dramatic form. The Expressionists were among the first to realize that theatrical performance had to suffer a similar assault in order to be of any historical utility. Whether or not twentieth-century life in fact has been more catastrophic than any other epoch is beside the point; what is unprecedented, as I say, is our ability to imagine and represent it so. This is the general heritage that, repeatedly over the last eighty years, has suggested the viability of specific Expressionist methods in theatrical representation. Chief among these legacies, the strategy of coming to terms with historical crisis by anthropomorphizing it in the body and voice of the actor remains evident to the present day. From the Expressionist theatre, in short, we have learned much about how to use the actor to help us imagine history rhetorically, both as actuality and possibility.

Notes

INTRODUCTION

1 Ulrich Weisstein, *Expressionism as an International Literary Phenomenon* (Paris: Didier, 1973), 17.

2 Reinhardt's Regiebücher, of course, contain important information about his approach to Expressionist scripts; and I shall have occasion to draw upon this source material for my discussion in Chapter Three of the Das junge Deutschland première of Sorge's *Der Bettler*. To be sure, Reinhardt was among the pioneers of Expressionist staging. However, he never became so involved with the movement's aesthetic principles as to be considered an "Expressionist" director in the programmatic sense of directors like Schreyer, Karlheinz Martin, or Leopold Jessner. Moreover, Expressionist performance in Reinhardt's productions appears to have been based on powerful, essentially realistic, character acting. It was not governed by the kind of broadly abstract directorial stylization typical of Jessner's work most notably, or that of Schreyer, Martin, and Jürgen Fehling. This study will argue that the productions of these directors developed the most "Expressionist" quality of Expressionist performance – its ability to transform the actor into a non-mimetic, abstract medium of expression.

   Aside from Schreyer, the directors most associated with the heyday of theatrical Expressionism were Jessner, Martin, Fehling, Gustav Hartung, Richard Weichert, and Otto Falckenberg. Jessner's *Schriften* (ed. H. Fetting, East Berlin, 1979) and Fehling's *Die Magie des Theaters* (1965) both make occasional references to Expressionist production as a part of the larger, more stylistically varied bodies of their directorial work. But neither identifies himself so exclusively and comprehensively with Expressionism as Schreyer, for whom it was a life-long preoccupation.

3 It is true that a figure like the revolutionary leader Sonja in Ernst Toller's *Masse Mensch* [1921] represents a positive female image. Also, the principal female character in his *Hoppla, wir leben!*, Eva Berg, is a figure of revolutionary integrity. But this latter play of Toller's, written for production by the Piscator-Bühne in 1927, is not really an Expressionist drama in conception or theme. It does, however, retain

248

something of Toller's earlier style in its diction and in the lyricism with which the role of the central character is written.

4   *See* Roy F. Allen, *Literary Life in German Expressionism and the Berlin Circles* (Ann Arbor: University of Michigan Press), 1983.

5   Historically, the phrase operated either as the contemporary shibboleth developed and invoked by adherents of the movement itself working in the theatre, or as a retrospective category applied, sometimes indiscriminately, by later critics and theatre historians. In either case, certain artists whose theatre work is often considered seminal for the movement – Oskar Kokoschka, say, or Ernst Barlach – sometimes protested such categorization. *See* Oskar Kokoschka, *My Life*, trans. David Britt (New York: MacMillan, 1974), 30. For the April 1921 Staatstheater production of his play *Die echten Sedemunds* (1920), Barlach had expected a more or less realistic presentation. However, the markedly Expressionist staging given it by Leopold Jessner drew the following quip from the author: "I was at the second performance and saw a play by Herr Jessner, but not by me. Film tempo and expression. I'll have nothing to do with it." *See* Ernst Barlach, *Prosa aus vier Jahrzehnten*, ed. Elmer Jansen (Berlin: Union Verlag, 1966), 471. It is true that Kokoschka was closely associated from 1910 to 1911 with the *Sturm* Circle, serving as Walden's Austria-Hungary editor of *Der Sturm* during that time and frequently contributing to the periodical for years afterward. Consequently, as Allen notes, he "left a decisive imprint on the journal especially [in] its formative years." *See* Allen, *Literary Life in German Expressionism*, 94. *Mörder, Hoffnung der Frauen* (1909), arguably Kokoschka's most influential Expressionist play, was written and initially staged before his association with the *Sturm* Circle began. However, the illustrations to the play Kokoschka published in *Der Sturm* in the years 1911–12 left a strong impression on everyone connected with the *Sturm* association.

6   *See* for example, respectively, Peter Hohendahl, *Das Bild der bürgerlichen Welt im expressionistischen Drama* (Heidelberg: Winter), 1967; Horst Denkler, *Drama des Expressionismus: Programm, Spieltext, Theater* (Munich: Fink), 1967; and Annalisa Viviani, *Dramaturgische Elemente im expressionistischen Drama* (Bonn: H. Bouvier Verlag), 1970.

7   Mel Gordon, "German Expressionist Acting," *Drama Review* 19, no.3 (1975):34–55. The terms of Gordon's taxonomy of performance styles – "Geist," "Schrei," and "Ich" – are borrowed, he acknowledges, from Diebold's *Anarchie im Drama*. This appropriation, however, is somewhat loose in that Diebold himself never actually identifies a "Geist" type of Expressionist play. Further, scripts which, according to Gordon, particularly lent themselves to the "Schrei" production style (Hasenclever's *Der Sohn*; von Unruh's *Ein Geschlecht*), Diebold classifies as *Ich-Dramen* and *Pflichtdramen* (dramas of "duty" or "responsibility") respectively. While Karl Heinz Martin's Tribüne Theater production of *Die Wandlung* (Berlin, 1919) exemplifies the "Ich"

performance mode for Gordon, Diebold sees Toller's play merely as a type of revolutionary drama.

8 *See* Dennis Calandra, "Georg Kaiser's *From Morn to Midnight*: the Nature of Expressionist Performance" *Theatre Quarterly*, no. 6 (Spring, 1976): 45–54.

9 Among the titles I have found helpful the following might be particularly noted: Arthur Rosenberg, *A History of the German Republic*, trans. Ian F. D. Morrow, 1936; Carl E. Schorske, *German Social Democracy: 1905–1917*, 1955; Ralf Dahrendorf, *Gesellschaft und Demokratie in Deutschland*, Munich, 1965; E. K. Bramsted, *Aristocracy and the Middle Classes*, 2nd ed. Chicago, 1964; Dieter Rückhaberle, *et al.*, *Theater in der Weimarer Republik*, Berlin, 1977.

10 Herbert Ihering, *Begegnungen mit Zeit und Menschen* (Bremen: n.p., 1965), 25. This quotation is translated and cited in Allen, *Literary Life in German Expressionism*, 15.

1. ABSTRACTION AND EMPATHY

1 In one relatively early study of the movement, no less than four distinct viewpoints are identified: activism, cynicism, nationalism, and spiritual universalism. According to this account, the methods of the first two were generally rationalist, while the last (and apparently the third as well) were more emotionally and spiritually oriented, resulting in a basic artistic strategy of irrationalism. While it offered little hope of positive renewal, the cynical perspective at least promised an uncompromising penetration to the essential truth of the human condition. Presumably, to give even this negative stance ardent expressive form was a redemptive act. See R. Samuel and R. Hinton Thomas, *Expressionism in German Life, Literature and the Theatre (1910–24)* (Cambridge: Heffer, 1939), 14.

2 The same was true for the Russian Futurists, whom Lenin contemptuously dismissed in 1919 as a "plethora of bourgeois intellectuals, who very often regarded the new type of workers' and peasants' educational institution as the most convenient field for testing their individual theories in philosophy and culture." *See* Leon Trotsky, "First All-Russian Congress on Adult Education, 6–19 May 1919," in *Collected Works* (Moscow: Progress, 1965), 29:336. *Cited in* Marjorie Perloff, *The Futurist Movement* (Chicago: University of Chicago Press, 1986), 33.

3 *Abstraction and Empathy: a Contribution to the Psychology of Style*, 1908, trans. Michael Bullock (London: Routledge and Kegan Paul Ltd., 1968), 3, 11, 9. Worringer borrowed this term from the Viennese art historian Alois Riegel, who used it to designate the fundamental psychic drive within all artistic activity. However, this basic urge concretizes itself *distinctively*, Riegel argued, in every epoch of art; accordingly, the style of every

period is dependent on its own particular type of artistic volition or "will to form." See Weisstein, *Expressionism as an International Literary Phenomenon*, 49.

4 Rudolf Blümner, *Der Geist des Kubismus* (Berlin: n.p., 1921), 66.

5 John Willett, *Expressionism* (New York: McGraw, 1970), 25.

6 Samuel and Thomas, *Expressionism in German Life, Literature and the Theatre*, 10; Armin Arnold, *Die Literatur des Expressionismus: sprachliche und thematische Quellen* (Stuttgart: Kohlhammer, 1966), 9–15; Christopher Innes, *Holy Theatre: Ritual and the Avant Garde* (Cambridge: Cambridge University Press, 1981), 39.

7 At the same time, it should be noted that several scripts widely regarded as Expressionist during and after the era pre-date Hasenclever's play – among them: Oskar Kokoschka's *Mörder, Hoffnung der Frauen* (1909), Barlach's *Der tote Tag* (1912), Georg Kaiser's *Von morgens bis mitternachts* (1912) and most notably, Reinhard Sorge's *Der Bettler* (1912). Moreover, as John Willett has noted, there was an unusual time lag of several years between the publication of many of these early Expressionist scripts and their stage premières. In general, this time lag can be attributed to the typical hesitance of established commercial theatres in taking financial risks. See Willett, *The Theatre of the Weimar Republic*, 47. Though *Der Bettler* is often thought of as the earliest fully "Expressionist" play, it was Hasenclever who first presented his play, *Der Sohn*, on stage in 1916 under this rubric.

8 Kurt Pinthus, editor of the first Expressionist anthology, *Menschheitsdämmerung* (Twilight of Mankind), actually dates the beginning of literary Expressionism as a movement from novelist Max Brod's 1910 public reading of the Franz Werfel poem "An den Leser" to a group of Berlin students and literati. Others have attributed this inaugural honor to Franz Pfemfert's publication in *Die Aktion* of the poem "Weltende" by Jakob van Hoddis in 1911.

9 Peter Gay, *Weimar Culture: the Outsider as Insider* (New York : Harper, 1970), 67.

10 Albert Soergel, *Dichtung und Dichter der Zeit: Eine Schilderung der deutschen Literatur der letzten Jahrzehnte. Neue Folge: Im Banne des Expressionismus* (Leipzig: Voigtländer, 1925), 636, 599, 641.

11 Walter Sokel, *The Writer in Extremis: Expressionism in Twentieth-Century German Literature* (Stanford: Stanford University Press, 1959), 76.

12 Immanuel Kant, *Critique of Aesthetic Judgment*, trans. James C. Meredith (Oxford: Clarendon, 1911), 175. In the ensuing discussion of the philosophical tradition, my observations on the relevant ideas of Kant and Schiller, as well as Schopenhauer's concepts of music and "the Will," have been guided by Walter Sokel's presentation of this material in his *The Writer in Extremis*, 7–28.

13 Friedrich Schiller, *On the Aesthetic Education of Man*, ed. Elizabeth Wilkinson and L. A. Willoughby (Oxford: Clarendon, 1967), 154–57.

The rendering of this passage is the product of my negotiation with the editors' translation, which I find not altogether satisfactory.

14 Vassily Kandinsky, *Concerning the Spiritual in Art*, trans. Michael Sadleir (New York: Wittenborn, 1947), 47–48. It is important to note that, as applied to the stage, Kandinsky's principle of the self-sufficiency of form was not unprecedented in German theatre theory. The tradition of "Kulturtheater" and its central concept of the "Stilbühne" dates back to the turn of the century. Peter Behrens's influential pamphlet, *Feste des Lebens und der Kunst* (1900) [*Celebrations of Life and of Art*], for example, bears the telling subtitle, "a consideration of the theatre as the highest cultural symbol." Style, argued Behrens, is "the symbol of the totality of the emotional and philosophical response of an age . . . It is not the illusion of nature that is to be created but of our sublime aloofness from nature. The name of this illusion is culture." See Wilhelm Hortmann, *Shakespeare on the German Stage* (Cambridge: Cambridge University Press, 1985), 2:17–18. The Expressionist idea of a spiritual theatre drew upon this immediate precedent of the Stilbühne movement along with the general tradition of theatrical "Bildung" as articulated by Schiller and first attempted by Goethe with his classicist approach to staging at Weimar. As Hortmann notes, proponents of the Stilbühne "wanted to abolish the tawdry realism of the average set and the grating stylistic dissonances from one set to the next in the same play. They sought to achieve this by fewer scene changes, simpler and more versatile stage architecture, and by *décor* of a unified and recognizable style, hence 'Stilbühne'." (p.22) The Expressionist directors would infuse this formalist idea of unity and simplicity with the intense accents and distortions which registered the urgency of their commitment to social activism.

15 Arthur Schopenhauer, *The World as Will and Idea*, 3rd ed., 3 vols., trans. R. B. Haldane and J. Kemp (London: Paul, Trench, Trübner, 1888), 1:333.

16 *Ibid.*, 1:130–41, 2:482.

17 The words "changing complex of behavior" are Joseph Bernstein's rendering of Kornfeld's phrase "wechselnde Summe." See Walter Sokel, ed., *An Anthology of German Expressionist Drama* (New York: Anchor Doubleday, 1963), 7.

18 Paul Kornfeld, "Nachwort an den Schauspieler," in *Literaturrevolution 1910–1925*, 2 vols., ed. Paul Pörtner (Darmstadt: Luchterhand, 1960), 1:351.

19 Kasimir Edschmid, *Über den Expressionismus in der Literatur und die neue Dichtung* (Berlin: Reiss, 1919), 55.

20 See Günther Rühle, ed., *Zeit und Theater: Vom Kaiserreich zur Republik 1913–1925*, 2 vols., (N.p.: Propyläen, N.d.), 1:59–60.

21 *The Writer in Extremis*, 51.

22 See Ludwig Lewin, *Die Jagd nach dem Erlebnis: Ein Buch über Georg Kaiser* (Berlin: Die Schmiede, 1926), 133.

23 The popularity of Nietzschean thought among young German artists and intellectuals at this time cannot be overstressed. The Expressionists first encountered his writings under the influence of their literary circles, but also as a function of the general Nietzsche craze in the first two decades of the twentieth century. In the context of theatre his impact extended even to paratheatrical contexts such as cabaret, a point to be discussed in the next chapter. So wide-ranging was Nietzsche's appeal that, in the words of Peter Jelavich, "people of every imaginable persuasion – from anarchists and Social Democrats to anti-Semites and the far Right – were attempting to appropriate Nietzsche to their causes . . ." See Peter Jelavich, *Berlin Cabaret* (Cambridge: Harvard University Press, 1993), 28.

24 *Nietzsche-Wagner Correspondence*, ed. Elizabeth Foerster-Nietzsche, trans. Caroline V. Kerr (New York: Liveright, 1921), 167.

25 Friedrich Nietzsche, *The Birth of Tragedy and the Case of Wagner*, trans. Walter Kaufmann (New York: Random House, 1967), 183.

26 Henri Bergson, *Creative Evolution*, trans. Arthur Mitchell (New York: Modern Library, 1944), 146.

27 *Thus Spake Zarathustra*, trans. Thomas Common (New York: Heritage, 1967), 5, 8.

28 *Beyond Good and Evil: Prelude to a Philosophy of the Future*, trans. Helen Zimmern (New York: MacMillan, 1924), 162.

29 Egbert Krispyn, *Style and Society in German Literary Expressionism* (Gainesville: University of Florida Press, 1964), 15.

30 *The Writer in Extremis*, 99.

31 His famous performance as Gessler in Jessner's 1919 Staatstheater production of *Wilhelm Tell*, for example, was modeled on a tyrannical geometry teacher. See *Aller Tage Abend* (Munich: Kindler, 1959), 51–52.

32 Indeed, all of the Expressionist circles and affiliations were characterized by strong leadership; and, not infrequently, new associations resulted from the clash of dominant personalities. Kurt Hiller, for example, having quarreled with other leaders of "Der neue Club" in 1911 seceded to organize the circle known as "Das Gnu." Subsequently, his break in 1913 with Ernst Blass, another secessionist, spelled the end of Das Gnu. Herwarth Walden's founding of *Der Sturm* follows a similar story of stormy relations with journalistic associates.

33 In Sorge's *Der Bettler* (1912) these two functions are somewhat combined in the central figure who murders his father not out of hatred but as a gesture of loving mercy towards a representative figure, who, rather uncharacteristically, realizes that the time has come for his generation to step aside.

34 See Ernest K. Bramsted, *Aristocracy and the Middle Class in Germany*, 2nd ed. (Chicago: University of Chicago Press, 1964), 229.

35 Ralf Dahrendorf, *Society and Democracy in Germany* (New York: Anchor-Doubleday, 1969), 51.

36 *Style and Society in German Literary Expressionism*, 8–11.

37 Franz Werfel, *Nicht der Mörder, der Ermordete ist schuldig* (Munich: Wolff, 1920), 137.

38 Franz Kafka, "Brief an den Vater," *Die neue Rundschau* 63, no.2 (1952):12.

39 With reference to Hasenclever's representative play *Der Sohn*, for example, the Expressionist theorist Rudolf Kayser wrote that "the protest against fathers can only signify a protest against the inhibitions on the vitality of the young [*jugendlichen Lebens*] by state, society, family." See Rudolf Kayser, "*Der Sohn*: Anmerkungen zur neu-Aufführung," *Das junge Deutschland* 1 (1918):315. However, it should be noted that the father–son conflict was also fueled by specific instances of parental abuse. A shocking case in point was that of Otto Gross, a young physician and psychoanalyst influential in Expressionist literary circles, whose father had him forcibly carried off to a mental institution in 1913 apparently for no other reason than that Gross's bohemian life-style and associations displeased him. This affair excited great outrage in the German avant-garde literary community, and Gross predictably became a sensational *cause célèbre* as a chilling real-life type of the aggrieved younger generation. See Thomas Anz and Michael Stark, eds., *Expressionismus: Manifeste und Dokumente zur deutschen Literatur 1910–1920* (Stuttgart: Metzler, 1982), 145. The rather comic flip-side of this situation is evident in the case of Max Brod, who, according to Roy Allen, "felt that the father–son conflict was so crucial to Expressionism that he was induced to assert that he himself, although he felt he was an Expressionist, held an 'isolated position' in the movement because of the absence of [this conflict] in his life." See Allen, *Literary Life in German Expressionism*, 275, n.32.

40 Michael Patterson, *The Revolution in German Theatre: 1900–1930* (Boston: Routledge, 1981), 14.

41 Ernst Toller, "Bemerkungen zu meinem Drama *Die Wandlung*," in *Schöpferische Konfession* (Berlin: Reiss, 1922), 46.

42 Peter Jelavich, *Munich and Theatrical Modernism* (Cambridge, MA: Harvard University Press, 1985), 6. Jelavich argues that artists in the Munich avant-garde community responded to censorship in one of two basic ways: either they became apolitical and "aesthetically introverted," or they tended towards activism. In the latter group, a minority adopted a proto-fascist ideology of cultural totalitarianism, while the majority espoused anarchism (7). Arguably, the utopianism of these right- and left-wing factions was no less politically escapist than the introversion of the aesthetes. It was a general susceptibility to idealism which politically enfeebled the avant-garde in its losing battle with censorship before the war and prevented even the left-wing activists from developing a practical and effective political discourse after the war. At any rate, the anarchist view, as noted above, was not characteristic of Expressionist associations specifically. Both philosophically and practically, it accorded

much more readily with a general bohemian life-style, from which, as Allen argues, Expressionist literary life is distinguishable by its consistent tendency toward formal organization and structuring of its activities. See *Literary Life in German Expressionism*, 22–23.

43 Patterson, *The Revolution in German Theatre: 1900–1930*, 28–29.

44 The other side of this coin, of course, was that such rejection was deemed a sign of both artistic merit and social worth by artists who saw cultural outsidership as the very *raison d' être* of their work.

45 Istvan Deak, *Weimar Germany's Left-Wing Intellectuals* (Berkeley: University of California Press, 1968), 28.

46 *Style and Society in German Literary Expressionism*, 16–17.

47 Franz Werfel, "Aphorismus zu diesem Jahr," *Die Aktion* 4 (1914):904; Ludwig Rubiner, "Der Kampf mit dem Engel," *Die Aktion* 7 (1917):226; Ernst Toller, *I Was a German*, ed. Edward Crankshaw (New York: Morrow, 1934), 19–23, (originally published in 1933 under the title *Eine Jugend in Deutschland* [A Youth in Germany]); *Aller Tage Abend*, 383.

48 Paul Kornfeld, "Der beseelte und der psychologische Mensch," *Das junge Deutschland* 1, no.1 (1917):1–2.

49 Ernst Blass, "The Old in Café des Westens," *The Era of German Expressionism*, ed. Paul Raabe, trans. J. Ritchie (New York: Overlook, 1974), 30.

50 *The Writer in Extremis*, 3.

2. THE POETICS OF EXPRESSIONIST PERFORMANCE

1 John Willett, *Expressionism* (New York: McGraw, 1970), 6.

2 Rudolf Kayser, "Das neue Drama," *Das junge Deutschland* 10 (1917):1–2; reprinted in *Literaturrevolution, 1910–1925. See* Pörtner, 2:235.

3 More than simply a character he created, this figure was transparently autobiographical, a deliberate self-portrayal in terms of his struggle with censorship. The unique qualities of Wedekind's performance style stem from its reflexivity. For him, the stage was a highly personal arena in which he worked through the aesthetic, moral, and social problems which arose out of his dramatic writing. Of *Die Zensur* he once wrote:

Had I wished to call the child by its true name, I would have had to call the one-acter "Exhibitionism" or "Self-Portrait." The critics have often reproached me that my dramas are about myself. I would like to show that it's worth the trouble to bring myself onto the stage.

See Günther Seehaus, *Frank Wedekind und das Theater* (Munich: Laokoon Verlag, 1964), 613.

4 Hugo Ball, "Wedekind als Schauspieler," *Phöbus* 1, no.3 (1914):105–08; reprinted in Pörtner, *Literaturrevolution 1910–1925*, 1: 339–40.

5 Kortner, *Aller Tage Abend*, 197.

6 Bertolt Brecht, "Frank Wedekind," *Augsburger Neueste Nachrichten*, 12

March, 1918; reprinted in *Brecht on Theatre*, ed. and trans. John Willett (New York: Hill, 1964), 3–4. It should be noted that these are the comments of a young Brecht who, as Günther Seehaus remarks, hadn't yet developed "the cool, de-emotionalizing, data-recording [*Protokollierung*]" style of his later analytical prose. "Nonetheless," Seehaus continues, "Brecht never again experienced an encounter with another author – both his work and his personality – so immediately and so personally." *See* Günther Seehaus, *Frank Wedekind* (Reinbek: Rowohlt, 1974), 9–10.

7 Like contemporary media personalities, Wedekind's presence, more often than not, seems to have carried with it a theatricality that transformed real-life situations into stage events. At times, an unfortunate and certainly unintended by-product was self-parody. In a 1914 public address, Wedekind shocked many of his admirers by expressing sympathy for the war effort. According to the Expressionist poet Johannes Becher, he "welcomed the German invasion of Holland and Belgium and pointed out how this military operation would be of great economic advantage, especially because it opened up a rich field of activity for the German Civil Service. The German Civil Servant was lauded by Wedekind as a new type of human being, far surpassing the English Colonial Official, who would see his calling in spreading efficiency and reliability throughout the world. The Age of the German Civil Servant had arrived. In his lofty ethical mission only the Christian missionary was in any way comparable to him. The public, at first not sure whether Frank Wedekind was being serious or facetious, was slow to applaud – but in fact Wedekind was in deadly earnest about everything he had said and he complained bitterly in the wings that, once again, he had not been taken seriously." *See* Paul Raabe, ed., *The Era of German Expressionism*, trans. J. M. Ritchie (Woodstock, NY: Overlook, 1974), 367.

For the last twenty years of his life, the question of Wedekind's public character was repeatedly and hotly debated in the courtroom and in the press. To advocates he was a champion of free speech and moral freedom; to opponents, a dangerous perverter of public morals. Constructed and re-constructed thus by friend and foe alike, his public identity took on a notorious life of its own over which he was never quite able to gain control. Even his funeral and interment degenerated into a histrionic circus. *See* Tilly Newes Wedekind, *Lulu: die Rolle meines Lebens* (Munich: Rütten und Loening Verlag, 1969), 201–03; also, Seehaus, *Frank Wedekind*, 11.

8 The many testimonials to Wedekind by his contemporaries as *the* representative figure of their era are most comprehensively presented in *Das Wedekindbuch*. This was a collection of laudatory essays published as part of a celebration sponsored by many of Germany's leading literary and theatrical figures on the occasion of his fiftieth birthday in 1914. As

Kurt Pinthus later succinctly put it: "We all worshiped [him]." *See* Raabe, 71.

9 For a full description of the features of Wedekindstil in performance, see David F. Kuhns, "Wedekind, the Actor: Aesthetics, Morality, and Monstrosity," *Theatre Survey* 31.2 (November 1990): 144–64.

10 Artur Kutscher, *Frank Wedekind: Sein Leben und seine Werke*, 3 vols. (Munich: Georg Müller, 1931), 2:185.

11 Kutscher, 2:71; Sol Gittleman, *Frank Wedekind* (New York: Twayne, 1969), xi.

12 Kutscher, 2:192.

13 Julius Bab, *Das Theater der Gegenwart* (Leipzig: Weber, 1928), 175.

14 Hans-Jochen Irmer, *Der Theaterdichter Frank Wedekind* (Berlin: Henschelverlag, 1975), 260.

15 *Ibid.*, 264, 266.

16 *Ibid.*, 261.

17 Heinrich Mann, "Erinnerungen an Frank Wedekind," Wedekind Archive – MS.L3681, Handschriften-sammlung der Stadtbibliothek Munich.

18 Seehaus, *Frank Wedekind und das Theater*, 410.

19 Irmer, 262–63. This analysis is particularly significant in that Wedekind himself validated it in a letter thanking Zeiss for his defense of Wedekind's acting in an essay written for *Das Wedekindbuch*, mentioned above in note 8. *See* Frank Wedekind, *Gesammelte Briefe*, 2 vols., ed. Fritz Strich (Munich: Müller Verlag, 1924), 2:300 (Letter No.423).

20 Tilla Durieux, *Eine Tür steht offen* (Berlin: Herbig, 1965), 75.

21 *Ibid.*, 75, 146.

22 *See* his essay on Wedekind as both playwright and actor in Joachim Friedenthal, ed., *Das Wedekindbuch* (Munich: Müller, 1914), 257.

23 Having developed the basic features of this unique performance style before 1905, he anticipates the Futurists and Dadaists by nearly a decade.

24 Peter Jelavich argues that, in terms of dramaturgy, Wedekind's technique becomes one of "negative characterization" with respect to Lulu. "He could not show what Lulu's personality was," says Jelavich, "but he could indicate what it was not" – e.g., she has no parentage, no social class, not even a unique proper name (Nellie, Eve, Mignon, Lulu, etc.). See *Munich and Theatrical Modernism* (Cambridge: Harvard University Press, 1985), 111. Clearly, however, her victims share in the responsibility for their destruction in that they all rhetorically evade or deny the moral accountability with which they are confronted in the person of Lulu, the mirror of their own depravity.

25 Edschmid's real name was Eduard Schmid. Presumably this pseudonym – in which the last name is a contraction of the full name and the first name an exotic substitute for the Christian name – was taken up, to some degree, tongue-in-cheek. However, other prominent Expression-

ists – notably the impresario Herwarth Walden (*né* Georg Levin) and the influential poet Jakob von Hoddis (*né* Hans Davidsohn) – made the same gesture. It perhaps reflects a self-conscious sense of role-playing as a strategy of cultural struggle. See M. S. Jones, *Der Sturm: a focus of Expressionism* (Columbia, S.C.: Camden House, 1984), 2; and Willett, *Expressionism*, 74. According to Jones, Walden's pseudonym was given him by his first wife, the prominent Expressionist poet Else Lasker-Schüler, "who considered his family name too bourgeois. She therefore invented a new one with a more 'artistic' and 'mysterious' ring to it."

26 Kasimir Edschmid, "Schauspielkunst," in *Das deutsche Theater der Gegenwart*, ed. Max Krell (Munich: Rösl, 1923), 118, 120. However "helpless" he may have seemed to Edschmid, for the critic Felix Salten Wedekind conveyed the dazzling impression of a playwright composing in the course of performing as an actor. Salten observed that,

> Frank Wedekind didn't transform himself; rather it was as though he somehow doubled himself. One always saw the poet himself, but one also saw the Marquis of Keith . . . We had before us the creator and the creation all in one . . . entirely as a poet, he created a character, and now on the stage he once again created it anew, completely filled with the ecstasy of forming it . . . and while doing so he devised for himself an acting technique, improvised the means of presentation, discovered for himself in them the limitations and the surprising little difficulties of the scene, of the speech, of stasis and movement on the stage, of the pauses and the attacks. He struggled with them and conquered them by means of instantaneously devised expedients.

See Irmer, 265.
27 Ball, "Wedekind als Schauspieler," 340.
28 Frank Wedekind, "Zirkusgedanken," in *Werke*, 3 vols., ed. Manfred Hahn (Berlin: Aufbau Verlag, 1969), 3:156.
29 *Ibid.*, 161, 155.
30 *Ibid.*, 154, 155.
31 Alan Best, *Frank Wedekind* (London: Wolff, 1975), 16.
32 Quoted in Kutscher, 2:89.
33 Kutscher, 2:79.
34 At the same time, Bierbaum also took note of how, after a few years as cutting-edge centers of avant-garde experimentation, such pioneering ventures as the French cabaret, "Le Chat noir," had become kitsch tourist traps. In his 1897 novel, *Stilpe*, he had both advocated the variety stage as a vehicle for the Jugendstil renewal of everyday life and cautioned against the threat posed by commercialism to such an enterprise. See Jelavich, *Berlin Cabaret*, 27.
35 Kutscher, 2:80.
36 Von Wolzogen, founder of Berlin's first cabaret, even claims in his memoir that Nietzsche's key term "Übermensch" was the inspiration

for his own coinage of the word "Überbrettl," which quickly became a standard designation for the cabaret as a specific kind of avant-garde alternative stage. *See* Jelavich, *Berlin Cabaret*, 29.

37 Gottfried Reinhardt, *The Genius: a Memoir of Max Reinhardt* (New York: Knopf, 1979), 277.

38 Harold B. Segel, *Turn-of-the-Century Cabaret* (New York: Columbia, 1987), 137.

39 Jelavich, *Berlin Cabaret*, 184–85.

40 Lisa Appignanesi, *The Cabaret* (New York: Universe, 1976), 30.

41 Charlotte W. MacArthur, "Portraitists in performance – four women originals," Ph.D. Diss. (University of Pittsburgh, 1987), 3, 11, 4–5. I am indebted to Ms. MacArthur for the term "portraitist performance."

42 Kutscher 2: 88

43 Jelavich, *Berlin Cabaret*, 1.

44 *See* Allen, *Literary Life in German Expressionism*, 77, for a detailed discussion of how such cabarets fostered the growth of political thought in specifically literary terms.

45 Quoted in J. M. Ritchie, *German Expressionist Drama* (Boston: Twayne, 1976), 34.

46 *See* Jelavich, *Berlin Cabaret*, 34–35. Here Jelavich shows how on the one hand the police could and did suppress radically subversive cabaret stage activity; yet, on the other, they were sensitive about preserving Berlin's reputation as a sophisticated "Weltstadt." In any case, because the actions of the censor were routinely a matter of public record in the newspapers, they certainly wanted to avoid any unnecessary publicity that would create a succés de scandale. The authorities, unwilling to act too quickly or heavy-handedly, and the cabarets, constantly experimenting to see how much they could get away with, played a lively game of cat and mouse that hurt nobody and apparently amused most of the players most of the time.

47 "On the Art of Living Theatre," in Oliver M. Sayler. ed., *Max Reinhardt and His Theatre*, 1924 (New York: Blom, 1968), 64.

48 Max Reinhardt, "On the Art of the Theatre," in *Max Reinhardt and His Theatre. See* Sayler, 57–58.

49 For a detailed account of this initial program, see Jelavich, *Berlin Cabaret*, 64–88.

50 A fictitious noble ruler of a small principality, Serenissimus was the consummate philistine, devoid of any political or cultural sophistication. His adviser, therefore, had to interpret the significance of every dramatic situation on stage. Often Serenissimus would stand to make a comment or ask a naive question from his seat in the Kaiser's box, the subscription to which the real-life Wilhelm had cancelled in protest over Schall und Rauch's satirical representation of life in his regime. *See* Jelavich, *Berlin Cabaret*, 73.

51 *See* Max Reinhardt, *Ich bin nichts als ein Theatermann: Briefe, Reden, Aufsätze,*

Interviews, Gespräche, Auszüge aus Regiebüchern, ed. Hugo Fetting (Berlin: N.p., 1989), 61.

52 Carl Heine, "The Actor of Reinhardt's Ensemble," in *Max Reinhardt and His Theatre*. *See* Sayler, 112.

53 Martin Esslin, "Max Reinhardt – High Priest of Theatricality," *Drama Review* 21, no.2 (June 1977): 7.

54 Gertrud Eysoldt, "How Reinhardt Works With His Actors," in *Max Reinhardt and his Theatre*. *See* Sayler, 102–03.

55 Ernst Deutsch, "Reinhardt and the Young Actor," in *Max Reinhardt and His Theatre*. *See* Sayler, 107–08.

56 "The Actor of Reinhardt's Ensemble," 112.

57 Edward Braun, *The Director and the Stage: from Naturalism to Grotowski* (New York: Holmes, 1982), 95.

58 Edward Gordon Craig, *On the Art of the Theatre* (Boston: Samuel, 1925), 55, 58.

59 *Ibid.*, 61.

60 *Ibid.*, 61, 93, 81, 82, 84–85.

61 Ritchie, *German Expressionist Drama*, 30.

62 Craig's exhibitions of his scenic designs between December 1904 and October 1905 in Berlin, Düsseldorf, Cologne, Dresden, Munich and Vienna also greatly influenced German theatre production. *See* Braun, 87. In particular, Max Reinhardt was "deeply and decisively" impressed by Craig's work. *See* Gottfried Reinhardt, *The Genius*, 16.

63 Emile Jacques Dalcroze, *Eurhythmics, Art and Education*, ed. Cynthia Cox, trans. Frederick Rothwell (1930; reprint, Salem, NH: Ayer, 1985), 7, 11.

64 Vera Maletic, *Body – Space – Expression: the Development of Rudolf Laban's Movement and Dance Concepts* (Berlin: Mouton de Gruyter, 1987), 6–7.

65 John Foster, *The Influence of Rudolf Laban* (London: Lepus, 1977), 16–17, 21.

66 Rudolf Laban, *A Life for Dance*, trans. Lisa Ullmann (1935; reprint, New York: Theatre Arts Books, 1975), 146–47.

67 Maletic, 7–8, 27.

68 John Schikowski, *Geschichte des Tanzes* (Berlin: Büchergilde Gutenberg, 1926), 137.

69 Foster, 40.

70 Maletic, 97–98.

71 Laban, *A Life for Dance*, 87, 129, 84.

72 Quoted in Maletic, 7.

73 Maletic, 34.

74 In a recent essay, the German dance critic Hedwig Müller stresses that this term referred not simply to a single style or technique but rather to a wide range of quite distinct styles whose common element was, presumably, the general intention of making some sort of personal or social statement through dance. *See* Hedwig Müller, "Jooss and Expressionism," in *Jooss: Dokumentation von Anna und Hermann Markard* (Cologne: Ballet-Bühnen-Verlag, 1985), 13.

75 In the case of Futurism, this originally loose identification – vociferously repudiated by the Italian cultural establishment – modulated into a militant nationalism with the outbreak of war. In its origins, however, Futurism draws heavily upon the distinctive spirit of such French avant-garde figures as Apollinaire and Jarry, with both of whom Marinetti had extensive contact in Paris from the late 1890s onward. For a discussion of the "Franco-Italian" character of early Futurism, and the particularly profound influence of Jarry on Marinetti, see R. W. Flint's introduction to F. T. Marinetti, *Selected Writings*, ed. and trans. R. W. Flint and Arthur A. Coppotelli (New York: Farrar, Straus, and Giroux, 1972), 13–17.

76 Having arrived in Paris as a young man of seventeen, Marinetti was initially drawn to the declining Symbolist school. But he was more attracted to its general reputation as a revolutionary movement than to its actual poetic methods or metaphysical vision. Subsequently, he embraced the emergent aesthetic program of "naturisme," championed by Saint-Georges de Bouhélier. Arising out of the modern urban environment, this movement, wrote the poet Apollinaire, "impressed the spirits of the young men of my generation . . . [who] . . . discovered themselves the sons of Naturalism and chose Emile Zola as their master." Quoted in Marianne W. Martin, *Futurist Art and Theory: 1909–1915* (Oxford: Clarendon, 1968), 29. The poetry Marinetti himself composed from the late 1890s on substituted an extroverted, exuberant, at times violent, celebration of modern life for the introverted, melancholy escapism of high Symbolist French poetry. Yet the Symbolists' imagistic expressive economy was to be become the hallmark of Futurist literary and performance art.

77 R. S. Furness, *Expressionism* (London: Methuen, 1973), 12–13.

78 Particularly in terms of influence on the German literary and theatrical avant-garde, a distinction must, of course, be drawn between Italian Futurism and its Russian variant. Though Mayakovsky and others of the pre-war Russian avant-garde were influenced by Italian Futurism, even to the point of adopting its name, the Russian Futurist movement from early on was less international in character. The profound influence of Marinetti's 1909 founding manifesto, when it came out simultaneously in Russia as well as Paris, was that it opened a new way for the young Russian avant-garde to address their concern for developing a distinctly Russian cultural revolution. Not surprisingly, this nationalist appropriation of Futurism modulated into an aesthetics of specific political action in the early years of the Soviet revolution and its immediate aftermath. As I noted earlier in this study, however, Lenin contemptuously rejected, as mere politicized bourgeois formalism, the aesthetic strategies Russian Futurism offered as a socio-political praxis. See Chapter 1, n.2.

79 It is a curious paradox in the histories of modern art and performance

that the most revolutionary of movements – Futurism, Dada, Surrealism – ultimately became the most codified in writing. Futurism was particularly notable in this regard, as well as in the dogmatic fidelity to its aesthetic principles demanded of its disciples. In a letter written in 1910 describing the requirements of the "complete Futurist," the painter Boccioni wrote that "fidelity to the movement must be complete and without mental reservation . . . We need young men (and there are few) of secure faith and self-denial; [young men] of culture and of action who aspire in their works – as yet uncertain – towards the total perfection which will indicate the radiant path of the ideal." Quoted in Martin, *Futurist Art and Theory: 1909–1915*, 61. It would be mistaken, however, to assume from this a complete unanimity of opinion among the Futurists. By the time Futurism had achieved international recognition in 1913, the movement was in fact a tenuous and volatile coalition of Marinetti's Milanese group and the so-called "Florentine Movement," active since 1903 and lead by Giovani Papini and Ardengo Soffici. Less than a year later, this union was already beginning to disintegrate. In September 1913, the Florentine painter Severini wrote to his colleague Soffici complaining that a plethora of manifestos by individual members of the movement were being published "without being known to the others, as if each feared being robbed or outdone by another." Marinetti, for his part, was hard pressed to mediate the many theoretical disagreements that threatened the movement's cohesion. By December 1914, the Florentines had seceded and their periodical, *Lacerba* was no longer available as a venue for Milanese Futurism. For a detailed account of the dissolution of the early Futurist movement, see Martin, 183–88, 202–04.

80 Quoting Karl Kraus, *Die Aktion* dismissed them as "protests of a rabid poverty of mind." *See* Peter Demetz, "Italian Futurism and the German Literary Avant-Garde," in *Bithell memorial Lecture Series* (London: Institute of Germanic Studies, University of London, 1987), 6–7. However, as Paul Pörtner has argued, it is likely that *Aktion*'s initial reaction to Futurism was also a Pfemfert stratagem directed more at his chief avant-garde periodical competitor, Walden, than at the Futurists themselves. *See* Pörtner, *Literaturrevolution 1910–1925*, 2:8.

81 Demetz, *Ibid.* Demetz maintains that Pfemfert's change of attitude was due in part to his admiration for the Futurist poetry of the self-exiled German Theodor Däubler and partly to his desire to make an internationalist statement in the face of rampant nationalism throughout Europe. Indeed, as Marjory Perloff observed in her fine study of Futurism, "the curious tension between nationalism and internationalism is at the heart of *avant-guerre* consciousness." *See* Perloff, *The Futurist Movement* (Chicago: University of Chicago Press, 1986), 6. Walden's advocacy of Futurism continued through the war years and into the early twenties; even as, from 1919 onward, he began moving

steadily and irrevocably toward Communism. It would appear that he sought to transcend or simply evade the conflict between nationalism and internationalism – not to mention that between the fascist orientation of Futurism and his own growing socialist sympathies – through concentrating on the purely aesthetic issues raised by the work of the Futurists. On the other hand, the Walden of the pre-war and war years – and many Expressionists like him – can be viewed as typical of the kind of cultural activists that place complete reliance on artistic revolution alone.

82 In this regard, Italian Futurism can been seen as one of the important progenitors of what today is known in America and Europe as "performance art." For an account of this legacy, see Rosalee Goldberg, *Performance: Live Art 1909 to the Present* (New York: Abrams, 1979).

83 Edschmid, *Über den Expressionismus in der Literatur und die neue Dichtung*, 49.

84 Pörtner, *Literaturrevolution 1910–1925*, 2:6.

85 F. T. Marinetti, "The Variety Theatre," *Lacerba* 1 October, 1913, reprinted in *Futurist Manifestos*, ed. Umbro Apollonio, trans. R. W. Flint (New York: Viking, 1973), 130.

86 The Futurists' idea of theatre – like that of Wedekind – was inspired by variety theatre models such as the music hall, the circus, the cabaret and the carnival. In his well-known essay entitled "The Variety Theatre" (1913), Marinetti celebrated the rapidly episodic, multimedia nature of these popular performance genres. The variety theatre, he argued, is "fed by swift actuality" which dynamically charges the interaction of performer and spectator, and thus performs the beneficial function of breaking down the barrier between them. See *Futurist Manifestos*, 126. Donald Marinelli's biographical study of Marinetti's early career provides a detailed account of how Marinetti's life itself was a model for the Futurist's confrontative notion of the performer–audience relationship. *See* "Origins of Futurist Theatricality: the Early Life and Career of F. T. Marinetti." Ph.D. Diss.,(University of Pittsburgh, 1987). It should be noted that the Variety Theatre manifesto, despite its prescriptive attitude, was the product of much prior experimentation; it thus represents a digest of performance principles acquired over several years by the Futurists through trial and error ("error" in this case presumably being any tactic that failed to outrage an audience).

87 F. T. Marinetti, "Dynamic and Synoptic Declamation," in *Selected Writings*, 142–44.

88 One of these performers, the Futurist architect Virgilio Marchi, recalled that he was instructed "to repeat with violence the syllable 'STA'." For this quotation, as well as a more detailed description of *Macchina tipografica*, see Goldberg, *Performance: Live Art 1909 to the Present*, 16.

89 *Plastic Dances* (Clavel and Depero, 1918) and *The Merchants of Heart* (Prampolini and Casavola, 1927), respectively, are cases in point.

90 "Manifesto of the Futurist Dance," in *Selected Writings*. See Flint, 141.

91 In Michael Kirby, *Futurist Performance*, trans. Victoria Nes Kirby (New York: Dutton, 1971), 205–06, 229.

92 Willett, *Expressionism*, 93.

93 In the manifesto entitled "The Pleasure of Being Booed," Marinetti argued that authors and performers must "despise" the audience in order for their work to be effective. See *Selected Writings*, 113. Specific suggestions for stimulating spectators in this provocative spirit included double-booking their seats and coating them with glue, giving free seats to notoriously irritable or eccentric people, sprinkling the seats with powder to make spectators itch and sneeze. *See* "The Variety Theatre," in *Futurist Manifestos*, 130.

94 Alfred Döblin, "Futuristische Worttechnik," *Der Sturm*, March 1913: 280–82. Interestingly, much of what Döblin objected to in Futurist performance, he later praised in the context of the modernist revolution in narrative form. The novel, he argued, stood to benefit greatly from the Futurist demolition of logic and syntax which yields "the a-logical and the individual word. Here is clarity." *See* Demetz, 14.

95 Oskar Kokoschka, *My Life*, trans. David Britt (New York: MacMillan, 1974), 28–29.

96 *Ibid.*

97 Both of these review excerpts are cited by Dorothy Pam in her article, "Murderer, the Women's Hope," *Drama Review* 19, no.3 (1975):8–9.

98 Ludwig Goldscheider, *Kokoschka* (London: Phaidon, 1963), 14.

99 Oskar Kokoschka, "Vom Erleben," in *Oskar Kokoschka – vom Erlebnis im Leben* (Salzburg: Verlag Galerie Welz, 1975), 136.

100 *My Life*, 29.

101 "Vom Erleben," 136.

102 J. P. Hodin, *Oskar Kokoschka, the Artist and His Time* (New York: New York Graphic Society, 1966), 69–70.

103 *My Life*, 28.

104 Kokoschka, *Mörder, Hoffnung der Frauen*, trans. Michael Hamburger, in *Anthology of German Expressionist Drama*, ed. Walter Sokel (New York: Anchor, 1963), 17–21.

105 *My Life*, 22–27.

106 In a turn-of-the-century work entitled *Geschlecht und Charakter* [*Sex and Character*, 1902], the Viennese psychologist Otto Weininger had posited an androgynous idea of human personality in which history is shaped by the clash between a positive, spiritual, "male principle" and a negative, animalistic, "female principle" in the individual psyche. The extent of Weininger's influence on the young Kokoschka, and in particular on his first play, is unclear. For representative opinions see Horst Denkler, *Drama des Expressionismus: Programm, Spieltext, Theater* (Munich: Fink, 1967), 46–47, and Hans Schwerte, "Anfang des expressionistischen Dramas," *Zeitschrift für Deutsche Philologie* 80, no.2 (1964): 175.

107 Interview with Wolfgang Fischer in *Kokoschka Lithographs* (London: The Arts Council, 1966), 12.

108 This pronouncement, first made by Loos and later corroborated by Kraus and other close associates of Kokoschka, is quoted in an essay by Peter Scher entitled "Als Kokoschka mich malte" ["When Kokoschka Painted Me"], a portion of which appears in Raabe, *The Era of German Expressionism*, 333.

109 Bernhard Diebold, review of *Mörder, Hoffnung der Frauen, Hiob*, and *Der brennende Dornbusch*, by Oskar Kokoschka, Neues Theater, Frankfurt; *Frankfurter Zeitung*, 12 April 1918; reprinted in Günther Rühle, ed., *Theater für die Republik 1917–33 im Spiegel der Kritik* (Frankfurt am Main: S. Fischer Verlag, 1967), 66–67. A similarly negative (and evidently also minority) response was registered by F. H. Geissler's review on the occasion of the Dresden première of the plays in June of the previous year. The majority of the (again) invited spectators, he observed, "had applauded, partly out of goodwill and partly because they lacked sufficient judgment . . . [but] the aesthetically discriminating members of the audience made no secret of such a misuse of artistic resources." Kokoschka Archive, Item No.94435, Theatermuseum des Instituts für Theater-, Film- und Fernsehwissenschaft der Universität zu Köln.

110 Paul Kornfeld, *Kokoschka*. In *Programm zur Uraufführung der Einaker Mörder, Hoffnung der Frauen, Hiob, und Der brennende Dornbusch*, 3 Juni 1917, Albert-Theater, Dresden. Reprinted in Thomas Anz and Michael Stark, eds., *Expressionismus: Manifeste und Dokumente zur deutschen Literatur 1910–1920* (Stuttgart: Metzler, 1982), 686. A minority dissent, again expressed by Geissler, was that the language in these plays of "the rather Futurist-inspired painter Oskar Kokoschka . . . is so stilted that it almost becomes incomprehensible; in conjunction, the author places great value on pantomimic acting, whose exhaustive employment is supposed to constitute an essential element of his new style."

111 For Geissler, however, the settings resembled "puppet theatre furnishings fashioned by children's hands."

112 Zehder, *Tägliche Rundschau*, Kokoschka Archive, Item No.94432; von Lücken, *Kölner Tageblatt*, Kokoschka Archive, Item No.94434, Theatermuseum des Instituts für Theater-, Film- und Fernsehwissenschaft der Universität zu Köln.

113 Faktor, *Berliner Börsen-Courier* 4 Juni 1917, Kokoschka Archive, Item No.99436; Grossman, *Vossische Zeitung*, Kokoschka Archive, Item No.94438; unsigned review, Kokoschka Archive, Item No.94430, Theatermuseum des Instituts für Theater-, Film- und Fernsehwissenschaft der Universität zu Köln.

114 Felix Emmel, *Das ekstatische Theater* (Prien: Kampmann, 1924), 25. It should be noted that Emmel's book post-dates the heyday of theatrical Expressionism by some five years. As such it can only constitute a retrospective synthesis of "ecstatic" performance theory. Though no

Expressionist actor or director could have read or been influenced by Emmel's work, the book is nonetheless a valuable representation of the kind of rhetoric employed by performance theorists who were writing, between 1916 and 1921 or 1922, about what they were seeing – or thought they were seeing, or hoped they would see – in the acting of Expressionist drama. To the extent that the performers themselves read such contemporary theoretical reactions to their production work, the rhetoric of theatrical "ecstasy" doubtless had some bearing on the choices they made in Expressionist performance. Surely, however, such theoretical influence was relatively minor in comparison with the impact of Stanislavsky, for example, whose theoretical discourses arose out of a distinctly pedagogical agenda. Most Expressionist actors were firmly grounded in the tradition of Naturalism and reached the extremities of Expressionist performance through exposure to Reinhardt's eclectic theatrical stylizations. But the practical experience and images they brought with them to the Expressionist stage were nothing like the dense cocoon of theoretical discourse through which, to this day, young actors who are trained in the Stanislavsky system must chew.

115 *Expressionismus*, 66.
116 Paul Kornfeld, "Nachwort an den Schauspieler," afterword to *Die Verführung: eine Tragödie in fünf Akten* (Berlin: S. Fischer Verlag, 1916); reprinted in Pörtner, *Literaturrevolution 1910–1925*, 1:350.
117 Leontine Sagan, "Expressionism: Germ of the Sound Film," *Cinema Quarterly* 10, no.5 (Summer 1933):229.
118 Walther von Hollander, "Expressionismus des Schauspielers," *Die neue Rundschau* 1 (1917):575–76; reprinted in Pörtner, *Literaturrevolution 1910–1925*, 2:239.
119 *Ibid.*, 240.
120 To a historical materialist like Brecht, such a concept of revolutionary praxis was just plain silly in its avoidance of any methodical socioeconomic analyses of contemporary culture. The basic argument of the Expressionists, however, was simply that history was a product of motives ultimately determined at the spiritual level of human consciousness. Granting this assumption, it then made sense to seek poetically, rhetorically, to move the human spirit to a committed attitude of "universal brotherhood" and so transform the sad course of contemporary German history. This strategy was really not so far afield of the Brechtian theatre's attempt to induce the audience into a critical frame of mind. Both the Expressionist idea of "inspiration" and the Brechtian concept of "alienated" reflection depended on the rhetorical power of the stage. In both cases, any actual revolutionary change – whether motivated by emotional stimulation or dialectical argument – depended on audience members making a commitment on the basis of what they had seen and heard in the theatre. No less than

the Expressionists, Brecht staked his faith on the rhetorical force of word and image.

121 Lotte Eisner, *The Haunted Screen* (Los Angeles: University of California Press, 1969), 144.
122 *Expressionismus*, 55.
123 Quoted in Foster, 22.
124 Sokel, *The Writer in Extremis*, 87.

3. SCHREI ECSTATIC PERFORMANCE

1 That these scripts were not actually performed until some four years after their composition is a significant aspect of the particular historical nature of Expressionist staging. Following an examination of the scripts and the history of their first productions, I will return to this question in a concluding discussion of Schrei performance as a mode of crisis inscription in the body of the Expressionist actor. At this juncture, however, John Willett's pragmatic characterization of the pre-war German theatre vis-à-vis the new drama might be noted:

. . in the theatre the older writers still held the stage, because although the early Expressionist playwrights were already writing there was as yet no director to stage their work in a suitable form and precious little chance of it getting put on at all. The apparatus still had to be won over; and convincing an editor (or a picture dealer for that matter) was a good deal simpler than convincing a state-, court- or municipally appointed theatre Indendant. (Willett, *Expressionism*, 97–98)

In the period 1910–14, early Expressionist drama had drawn upon the same distorted imagery of the city, the landscape, and the human form as early Expressionist poetry and painting. However, when "early" Expressionist *performance* took the stage in 1916, the pre-war sense of cultural alienation expressed in scripts such as those under present consideration had given way to the new, horrifying experience of the war. It is, then, all the more striking that early Expressionist theatre not only emerged but developed with productions of the pre-war Expressionist drama. Between 1914 and 1918, when battle stilled the pens and brushes – in all too many cases, forever – of the pre-war Expressionist movement, the theatre not only kept Expressionism alive but became its dominant venue. Indeed, aside from scattered Expressionist developments in prose fiction and criticism – in the war-time writings of Alfred Döblin and Kasimir Edschmid, for example – "late" Expressionism, in the literary and visual arts, developed chiefly in the dramaturgy and scenic designs of the Expressionist stage. By 1919, as the November Revolution petered out and Weimar Germany settled down to the practical tasks of reconstruction, poets and painters were already turning either to constructivism or to a "new objectivity." Yet it was at precisely this point that theatrical Expressionism moved into its final culminating phase in Berlin and the twin themes of war and politics took center stage. Interestingly, where an immediacy of experience typically galvanized Expressionist literary and visual art – both before and during the war – theatrical Expressionism appears to have performed something of a therapeutic post-mortem function: pre-war scripts were first staged during the war; and war-time scripts such as those of Toller, Unruh and Goering did not begin to première until early 1918, when defeat was looming. Thus, the Expressionist stage created powerful images of very recent cultural history that arguably enabled in audiences a kind of initial cathartic processing of traumatic events.

2 By contrast, idealism had "disintegrated" in Berlin, the "Großtadt, which from 1918 on was rapidly changing." *Theater für die Republik*, 19.

3 *See* Patterson, *The Revolution in German Theatre: 1900–1930*, 43; Samuel and Thomas, *Expressionism in German Life, Literature and the Theatre*, 9. Productions of *Ghost Sonata* at the Munich Kammerspiele in 1915 and *A Dream Play* at the Berlin Theater in der Königgrätzerstraße in 1916 both ran for over a hundred performances. See Klaus van den Berg, *Strindberg's Post-inferno Plays on the German Stage: Studies in Modern Spatial and Temporal Consciousness* (Ph.D. diss., Indiana University, 1993), 4.

4 Quoted in Rühle, *Theater für die Republik*, 15.

5 Van den Berg, 2, 13, 92, 68.

6 *Ibid.*, 65, 192.

7 *Ibid.*, 160, 108. It should also be noted that Bernauer, at this time, had gathered about him an ensemble of actors specifically oriented toward playing avant-garde drama. Among them, Friedrich Kayssler in particular would later become prominent in theatrical Expressionism as an actor and a performance theorist.

8 Rühle, *Theater für die Republik*, 20.

9 *Ibid.*, 18–20.

10 Schroeder's position is well represented in the following remarks on acting made by him in a conversation with one Jens Baggesen reported by Karl Mantzius in his *History of Theatrical Art*:

BAGGESEN: ". . . then you are not King Lear on the stage, while illuding others you are not under the illusion yourself?"

SCHROEDER: "Do you think that I should succeed in making the spectators forget Schroeder if for one moment I myself were Lear – or make them fancy they were seeing Lear, if for a moment I forget Schroeder."

BAGGESEN: "So you remain cold all the time you are acting?"

SCHROEDER: "So cold that between the scenes and acts I play the part of manager as if I had done nothing but stand in the wings. My warmth is physical, not mental; it is the heat of bodily exertion, not of enthusiasm."

Quoted in Toby Cole and Helen Chinoy, eds., *Actors on Acting* (New York: Crown, 1970), 277.

11 *Ibid.*, 288.

12 Munch, it will be remembered, designed Expressionist settings for Reinhardt's famous 1906 production of Ibsen's *Ghosts*, inaugurating the Kammerspiele at the Deutsches Theater.

13 Willett, *Expressionism*, 64.

14 *Ibid.*, 85. This show, at Munich's Tannhäuser Galerie, was staged in secession from Neue Künstlervereinigung as a result of the secessionists movement toward a more abstract, Cubist aesthetic.

15 Cited by Patterson, *The Revolution in German Theatre*, 9.

16 Bernhard Diebold, *Anarchie im Drama* (Frankfurt: Frankfurter Verlags-Anstalt, 1921), 5.

17 Edschmid, "Schauspielkunst," 118.

18 Emmel, *Das ekstatische Theater*, 31, 36.

19 Rühle, *Theater für die Republik*, 16.

20 Edschmid, *Über den Expressionismus in der Literatur und die neue Dichtung*, 64.

21 Quoted in Emmel, 37.

22 "Sie haben, und deswegen mag man sie, wenn es durchaus sein muß, 'Expressionisten' nennen, den Sinn für die große Linie, den Mut zu gewissen rhythmischen Vereinfachungen gemein." *Schauspieler und Schauspielkunst*, 132.

23 Gustav Hartung, "On the Essence of Directing," in *Das deutsche Theater der Gegenwart. See* Krell, 101.

24 *Schauspieler und Schauspielkunst*, 134.

25 *Theater für die Republik*, 17. From a purely rhetorical point of view, this description is noteworthy because its words are not those of a contemporary critic writing in the heyday of theatrical Expressionism under the influence of its amplified linguistic climate. Rather, Rühle's characterization of Krauss's acting, written nearly half a century later, suggests the durability of original critical estimations of Krauss's work expressed in similarly superlative terms..

26 Kurt Wallstab, *Werner Krauss – Rollenchronik*, 1977. Sammlung: Wilhelm Richter, Akademie der Künste, Berlin / Abteilung 5 – Darstellende Kunst, 13, 22. Having first worked with Krauss in a 1911 production of his play *Der Kammersänger* (Stadttheater, (Nuremberg), Wedekind was so impressed that he concluded he had finally found an actor who understood how to play his characters. When Reinhardt produced the 1913–14 Deutsches Theater Wedekind-cycle, the playwright insisted that Reinhardt use Krauss in several of the principal roles. *See* Wolfgang Goetz, *Werner Krauss* (Hamburg: Hoffman und Campe, 1954), 98–102. This work is also available at the Akademie der Künste, Wolfgang Goetz Archiv.

27 Richard, *Phaidon Encyclopedia of Expressionism*, 205.

28 Quoted in Rühle, *Theater für die Republik*, 17.

29 Fritz Engel, review of *Advent*, Kammerspiele des Deutschen Theater,

Berlin; *Berliner Tageblatt*, 10 December 1919; reprinted in Rühle, *Theater für die Republik*, 181.

30 Rudolf Frank, *Das neue Theater* (Berlin: n.p., 1928), 32.

31 *Schauspieler und Schauspielkunst*, 134.

32 *Ibid.*, 134–35.

33 Alfred Hitchcock exploited this principle magnificently in his film *Psycho*, where every time the psychotic killer struck the physical action was accompanied by a high-pitched, fast-paced series of scream-like noises. To the casual viewer, these pulsing screeches as such are not consciously perceptible; yet a careful study of the murder scenes quickly reveals the technique of this sound trick. The source of the sound is clearly artificial – perhaps high notes roughly stroked on a violin. But the pitch of the sound resembles that of a human scream, and its tempo suggests that of blood spurting from a gashed artery. The effect is to fuse all these images into one electrifying total experience, whose locus is primarily, but not at all exclusively, visual.

34 *Schauspieler und Schauspielkunst*, 134.

35 Aside from the acting style it describes, such an account in its florid rhetoric might be considered an Expressionist performance in its own right. Clearly Bab was among the most sympathetic of critics as regards Berlin stage Expressionism. His rhetoric here reveals the general influence of Expressionist cultural discourse as it constructs an audience literally overwhelmed by an actor. In its dependence upon lurid physical imagery – "blood-surfeited voice vibrating in wrath . . . fear-instilling paralysis . . . red, piercing flame . . . takes our breath away . . . physical fear . . . flash of lightning" – Bab's rendering of the effect of Kortner's stage voice reflects the Expressionist conception of the theatre as a powerful historical force. Lest this view of the stage-audience relationship seem far-fetched, we have only to recall the effect of Nazi rhetoric in the mouth of an orator like Hitler.

36 *Das ekstatische Theater*, 39. Here, Emmel is referring to Jessner's 1921 Staatstheater production.

37 Kortner, *Aller Tage Abend*, 25–26.

38 Quoted in Cole and Chinoy, *Actors on Acting*, 289.

39 *Das ekstatische Theater*, 37.

40 Cole and Chinoy, 289.

41 *Aller Tage Abend*, 166–67.

42 Kortner's phrase in the original is "die lange in mir rumort hatte." In context, the sense seems to be that Chaplin's example *confirmed* earlier, troubling misgivings about privileging the vocal over the gestural element in his acting. The verb "rumoren" literally means to "make a noise" or "stir up a row"; hence, the voice of disquietude within him refused to shut up until he began to study Chaplin's work.

43 Ernst Deutsch, "Reinhardt and the Young Actor," in *Max Reinhardt and His Theatre*. *See* Sayler, 108.

44 *Schauspieler und Schauspielkunst*, 172–73. The ironic tone here is more charitable, I think, than not. However, Bab's point is that for all their insistence that the youthful poet of intense passion was a "new man," the Expressionists were really drawing upon a well-established tradition of German theatre in which the term "Liebhaber" referred basically to the stock figure of the "juvenile lead."

45 *Aller Tage Abend*, 236, 271.

46 *Schauspieler und Schauspielkunst*, 175.

47 *Aller Tage Abend*, 236, 146–47.

48 *Schauspieler und Schauspielkunst*, 176, 174.

49 Sokel, *Anthology of German Expressionist Drama*, 40.

50 Ernst Leopold Stahl, review of *Der Sohn*, by Walter Hasenclever. Nationaltheater, Mannheim; *Neue Badische Landeszeitung*, 19 January 1918; reprinted in Rühle, *Theater für die Republik*, 108.

51 Interestingly, however, whereas the children of *Frühlings Erwachen* are pitted rather broadly against Wilhelmine culture in the contexts of the both family and educational structures, the conflict for the young hero of *Der Sohn* is sharpened into an intense focus on the confrontation with his father. The Tutor, who represents the Wilhelmine educational establishment, is actually a rather sympathetic figure in his accepting attitude toward the Son's alienation.

52 Walter Hasenclever, *Der Sohn*, in *Gedichte Dramen Prosa*, ed. Kurt Pinthus (Reinbek bei Hamburg: Rowohlt, 1963), 102.

53 Camill Hoffmann, review of *Der Sohn*, Albert-Theater, Dresden; reprinted in Rühle, *Theater für die Republik*, 106.

54 Rühle, *Theater für die Republik*, 106.

55 *Ibid.*

56 The basic problem was to find a style whose scale would both fit the vast egotistical dimensions of the dramaturgy and yet enthrall the audience. Deutsch's achievement is the more notable because he avoided the kind of pitfall noted by the critic Fritz Mack in his review of a contemporaneous Leipzig production: "To me, Friedrich Berthelen as the Son was too weak in the lyrical parts and in the later explosions of feeling more loud than convincing." Review of *Der Sohn*, Leipzig Schauspielhaus 1918. Expressionist Theatre Archive, Item No.71001, Theatermuseum des Instituts für Theater-, Film- und Fernsehwissenschaft der Universität zu Köln. Even in the original Dresden production, complained one critic, the actors "often spoke more rhetorically than expressively [pathetisch]. In the process, the ideas all mingled together in a juvenile lack of clarity." Review of *Der Sohn*, Dresden Albert-Theater, [journal unidentified] 8 October 1916, reviewer unidentified. Expressionist Theatre Archive [item unnumbered; can be located under reviews of *Der Sohn*], Theatermuseum des Instituts für Theater-, Film- und Fernsehwissenschaft der Universität zu Köln.

57 Siegfried Jacobsohn, review of *Der Sohn*, Das junge Deutschland,

Deutsches Theater, Berlin; *Die Weltbühne*, 1918; reprinted in Rühle, *Theater für die Republik*, 112.

58 Review of *Der Sohn*, *Berliner Börsen Courier* 25 March 1918. Expressionist Theatre Archive, Item No.71005, Theatermuseum des Instituts für Theater-, Film- und Fernsehwissenschaft der Universität zu Köln.

59 According to Pinthus, Deutsch was such a sensation in the Dresden *Der Sohn* that Reinhardt engaged him to work in Berlin "literally on the day following" the opening. See his introduction to *Gedichte Dramen Prosa*, 20.

60 Stephen J. Shearier, "Das junge Deutschland: the Late Expressionist Association in Berlin, Its Journal and Series of Twelve Dramatic Productions," Ph.D. diss. (University of Wisconsin-Madison, 1986), 211–12. Hasenclever's chagrin may have been compounded by the fact, mentioned in two or three of the reviews I have seen, that he himself appeared in this production in the small supporting role of the Prince.

61 Quoted in Rühle, *Theater für die Republik*, 106.

62 Fritz Droop, review of *Der Sohn*, Nationaltheater, Mannheim; *Mannheimer Tageblatt*, 20 January 1918; reprinted in Rühle, *Theater für die Republik*, 107.

63 Jacobsohn, review of *Der Sohn*, 112.

64 Stahl, review of *Der Sohn*, 109.

65 Frank, *Das neue Theater*, 32.

66 Richard, *Phaidon Encyclopedia of Expressionism*, 212.

67 Willett, *Expressionism*, 124.

68 Richard, *Phaidon Encyclopedia of Expressionism*, 211.

69 Quoted in Rühle, *Theater für die Republik*, 106. The term *Lichtregie* is used by Rühle, not Grossmann.

70 Kornfeld, "Nachwort an den Schauspieler," 352.

71 Kasimir Edschmid, review of *Die Verführung*, by Paul Kornfeld, Schauspielhaus, Frankfurt; *Vossische Zeitung*, 12 December 1917; reprinted in Rühle, *Theater für die Republik*, 95.

72 One means of Expressionist character typification in this play is the use of an allegorical naming code for the two principal characters. The word "vogelfrei" means both "free as a bird" and "outlaw."

73 Quoted in Rühle, *Theater für die Republik*, 91.

74 Bernhard Diebold, review of *Die Verführung*, Schauspielhaus, Frankfurt; *Frankfurter Zeitung*, 10 December 1917; reprinted in Rühle, *Theater für die Republik*, 93.

75 *Ibid.*, 94.

76 Edschmid, review of *Die Verführung*, 95.

77 Alfred Polgar, review of *Die Verführung*, Neue Wiener Bühne, Vienna; *Prager Tageblatt*, 15 February 1918; reprinted in Rühle, *Theater für die Republik*, 96. That crucifixion, the single most durable symbol of communal self-sacrifice in Western culture, should be appropriated for the semiotics of the play's inescapably egoist vision of a fulfilled life seems a fundamental contradiction. Indeed, the script itself runs far afield of the appeals to universal brotherly love one often associates with

theatrical Expressionism. However, the thematic core of Expressionist drama is the question of the relationship between experience and its expression; expression itself being an important part of the experience expressed. Whether the plays envision utopian communal self-sacrifice or solipsistic experiential self-gratification, the critical issue is always the liberation of consciousness through a revolutionary breakthrough in self-expression.

78 Viviani, *Dramaturgische Elemente im expressionistischen Drama*, 117.
79 Friedrich Michael, "Steil," *Das literarische Echo* 22 (1919): 257.
80 Wolfgang Paulsen, *Expressionismus und Aktivismus: Eine typologische Untersuchung* (Bern: n.p., 1938), 166–67.
81 Sokel, *Anthology of German Expressionist Drama*, 33.
82 Emil Faktor, review of *Der Bettler*, by Reinhard Sorge, Deutsches Theater, Berlin; *Berlin Börsen-Courier*, 24 Decembert 1917; reprinted in Rühle, *Theater für die Republik*, 99..
83 Fritz Engel, review of *Der Bettler*, Deutsches Theater, Berlin; *Berliner Tageblatt*, 24 December 1917; reprinted in Rühle, *Theater für die Republik*, 100.
84 John Styan, *Max Reinhardt* (Cambridge: Cambridge University Press, 1982), 43. Das junge Deutschland (hereafter referred to as DjD) was founded in December 1917 at the Deutsches Theater for the purpose of promoting new directions in the arts. Although Reinhardt provided the facilities both for the association's productions and for the publication of its journal, Heinz Herald was the single greatest moving force in DjD. Along with him, Arthur Kahane (co-editor with Herald of the journal), Felix Hollaender (dramaturge), Ernst Stern (designer) and Paul Kornfeld (aesthetician and editor of the journal's first volume) were in effect DjD's board of directors. Reinhardt himself, after directing the first two productions of the première DjD season, *Der Bettler* and *Seeschlacht*, virtually ceased to participate in DjD's stage activities. Furthermore, he never wrote any articles for the journal. His main contribution seems to have been the gathering together of the above-mentioned figures. Following the two initial Reinhardt productions, this group appears to have more or less collectively mounted the rest of DjD's dramatic series and to have edited its journal in the same way. In the Spring of 1920, the association voluntarily disbanded, having concluded that its founding purposes were accomplished. *See* Shearier, *Das junge Deutschland: the Late Expressionist Association in Berlin*, 26, 25, 17.
85 Shearier, 8.
86 Sokel, *Anthology*, 42.
87 Styan, 45–46.
88 Emmel, *Das ekstatische Theater*, 41.
89 Frank Witford, "Expressionism in the Cinema," *Studio International* 179 (1979): 26.
90 Gordon, "German Expressionist Acting," 45.

4. GEIST ABSTRACTION IN PERFORMANCE

1 Other principal sources of information about the Kampfbühne are to be found in Schreyer's correspondence with Herwarth Walden, the relevant portions of which I will discuss as needed.

2 Lothar Schreyer, *Expressionistisches Theater* (Hamburg: Toth, 1948), 204. John Willett's remark that Expressionism "was never, like Futurism or Surrealism, a conscious grouping which can be related to a common programme (however loosely worded) or to certain collective demonstrations and publications" (*Expressionism*, 7) is not true of the *Sturm* association. What characterizes this faction of Expressionists was precisely their preoccupation with the concept of Expressionism as they uniquely defined it. See, for example, the preface to Schreyer's essay, "Vom Leben des Sturms," *Imprimatur* [New Series] 3 (1961–62):223–27, where he distinguishes between Expressionism and pseudo-Expressionism in the context of Walden's tutelage. According to Schreyer, "what the group meant by Expressionism was rather different from the accepted meaning." Walden employed the term Expressionism in "a very restricted usage [to] appl[y] more or less exclusively to the artists of the *Sturm*"; everything else he "dismissed as pseudo-Expressionism."

3 "Wir waren – und sind, soweit wir heute noch leben – überzeugt, dass ein jeder Mensch, wenn auch in verschiedenem Grade, die Möglichkeit zu künstlerisch-schöpferischem Werk hat". *See Expressionistisches Theater*, 127.

4 Wassily Kandinsky, "On Stage Composition," in *Blaue Reiter Almanac*. *See* Kandinsky and Marc, 191.

5 This prohibition took effect, however, only after Schreyer's removal of his ensemble to Hamburg and its reconstitution as the Kampfbühne.

6 Awareness of Symbolist aesthetics first arose in Germany through the work and influence of such groups as the Munich Secession and the literary circle around the Symbolist poet Stefan George. Also, of course, Freud's research on dream experience together with the symbolic dramaturgy of August Strindberg were tremendously influential on the German theatrical avant-garde. In terms of production staging, theorists such as Georg Fuchs and Peter Behrens advanced and attempted to implement proposals for a specifically Symbolist theatrical performance space. But the practical achievements of Reinhardt, the brilliant eclecticist, made the greatest impact on the pre-war German theatre in terms of suggesting alternatives to the Naturalist hegemony. None of these precursors, however – with the possible exception of Kokoschka in his original staging of *Mörder, Hoffnung der Frauen* – took stage performance as far in the direction of pure formal abstraction as Schreyer.

7 *See* also *Briefe.* Sturm-Archiv: Lothar Schreyer. Staatsbibliothek zu Berlin, Preussischer Kulturbesitz. The first Sturm-Bühne performance had been Schreyer's staging of Stramm's *Sancta Susanna* on 26 October

1918 in the Berliner Künstlerhaus. A second performance planned for early December was canceled because of the social chaos attendant upon the November revolution. Domestic political violence, of course, would continue sporadically in Germany for the next four years – well beyond the passing of Expressionism, after approximately 1921, from the theatre. In a letter to Walden dated 19 March 1920 – just days after the abortive right-wing Kapp putsch – Schreyer makes routine mention of the latest upheavals: "Hopefully all is well with you after the chaos in Berlin. Following a few gunfights, all is quiet here [in Hamburg]."

8   Quite apart from the idealistic goals of the Kampfbühne, a commercial agenda is evident in Schreyer's correspondence with Walden, where financial concerns and strategies are a frequent theme. See, for example, the letter dated 5 August 1919 where he suggests a 15 percent royalty charge for the Stramm pieces *Heidebraut* and *Kräfte* performed separately, and 10 percent when performed together. The letter in fact amounts to a proposed contract between the *Sturm* Association and Schreyer stipulating, along with royalties, his exclusive right to direct the performances and to determine when they are to take place. He further requests a timely answer from Walden so he can report to "the board" (i.e., drawn from the membership of the Kampfbühne theatre collective). It does seem, however, that these contractual negotiations are in the interest of the collective and not merely selfish. Indeed, Schreyer appears to have felt a keen sense of material stewardship with respect to the collective which he carefully correlated with the group's philosophical identity. In a letter to Walden dated 19 September 1919 he notes proudly that the Kampfbühne's expenses are minimal because, among other things, the actors perform simply out of personal commitment and not for hire.

Nonetheless, he is frequently concerned about his personal financial and employment status with regard to the *Sturm* Association. In a letter written just five days later, Schreyer proposes sending Walden his *Reichsversicherungskarte* ["federal health insurance card"], and asks whether it is necessary for him to be designated as Walden's employee. He further suggests that he be given the official job title of "Vertreter des Sturms für Hamburg" [Sturm representative for Hamburg] and proposes a salary of 300 Deutsche Marks.

9   In a 1921 critique of Reinhardt's production of the Stramm play *Kräfte* [*Forces*], Emil Faktor recalled that "the pompously exotic, contrived staging of Stramm's *Sancta Susanna* by the Sturm people was regarded as laughable dilettantism." *See* Rühle, *Theater für die Republik*, 305. On the other hand, Mel Gordon asserts, in his article "Lothar Schreyer and the Sturm-Bühne," that a September 1920 staging of two highly abstract plays by Walden was "surprisingly well received" in Dresden. "Evidently," he adds, "there were audiences for this kind of performance, but not in Berlin, oddly enough." See *The Drama Review* 24 (1980):85–102.

10 *See* M. S. Jones, *Der Sturm: a Focus of Expressionism* (Columbia, S. C.: Camden House, 1984), 7–8, 15. When the war was acknowledged it was typically in obituaries to fallen colleagues, and even then it was not directly or critically dealt with as a subject. "Walden even goes so far," says Jones, "as to declare in the article "Die ernste Kritik" ["Genuine Criticism"] (*Der Sturm* 6 (1916):86 "Aber mit dem Krieg wird weder für noch gegen Kunst etwas bewiesen" [But with the war nothing either for or against art is proven]. By 1919, however, the chaotic and frequently violent political aftermath of the revolution could hardly be ignored and Walden's dawning interest in politics dates from this time. He joins the German Communist Party, seeks to establish cultural links with the revolutionary regime in Russia, and begins to re-theorize his formalist aesthetics in terms of Socialism.

11 Blümner stressed that theatre should remain free of any specific political or other external commitment so as not to compromise its inherent aesthetic qualities. He held to this view, in fact, long after Walden had become a committed Socialist. As late as 1932, the year of Walden's emigration to Moscow, Blümner, in an article entitled "Individuum und Masse" [*Das Nationaltheater* 2 (1932):130–35], dismissed both Toller's *Masse Mensch* and Brecht's *Mann ist Mann* by insisting on the absolute nature of art in relation to any individual situation. In another and earlier *Das Nationaltheater* article [2 (1928–29):1–4] entitled "Zeitgeist und Weltanschauung im Drama" he had argued that "the artwork is not a fragment of the times but a little piece of eternity!" *See* Jones, 48.

12 In a 1918 *Der Sturm* article entitled "Der Sinn des Mitleids" (9, no. 11:138), Schreyer argued that through accepting one's own suffering one becomes aware of the suffering of all mankind. In this way, one acquires a unique kind of "sympathy" which has greater power than sympathy, as it is usually understood, to build communal bonding between human beings. *See* Jones, *Der Sturm: a Focus of Expressionism*, 50, for a full dicussion of Schreyer's gloss on "Mitleid." It may be, as Brian Keith-Smith argues, that Schreyer's sense of the spiritual compensations of suffering arose autobiographically as a compensation for the domestic chaos of his parents' horrible marriage. See his book, *Lothar Schreyer: ein vergessener Expressionist* (Stuttgart: Hans-Dieter Heinz Akademischer Verlag, 1990), 6. However, for Schreyer, acceptance of one's own suffering and sympathy for that of other people's had nothing to do with political activism. Rather, the historical process was only to be comprehended through artistic revelation. Schreyer in fact directly equated transformations in art with historical change. See, for example, his article "Die neue Kunst" where he declares that "turning points in art are turning points in history," in *Der Sturm* 10, no.5 (August 1919), 68.

In place of a political idea of community, Schreyer developed a specialized sense of the term "Volk" which denoted the ideal expression of human spirit in terms of abstract aesthetic form. But this aesthetic concept of "Gemeinschaft" apparently excluded from its sense of universal humanity any practical commitment to internationalism; and, as early as 1920, it had begun to resonate in Schreyer's thinking with another, rather more disturbing, idea of "Volk." In an article published in *Deutsche Vierteljahresschrift* entitled "Theaterdämmerung" (1920, 109–12), Schreyer complains that German theatre no longer related to the German people. "For example," he argues, "we need only take a look at the repertoires of small and large theatres. It is completely international. And where it features new poets of the German language, these poets are typically authors rooted in Jewish heritage. It's no wonder, for all the leading theatre people in Germany, directors, actors, and publishers are alien to our nationality. Therefore they have no feeling for the German people." Notably, this is not a *Der Sturm* article, and, as Jones observes, one may well wonder what Walden, a Jew, thought of the reference to Jews as alien to German nationality. *See* Jones, 61.

This nationalist turn in Schreyer's thought is all the more bizarre given the internationalist attitude explicitly adopted by *Der Sturm*, which Schreyer edited from 1917 through 1928. As Walden moved in the direction of Bolshevism, Schreyer, for his part, followed his long-standing attraction to the German medieval mystic tradition, which ultimately led him to become a Catholic Christian in 1933. Though Walden apparently respected Schreyer's mystical orientation, it seems to have set him at odds with colleagues at the Bauhaus, where he had undertaken direction of the drama program in 1921, and two years later he resigned.

13 John Willett, for example, dismisses the Sturm-Bühne as "a somewhat amateurish fringe group." *Theater in the Weimar Republic*, 69.
14 Wassily Kandinsky, *Concerning the Spiritual in Art*, trans. Michael Sadleir (New York: Wittenborn, 1947), 33.
15 Kandinsky elaborates on this faculty in his essay, "On the Question of Form," *Blaue Reiter Almanac, See* Kandinsky and Marc, 147–87, 156.
16 Wassily Kandinsky, "On Stage Composition," in *Blaue Reiter Almanac.* *See* Kandinsky and Marc, 190–91.
17 Sixten Ringbom, "Art in the 'epoch of the Great Spiritual': Occult Elements in the Early Theory of Abstract Painting," *Journal of the Warburg and Courtauld Institutes* 29 (1966):390–91.
18 Quoted in Ringbom, 406.
19 *Concerning the Spiritual in Art*, 34.
20 *Munich and Theatrical Modernism*, 230.
21 *Concerning the Spiritual in Art*, 66.
22 Wassily Kandinsky and Franz Marc, eds., *Blaue Reiter Almanac*, trans. Henning Falkenstein (1912; New York: Viking, 1974), 201, 206.
23 And ". . .this," Kandinsky adds, "in contrast to the claim of the

impressionists that they could explain nothing, that their art came by inspiration" (*Concerning the Spiritual in Art*, 77).

24 *Ibid.*

25 "On Stage Composition," 205.

26 *See* Walden's article, "Theater," *Der Sturm* 5.22 (Feb. 1915): 147.

27 This language was used in an advertisement for the school which began to appear regularly in *Der Sturm* beginning with the March 1917 issue.

28 Interestingly, both Blümner and Schreyer trained as lawyers but decided to pursue theatre instead. Beginning in 1905, Blümner collaborated with Walden on the precursors of *Der Sturm*, *Das Magazin* and *Das Theater*. He was one of Walden's few personal friends and the only original member of the *Sturm* Association to stay with the organization until its dissolution in 1932. In the operation of *Der Sturm* Blümner served as Walden's business manager while Schreyer did the day-to-day editing of the periodical from 1917 through 1928. Working for Walden brought little financial security, so Blümner also worked for Reinhardt and at the Lessing-Theater school of acting as a speech teacher. After Walden went to live and work in Moscow, Blümner, who did not share his political idealism, declined Walden's offer of money and a position in Moscow. *See* Jones, *Der Sturm: a Focus of Expressionism* 2, 39–41. In his monograph, "Italian Futurism and the German Literary Avant-garde," Peter Demetz records the sad irony that Blümner died of hunger "in the ruins of Berlin" after WW II, "while his Jewish wife, fortunately, survived" (8).

29 *Expressionistisches Theater*, 198.

30 The non-traditional idea of a theatrical company common to all of these coterie organizations is paralleled by the particularly imagistic nature of their productions. Schreyer obviously felt that amateur actors would be less hindered by egotism than professionals from experimenting with radical new ideas of "acting." In fact, all of these directors link the integrity – indeed, the very possibility – of their kind of theatre with an intimate and anonymous performance ensemble. For Wilson, moreover – whose extravagant, lengthy and technically elaborate early works required literally hundreds of actors, designers and technicians – a volunteer work force of "disciples" was an economic imperative.

31 All but two of the Kampfbühne stagings were presented in the Hamburg *Kunstgewerbeschule* ["arts and crafts school"]. A letter to Walden written 13 November 1919, describes the negative public reaction to this performance of the double-bill, *Heidebraut/Kräfte*. Schreyer stoped the performance during the *Kräfte* part of the program because of "reactionary" protesters led by a "Volksschullehrer [primary school teacher] who looks like Otto Ernst and is named Richard Wagner." He mentions fearing that worse disturbances may be expected in Berlin and suggests playing before a "somewhat" carefully selected audience, perhaps with the added protection of a "Sturm-

Bühnewache" [i.e., security staff]. Another letter, written 19 September 1919, also speaks of internal dissension at the Kampfbühne and states Schreyer's intention of getting rid of one Herr Wlach from the board of directors because he is the "chief obstructor." This done he estimates he could build a 500-person circle of supporters.

32 "On Stage Composition," 191.

33 Actually, these performance "scores" are rather complicated diagrams of symbolic figures indicating Schreyer's plan for the progression of physical and vocal relationships between performers in a given production. They appear more substantial than mere blocking plots, however, but seem "easily readable" only to those carefully initiated into Schreyer's symbolic performance language of symbols, shapes, and colors.

34 "Das Bühnenkunstwerk," *Der Sturm* 8, no. 2 (May 1917): 19.

35 "Die neue Kunst," *Der Sturm* 10.8 (November 1919):119. Like the treatise, "Das Bühnenkunstwerk," this extended monograph appeared over several installments in *Der Sturm*.

36 "Das Drama," *Der Sturm* 7, no. 10 (1916):119.

37 "Die neue Kunst," *Der Sturm* 10, no. 8 (November 1919):119; 10, no. 6 (September 1919):84.

38 "Das Bühnenkunstwerk," *Der Sturm* 8, no.3 (June 1917):38.

39 *Expressionistisches Theater*, 146–48.

40 "Expressionistische Dichtung," *Sturm-Bühne*, no. 4–6, 1918/1919; reprinted in Pörtner, *Literaturrevolution 1910–1925*, 1:439–43.

41 *Expressionistisches Theater*, 151.

42 In the case of the Kampfbühne, the ambiguity arose from the fact that each Bühnenkunstwerk received "a minimum of one-hundred rehearsals" but no Bühnenkunstwerk was performed more than three times. *See Expressionistisches Theater*, 199, 201. This extraordinary emphasis on rehearsal was one of the ways in which Schreyer's ensemble, as we noted earlier, was a prototype of later avant-garde performance groups such as those of Grotowski and Schechner.

43 Rudolf Blümner, "August Stramm: zu seinem zehn-jährigen Todestag," *Sturm*, September 1924:124.

44 Kenneth Burke, *A Grammar of Motives* (Berkeley: University of California Press, 1969), 261–62.

45 "In this community" [i.e., the Kampfbühne ensemble]," Schreyer notes, "each member had to be able, and was able, to take on a great solo role or to be an element in the chorus" (*Expressionistisches Theater*, 154).

46 *Munich and Theatrical Modernism*, 222.

47 *Expressionistisches Theater*, 33.

48 Heinrich von Kleist, "Über das Marionettentheater," in *Sämtliche Werke*, ed. Curt Grützmacher (Munich: Winkler Verlag, 1967), 945ff.

49 *Expressionistisches Theater*, 51.

50 Walter Gropius, ed., *The Theater of the Bauhaus*, trans. Arthur S. Wensinger (Middletown, CT: Wesleyan University Press, 1961), 22.

51 Quoted in Oscar Brockett and Robert R. Findlay, *Century of Innovation: a History of European and American Theatre and Drama Since the Late Nineteenth Century*, 1st ed. (Englewood Cliffs: Prentice-Hall, 1973), 427–28.

52 *Expressionistisches Theater*, 56.

53 Each primary color, Schreyer maintained, has an essential nature "with a positive and negative effect." Blue, for example, "binds all colors" and is the symbol of "faith, fidelity, and piety." Its positive character is "endurance"; its negative character is "envelopment." Yellow's "force" is the opposite of blue, and it is the symbol of "revelation" and "knowledge" (*Expressionistisches Theater*, 65–66), and so on. Furthermore, the fundamental colors have corresponding fundamental forms which they take when they appear unmixed and pure: Yellow -> equi-lateral triangle; Blue -> circle and sphere; red -> square and cube; green -> waveform; orange -> the "manifolding" [*Vervielfältigung*] of form; violet -> the "partitioning" [*Teilung*] of form; white -> oval; black -> point. Each of these fundamental forms have a surface and an outline which articulates it; and the outlines indicate both "the directions of the surface" and "the directions of the forces which live in the surface" (82). Schreyer's spiritual "force" theory of color is clearly indebted to Kandinsky's discussion of "the study of color and its effects on men" in *Concerning the Spiritual in Art. See* pp. 55–67.

54 "Das Bühnenkunstwerk," 8.3: 38.

55 *Expressionistisches Theater*, 58. This is almost certainly a swipe at the purely geometrical formalism in the work of Schlemmer and others, whose opposition to Schreyer's mystical orientation led to his resignation from the Bauhaus in 1923.

56 *Dramaturgische Elemente im expressionistischen Drama*, 6.

57 *The Theatre of the Bauhaus*, 91.

58 "Das Bühnenkunstwerk," 8.2: 22.

59 "Die neue Kunst," 10.5: 68.

60 "Die neue Kunst," 10.8: 124; *Expressionistisches Theater*, 141.

61 Rühle, *Theater für die Republik*, 301.

62 *Expressionistisches Theater*, 153, 197.

63 Herbert Ihering, *Von Reinhardt bis Brecht* (Berlin: Aufbau Verlag, 1961), 81.

64 *Aller Tage Abend*, 25–26; *Expressionistisches Theater*, 127.

65 *Der Sturm* 11, no. 2 (1920):32, indicates May 16 as the date of the première.

66 *Expressionistisches Theater*, 202.

67 *Theater für die Republik*, 302.

68 Alfred Kerr, review of *Forces*, Kammerspiele, Berlin; *Berliner Tageblatt*, 13 April 1921; reprinted in Rühle, *Theater für die Republik*, 302, 304.

69 Such a scenario well exemplifies the misogynist tendency in Stramm's work. To varying degrees, it occurs throughout Expressionist dramatic literature.

70 Emil Faktor, review of *Forces*, Kammerspiele, Berlin; *Berliner Börsen-Courier*, 13 April 1921; reprinted in Rühle, *Theater für die Republik*, 305.
71 Siegfried Jacobsohn, review of *Forces*, Kammerspiele, Berlin; *Die Weltbühne*, 1921; reprinted in Rühle, *Theater für die Republik*, 307.
72 Rühle, *Theater für die Republik*, 302.
73 Rudolf Blümner, "August Stramm: zu seinem zehn-jährigen Todestag," *Der Sturm*, September 1925:124.
74 Alfred Kerr, *Mit Schleuder und Harfe*, ed. Hugo Fetting (Berlin: Severin, 1982), 307.
75 "Das Bühnenkunstwerk," *Der Sturm* 7, no.5 (April 1916): 51.
76 In a letter to Walden dated 14 October 1919, he regrets an ongoing quarrel with one Wilhelm Schlichtkrull and reproaches Walden for printing an attack on Schreyer written by Schlichtkrull in *Der Sturm*. He further accuses Schlichtkrull of attempting to force Schreyer out of the inner circle of *Sturm* and discredit him as an artist and a person in Walden's eyes. *Briefe*. Sturm Archiv: Lothar Schreyer. Staatsbibliothek zu Berlin, Preussischer Kulturbesitz.
77 *See* W. Rittich, *Kunsttheorie, Wortkunsttheorie und lyrische Wortkunst im Sturm* (Bamberg: Universitätsverlag, 1933), 6. Walden had been involved in this sort of performance venue since 1904 when had founded the prototype of the *Sturm* Association called the "Verein für Kunst." The evening recitals of this association featured presentations of the latest experimental work in poetry and musical composition. The *Sturm-Abende* – staged occasionally before 1916 and more regularly after Schreyer became involved that year – continued the Verein für Kunst's practice of featuring unknown artists as well as those who were established pioneers of "the new art." Of course, there were many such associations founded for the promotion of new directions in the arts throughout the early modern era in Germany, as I have noted in earlier chapters of this study. Groups such as *Sturm* and Kurt Hiller's "Neo-pathetisches Cabaret" were simply among the most visible and active.
78 That he retained ambitions of moving back into the limelight, however, is clear from his 19 September 1919 letter to Walden where he talks of planning the take-over of the Kampfbühne by the Sturm-Bühne and even mentions the possibility of enlisting support from a well-established public theatre organization, the Berlin Volksbühne.
79 *Expressionistisches Theater*, 206–07.

5. LATE EXPRESSIONIST PERFORMANCE IN BERLIN: THE EMBLEMATIC MODE

1 This is the basic semiotic principle of the abstract unit set, which may appear, for example, to be a throne room in one scene and a battle field in another simply through the use of a few well-chosen props and/or

movable set pieces. The function of these latter is imagistically to prompt the audience's imagination to fill in the details of the setting. As regards specific props, to cite one of Elam's examples, what is a sword hilt in one scene might become inverted to represent iconically a cross in another.

2 *See* Keir Elam, *The Semiotics of Theatre and Drama* (London: Routledge, 1988), 12–16.

3 Quoted in Günther Rühle, *Theater in unserer Zeit* (Frankfurt am Main: Suhrkamp, 1976), 62.

4 *The Revolution in German Theatre*, 85–86.

5 Quoted in Rühle, *Theater für die Republik*, 58.

6 Franz Servaes, review of *Von morgens bis mitternachts*, Lessing-Theater, Berlin; *Berliner Lokal-Anzeiger*, 15 April 1921.

7 Fritz Engel, review of *Von morgens bis mitternachts*, Lessing Theater, Berlin, *Berliner Tageblatt*, 24 December 1919; Emil Faktor, review of *Von morgens bis mitternachts*, Deutsches Theater, Berlin; *Berliner Börsen-Courier*, 2 February 1919 [Georg Kaiser Archiv-Akademie der Künste, Berlin]; Alfred Kerr, *Mit Schleuder und Harfe*, ed. Hugo Fetting (Berlin: Severin, 1982), 150; Alfred Polgar, *Max Pallenberg* (Berlin: n.p., n.d.), 22.

8 Georg Kaiser, *From Morning to Midnight. Five Plays*, trans. and ed. J. M. Ritchie (London: Calder, 1971), 73.

9 Herman George Scheffauer, *The New Vision in the German Arts* (London: Kennikat, 1924), 53–54.

10 Here Martin may well have intended a reference to the famous Munch painting, *Der Schrei*, which became something of a logo for Expressionism as a whole during the life span of the movement. As an emblem of the quintessential Expressionist posture of "Aufbruch" [awakening], the Schrei was clearly an important inspiration in the stylistic explorations first of painters, such as Kokoschka, and later of actors and directors, like Deutsch and Martin.

11 This strategy is particularly effective during testimonials at the Salvation Army in the film's final scene: as several penitents bear witness to their conversions, each of their faces suddenly become Deutsch's as he looks at them one by one.

12 The prolonged staring encounter with the mother-in-law in particular is clearly intended as comic relief. But there is in fact a sense of tongue-in-cheek about the stylization throughout the entire film, as in the blowing snow that finds its way into a comically excessive number of scenes.

13 This sculptural plasticity in emblematic performance was most characteristic of the Expressionist stage productions of Fehling and Jessner.

14 Dennis Calandra, "Georg Kaiser's *From Morn to Midnight*: the Nature of Expressionist Performance," *Theatre Quarterly* 6 (Spring 1976):50. As Calandra says, "in particular moments of the film there is something genuinely terrifying in seeing Deutsch as a man possessed." It is all the more remarkable that Deutsch was able to achieve this impact having

only the visual dimension of expression to work with on the silent screen. Yet even with the availability of speech, this kind of acting was undoubtedly more difficult on stage than in the cinema, where the magnified abstracting power of film construction itself came to the aid of the emblematic actor.

15 Richard Braungart, review of *Von morgens bis mitternachts*, Kammerspiele, Munich; *Municher Zeitung*, 30 March 1917; reprinted in Rühle, *Theater für die Republik*, 61.

16 P. S. review of *Von morgens bis mitternachts*, by Georg Kaiser. Kammerspiele, Munich, *Frankfurter Zeitung*, 20 April 1917; reprinted in Rühle, *Theater für die Republik*, 62.

17 Paul Wiegler, review of *Von morgens bis mitternachts*, Deutsches Theater, Berlin; *BZ*, 2 February 1919, Georg Kaiser Archive – Theatermuseum des Instituts für Theater, Film- und Fernsehwissenschaft der Universität zu Köln.

18 Herbert Ihering, *Regisseure und Bühnenmaler* (Berlin-Wilmersdorf: Bibliophiler Verlag, 1921), 22.

19 Georg Kaiser, "Der Mensch im Tunnel," *Das Kunstblatt* 6, no.1 (1922):516; reprinted in Pörtner, *Literaturrevolution 1910–1925*, 1:389.

20 Richard Specht, review of *Von morgens bis mitternachts*, Volksbühne, Vienna; *Berliner Börsen-Courier*, 28 December 1917; reprinted in Rühle, *Theater für die Republik*, 63.

21 *Theater für die Republik*, 157.

22 Though it is often said that the Tribüne opened its doors with this production, actually *Die Wandlung* was the second offering of the season following Martin's productions of two less memorable pieces, *Der Retter* [*The Savior*] and *Die Entscheidung* [*The Decision*]. See Willett, *Theatre of the Weimar Republic*, 259.

23 Willett notes that "the play ran for 115 performances and not only put Kortner instantly into the first rank of Weimar actors but also established Toller for a time as something close to a Socialist messiah in the theatre, several of his plays subsequently being staged in the new Russia." See *Theatre of the Weimar Republic*, 62.

24 *Aller Tage Abend*, 343.

25 Rühle, *Theater für die Republik*, 156.

26 Quoted in Bab, *Das Theater der Gegenwart*, 178.

27 Michael Patterson credits Martin with being the first director in Germany to use the black-out as an alternative to the traditional curtain method of ending a scene. See *The Revolution in German Theatre*, 102.

28 Alfred Kerr, review of *Die Wandlung*, Tribüne Theater, Berlin; *Berliner Tageblatt*, 1 October 1919; reprinted in Rühle, *Theater für die Republik*, 164.

29 Karl Heinz Martin, "Die Bühne und ich," *Die vierte Wand, Organ der deutschen Theaterausstellung* (1927):77. The emphases in the quote are Martin's.

30 In his 1918 article "Bühne und Expressionismus," however, Martin

indicated the influence of the abstract stylization in Japanese acting on his own ideas about working with actors in the context of stage Expressionism. *See* the periodical *Neue Hamburger Zeitung*, no. 230.

31 Herbert Ihering, review of *Die Wandlung*, Tribüne Theater, Berlin; *Der Tag*, 2 October 1919; reprinted in Rühle, *Theater für die Republik*, 159.

32 *Aller Tage Abend*, 343.

33 During his subsequent association with Jessner, however, Expressionist acting stylization was clearly a directorial mandate and it finally became programmatic for him. At that point, he recalls in his memoir, he abandoned it for a more restrained style which he felt would foster his growth as an actor.

34 *Aller Tage Abend*, 384–85. The durability of this assessment of Ihering is confirmed by Rühle, writing from one generation's distance in 1967, who states flatly that "he was the most important critic of our epoch in Berlin and for the theatre of the Reich. Instinctively, he recognized the problems of the new theatre which began to define itself after 1910 . . . The theatre for him was a means of shaping political consciousness" (*Theater für die Republik*, 1167). And again, from the vantage point of the late 1980s, John Willett writes that of all the critics of the Weimar Era, "much the most impressive to reread today is the Hannoverian Ihering, who was no great stylist but . . . cared deeply for quality, and worked with astonishing persistence to establish a broad idea of socially relevant theatre based on the original principles of the Volksbühne. Like Kortner, Fehling, and Agnes Straub, he worked for the Vienna Volksbühne in the First World War, becoming its dramaturg . . . Starting work as a critic on his return to Berlin in 1918 at the age of thirty, he soon distinguished himself from his colleagues by discussing the real shifts of power, administrative structure, and artistic intention among the Berlin theatres as well as covering their individual productions" (*Theatre of the Weimar Republic*, 174).

35 Bab, *Das Theater der Gegenwart*, 179.

36 Review of *Die Wandlung*, 159.

37 Rühle, *Theater für die Republik*, 156.

38 Emil Faktor, review of *Die Wandlung*, Tribüne Theater, Berlin; *Berliner Börsen-Courier*, 1 October 1919; reprinted in Rühle, *Theater für die Republik*, 162.

39 Kurt Tucholsky, review of *Die Wandlung*, Tribüne Theater, Berlin, *Die Weltbühne* 15 (1919): 635.

40 Ernst Toller, *Transfiguration*, trans. Edward Crankshaw, in *Modern Continental Dramas*, ed. Harlan Hatcher (New York: Harcourt, 1941), 670.

41 Review of *Die Wandlung*, 158.

42 *Regisseure und Bühnenmaler*, 50–51.

43 *Aller Tage Abend*, 54.

44 Scheffauer, *The New Vision in the German Arts*, 230.

45 Rühle, *Theater für die Republik*, 156.

46 *The New Vision in the German Arts*, 234–35.

47 Quoted in Rühle, *Theater für die Republik*, 321.

48 Siegfried Jacobsohn, review of *Masse Mensch*, Tribüne Theater, Berlin; *Die Weltbühne*, 1921; reprinted in Rühle, *Theater für die Republik*, 325.

49 Scheffauer, 240.

50 Patterson, *The Revolution in German Theatre*, 77.

51 Rühle, *Theater in unserer Zeit*, 61. It should be noted that this monumental rigidity which Jessner required of his actors was characteristic of his Expressionist phase, roughly from 1919 through 1922. According to Rühle, as time passed and Jessner moved toward "New Objectivity" aesthetics, "he liberated the actor from his initial stiffness."

52 Quoted in Rühle, *Theater in unserer Zeit*, 62–63.

53 *Aller Tage Abend*, 369.

54 *Das Theater der Gegenwart*, 181.

55 Quoted in Rühle, *Theater in unserer Zeit*, 60.

56 *Aller Tage Abend*, 370.

57 Siegfried Jacobsohn, review of *Richard III*, Staatliches Schauspielhaus, Berlin; *Die Weltbühne*, 1920; reprinted in Rühle, *Theater füür die Republik*, 263. It will become apparent in the course of the following discussion that emblematic production values and acting, considered semiotically, most have to do with what the American semiotic theorist Charles Peirce called the "iconic" and the "indexical" functions of signification. Thus, for example, the predominance of the color red in the lighting and costuming of *Richard III*, or Kortner's spider-like movements in his playing of the title role, are modes of theatrical signification which employ iconic *likeness* to the color of blood and the movements of a predatory insect, respectively. Moreover, in this particular dramatic context, the blood imagery indexically signifies – that is, *points to, gives evidence of* – murder, just as Kortner's movements point to the spider-like strategy of entrapment by stealth that characterizes Richard's diabolic progress toward the throne. In this latter case, the pointing may again be seen as iconic in that it is *metaphorical*, – metaphor, for Peirce, being a special case of iconic signification where iconic likeness "is asserted rather than apparent." *See* Elam, *The Semiotics of Theatre and Drama*, 21–27. Having said all of this, it must be stressed that these instances of iconicity and indexicality are also a function of Jacobsohn's particular *reading* of the performance text, whatever the intentions of Jessner and Kortner in their "writing" of that text.

58 Ihering, *Regisseure und Bühnenmaler*, 64; Jacobsohn, 262.

59 Alfred Polgar, "Shakespeare, Jessner und Kortner," *Die Weltbühne* 3 (1922):71.

60 Alfred Kerr, review of *Richard III*, Staatliches Schauspielhaus, Berlin; *Die Weltbühne*, 1920; reprinted in Rühle, *Theater für die Republik*, 260.

61 Ihering, 64; Rühle, *Theater in unserer Zeit*, 60.

62 Artur Michel, review of *Richard III*, Staatliches Schauspielhaus, Berlin;

Deutsche Allgemeine Zeitung, 7 November 1920; reprinted in Rühle, *Theater für die Republik*, 264.

63 See Thomas Sidney, *The Antic Hamlet and Richard III* (New York: King's Crown Press, 1943), 19.

64 The return of Naturalistic representation associated particularly with New Objectivity cinema, of course, is not related to *Richard III*. However, Jessner's productions in the mid to late twenties do reflect a renewed sense of realism.

65 *Theater in unserer Zeit*, 58. Jessner is quoted from an interview in *Die Szene*, 1928, p. 66.

66 *Theater in unserer Zeit*, 59.

67 Quoted in Rühle, *Theater in unserer Zeit*, 58.

68 Quoted in Rühle, *Theater für die Republik*, 190.

69 The most direct impact on the theatre of this political situation occurred during the revolution when, for a time, control of some theatres in Germany was commandeered by "workers' councils." These local soviets were composed of actors, wardrobe attendants, stage hands and house attendants. According to Julius Bab, they assumed decision-making power in every area, from engagement of scripts to the casting of roles. In one case, says Bab, the manager of a theatre in Düsseldorf was forced to resign even though he had agreed before the revolution to allow the staff to participate in the administration of the theatre. Interestingly, the principal actors at this theatre sided with management by refusing to work with the radicalized choral actors in a scheduled production of Kaiser's play *Gas*. In Berlin the prestigious Volksbühne was temporarily closed when management refused to pay the workers 40,000 Marks which they had demanded as their fair share of profits during the war years. However, Bab claims that even before the revolution was suppressed the "majority" of producers, directors, playwrights and "many sensible [einsichtig] actors" formally denounced the theatre workers' councils (*Das Theater der Gegenwart*, 161–62).

70 Paul Fechter, review of *Wilhelm Tell*, Staatliches Schauspielhaus, Berlin; *Deutsche Allgemeine Zeitung*, 13 December 1919; reprinted in Rühle, 194.

71 *Aller Tage Abend*, 354–55. I have not been able to find corroborating primary evidence for all of the details of this backstage anecdote – notably, the surprise curtain raising incident. However, no less an authority on the Expressionist era than John Willett accepts Kortner's general reliability as a source of information about this première. (See *The Theatre of the Weimar Republic*, 67.) Although Kortner's account may be peppered with some exaggerations, it seems clear, as Willett notes, that the audience uproar was both racially motivated (as Kortner alleges) and profoundly unsettling to the production staff backstage. The apparent result was that the chaos in the auditorium induced something like a euphoric loss of control backstage – a climate in which the events described by Kortner become quite plausible.

72 Alfred Kerr, review of *Wilhelm Tell*, Staatliches Schauspielhaus, Berlin; *Berliner Tageblatt*, 13 December 1919; reprinted in Rühle, *Theater für die Republik*, 194.

73 Siegfried Jacobsohn, review of *Wilhelm Tell*, Staatliches Schauspielhaus, Berlin; *Die Weltbühne*, 1919; reprinted in Rühle, *Theater für die Republik*, 193.

74 *Theater für die Republik*, 190.

75 "Wenn die Leute Sie erst sehen, dann ist es ganz aus."

76 Norbert Falk, review of *Wilhelm Tell*, Staatliches Schauspielhaus, Berlin; *BZ am Mittag*, 13 December 1919; reprinted in Rühle, *Theater für die Republik*, 197–98.

77 *Das Theater der Gegenwart*, 183.

78 *Theater in unserer Zeit*, 19, 22.

79 *Ibid.*, 59–60.

80 Alfred Kerr, review of *Macbeth*, Staatliches Schauspielhaus, Berlin; *Berliner Tageblatt*, 11 November 1922; reprinted in Rühle, *Theater für die Republik*, 411.

81 Ludwig Sternaux, review of *Macbeth*, Staatliches Schauspielhaus, Berlin; *Berliner Lokal-Anzeiger*, 11 November 1922; reprinted in Rühle, *Theater für die Republik*, 413.

82 Alfred Kerr, review of *Masse Mensch*, Volksbühne am Bülowplatz, Berlin; *Berliner Tageblatt*, 30 September 1921; reprinted in Rühle, *Theater für die Republik*, 324.

83 Quoted in Edward Braun, *The Director and the Stage: from Naturalism to Grotowski* (New York: Holmes, 1982), 90, 92.

84 Norbert Falk, review of *Macbeth*, Staatliches Schauspielhaus, Berlin; *BZ am Mittag*, 11 November 1922; reprinted in Rühle, *Theater für die Republik*, 415.

85 Herbert Ihering, review of *Macbeth*, Staatliches Schauspielhaus, Berlin; *Berliner Börsen-Courier*, 11 November 1922; reprinted in Rühle, *Theater für die Republik*, 417.

86 *Theater in unserer Zeit*, 22.

87 See Gottfried Reinhardt, *The Genius: a Memoir of Max Reinhardt*, 42.

88 Rühle, *Theater für die Republik*, 410.

CONCLUDING OBSERVATIONS

1 Goering wrote *Seeschlacht* in a sanatorium while recuperating from battle trauma suffered in the fighting at Skagerrak; Unruh composed *Ein Geschlecht* while fighting at the front.

2 Certainly among the most significant of these administrative changes was Jessner's being named to the position of Intendant at the Berlin Staatstheater. This, according to Willett, was a "consciously political appointment, Jessner being not merely a republican but also a member of the SPD." *Theatre of the Weimar Republic*, 66.

3 Jean Alter, *A Sociosemiotic Theory of Theatre* (Philadelphia: University of Pennsylvania Press, 1990), 263.
4 *Ibid.*, 32, 63.
5 Erika Fischer-Lichte, "Theatre and the Civilizing Process: an Approach to the History of Acting," in *Interpreting the Theatrical Past*, ed. Thomas Postlewait and Bruce McConachie (Iowa City: University of Iowa Press, 1989), 32–33.
6 See the Camill Hoffman review of *Der Sohn* cited in note no.53 of Chapter Three.
7 See the *Richard III* reviews of Siegfried Jacobsohn and Alfred Kerr, cited on p. 198.
8 See Chapter Three, pp. 118–19.
9 As one commentator on Expressionist staging has quipped, "there are (naturally) no transfigured audiences on record." *See* Christopher Innes, *Holy Theatre: Ritual and the Avant-Garde* (Cambridge: Cambridge University Press, 1981), 263.
10 *Theater in unserer Zeit*, 22.
11 Quoted in W. Petzet, *Die Münchner Kammerspiele 1911–1972* (Munich: Kurt Desch Verlag, 1973), 130.
12 Quoted in Calandra, "George Kaiser's *From Morn to Midnight*: the Nature of Expressionist Performance," 48.
13 *Holy Theatre: Ritual and the Avant-Garde*, 47–48. Innes notes that the phrase "tremendous spiritual ecstasies" is quoted from Kayssler's acting notes by Felix Emmel in *Das ekstatische Theater*, 37. Though such rhetoric clearly typifies the views of one or two individual actors such Kayssler and Kalser, I disagree with the suggestion that it is representative of the majority of actors who worked on the Expressionist stage.
14 "Expressionism: Germ of the Sound Film," 229.
15 *Expressionism*, 192.
16 Quoted in Willett, *Theatre of the Weimar Republic*, 76.
17 It is true that from approximately 1922 to 1924 dramatists such as Bronnen, Essig, and Jahn continued to produce a kind of self-styled Expressionist drama characterized more by violent sensationalism than meliorating social vision. This period of "Black Expressionism," so-called, was as much an attempt to kick-start moribund box-office interest as it was an articulation of cultural cynicism.
18 *Aller Tage Abend*, 343ff.
19 This issue had largely been forgotten in German theatre after the era of Schiller and Goethe. The one exception, of course, was the Socialist-based Volksbühne movement beginning in the late 1880s. But though Volksbühne membership grew phenomenally over the next several decades, the movement *qua* movement was never able to define a clear and cogent position on the relationship between theatrical art and other processes of historical development. It was prevented from doing so basically because of on-going internal dissension as to whether a

"theatre for the people" ought to educate the working class for political action or simply provide it access to "higher" culture, entrusting its betterment to the traditional idea of *Bildung*. In relation to this question, there was also disagreement as to whether or not the Volksbühne movement should organize to produce plays or simply act as a liaison between the working class and the theatre. In both capacities, as it turned out, the movement did much to identify the working class as a viable and important audience. Unfortunately, in the commercial theatre the market potential of this audience was more readily appreciated than its class interests, a problem whose articulation would await serious attention until the emergence of the political theatre of the 1920s. On the other hand, it also became clear during the four decades between the founding of the Volksbühne movement and the advent of National Socialism that the majority of the proletarian audience actually preferred Naturalism and the classical repertoire. Ironically, experimental activist theatre – of the kind, for instance, that Piscator and Brecht would later develop – found its financial base and critical success with the very bourgeois audience it vilified. To his credit, Piscator did make a concerted attempt to develop the proletarian audience in the early years of the Weimar Republic. By the end of the decade, however, he had to acknowledge that the economic base of that audience was still too weak for it to sustain its own revolutionary theatre.

20 In all, some nineteen administrations were formed and dissolved between the founding of the Republic in November 1918 and Hitler's accession to power in January 1933. The abortive Kapp Putsch of March 1920 and the Munich "Beer Hall Putsch" in November 1923 are two of the best known illustrations of republican vulnerability in the face of political agitation. The former precipitated the resignation of Chancellor Bauer in late March, followed by the collapse of his coalition in June when Reichstag elections significantly decreased republican and increased nationalist parliamentary strength. In the treason trials associated with the latter coup attempt, the radical right perpetrators escaped with disgracefully lenient sentences while enjoying the opportunity, Hitler in particular, of publicizing their propaganda in grandiose courtroom testimony and widespread media coverage.

21 *Weimar Culture*, 156–57.

22 These and similar statements are quoted in Samuel and Thomas, *Expressionism in German Life, Literature and the Theatre (1910–24)*, 176.

23 Erwin Piscator, *Das politische Theater* (1929), in *Schriften* (Berlin: Henschelverlag, 1968), 83. Michael Patterson has noted that near the end of the Weimar era, Piscator did finally arrive at a specifically "epic" idea of acting in his 1931 production of Friedrich Wolf's *Tai Yang Wakes Up*. See *The Revolution in German Theatre*, 129. Here Piscator employed techniques such as having the actors change into their costumes and create various

settings with movable political placards while discussing with the audience the message of the play and its relevance to contemporary events.

24 In the case of the *Storm Over Gothland* production, the specific mode of semiosis is iconic: Piscator transformed Granach into a picture of Lenin.

25 *See* Patterson, 148.

26 *Schriften zum Theater*, 1:124–25. See also page 128, where Brecht admits that Kaiser's dramaturgy has been "decisively important" and that "he has altered the situation of European drama."

27 *See* "Über die Verwendung von Musik für ein episches Theater," in *Schriften zum Theater*, 3:267.

28 Of course, the late plays of Strindberg, nearly all of Wedekind's work, Büchner's *Woyzeck*, and Shakespeare's history plays were also exemplary models of interruptive dramaturgy for Brecht.

29 *Schriften zum Theater*, 2:27. This production featured Alexander Granach as the Cashier.

30 Willett, *Brecht on Theatre*, 233.

31 *Ibid.*, 231.

32 Piscator himself had emigrated to the Soviet Union in 1931.

33 Antonin Artaud, *Collected Works*, 4 vols., trans. Victor Corti (London, 1968–74), 4:85.

34 *The Theatre and Its Double*, trans. Mary Caroline Richards (New York: Grove, 1958), 13. Anaïs Nin's description of Artaud's famous 1933 Sorbonne lecture on "The Theatre and the Plague" runs, in part, as follows: "His face was contorted with anguish, one could see the perspiration dampening his hair. His eyes dilated, his muscles became cramped, his fingers struggled to retain their flexibility. He made one feel the parched and burning throat, the pain, the fever, the fire in the guts. He was in agony. He was screaming. He was delirious. He was enacting his own death, his own crucifixion." *See* Ronald Hayman, *Artaud and After* (Oxford: Oxford University Press, 1977), 89.

35 In the post-Vietnam era, many directors have come to believe that theatre can only be efficacious through a combination of both traditions: Brecht's Marxist rationalism and Artaud's surreal intensity.

36 An early section of Grotowski's influential work *Towards a Poor Theatre* features a description of acting that could have been written by Kasimir Edschmid or Paul Kornfeld: "The actor makes a total gift of himself. This is a technique of the 'trance' and of the integration of all the actor's psychic and bodily powers which emerge from the most intimate layers of his being and his instinct, springing forth in a sort of 'translumination'." On the very next page, however, Grotowski writes: "The forms of common 'natural' behavior obscure the truth; we compose a role as a system of signs which demonstrate what is behind the mask of common vision: the dialectics of human behavior." Jerzy Grotowski, *Towards a Poor Theatre* (New York: Simon and Schuster, 1968), 16–17.

37 Patterson notes Beckett's "considerable interest" in Expressionist drama after seeing some of the plays performed in Dublin during the war years. See *The Revolution in German Theatre*, 184. However this may have influenced his dramaturgy, a more telling point of relationship between Beckett and Expressionist acting specifically is seen in Günther Rühle's observation, noted by Patterson, that it was Jessner-trained actors like Kortner who found the greatest success playing Beckett on the German stage.

38 The only purpose in their performance of the fiction that Godot's arrival will bring redemptive change is to hold full acceptance of the unchanging existential self at bay. Depending upon one's point of view, the play in this aspect represents either a denial of any redemptive hope for human identity or else a heroic attempt to negotiate that hope in the only way possible, as Beckett saw it, within the particular historical moment of the play's composition.

39 *See* Marc Robinson, "Performance Strategies," *Performing Arts Journal* 10, no.3 (1987):31–55. In the sprawling monologues of a performer like Spaulding Gray, the comedic representation is no less than that of completely reconstituting the performer's identity right there in the presence of the audience.

40 *KA MOUNTAIN* (1972) took seven full days to perform, and *CIVIL warS* (1984) utilized performance venues ranging from West Germany, France and Italy to Japan and the United States.

41 Brecht found it necessary to argue for a similar distinction in regard to his "scientific" idea of theatre. In his prologue to the *Kleines Organon*, he stipulated that "what we practiced as theatre of a scientific age was not science but theatre . . . By any chance it would be too difficult to explain the theory of theatrical defamiliarization outside of an aesthetic framework." *See* Bertolt Brecht, "Kleines Organon für das Theater," in *Gesammelte Werke*, ed. Werner Hecht, 20 vols. (Frankfurt am Main: Suhrkamp, 1967), 16:697, 662. I have rendered "Verfremdung" as "defamiliarization" because this word seems best to capture the sense of fresh, unbiased perception that Brecht chiefly had in mind. Though renderings such as "alienation" or "astonishment" are more usual, they are also, I fear, more susceptible of misunderstanding.

42 Richard Strayton, "Hell Raiser," *American Theatre* (February 1992):26.

43 *Ibid.*, 28.

44 As Peter Hacks, one of his early post-war disciples in the GDR, has written: "Brecht's reality was that of the first half of the twentieth century. Our reality is already different; our methods have to differ from his if they are to be called Brechtian. Like every intellectual achievement Brecht's remains an historical one. It is both ephemeral and eternal. To take his work further one must negate not prolong it." *See* Anthony Waine, "The Legacy for German-speaking Playwrights," in *Brecht in Perspective*, ed. Graham Bartram and Anthony Waine (New

York: Longman, 1982), 197. In general, as Waine notes, this negation took the form of either documentary dramas, such as Rolf Hochhuth's *The Representative* (1963), or parable plays like Dürrenmatt's *The Physicists* (1962) Brechtian theatricality, Waine argues, was more apt for dealing with an age dominated by extensive systems of ideological rhetoric on both the left and the right. By contrast, Marxism's traditional rhetorical model of "class struggle" had little resonance for the more prosperous post-Auschwitz/post-Hiroshima generation haunted by questions of individual moral responsibility. Theirs was a new truth which they felt required new, more formally realistic, methods of access.

Select bibliography

Allen, Roy F. *Literary Life in German Expressionism and the Berlin Circles*. Ann Arbor: University of Michigan Press, 1983.

Anz, Thomas, and Michael Stark, eds. *Expressionismus: Manifeste und Dokumente zur deutschen Literatur 1910–1920*. Stuttgart: Metzler, 1982.

Apollonio, Umbro, ed. *Futurist Manifestos*. London: Thames and Hudson, 1973.

Arnold, Armin. *Die Literatur des Expressionismus: Sprachliche und thematische Quellen*. Stuttgart: Kohlhammer, 1966.

Artaud, Antonin. *Collected Works*. Translated by Victor Corti, 4 vols. London, 1968–74.

The Theatre and Its Double. Translated by Mary Caroline Richards. New York: Grove, 1958.

Bab, Julius, *Schauspieler und Schauspielkunst*. Berlin: Österheld, 1926.

Das Theater der Gegenwart. Leipzig: Weber, 1928.

Ball, Hugo, "Wedekind als Schauspieler." *Phöbus* 1, No. 3 (1914):105–08. Reprinted in Pörtner, *Literarurrevolution 1910–1925*, 1:338–40.

Barlach, Ernst. *Prosa aus vier Jahrzehnten*. Edited by Elmer Jansen. Berlin: Union Verlag, 1966.

Bergson, Henri. *Creative Evolution*. Translated by Arthur Mitchell. With a foreword by Irwin Edman. New York: Modern Library, 1944.

Blass, Ernst. "The Old Café des Westens." In Raabe, *The Era of German Expressionism*, 27–33.

Blümner, Rudolf. "August Stramm: Zu seinem zehn-jährigen Todestag." *Der Sturm*, September 1925, 121–26.

Der Geist des Kubismus. Berlin: N.p., 1921.

Bramsted, Ernest K. *Aristocracy and the Middle Class in Germany*. 2nd ed. Chicago: University of Chicago Press, 1964.

Brecht, Bertolt. "Frank Wedekind." *Augsburger Neueste Nachrichten*, 12 March, 1918. In *Brecht on Theatre*, edited and translated by John Willett. New York: Hill, 1964.

Calandra, Dennis. "Georg Kaiser's *From Morn to Midnight*: the Nature of Expressionist Performance." *Theatre Quarterly* 6 (Spring 1976):45–54.

Carter, Huntley. *The New Spirit in the European Theatre 1914–1924*. London: N.p., 1925.

Craig, Edward Gordon. *On the Art of the Theatre.* Boston: Samuel, 1925.

Dahrendorf, Ralf. *Society and Democracy in Germany.* New York: Anchor-Doubleday, 1969.

Dalcroze, Emile Jaques. *Eurhythmics, Art and Education.* Edited by Cynthia Cox. Translated by Frederick Rothwell. 1930. Salem, NH: Ayer, 1985.

Deak, Istvan. *Weimar Germany's Left-Wing Intellectuals.* Berkeley: University of California Press, 1968.

Demetz, Peter. "Italian Futurism and the German Literary Avant-garde." Lecture. Bithell Memorial Lecture Series. London: Institute of Germanic Studies, University of London, 1987.

Denkler, Horst. *Drama des Expressionismus: Programm, Spieltext, Theater.* Munich: Fink, 1967.

Diebold, Bernhard. *Anarchie im Drama.* Frankfurt: Frankfurter Verlags-Anastalt, 1921.

Döblin, Alfred. "Futuristische Worttechnik." *Der Sturm*, March 1913. 280–82.

Durieux, Tilla. *Eine Tür steht offen.* Berlin: Herbig, 1954.

Edschmid, Kasimir. "Schauspielkunst." In Krell, *Das deutsche Theater der Gegenwart*, 116–120.

Über den Expressionismus in der Literatur und die neue Dichtung. Berlin: Reiss, 1919.

Eisner, Lotte. *The Haunted Screen.* Los Angeles: University of California Press, 1969.

Elam, Keir. *The Semiotics of Theatre and Drama.* London: Routledge, 1988.

Emmel, Felix, *Das ekstatische Theater.* Prien: Kampmann, 1924.

Fischer-Lichte, Erika. "Theatre and the Civilizing Process: An Approach to the History of Acting." In *Interpreting the Theatrical Past*, edited by Thomas Postlewait and Bruce McConachie, Iowa City: University of Iowa Press, 1989, 19–36.

Foster, John. *The Influence of Rudolf Laban.* London: Lepus, 1977.

Frank, Rudolf. *Das neue Theater.* Berlin: N.p., 1928.

Friedenthal, Joachim, ed. *Das Wedekindbuch.* Munich: Müller, 1914.

Furness, R. S. *Expressionism.* London: Methuen, 1973.

Gay, Peter, *Weimar Culture: The Outsider as Insider.* New York: Harper, 1970.

Gittleman, Sol. *Frank Wedekind.* New York: Twayne, 1969.

Goetz, Wolfgang. *Werner Krauss.* Hamburg: Hoffmann und Campe, 1954.

Goldberg, Rosalee. *Performance: Live Art 1909 to the Present.* New York: Abrams, 1979.

Goldscheider, Ludwig. *Kokoschka.* London: Phaidon, 1963.

Gropius, Walter, ed. *The Theatre of the Bauhaus.* Translated by Arthur S. Wensinger. Middletown, CT: Wesleyan University Press, 1961.

Grotowski, Jerzy. *Towards a Poor Theatre.* New York: Simon and Schuster, 1968.

Hasenclever, Walter. *Der Sohn.* In *Gedichte Dramen Prosa*, edited by Kurt Pinthus, Reinbek bei Hamburg: Rowohlt, 1963, 99–156.

Hayman, Ronald. *The German Theatre.* New York: Harper, 1975.

Hohendahl, Peter. *Das Bild der bürgerlichen Welt im expressionistischen Drama.* Heidelberg: Winter, 1967.
Hollander, Walther von. "Expressionismus des Schauspielers." *Die Neue Rundschau* 1 (1917):575–76. Reprinted in Pörtner, *Literaturrevolution 1910–1925,* 2:239–40.
Hortmann, Wilhelm. *Shakespeare on the German Stage.* Vol. 2. Cambridge: Cambridge University Press.
Ihering, Herbert. *Begegnungen mit Zeit und Menschen.* Bremen: N.p., 1965.
Regisseure und Bühnenmaler. Berlin-Wilmersdorf: Bibliophiler Verlag, 1921.
Von Reinhardt bis Brecht. Berlin: Aufbau Verlag, 1961.
Die Zwanziger-Jahre. Berlin: Aufbau Verlag, 1948.
Innes, Christopher. *Holy Theatre: Ritual and the Avant-Garde.* Cambridge: Cambridge University Press, 1981.
Jelavich, Peter. *Berlin Cabaret.* Cambridge, MA: Harvard University Press, 1993.
Munich and Theatrical Modernism. Cambridge, MA: Harvard University Press, 1985.
Jones, M. S. *Der Sturm: A Focus of Expressionism.* Columbia, SC: Camden House, 1984.
Kafka, Franz. "Brief an den Vater." *Die Neue Rundschau* 63, no. 2 (1952):10–12.
Kaiser, Georg. *From Morning to Midnight. Five Plays.* Translated and edited by J. M. Ritchie. London: Calder, 1971.
"Der Mensch im Tunnel." *Das Kunstblatt* 6, no. 1, 1922, 516. Reprinted in Pörtner, *Literaturrevolution 1910–25,* 1:389–91.
Kandinsky, Wassily. *Concerning the Spiritual in Art.* Translated by Michael Sadleir. New York: Wittenborn, 1947.
Kandinsky, Wassily, and Franz Marc, eds. *Blaue Reiter Almanac.* Translated by Henning Falkenstein, 1912. New York: Viking, 1974.
Kant, Immanuel. *Critique of Aesthetic Judgment.* Translated by James C. Meredith. Oxford: Clarendon, 1911.
Keith-Smith, Brian. *Lothar Schreyer: Ein vergessener Expressionist.* Stuttgart: Hans-Dieter Heinz Akademischer Verlag, 1990.
Kerr, Alfred, *Mit Schleuder und Harfe.* Edited by Hugo Fetting. Berlin: Severin, 1982.
Kirby, Michael. *Futurist Performance.* New York: Dutton, 1971.
Kleist, Heinrich von. "Über das Marionetten-theater." In *Sämtliche Werke,* edited by Curt Grützmacher, Munich: Winkler-Verlag, 1967, 945–51.
Kokoschka, Oskar. *My Life.* Translated by David Britt. New York: MacMillan, 1974.
Kornfeld, Paul. "Der beseelte und der psychologische Mensch." *Das Junge Deutschland* 1, no. 1 (1917):1–13.
Die Verführung. Berlin: Fischer, 1916.
Kortner, Fritz. *Aller Tage Abend.* Munich: Kindler, 1959.
Krell, Max. *Das deutsche Theater der Gegenwart.* Munich: Rösl, 1923.

Krispyn, Egbert. *Style and Society in German Literary Expressionism.* Gainesville: University of Florida Press, 1964.

Kuhns, David F. "Wedekind, the Actor: Aesthetics, Morality and Monstrosity." *Theatre Survey* 31 (November 1990):144–64.

Kutscher, Artur. *Frank Wedekind: Sein Leben und seine Werke.* 3 vols. Munich: Georg Müller, 1931.

Laban, Rudolf. *A Life for Dance.* Translated by Lisa Ullmann. 1935. New York: Theatre Arts Books, 1975.

Lewin, Ludwig. *Die Jagd nach dem Erlebnis: Ein Buch über Georg Kaiser.* Berlin: Die Schmiede, 1926.

Maletic, Vera. *Body – Space – Expression: the Development of Rudolf Laban's Movement and Dance Concepts.* Berlin: Mouton de Gruyter, 1987.

Marinetti, F. T. *Selected Writings.* Edited by R. W. Flint. Translated by R. W. Flint and Arthur A. Coppotelli. New York: Farrar, Straus, and Giroux, 1972.

"The Variety Theatre." *Lacerba,* 1 October 1913. Reprinted in Apollonio, *Futurist Manifestos.*

Martin, Marianne W. *Futurist Art and Theory: 1909–1915.* Oxford: Clarendon, 1968.

Nietzsche, Friedrich. *Beyond Good and Evil: Prelude to a Philosophy of the Future.* Translated by Helen Zimmern. New York: MacMillan, 1924.

The Birth of Tragedy and the Case of Wagner. Translated and with commentary by Walter Kaufmann. New York: Random House, Vintage, 1967.

Thus Spake Zarathustra. Translated by Thomas Common. New York: Heritage, 1967.

Nietzsche–Wagner Correspondence. Edited by Elizabeth Foerster-Nietzsche. Translated by Caroline V. Kerr. New York: Liveright, 1921.

Patterson, Michael. *The Revolution in German Theatre: 1900–1930.* Boston: Routledge, 1981.

Paulsen, Wolfgang. *Expressionismus und Aktivismus: Eine typologische Untersuchung.* Bern: N.P., 1938.

Perloff, Marjorie. *The Futurist Movement.* Chicago: University of Chicago Press, 1986.

Petzet, W. *Die Münchner Kammerspiele 1911–1972.* Munich: Kurt Desch Verlag, 1973.

Piscator, Erwin. "Das politische Theater." In *Schriften.* Berlin: Henschelverlag, 1968.

Polgar, Alfred. *Max Pallenberg.* Berlin: N.p., n.d.

"Shakespeare, Jessner und Kortner." *Die Weltbühne* 3 (1922):69–71.

Pörtner, Paul, ed. *Literaturrevolution 1910–1925.* 2 vols. Darmstadt: Luchterhand, 1960.

Raabe, Paul, ed. *The Era of German Expressionism.* Translated by J. M. Ritchie. Woodstock, NY: Overlook, 1974.

Reinhardt, Gottfried. *The Genius: A Memoir of Max Reinhardt.* New York: Knopf, 1979.

Reinhardt, Max. *Ich bin nichts als ein Theatermann: Briefe, Reden, Aufsätze, Interviews, Gespräche, Auszüge aus Regiebüchern.* Edited by Hugo Fetting. Berlin: N.p., 1989.

Ringbom, Sixten. "Art in the 'epoch of the Great Spiritual': Occult Elements in the Early Theory of Abstract Painting." *Journal of the Warburg and Courtauld Institutes* 29 (1966):386–418.

Ritchie, J. M. *German Expressionist Drama.* Boston: Twayne, 1976.

Rittich, W. *Kunsttheorie, Wortkunsttheorie und lyrische Wortkunst im Sturm.* Bamberg: Universitätsverlag, 1933.

Rühle, Günther. *Theater in unserer Zeit.* Frankfurt: Suhrkamp, 1976.

Rühle, Günther, ed. *Zeit und Theater: Vom Kaiserreich zur Republik 1913–1925.* Vol. 1, n.p.: Propyläen, n.d.

Theater für die Republik 1917–1933 im Spiegel der Kritik. Frankfurt, S. Fischer Verlag, 1967.

Sagan, Leontine. "Expressionism: Germ of the Sound Film." *Cinema Quarterly* 10 (Summer 1933):229–31.

Salten, Felix. "Wedekind als Schauspieler." *Blätter des deutschen Theaters,* no. 19 (1 Juni 1912):292–94.

Samuel, R., and R. Hinton Thomas. *Expressionism in German Life, Literature and the Theatre (1910–24).* Cambridge: Heffer, 1939.

Sayler, Oliver M., ed. *Max Reinhardt and His Theatre.* 1924. New York: Blom, 1968.

Scheffauer, Herman George. *The New Vision in the German Arts.* London: Kennikat, 1924.

Schikowski, John. *Geschichte des Tanzes.* Berlin: Büchergilde Gutenberg, 1926.

Schiller, Friedrich. *On the Aesthetic Education of Man.* Translated by Reginald Snell. New York: Frederick Ungar, 1954.

On the Aesthetic Education of Man. Edited by Elizabeth Wilkinson and L. A. Willoughby. Oxford: Clarendon, 1967.

The Aesthetic Letters, Essays, and the Philosophical Letters. Translated by J. Weiss. Boston: Little, 1845.

Schopenhauer, Arthur. *The World as Will and Idea.* Translated by R. B. Haldane and J. Kemp. 3rd ed. 3 vols. London: Paul, Trench, Trübner, 1888.

Schreyer, Lothar. "Das Bühnenkunstwerk." *Der Sturm* 7, no. 5 (April 1916):50–51; 8, no. 2 (May 1917):18–22; 8, no. 3 (June 1917):36–40.

Erinnerungen an Sturm und Bauhaus: Was ist des Menschen Bild? Munich: N.p., 1956.

Expressionistisches Theater. Hamburg: Toth, 1948.

Sechaus, Günther. *Frank Wedekind und das Theater.* Munich: Laokoon Verlag, 1964.

Segel, Harold B. *Turn-of-the-century Cabaret.* New York: Columbia, 1987.

Shearier, Stephen J. "Das Junge Deutschland: the Late Expressionist Association in Berlin, Its Journal and Series of Twelve Dramatic Productions." Ph.D. Diss., University of Wisconsin-Madison. 1986.

Soergel, Albert. *Dichtung und Dichter der Zeit: Eine Schilderung der deutschen Literatur der letzten Jahrzehnte. Neue Folge: Im Banne des Expressionismus.* Leipzig: Voigtländer, 1925.

Sokel, Walter. *The Writer in Extremis: Expressionism in Twentieth-Century German Literature.* Stanford: Stanford University Press, 1959.

Styan, John. *Max Reinhardt.* Cambridge: Cambridge University Press, 1982.

Toller, Ernst. "Bemerkungen zu meinem Drama *Die Wandlung.*" In *Schöpferische Konfession.* Berlin: Reiss, 1922.

I Was a German. Edited by Edward Crankshaw. New York: Morrow, 1934.

Transfiguration. Translated by Edward Crankshaw. In *Modern Continental Dramas,* edited by Harlan Hatcher, New York: Harcourt, 1941, 656–87.

Ude, Karl. *Frank Wedekind.* Muhlaker: Stieglitz-Verlag, 1966.

Viviani, Annalisa. *Dramaturgische Elemente im expressionistischen Drama.* Bonn: H. Bouvier Verlag, 1970.

Wedekind, Frank. *Gesammelte Briefe.* Edited by Fritz Strich. 2 vols. Munich: Müller Verlag, 1924.

"Zirkusgedanken." In *Werke,* edited by Manfred Hahn, Berlin: Aufbau-Verlag, 1969, 3:153–62.

Wedekind, Tilly Newes. *Lulu: Die Rolle meines Lebens.* Munich: Rütten und Loening Verlag, 1969.

Weisstein, Ulrich. *Expressionism as an International Literary Phenomenon.* Paris: Didier, 1973.

Willett, John. *Expressionism.* New York: McGraw, 1970.

The Theatre of the Weimar Republic. New York: Holmes & Meier, 1988.

Worringer, Wilhelm. *Abstraction and Empathy: a Contribution to the Psychology of Style.* Translated by Michael Bullock. 1908. London: Routledge and Kegan Paul, Ltd., 1968.

Index